The bunyan
of
brooklyn

The bunyan of brooklyn

The Life and Practical Sermons of Ichabod Spencer

by

James M. Sherwood

Solid Ground Christian Books
Birmingham, Alabama USA

SOLID GROUND CHRISTIAN BOOKS
PO Box 660132, Vestavia Hills, AL 35266
205-443-0311
sgcb@charter.net
http://www.solid-ground-books.com

The Bunyan of Brooklyn:
The Life and Practical Sermons of Ichabod Spencer

by James M. Sherwood (1851-1921)

Published by Solid Ground Christian Books

Classic Reprints Series

First printing of hardcover edition July 2003
First printing of paperback edition October 2004

ISBN: 1-932474-00-5 (hardcover)
ISBN: 1-932474-58-7 (paperback)

Manufactured in the United States of America

PREFACE.

WE have stated in the *Sketch of Dr. Spencer's Life and Character*, the circumstances connected with the issue of these volumes of posthumous sermons from his pen. We have also preferred to express there what we have on other matters, which more properly belong to a Preface.

As to the *form* given to the present volumes, we have consulted what was supposed would be the wish of the numerous possessors of *A Pastor's Sketches*, making them uniform with them. Our only regret in doing this has been, that, after making the most of our space, and condensing the *Sketch*, we were still obliged to withhold so many sermons of a very superior character, which we should have gladly added to the number hereby given to the public.

In the *arrangement* of the Sermons, the Editor has followed what seemed to him the most natural course, embodying in one volume, and, as nearly as might be, in systematic order, those mainly of a *doctrinal* character; and in the other, grouping together subjects of a kindred nature, those which may be denominated *practical* or *experimental*.

A fastidious critic might possibly complain of the frequent use of *italics* in the Sermons. This was according to the Author's taste and judgment, and the Editor did not feel at liberty to violate them, at least in those of them which he himself had prepared for the press. Besides, our own judgment coincides with his in the propriety and wisdom of making a thought clear to the *common* mind (scholars need not such aids); and especially where so much Scripture is woven into the Sermon, to distinguish it thus to the eye, rather than by quotation marks.

For the *sentiments* contained in the *Sermons*, the Editor is of course in no wise responsible. Nor has he even ventured to characterize the Theology of them, according to the standard of any human system or school. He believes that it will be found in substantial agreement with the Bible ; and further than this, he feels no sort of solicitude. Perhaps we owe it to the memory of a Friend, to allude to a single Sermon, and give it the benefit of a brief remark, if it shall need any in the judgment of the reader. We allude to the Sermon on "The Light of Nature," in the second volume. It was preached by the Author several times, and in the hearing of many of his ministerial brethren, some of whom we know have severely condemned the doctrine and reasoning of the Sermon as unscriptural. It was one chosen by himself for publication, and therefore the Editor is not responsible for its appearance in this selection. We are inclined however to the opinion, that the *true* doctrine and reasoning of the Sermon was somewhat misapprehended by a portion of those who heard him preach it. We conclude so from the fact, that in *another* sermon on the same branch of Theology, written late in life, the commonly received opinions as to the measure of light there is revealed in Nature, are clearly stated and ably vindicated; and also from his own remark in relation to this same sermon. Knowing how some of his brethren viewed the leading sentiments of it, (we had heard it twice preached,) we took the liberty of repeating to him the criticisms which were made upon it. He seemed surprised. He thought for a moment, and then with emphasis said, bringing down his hand with force: " Why, the light is *there*. I do not dispute *that*. The lesson *is* in Nature. But man fails to *see* it, to read it. Sin has put out his eyes. He is *blind*. He *must* have the Bible or he cannot know God—cannot interpret Nature." By referring to the seventeenth and eighteenth pages of the Sermon, it will be seen that he there brings out this as the real doctrine of the discourse, which he argues to prove. Whether the point he was aiming at in his forcible and magnificent argumentation, was made sufficiently clear and prominent, is for the reader to judge.

It will be seen, that in the Sketch, in order to do justice to the life and position of the subject of it, it was necessary to go over ground delicate and difficult. We have aimed to be strictly impartial, discriminating, and just. If we have erred, it has been the fault of judgment. We had no personal feeling to gratify, or ecclesiastical interest to advance. What we have written has been submitted to Brethren whose relations and character qualify them to judge impartially; "and in whose judgment and taste" our lamented Brother publicly affirmed, that "he had great confidence." They have kindly signified their approval of our humble labor.

BLOOMFIELD, N. J., March, 1855.

CONTENTS.

	PAGE
SKETCH OF LIFE AND CHARACTER	9

I.
A DEVOTIONAL SPIRIT.. 129

II.
SORROW FOR THE DEATH OF FRIENDS 145

III.
REASONS FOR AFFLICTIONS.................................. 166

IV.
CHASTISEMENTS DISCIPLINARY............................... 183

V.
ENDURING TEMPTATIONS...................................... 198

VI.
THE DEPRESSION OF BELIEVERS............................. 217

VII.
THE WOMAN OF CANAAN IN PRAYER......................... 233

VIII.
THE BLIND LED IN A WAY THEY KNOW NOT.................. 247

IX.
MINGLED LIGHT AND DARKNESS.............................. 263

X.
Contentment.. 278

XI.
Assurance Attainable....................................... 298

XII.
Sanctification at Death.................................... 317

XIII.
The Chief of Sinners....................................... 336

XIV.
Delay of Conversion.. 351

XV.
Delay of Conversion, continued............................. 369

XVI.
Delay of Conversion, continued............................. 386

XVII.
The Rich and Poor Meet Together........................... 404

XVIII.
The Rich and Poor Meet Together, continued................ 419

XIX.
Lessons from Ecclesiastes.................................. 435

XX.
Lessons from Ecclesiastes, continued....................... 453

SKETCH

OF

LIFE AND CHARACTER.

IN giving to the public a selection from the sermons of the author of "A Pastor's Sketches," we are discharging, it is believed, a sacred duty to the dead and the living—meeting alike the demands of Christian feeling and the claims of truth and righteousness. It is also the conviction of his friends, that a sketch of his life and character accompanying these volumes of Sermons, will add not a little to their interest and value, and prove an acceptable service to the numerous readers of his own "Sketches."

We are not unconscious of the inadequacy of our powers for such an undertaking, or of the difficulties and embarrassments in the way of executing it satisfactorily. Dr. Spencer kept no journal, made no record whatever of his personal history or feelings, and seldom alluded to himself in his intercourse with others. Our knowledge of him, beyond what we gained from years of friendly intercourse and personal observation, had to be gleaned from a great variety of sources—from hints scattered through his sermons and "Sketches"—from his extensive memoranda of his pastoral labors—from his correspondence with a few intimate friends—and from the treasured recollections of his family and people. Besides, he was a *peculiar* man. The world, his friends and people in general knew him not fully. Such was his modesty and shrinking diffidence and reserve that but little of his interior life and genial spirit and noble character found free expression to the eye and ear of the world. He had to be judged of mainly by means of his *works*, his daily *life and conversation*. Hence it is exceedingly difficult to draw a life-sketch of him that shall satisfy those who knew him personally and intimately—whom he admitted to his heart's full confidence and love—and also his people, among whom for two-and-twenty years he wrought the signs of a faithful minister, and upon whom he lavished the affluence of his talents, piety and Christian devotedness, and at the same time escape, in the judgment of the public, the charge of panegyrizing or greatly exaggerating the virtues and abilities of the dead. And this charge we are most anxious to escape, knowing how intensely the subject of this sketch abhorred flattery and all extravagant praise. But honored with the personal friendship and confidence of this man of God far beyond our desert; having had some little responsibility in bringing his "Sketches" before the public; having frequently urged him to do what after his death it was found he had done; and being solicited to do what was needful in the case by one who sustained the nearest earthly relation to him;— we did not feel at liberty to decline the service. Still have we had to do it amid the pressing and exhausting demands of a large pastoral charge. We claim therefore the sympathy and indulgence of the reader, only adding, that in the brief space allotted to this Sketch we can not always give the *proof* of our statements respecting the opinions, etc., of the subject of this memoir; but we have aimed carefully to state nothing unwarrantably, and to fall short rather than transcend the truth in the matter of praise.

It will afford the reader no little pleasure to learn, that before his death, Dr. Spencer made a careful selection from his sermons, to the number of one hundred and thirty-seven, which he himself regarded as most worthy of publication. Out of this number he had selected twenty-three (all of which are given in these volumes) and prepared them for the press. He also authorized a *selection* from the remaining one hundred and fourteen, or from the mass of his sermons, if it should be thought best by his family after he was gone; and he likewise left hints of essential aid to guide one in making the selection. The public therefore have the assurance that we have violated no wish of the dead, and that the selection hereby given from his thousand manuscript sermons is based upon the author's own judgment and taste. The editor's responsibility has been greatly lessened by this fact, and, we add, his labor sweetened by the thought that he is but carrying out the wish of a friend who is no longer alive to speak for himself. With the additional remark that we have scrupulously regarded the author's *wish* and *taste* on every point, so far as we had a hint to guide us, or knew from personal intercourse his mind, we pass to the particular work of this Sketch.

HIS EARLY LIFE.

We know but little, comparatively, of the childhood and youth of our friend; and few of the incidents which we have gathered is it deemed necessary to state. He was the seventh in descent from Thomas Spencer, one of the first settlers of Hartford, Connecticut, who died in 1687. The son of this Thomas Spencer settled in Suffield, in the same State, where the family resided until about 1786, when the father of Dr. Spencer removed to the town of Rupert, county of Bennington, in the State of Vermont. Here ICHABOD SMITH SPENCER was born, on the 23d day of February, 1798, the youngest but one of eleven children. Four of his sisters and two of his brothers survive him. His father died while he was yet young, and his mother only a few years since. His father was an agriculturist in comfortable circumstances, able and desirous, it would seem, to give this son, whose earliest years were marked with decided promise, a collegiate education; but for some reason he remained at home until after his father's death, receiving only such an education as the excellent common schools of New England afford, in addition to his habits of meditation and self-application. He often said, as illustrating the influence of early impressions, that his destiny was settled, so far as a college education was concerned, by overhearing a remark of his father's in conversation with his uncle. Pointing to him, he said: "There is the collegian." He was too young then to know what the word meant; but it dwelt in his memory, and when his father was gone and he was cast upon the world and left to pursue the bent of his inclinations, that early impression decided his course.

His talents began to be developed quite early in life, especially his taste for poetry and a decided poetic genius. One of his first poetic effusions, written when only nine or ten years of age, possessed so much merit that his family questioned its originality, saying that it was "too good to be his." He often remarked what a trial this little incident was to his feelings; and it made him very careful and indulgent toward the early efforts of his own children and others. The *poetic* element was inborn in his nature, and he evidently nursed and cultivated it through all his early years by meditation, by reading, by solitary and frequent rambles in the fields, and musings on the mountains that were spread around his childhood's home. This fact should be borne in mind. His temperament was, by nature and early cultivation, singularly poetic. And that temperament was influential on his whole character and life. It gave form and color to not a few of his thoughts. It had not a little to do with one feature of his religious experience, which we shall have occasion to allude to hereafter. However recondite may be the philosophy of it, it is an admitted fact, that a poetic temperament is usually tinged with melancholy. It makes the impress of sadness on the heart. It cast a shadow on the mind and the pathway of this gifted man. It made his harp at times plaintive and sad, like the harp of the weeping prophet. It made him peculiarly sensitive to the infelicities and ills of this life; sighing in his inmost soul for higher forms of the beautiful, the true and the good. There are distinct traces of the influence of this temperament in his early years. It made him thoughtful and meditative. It made the field, the mountain, the murmuring brook, the flower, the birds, his own inner nature, his daily companions and the objects of his fondest musings. His father's death, which occurred when he had attained his seventeenth year, overwhelmed him with distress. Not long before his own death he poured into the bosom of confiding friendship* the tale of that early sorrow, and of life's gloominess and wretchedness as it then appeared to him, which will illustrate the above remarks.

"When in the year 1815 my father died, I felt that I was robbed, desolate, cut loose from my rock of hope and support. I had nothing to lean upon—nothing to trust—nothing to resort to. I came back from his funeral to my home, and it was home no longer. The house, the hills, the fields, the trees, the brooks, were not my old acquaintances. A change had passed upon them. Gloom hung over them. If the sun shone, it shone palely; if the birds sang, their song was turned into a dirge. I never got over that feeling. My rambles were gloomy; my favorite woods had become the abode of melancholy; the fields seemed to mourn under my eye; and when I climbed the old mountain on whose top I had spent so many happy hours, all the landscape before me, skirted with the distant mountains of blue, which had so often charmed me before, had now lost all its sweetness. The very malediction of God seemed to hang over it all. Earth was a wilderness, and I was a hermit. I could not live there. I tried it for a year, and never returned to it as a home. Young, unbefriended, and poor, I went forth upon the world."

None but a heart of profound sensibility and meditation could sorrow thus in life's fresh morn; and none but a highly poetic mind could thus picture it.

At this time he was living *without God in the world.* He grew up irreligious. There are no traces of any serious impressions made on his mind till after he left home. Indeed the

* In a letter addressed to Mrs. H., of C———, N. Y., one of his few intimate correspondents.

testimony of those who knew him in his youth is, that he belonged to the class of careless, thoughtless, and gay young men. There had been no decidedly religious influence exerted upon him. Neither of his parents made a profession of religion. They were moral and reputable, and inculcated the principles of the Bible on their children; but this was all. Young Ichabod was thrown upon the world without those early religious advantages which multitudes enjoy. God will be a sovereign in the choice of the subjects of his grace. The last are often first, and the first last. It is highly probable that his father's death, so deeply felt, and so great a trial, was sanctified to his soul, and overruled to lead his mind and heart, so dark and trembling, to the only *true* "Rock of hope and support." It was more than a year, however, after this event occurred, before the grace of God changed his heart, and turned his feet into the way of life.

Deeply as he loved his father, and ever venerated his memory, it would seem that, like most great men, he was not a little indebted to his *mother*. He gives a touching sketch of her life and character in a sermon delivered to his people the Sabbath after her death, which occurred only three years before his own. It was a noble son who could stand up before his people, and pour forth such a tribute to the memory of his mother.

"My own mother has died! And when I utter that expression, and remember what she was to me from my childhood till her last breath of life, no words, I am sure, could paint the traces of emotion that come over me. I expected her death. I knew it must be near; and yet anticipation has not made it a reality for which I was prepared. But she has gone! She has gone to the grave, and I honor her memory. She was an uncommon woman. Her decision of character has seldom been equaled, nor her endurance. Born in 1762, and dying in 1851, she lived through almost a century; and amid all the diversities of her lot, she certainly performed her earthly part well. Fond of her family, devoted to them, self-sacrificing and ever faithful, she spared no pains, and shrunk from no labor, and shunned no care or hardship which was demanded for the good of her family. Though timid by nature, and more inclined to despondency than hope, she met the cares of a numerous family and the troubles of a changeful life, without complaint or repining. She took the trials of her children as her own trials, adopted their sorrows as her own, and whenever she could, she shielded them from harm by the ready exposure of herself. She never sent the poor away from her door empty, and never made an extravagant expenditure under the impulse of pride or self-indulgence. Conscientious in every thing, and guided by her Bible, she wronged no one, and, so far as I ever knew, no one ever complained of her. She was above reproach as a neighbor, a mother, a friend. As she was on the down-hill of life, every year, for sixteen years, I have visited her with a mournful and foreboding pleasure. When I last saw her, she said to me, 'Well, I am glad to see you again; but I was in hopes I should have been dead before the time came round for you to come and see me; but I am slow to the grave!' And when I bade her farewell, expecting never to see her again, she simply said: 'Good-by; pray for me—pray for me.' She had long expected and desired to die, and I hope grace had prepared her. Honored woman! honored mother! affection will embalm and hallow the recollection of thy life, and tenderness make her tearful pilgrimage to thy grave."

Blessed man! thy "tearful pilgrimage" was even then nearly ended. A few more toils, a year of suffering, and thy hand swept the lyre in that world where there are no graves, no tears, no mourning, to give sadness or wailing to its notes.

In a letter to the friend already referred to, he speaks in a striking and feeling manner of the *impression* which his mother's death made upon him:

"Her body now rests on the banks of the Cattaraugus, and the last common tie which bound her children together and made them feel as one family, is severed for ever. Perhaps it is partly this which makes me feel her death in an unexpected manner. Though I had anticipated it often, and knew it could not be far off, yet I did by no means expect it to impress me as I find it does. The reality is far beyond the impression. The world is more of a dream to me than ever before—life more of a fancy—existence more of a nullity. I seem now to be cut loose from all that went before me; I seem to have done with all the past, and to be compelled to turn all my thoughts to the future—from my parents to my children—from the generation that went before me to the generation that shall come after me. As long as my mother lived I could be a child and could have some of the feelings of childhood, and could see a relict at least of my ancestry standing (apparently) betwixt me and death; but now I seem to be crowded on to take myself the border, to stand on the outskirts of society, making one of the front rank to face death. [Here follows the sketch of his feelings at his father's death.] But still my mother lived. But though I could not think of her any longer as one to lean upon, I *could* think of her as one to love, and think of her too as one to lean upon *me*. I endured and bore up on her account at times when nothing but the thought of her kept me from despair. *One* at least would honor me, do me justice, prize me; to *one* at least I might be useful. And from that day till the 27th of December [1851], through the period of thirty-five years, I have carried along with me that sustaining and stimulating idea—an idea which seemed to place me betwixt my children and my fathers in the midst of life. But now it is gone—I am on the last border of life. The generation before me has now vanished, and all the world has put on a new aspect. Surely I ought henceforth to live for eternity. I hope my mother has gone to glory. She never made any profession of religion, but I have no small reason, as I think, to believe that her trust was in her Saviour. * * * May I hope you will pray for me. I have need of more grace (if indeed I have any at all), and I beseech you, my very dear friend, offer to God one prayer for me."

His father's death threw upon him life's responsibilities, and thrust him out into the world to achieve life's serious purpose and end: his mother's was a voice from Heaven calling him to lay off his armor and meditate on "eternity," and in the furnace of bodily affliction seek to have his Master's image perfected on his soul, and his heavenly crown made brighter.

THROWN UPON HIS OWN RESOURCES.

Deeply as he lamented his father's death, it was doubtless converted into an immense blessing to him, and surely it was to the Church and the world. Had he lived only a few years longer, the son might have remained a tiller of the ground, and the powers of his extraordinary mind never have been developed; or had the son decided on an education, he would not have made, with his father to lean upon, the self-reliant, resolute, energetic and powerful man that he became. He needed to have this prop torn away, and be thrown entirely upon his own resources, in order to test fairly his own capabilities of success; to stimulate his courage, arouse his mental powers to thorough and healthful action; and school him, physically, mentally and morally, into a strong man, that he might be a bold and distinguished standard-bearer, and be able to *endure hardness as a good soldier of Jesus Christ.*

At eighteen—one year after his father's death—he left home: "Young, unbefriended and poor, I went forth upon the world." But a merciful Providence guided his decisions, and ordered his ways. He had a great and important work for him to perform, and he left home and kindred, not knowing what was to befall him. He was guided to the town of Granville, Washington county, New York, where he engaged in manual labor for something like a year. During this year a revival of religion visited this town, and young Spencer was among its hopeful subjects. He made a public profession of religion soon after, in connection with the Congregational Church of Middle Granville, then under the pastoral charge of Rev. Nathaniel Hall, who died in the year 1820. He was considered at this time a young man of decided talent, and, giving good evidence of piety, was urged to enter the ministry. In pursuance of an education, he soon after entered the academy at Salem, in the same county, where he was fitted for college. While here he enjoyed the ministry and friendly counsels of the excellent Dr. Alexander Proudfit. This intercourse, occurring just when it did, was of great benefit to him. The good doctor was a father to him, and his kind interest in his welfare touched him deeply, and he carried the memory of it to his grave. Here we think it was that his mind and heart were first seriously directed to the Gospel ministry. Were there more sympathizing Proudfits in the ministry, ready to counsel and befriend the young men who are struggling, often in poverty and despondency, to obtain an education, there would be fewer sad hearts and fewer failures among them.

While at the academy he sustained himself by teaching a portion of his time. This prolonged his preparatory studies, but it was far from being lost time. It tended to make him more thorough in his studies, more independent in his feelings, more industrious and economical of time in his habits. His thirst for improvement at that time was great. He went through a course of medical reading with the student with whom he roomed at Salem, for the mere pleasure of acquiring knowledge. Here was the secret of his knowledge of medicine, which often surprised his friends, and which he turned to good account in his many visits to the poor.

He entered the sophomore class of Union College in 1819, and graduated in 1822, at the age of twenty-four. Nothing very marked occurred during his college life. He became known as a young man of decided talent. He stood high in his class in point of scholarship, and already wielded the pen of a ready writer. He left the college halls among the most promising. Eight years had now passed since, in sadness and grief, he went forth from the home of his youth. They had been given to earnest toil and manly effort. He had, unaided by friends or any society, worked his own way through the academy and college, and stood now on the threshold of professional life. If there were more of his resolute, independent, indomitable spirit in our young men who are seeking an education for the ministry, not only would our Education Societies be less burdened, but we should have a hardier, more thoroughly trained and effective class of ministers.

At this period Dr. Spencer's mind seems to have been undecided in regard to the choice of a profession. He thought seriously of the Law, and devoted a considerable time to reading law-books. And there can be no doubt that he would have distinguished himself at the Bar, had he bent his studies and energies in that direction. With his masterly mind, his elements of sturdy manliness, and his powers of application, he would have succeeded in any field—in any profession. But the Lord had appointed him to a "holy calling," and interposed in his providence at this time, and directed his mind and choice in another channel. He was called to take charge of the Grammar-School in Schenectady, where he remained for about three years. This was an important post, and nobly did he sustain himself. He was enthusiastic and devoted as a teacher, and had he remained here would soon no doubt have risen to a professor's chair. President Nott highly appreciated his tact and ability as a teacher, and remarked, that he never ought to think of any other profession for life. He pronounced him one of the most thorough masters of the art he had ever known. He promised to use his influence to secure him a Professorship in Union College as soon as a vacancy should occur, or in some other, if he would wait. But God again interposed. He was a "chosen vessel" for the Sanctuary. This work was designed to be only *preparatory* to the great work of his life. God was leading his servant by a way of his own devising, to his true mission—to a field on which the whole splendor of his genius, the rich stores of his learning, the entire affection of his heart, and the tact and energy and power of his being, could be consecrated to the highest and noblest ends for which a man can live—the ministry of reconciliation.

So active was his mind and bent on acquisition, that, while discharging the duties of this onerous office, he engaged in the study of Theology under the direction of Dr. Andrew Yates, Professor of Moral Philosophy in Union College. There is some doubt, however, whether he was fully *decided* at this time to enter the Gospel ministry. He had read Medicine and Law, and now he took up the study of Theology; not from any fickleness of mind, or freak of fancy—no man was ever freer from these despicable traits of character—but to extend his knowledge, and prepare himself, as far as possible, for any future call which Providence might make upon him. He had thrown himself on God—devoted life and all to him, and held himself in readiness to follow the leadings of his providence; and while he waited for further light to know what he would have him do, he was anxious to master all science. God had an end in view in keeping his mind so long in this state of indecision. He was all the while most assiduously disciplining the powers of his mind, laying the foundations of a most noble character, and gathering materials from various fields of study—all to be laid at his Master's feet. He cultivated while here quite an extensive acquaintance with several Indian dialects.

But his fame as a teacher had gone abroad, and Canandaigua, in Western New York, was fortunate enough to secure his services as the Preceptor of her Academy. He removed thither in the autumn of 1825. The Academy, though richly endowed, and occupying a very important position, had greatly run down previous to his going there. He addressed himself to the work of its resuscitation and improvement, with his characteristic zeal, industry and energy; and he quickly gave it new life, and raised it to a high degree of prosperity, and to a commanding position among the primary educational institutions of the State. He was celebrated here, as he had been in Schenectady, for his skill and success as a teacher of youth. He infused into the students not a little of his own spirit; gained the perfect confidence of the community; exerted an excellent literary and religious influence; and made many warm personal friends, whose respect and affection for him were life-long, and by whom his occasional visits to the place in after years were greatly enjoyed. He was also, at this time, a decided, active, and useful Christian; possessing remarkable gifts of prayer and exhortation, and ready to assist his Pastor and do good in the exercise of them.

We have alluded to his poetic talent. He exercised this to a considerable extent while at Canandaigua, but mainly, it would seem, for his own gratification. Seldom were any of his productions given to the press; and the authorship of the few which did meet the public eye was carefully concealed. This was characteristic of him all through life; he dreaded any thing like newspaper notoriety; he seemed anxious to conceal himself from public observation. He wrote at this time a Poem on Time, of two hundred lines, which appeared from the press of the village, in the form of "The Carrier's Address of the Ontario Repository." It attracted at the time not a little attention, as altogether superior to the usual literature of this class: and it certainly possesses a good degree of poetic merit. The author of it was never known beyond the circle of a few particular friends. Quite recently a leading New England newspaper republished a portion of it, prefaced with the remark, that the Poem was by one of the best English poets. We give a passage or two from it, as a specimen of his poetic ability at this period.

"Heard you that knell? It was the knell of *Time.*
And is Time dead? I thought Time never died:
I knew him old, 'tis true, and full of years,
And bald except in front; but he was strong
As Hercules. I saw him grasp the oak,
It fell—the tower, it crumbled;—and the stone,
The sculptured monument that marked the grave
Of fallen greatness, ceased its pompous strain
As Time came by. Yes, Time was very strong,
And I had thought too strong for Death to grapple.

But I remember now, his step was light;
And though he moved at rapid rate, or trod
On adamant, his tread was never heard.
And there was something ghostly in the thought
That in the silence of the midnight hour,
When all was hushed as death, and not a sound
Crept o'er my chamber's stillness, or awoke
The echo slumbering there—in such an hour
He trod my chamber, and I heard him not.
And I have held my breath and listened close
To catch one foot-fall as he glided by.
But not a slumbering sound awoke, or sighed;
And the thought struck me then that one, whose step
Was so much like a spirit's tread, whose acts
Were all so noiseless, like the world unseen,
Would soon be fit for other worlds than this—
Fit for high converse with immortal minds,
Unfettered by the flesh, unchained to earth.
  * * * * *
"I strayed one night along the ocean's brink;
It was a lonely and a rugged place;
The rocky cliff hung beetling o'er my path,
And just beneath me slept the waveless deep,
Which the pale moonbeam kissed as soft and light,
As if it feared to break its slumberings.
In such a wild and solitary place,
I was surprised at that lone hour to see
A human form, a youth of wasted frame,
Was seated on the fragment of a rock.
His brow was knit, and every muscle braced,
As if to curb the feelings of his heart:
His moveless eye was resting on the wide
And 'moon-lit deep,' as shadows of the past
Moved o'er his memory. I listened still,
As in a deep and death-like tone he spoke:
 'The moonbeams sleep upon the wave,
 And cast their glimmer on the grave,
 As if to cheer the darksome tomb,
 As if to light the sailor home.
 But on the heart with anguish torn,
 The heart that meets with haughty scorn,

POEM ON TIME.

The heart that once has felt the fire,
Of Love, and felt its flame expire
Before the cold unfeeling look,
The scorn its feeling could not brook;
On such a heart no light can dawn,
Its hopes are crushed, its joys are gone;
In such a heart no lingering ray
Lights up the blank of hope's decay;
Its years of bliss are past and gone,
Its fondest, dearest joys are flown;
Its days of love have glided by,
And left a blank—its destiny!'

*   *   *   *

"Such strains we say are requiems on Time.
But if Time's dead, will he not rise again,
And meet us in the other world? Oh yes,
His spirit will, and in that other world
Will meet his *murderers*. And who are they?
The proud, the gay, the thoughtless, and the vain,
Who crowd to scenes of midnight revelry;
The heartless miser, brooding o'er his gold,
Deaf to the cries of want, and ignorant
That wealth has wings, and heaven cannot be bribed;
The countless throng, who make this world their all,
Lay up their treasures here, and spend their days,
As if eternity were but a song.
These are Time's murderers, though he has been
Their kind and constant friend, watchful and true.
He rocked their cradle in their infancy;
He soothed their griefs, and taught them to forget
The thrills of anguish and the throbs of woe;
He dried from childhood's cheek the tear that marred
Its mantling bloom; he knit their sinews firm,
And braced their nerves to youthful energy;
He spread before them all the bloom of earth,
Painted the landscape in its loveliest hues,
And breathed fresh fragrance on the rising gale;
He crowned their board with plenty, and their cups
Ran o'er with blessedness; he gave them friends,
And taught them friendship's joys; their hearts he framed
For love, and strung their souls to sympathy;

> Time was their real friend ; true to his trust,
> He told them he and all his race should die,
> And leave Eternity their guardian."

Dr. Ansel D. Eddy was the Pastor of the Congregational Church of Canandaigua while Mr. Spencer was engaged there in teaching. He also took a friendly interest in his comfort and welfare, and often cheered him in his lonely and desponding seasons. And he cherished the remembrance of this kindness so long as he lived. He was a man indeed who never forgot a friend; slow to make friends, he loved them when made with a true and unchanging affection. It was doubtless the remembrance of his own many sad and dispirited hours while struggling through an education, and the sweetness of those expressions of kindness which he received at times, which interested him so deeply in the friendless and the desponding. They always found a warm and a willing friend in him. Many a letter of counsel and cheering, bearing material aid, has he sent to poor and pious young men, who were striving to fit themselves for spheres of usefulness. Not a few now occupying important stations, owe a great obligation to his timely aid and sympathy. He obeyed in this, as in all his other charities, the Scripture injunction: *Let not thy left hand know what thy right hand doeth.*

While thus engaged in a most laborious occupation, Dr. Spencer so far completed his theological studies as to be licensed to preach the Gospel. He received his licensure in November, 1826, from the Presbytery of Geneva. It was not his purpose immediately to relinquish his present calling and devote himself to the pastoral office. He hoped, however, to be able to exercise his gifts to better advantage, and preach more or less on the Sabbath. Hence he continued his employment in the Academy nearly two years after this, occupying some neighboring pulpit frequently on the Sabbath, and improving every spare moment and every opportunity to obtain a more thorough knowledge of theological science.

His theological training at the time he entered the ministry, was, from the force of circumstances, considerably deficient. He had not enjoyed the advantages of a "seminary course," nor of the old course, "studying two or more years with some approved divine." He had studied and meditated much upon his Bible. He had read Dwight, Bellamy, and a few other standard theological writers. His mind had received a thorough training in general knowledge. He was familiar with the classics and the English poets. But a *trained, accomplished theologian*, in the modern sense, he was not. Learned in the literature of the Bible, a master of the wisdom and art of the schools, he was not. He often remarked this. He was left almost entirely to his own mental resources. But they were ample; they exceeded those of any man we ever knew. And his unwearied diligence, his trained mind, the native vigor and versatility of his intellectual powers, his commanding genius, and the fund of tact and good sense and manliness which characterized him, more than supplied the lack of any early deficiency in this respect, and made him truly "a master in Israel." *However* he got his education for the ministry—by whatever processes of culture he reached the result—he *was* educated for it as few men are. Few may have his mind or make his application, it may be; but certainly few of our most carefully educated ministers, on the modern system, will compare with him, we think, judged of by the standard of Bible, effective, successful preaching.

It is known to all who were favored with much personal intercourse with Dr. Spencer—indeed his "Sketches" more than hint as much, for he was a man who never sought to conceal his opinions—that he was not altogether satisfied with our present system of theological education for the ministry. He reflected much and deeply on this vital subject, especially during the last few years of his life. He most carefully observed and noted the workings and results of the "seminary" system, generally so popular, and it became his deep-seated conviction, growing stronger till death, that it is not a little defective—failing fully to answer the demands of the age on the Christian pulpit.

This view of the matter filled his own mind with anxiety and alarm. He attributed to this defect in ministerial training much of the inefficiency of our evangelical preaching—that loss of real power which, in common with many of his brethren and many observant laymen, he believed characterized the modern pulpit. He fully indorsed the views so timely expressed by Dr. Gardiner Spring, a few years since, in his *"Power of the Pulpit."* He thought also that our denomination adhered *too rigidly* to the rule requiring a regular and full course of study on the part of all those who enter the ministry; that in many cases, with the right sort of training, practical and highly useful men might be introduced into the ministry, whose age or circumstances debarred them from it under this rule.—How far the fact that he never personally enjoyed the advantages of a Seminary training ought to impair the force of a judgment so carefully formed, and based on so extended and sagacious an observation, the reader must judge for himself. We are only concerned to give his opinion publicity and due weight.

In May, 1828, Dr. Spencer was married to Miss Hannah Magoffin, youngest daughter of John Magoffin, Esq., of Albany, N. Y. Mrs. Spencer survives her husband. Four children— two sons and two daughters—also survive their father—all of them old enough to appreciate the greatness of their loss. The light of that once happy and favored home has gone out. Earth seems desolate to them now. And none will wonder at this who knew him in his own family.

This relation exerted a very decided and beneficial influence on the mind and character and future life of Dr. Spencer, and therefore deserves particular notice. His was a nature that peculiarly needed woman's cheerful presence and soothing influence. His heart was a deep fountain of love. He craved sympathy and social communion. His temperament was somewhat despondent. And in his case the proverb respecting "ministers' wives" did not hold true. The connection was both a blessing and a comfort to him personally. His dying testimony on this point is worthy of being pondered. There is no class of men on earth that so much *need* a wife's devoted, I had almost said exclusive, ministries, as our sensitive, over-worked and oft-dejected pastors. And yet, is it not true that the demands of the parish and of public charities upon her time and energy, almost deprive him of this home-solace and aid, so longed for and so indispensable to a healthy state of mind and body ? Mrs. Spencer believed that she owed her first and chief duty to her husband, and nothing was allowed to interfere with its discharge. He always felt that he could write better, having her with him in the study : and there in silence would she sit, long past the midnight hour, till his day's toil was ended. We have ventured to touch on this delicate point, that we might commend an example which, if emulated—if our congregations would suffer their pastors' wives to follow—would, we think, be mutually beneficial.

We have alluded to his occasional preaching in various pulpits while still engaged in teaching. He was heard with interest from the first. His preaching, in both style and matter, was attractive, marked by unusual freshness, a rich imagination, maturity of mind, a warm and earnest heart, and decided intellectual vigor. It was soon apparent that he was no common man in the pulpit, and needed only practice and development to make him distinguished. And the time had now come for him to enter upon that high career of ministerial usefulness for which Divine Providence had been so long and so singularly preparing him. Twelve years had passed away since he bade adieu to the home of his youth. He had urged his way manfully along amid trials many, and depressions great. He had been tossed about the world, and somewhat undecided as to what Providence meant for him to do. He had now attained to the ripe age of thirty, was well educated, was married, had made proof of his ministerial gifts satisfactory to his friends, if not to himself, and now Providence called him to abandon the sphere he had for years filled so ably, and occupy one of the most extensive and important pastorates in the land. The call of duty was clear to his mind; and yet he entered upon his new and responsible charge with no little misgiving and trembling.

HIS MINISTRY AT NORTHAMPTON.

In the summer of 1828, Dr. Spencer received and accepted a call from the Congregational Church in Northampton, Massachusetts, where he was ordained and installed as colleague-pastor with the venerable Williams, on the 11th of September following. Here his ministerial, we may say his true life, began. He here entered on a noted, congenial and widely-extended field of labor. The pulpit from which Jonathan Edwards had so long preached, and which his successors had so ably filled, was a justly distinguished one, and the Parish of Northampton was at that time one of the largest in all New England. It required a high degree of ability, and an iron frame, to meet the demands of such a field of labor; and Dr. Spencer brought to it all the elements and qualifications essential to a thorough and successful cultivation of it. Considering his theological training, his inexperience in the pastoral office, and the fact that he had been able to prepare very few sermons, the extraordinary results of his brief ministry here furnish proof of his superior powers of intellect and of grace. Few men, in similar circumstances, could have taken such a load on their shoulders and stood up under it. He bore it without fainting; grew ministerially strong under it; and rapidly developed into one of the most able, successful and justly distinguished preachers and pastors which have adorned the American Church.

He entered on his ministry with very exalted and solemn views of the sacredness and responsibility of the ministerial and pastoral office. He consecrated to the work his whole heart, soul and being. He brought to it all those elements of strength, application and endurance which had made him a master of the difficult art of teaching. From the first he aimed at a high order of excellence in his pulpit preparations, and nobly did he strive while he lived to attain it. His earliest sermons show a carefulness and thoroughness of study and composition which make his example a model to young preachers. With a brilliant fancy, a rich imagination, a good degree of poetic talent, and a ready, fluent speech, which might have enabled him to shine for a season even without close and painstaking application, he yet most rigorously subordinated all these gifts or elements to those that are solid, instructive and enduring. He studied with a resolute, unbending purpose, *to show himself approved unto God, a workman that needeth not to be ashamed, rightly dividing the word of truth.* And God honored his ministry, early and late, with frequent effusions of his Spirit.

His ministry of three and a half years at Northampton was characterized by unusual industry and energy, and by an entire, absorbing devotion to his work—by an amount of labor which seems almost superhuman—and by a signal visitation of Heavenly influence, which made its results truly extraordinary and glorious. He labored almost incessantly, frequently preaching at stations miles distant from his church. In heat and cold, in storm and sunshine, by day and by night, he was about his *Master's business,* burning with zeal, the care of souls weighing heavily on his heart, and the love of Christ constraining.

He had not labored here long before God was pleased to own and reward his ministry in a most pleasing manner. The years 1830 and 1831 were rendered memorable in the history of Northampton by one of the most extensive and blessed revivals of religion which even that favored place has known. The faithful, pungent, scriptural preaching of their new pastor— not exceeded in these characteristics perhaps since the days of Edwards—took effect, and the church was aroused and the whole place shaken by the mighty power of God; and for months the inquiry on anxious sinners' lips, was, "What must we do to be saved?" God's servant had *gone forth weeping, bearing precious seed,* and quickly was he permitted to return loaded down with *sheaves.* His labors, his fidelity, his tact and discretion amid these exciting, and, to an inexperienced pastor, naturally embarrassing scenes, were above praise.

This " great revival"—the memory of which is still sacredly cherished by that people—had a decided influence on the mind and character and future ministry of Dr. Spencer. It was just what he needed, and all that was wanting fully to qualify him for the sacred work to which he had devoted his life. It improved his religious feelings, and the character of his public ministrations, making them still more practical, instructive, biblical and spiritual. It brought him into stronger sympathy with anxious souls in all states of mind and feeling. It helped to make him a proficient and skillful guide to " anxious inquirers after the way of salvation." His labors are held in grateful remembrance by the people of his first ministerial charge, among whom he reaped the harvest of an ordinary life-time. He loved, also, to revisit the scene of his early toils and triumphs, where he would gladly have passed his days had Providence so ordered it.

Since writing the above, we have received, at our request, an interesting account of his Northampton life, from the Hon. Lewis Strong, of that place, which, as it is the testimony of an eye-witness and a former parishioner, we subjoin in his own language. After relating the incidents which led to the settlement of Dr. Spencer among them, which plainly show a guiding Providence in the thing, and bring out strongly some of the characteristics of the man, he says :

" From month to month afterward, as the desired result of his labors became more and more manifest, he seemed to be rapidly gaining, not only in knowledge and ministerial ability, but especially in devotedness to the great work in which he was engaged. Not an individual was to be found, old or young, in his whole parish, with whose name and countenance he was not familiar; and when the breathless silence, and riveted attention, and tearful eye, at the various gatherings of his people for prayer, or for public worship on the Sabbath, made it obvious that the influences of the Spirit were attending his ministry, his own earnestness and zeal were redoubled, and he seemed awakened to a new sense of his responsibilities and privileges, and to be watching for souls, as one who would be held to a strict account for his improvement of these opportunities of usefulness to his Master and Lord. So unwearied, indeed, (and more strikingly in 1830 and 1831,) were his efforts as a pastor, visiting from house to house, admonishing the careless, catching the first glimpses of penitence, and guiding the troubled spirit into the way of peace, that one would have thought that he had no leisure at all for study; and yet so tender and earnest and pungent were his public appeals to the impenitent, and his calls upon Christians for their coöperation and prayers, and so varied and thorough his public instructions, and especially those on the Sabbath, that we wondered where he could find time, beyond the necessary preparation for these various public services, for any thing else.

" In the spring of 1831, some of the members of his church, and among others one of his deacons, having determined to join a number of persons about to emigrate from this neighborhood to Princeton, in the State of Illinois, a public meeting was held here for the purpose of organizing the proposed emigrants into a church, and commending them to the guidance and keeping of the Shepherd and Bishop of souls. The meeting-house was thronged, and the public services, conducted mainly by Mr. Spencer himself, were of the most thrilling interest. Never shall we entirely forget the wise counsels he imparted to that little company of believers, or the earnestness with which he implored, in their behalf, the blessing of God, or the meltings of heart throughout every portion of that great assembly, as in their name, and with deep emotion, he bade the departing ones a final and most affectionate adieu.*

* He wrote them, also, a solemn farewell letter of instruction and counsel; and not long ago he learned that this letter was sacredly cherished by this people, and read once a year publicly on the anniversary of their leaving Northampton.—ED.

"Stern as his manner sometimes was, on such occasions as that just mentioned, he was peculiarly solemn and tender; awakening, on the part of his hearers, not only the closest attention, but something of the same sweet and noble enthusiasm of spirit which swelled and animated his own heart.

"Though his extemporaneous discourses were usually plain, and well adapted to the comprehension of the humblest capacity, yet in these, as well as in his written ones, he sometimes, bracing himself for an unusual effort, poured out a stream of eloquent remark or illustration absolutely overwhelming.

"His mind seemed always awake and active, and ready for any emergency. On one occasion our senior pastor, the Rev. Mr. Williams, was in the midst of his sermon suddenly taken ill, and when it was discovered, a few moments after, that he would be unable to resume it, Mr. Spencer arose, and throwing off his cloak, carried out the train of thought which had been proposed, and completed the discourse, thus providentially left unfinished, to the surprise and entire satisfaction of his audience.

"Dr. Spencer had, while here, many ardently attached friends, and many regard him still as their very *beau ideal* of ministerial excellence.

"As the fruits of his ministry while he was with us, there were received into the church in all two hundred and thirty-three. Some of these, no doubt, were received from other churches [thirty-two of them were]; but the accessions to this church, thus increasing from year to year, show conclusively that the blessing of God had attended, to an unusual extent, the labors of our deceased friend, and made him eminently wise in winning souls to Christ.

"On the 13th of February, he requested the concurrence of his people in calling an ecclesiastical Council for his dismission, and after repeated but unsuccessful efforts to retain him longer, they reluctantly yielded to his wishes, and on the 12th day of March he was dismissed.

"The intelligence of his death, a few weeks since, awakened in the hearts of great numbers of our people the deepest emotion; and on the ensuing Sabbath, notes were read in the old church and the Edwards church. and I think (though of this I am not quite certain) in the Baptist and Methodist churches also, desiring prayers that the event might be sanctified, not only to his family, and the church and people with which he had been of late connected, but to the hundreds here who still remembered him with the sincerest gratitude and affection."

As might have been feared, although blessed with a robust constitution, such severe labor—little time for rest or relaxation—his mind continually on the stretch, and his sensibilities excited—preparing and preaching four sermons a week (five during the year of the revival)—with hundreds of inquiring souls to instruct, over two hundred of whom were trained as converts under his ministry, and received by him into church-fellowship—and all the varied cares and anxieties of such an extensive Parish, was too much for mortal endurance, and his strength finally gave way; and at the close of this harvest-season his health was found to be so seriously impaired as to render a season of rest and a change to a less laborious charge needful. This was a great trial both to pastor and people. It was his first settlement, and first loves are strong. He was greatly attached and tenderly devoted to this people. God had signally honored his ministry among them. Many and sacred were the ties which bound him to Northampton. And his people had learned his worth. They had taken him untried, but found him to be a man after God's own heart. He had *fed them with the finest of the wheat;* made proof that his ministry was one of no ordinary character; secured the confidence and affection of all; and been the instrument of guiding a multitude to the Saviour. His brief trial had distinguished him among the orthodox pastors of New England. But Divine Providence interposed, as it had often done before in his life. This was not to be the resting-place of his soul—the permanent field of his important ministry. He was to occupy a pulpit where he was *not to build on another man's foundations*—where his influence would be wider still, and radiate from a central point—be felt just where such an influence was most of all needed, and would tell most advantageously on the interests of the Church at large.

No; the many earnest prayers of his Northampton people that his highly useful and appreciated ministry might be long continued among them, were not to be answered. The tie must be sundered, and pastor and people part just when their hearts were knit together in love, and the hallowed scenes and sympathies of a great revival made parting doubly painful. Such separations are among the bitterest trials of the ministry. Who that has drank this cup of sorrow can ever forget it? Fewer such separations would take place were the cost counted in time. If ever a pastor needs special sympathy and prayer, it is amid the trial and darkness of such an hour—not rashly chosen by him, but forced upon him in the providence of God. The ties of nature are scarcely so strong as the ties with which grace unites a devoted pastor and a loved and loving people. Dr. Spencer was a man to *feel* such a trial keenly, though he would strive to confine his grief to his own bosom. His impaired health, and the uncertainties of the future, added to it. But it was his only trial of the kind; he was kindly spared the repetition of it.

He had already become distinguished as a preacher. His fame had gone abroad in spite of his modesty, and humility, and almost exclusive devotion to his particular field of labor. His brethren, the wise and the good of New England, had their eye upon him, as a rising star of the first magnitude. And hence, when it was known that he contemplated leaving Northampton, he received numerous overtures and calls from important churches in various places—two or three from Boston, and one from Brooklyn, to name no others. The call from the Park Street Church, Boston, was a very important one; and wholly unsolicited on his part, was a distinguished testimony to his ministerial ability, and the reputation he had already achieved in New

England. The position and history of that Church are too well known to need any description. The call was urgent—backed by letters from many of the first men in Boston and elsewhere, and every inducement held out to influence his acceptance of it. But the state of his health, the onerous duties of such a city charge, and the entire absence of any thing like a worldly ambition in his heart, finally induced him to decline it. His letter conveying this decision is a model of its kind; full of Christian humility and sweetness of temper; and giving evidence, that what he believed to be "the will of his Divine Master," the simple question of "duty," ruled wholly his decision. He was a most conscientious man on such a point. He soon after accepted a call from the Second Presbyterian Church of Brooklyn, New York, and removed there in the Spring of 1832.

HIS MINISTRY IN BROOKLYN.

He was installed as the first Pastor of this Church on the 23d of March, 1832, and remained its Pastor until his death. Here he prosecuted his ministry, without interruption, with untiring zeal, with growing ability, and with eminent success, for a period of over two-and-twenty years. His influence was brought to bear here on a new and yet unmatured enterprise; on a new yet rapidly growing and important city. And it is not too much to say, that of all the able and useful ministers that have occupied, or do occupy, the pulpits of this "City of Churches"—and the same amount of talent is probably scarcely equaled in the world by any city of its size—none have taken a higher position, or exerted a happier and deeper influence on its rising greatness, or won more entirely the confidence and love of all classes and denominations. His death was felt to be a public calamity. It caused gloom and sorrow among its 150,000 inhabitants; and multitudes in the neighboring city of New York, where he was scarcely less known, sympathized in this feeling.

The Church to whose call he responded, had no importance

except prospectively. Its history was not yet written. It was an infant and weak colony from the First Church, numbering less than forty members. It had no house of worship, and no means had yet been taken to build one. The congregation was still to be gathered. Every thing was to be done that related to the building up and establishing of a new enterprise; and the most of it had to be done by himself. And experience has taught the extreme difficulty and arduousness of such a work. Many similar efforts, in Brooklyn and other cities, begun under more favorable auspices, have entirely failed. Many worthy pastors have struggled nobly and long in a similar field, and at last given up in despair, or broken down under the effort. There are *peculiar* embarrassments and trials connected with such a work. Few men are fitted for it; few ought ever to undertake it. Experience furnishes a sad and instructive history on this point. Say what men will, the tendency, in our cities at least, is to multiply churches faster than they can be well sustained. One strong church, well furnished and drilled, is worth a half dozen weak and dispirited ones, for efficiency and usefulness. Ambition, a desire to rule, restlessness, sectarian zeal, selfish considerations rather than the glory of God in the advancement of his kingdom, are too often the motives which originate these new churches—a large proportion of which have only a brief and sickly life to live.

Dr. Spencer succeeded in the enterprise to which he here gave himself. While many men would have failed in it, he raised it to the point of success, and carried it along through a noble career of prosperity and usefulness. But it cost even him a long, severe and earnest struggle. He labored as few men ever did. He brought to it the fruits of all his previous study and discipline; the experience of his Northampton ministry; and maturity of mind and judgment and character. He laid himself out on this field. He identified himself fully with the interests of this infant Church. He gave himself, heart and soul, to preaching, to visitation, and to measures to secure a suitable house for the worship of God. He was often at first greatly disheartened. The change from Northampton to a new and feeble church, such as this then was, was great, and he felt it sensibly. But he toiled on uncomplainingly. He was resolved that the enterprise should succeed, the Lord building the house. He was not a man, indeed, to let any thing fail on his hands.

The congregation worshiped for awhile in a school-room, but by dint of his energetic and persevering efforts, their fine and commodious church edifice and adjoining lecture-room were projected and soon completed, and entirely paid for years before his death. His preaching, too, soon began to attract an intelligent and influential class of hearers. For many years his congregation has been among the largest and noblest in the city. His Church too grew rapidly in numbers, strength and influence, and has for many years ranked among the first. Colonies have gone out from it to plant other churches. Dr. Spencer was unselfish in this. Whatever the feeling of his brethren, he was not anxious to retain any of his people, if they could be more useful in some destitute field, or in a new enterprise. He knew the wants of the city, fast stretching itself out on every side, and often advised his members to leave for some distant locality. And he entered himself heartily into efforts to build up new churches, talking, visiting, preaching and giving to aid them. More than one church now living, owes a lasting debt to his disinterested and active exertions. Few Brooklyn pastors, we apprehend, have done so much in this way.

His labors here were incessant and almost super-human, for the first twenty years. He preached *three* times on the Sabbath habitually—two carefully-written sermons, and one in the evening, thoroughly studied but unwritten. This *Sabbath evening* service, was perhaps the most interesting and profitable of the three. Though it taxed his strength very severely, and few men could sustain such a service for so long a period, he loved it; he threw into it all the strength of his vigorous mind and the warmth of his heart. His Biblical expository lectures, his lectures on the Shorter

Catechism, and his familiar practical discourses, on this evening, will never be forgotten by those who enjoyed them. We have no record or memorial of them, save what is found in the memories and hearts of his people. He has remarked to us that he owed more of his success to this evening service than to any thing else; indeed that he could never have sustained and lifted the enterprise into vigorous and permanent life without it. There can be no doubt that our denomination loses greatly by the infrequency of this habit.

Probably no man, in the same time, ever performed more pastoral labor than did Dr. Spencer during his ministry in Brooklyn. He was most indefatigable and laborious in this part of his office. His daily records of visits and conversations, persevered in for twenty-one years, form the most surprising and affecting testimonies of pastoral industry and fidelity that have ever met our eye. His visits were not visits of ceremony—visits to keep his people from fault-finding—but the visits of a man of God watching for souls, and anxious for their welfare; the visits of a kind spiritual shepherd looking after every member of his flock. Nor were they confined to his own people. He cared for the poor and the neglected. He explored the lanes and alleys of the city, literally preaching the Gospel from house to house, and warning those whom he met in the streets as God gave him opportunity. And not a little of his success was owing to these labors. Few ministers have done more good in this humble and unobtrusive way. He will be kindly remembered by hundreds of souls and families, beyond the sphere of his own congregation, to whose sad or lowly or neglected dwellings, he carried the messages of life, on lips of tender sympathy and with tearful eyes.

His removal to a city charge—his great prosperity and distinguished reputation—the gathering of fashionable churches about him, whose pulpits were filled with popular preachers—and the rivalry and emulation among churches and pastors which are incident to city life—did not change in the least the characteristics of his preaching. He remained to the last what he was in the pulpit of Edwards—free from pride and a worldly ambition—knowing nothing but Christ and him crucified—preaching the great doctrines of the Christian system, as they are held by the Presbyterian Church, with great boldness and fidelity, and without the least compromise with the spirit of a liberal and fastidious age or the demands of a flippant philosophy ; content to preach Divine sovereignty, election, total depravity, the vicarious death of Christ, the duty of all men to repent and obey the Gospel, the necessity of the Holy Spirit's influences, faith and holiness, and the eternal punishment of the wicked. No temptation, no pressure from any quarter, could ever draw him aside from these topics : they formed the staple of his ministry.

We fully believe that since Jonathan Edwards exercised his ministry at Northampton, no man has preached more real *divinity*, or preached it with more clearness, thoroughness, and unction, than he preached from the pulpit of the Second Church in Brooklyn, during the like period of time. The number and character of his sermons ; the ability and thoroughness with which the fundamental doctrines of the Gospel are discussed and vindicated in them ; the range of topics, the scope and depth of his investigations, and the vast amount of Biblical science and instruction embodied in them, will surprise any one who will be at the pains to examine them as we have done.

His preaching was never *popular*, in the modern sense of that term. There was too much weighty thought, too much doctrine, too much of God and duty, too much Edwardean plainness, honesty, and scripturalness, too much of the humility of the Cross in it, to be popular with the multitude, who love excitement and novelty, and seek after "wisdom" and a "sign." Neither his taste nor conscience would suffer him to bring *the glorious gospel of the blessed God* down to the level of modern taste, and superficiality, and sentiment, or philosophy and *science, falsely so called*. He held all such preaching in lofty contempt. He soared above it. His mind had no sympathy with the littlenesses or frivolities of fashionable preaching. But while not popular with or sought after by the mass, he drew around him many thinking minds—men of intelligence, character, and influence. And no minister was ever more appreciated and loved than was Dr. Spencer by the congregation which attended stately on his preaching.

And the Lord left not himself without a witness to his servant's fidelity. His ministry here was not more distinguished by ability and self-devotion, than it was by that highest of all tests of excellence—the conversion of souls. The Holy Spirit which had given him so many seals in Northampton, gave him many more in Brooklyn. Many hundreds of souls were added to the Lord as fruits of his labor. Several precious revivals of religion cheered his heart. He loved and prayed for, and was never more happy than when in the midst of such seasons of special interest. His preaching was adapted to arouse, to convict, to bring sinners to immediate repentance. He aimed at this. It was hard to be careless and unfeeling under such habitual preaching. A Church could not well be cold, inactive, lifeless, under such a faithful exhibition of the truth. Always engaged himself; never idle; his heart full of the love and tenderness of Christ; and his pulpit uttering, Sabbath after Sabbath, such doctrines as the Spirit has ever most honored in the conversion of souls, and the growth of the Church—it is not surprising that his ministry was almost one continued revival; that conversions should be all the while occurring; not a year without a considerable accession to his Church from the world; scarcely a month at a time in which he found not some new inquirer after the way of salvation. The facts, which we reserve for another place, will make this point clear.

We have alluded to his connection with "revivals." He was a revival preacher, in the best sense of that oft-abused word. He believed in revivals. He aimed steadily and prayerfully at such results among his own people; and he labored much, and with remarkable success, in such seasons of special Divine visitations, with other pastors and churches. But he did not *abuse* them, as too many have done. He did not place an undue reliance upon them. He did not fall into that wretched philosophy, or way of theorizing, which shuts God up to particular seasons or conditions. He honored the regular means of grace, and the ordinary operations of the Spirit. He had no partiality for the religion of revivals. He believed that salvation is as certainly and as easily attainable at any other time, as during a revival, if the soul will as diligently seek it. He accordingly, in much of his preaching, and in pastoral visitation, aimed directly, and with all the urgencies of religion and eternity, to bring men to immediate repentance—to compel them to a decision—to draw them at once to Calvary, and make them see the willingness of Christ to save them. "He had no fear of any excitements which divine truth produces; he would not undervalue revivals of religion because abuses have sometimes crept into the churches under that name; nor would he do any thing toward fostering those spurious excitements so often *called* revivals, which have done so much to distract the churches, and corrupt the religion of this country."* There was a time when he labored much in what were known as "eight days'" and "four days'" meetings. But at no time was he known to countenance any novel or rash measures to promote revivals. He was remarkable for his wisdom, and prudence, in times of religious awakening. Feeling, excitement, never swayed his judgment, or led him into extravagance. His sole reliance was the truth, blessed of the Spirit, in answer to the prayers of God's people. And a most safe guide; a thorough instructor; a master of the delicate and difficult science of guiding anxious inquirers was he, as his "Sketches," or "Conversations" with so many of them clearly prove. Probably no pastor ever felt a higher degree of responsibility than he, in this part of ministerial labor; or was more expert and thorough in it; or trained up a more intelligent and stable class of converts; or was at greater pains to acquit himself of the blood of the souls who

---

* See Preface to his *Sketches*, first series. See also in this connection that instructive Sketch in the second series, entitled "Unknown Presence of the Spirit."

sought his instruction. He believed that pastors are often far too careless—too superficial—not a little unfaithful, in their dealings with this class of sinners. He was anxious to set a worthy example. And there can be no doubt that that example, reluctantly made known to his brethren in *A Pastor's Sketches*, will be of essential benefit to them. Few men were better qualified by nature and grace, by observation and experience, to instruct others on this subject. And we account it as among the most important of his labors—these garnered fruits of his ministerial wisdom, fidelity, and experience. Thousands will willingly sit at his feet and learn.

Few pastors ever loved a people more devotedly than Dr. Spencer loved his Brooklyn charge. Few pastors ever made greater sacrifices for the sake of serving a people in the ministry of the Word. He *gave himself wholly to these things.* He sought not fame—he coveted no man's silver or gold—he scarcely gave himself the necessary rest—by day and far into the night-watches—amid the sweltering heat of summer and the rigor of winter, he toiled on with singleness of purpose, to win souls to Christ and train his people for heaven. He was always at his post; always ready for any service; always at work; always living for his people, giving them his best and undivided services. He subordinated most rigorously—as few we think ever did—the entire elements of his mind and heart and character, to the duties of the ministerial and pastoral office. Many and flattering were the "calls" made to him from various parts of the land; but believing that his Divine Master had put him into that field, and that *duty* required him to continue in it, no offer or solicitation could draw him away from it. Just after his settlement in Brooklyn, while the Church was still in its infancy, and before any particular attachment was formed, he declined a most pressing call to the Presidency of Hamilton College. He loved the ministry—he loved the pastoral office, notwithstanding its responsibilities and cares and severe trials. He had taken this weak people and enterprise to his heart, and for them would he live, for them shed his tears, till toils and cares shall end. Few people have had more reason to love a pastor and hold him in grateful remembrance than this recently bereaved Church. How much did he feel and do for them! What burdens did his kind heart bear for them! What anxious days and sleepless nights did he pass on their account! What an amount of consecrated talent, affection and endurance did he cheerfully devote for their highest good! Oh, who but the Lord can reward services like these! Weighed in the balances of eternity, how great their worth! It will not be easy to find his like. Any thing that we can write in praise of him, or rather in justice to his character and ministry, must appear tame to those among whom he labored so long, as one *eloquent and mighty in the Scriptures—not walking in craftiness, nor handling the word of God deceitfully ; but by manifestation of the truth commending himself to every man's conscience in the sight of God.*

CALLS TO OTHER FIELDS.

No man sought celebrity less than Dr. Spencer. He avoided every thing that looked like a flourish of trumpets, and was severe on those who resorted to newspapers and other usual ways to obtain notoriety or reputation. He seldom went abroad, except in exchanges with his brethren. He did not take a prominent part in the management of our Public Charities and Institutions; was never foremost on anniversary occasions; and never aimed to take the lead in ecclesiastical meetings. He was modest, as real merit usually is—would not push himself forward— was content to be a *worker*. Some of his friends felt that he did himself injustice in these matters. But it was characteristic of him. Still he became early and extensively known in the Church, and was highly appreciated by the wise and the good. Few men have received, wholly uninvited, more flattering and urgent solicitations than he. He seldom spoke of these; never trumpeted them through the land. And he observed one rule most conscientiously through life, which is too often violated by good men, and the violation of which, from whatever motive prompted, is productive of not a little mischief to the Church, and in the end injures those who indulge in it. Dr. Spencer received numerous overtures from various individuals and Churches soliciting his services and tendering him a formal call, if he would give the least encouragement; but in every instance, when advised of it, if he saw no probability of his accepting it, he took measures to forestall and prevent it. He would not sacrifice a good conscience to vanity; the interests of others for reputation.

Notwithstanding this caution, many important and urgent calls to other spheres of labor were put into his hands, at different periods of his ministry. In 1830 he was called to the Presidency of the University of Alabama; and in 1832 to the Presidency of Hamilton College of New York. This last call was long and most seriously considered by him. It was a most inviting and important post. Every inducement was held out to him. Numerous letters from distinguished men in Central and Western New York were written, urging his acceptance. It appealed to his literary taste and ambition and scholarship. He had superior qualifications for the office, and would unquestionably have distinguished himself in it. His resolution was shaken. But he could not be spared from the ministry, from Brooklyn. The Lord had a great work for him to do in the pastoral office. And the result, we think, shows the wisdom of his decision to remain where he was, and the guiding influence of Heaven in answer to prayer. This call was renewed in 1835.

We have alluded to the call from the Park Street Church, Boston, while he was yet at Northampton. He was again solicited to take upon him this important charge, in 1835, but declined having a call formally made out, as his mind remained unchanged. In 1833 he received a unanimous call to the Essex Street Church, Boston; and while he had the Park Street call under consideration, he received, through Dr. B. B. Edwards, the tender of a call from the Pine Street Church, in case he declined that, so "anxious" were the leading minds of that city, as Mr. E. expressed it, "to have him come to Boston." Many formal calls also were put into his hands, and numerous overtures made to him, from churches in New York, Philadelphia, Newark, Buffalo, Cincinnati, and various other places in the land. In 1853 he was elected to the Professorship of Pastoral Theology in East Windsor Theological Seminary, Ct. But he could not be induced to leave his Brooklyn charge. Salary, a wider field, a more conspicuous position, a splendid church edifice, literary ambition and leisure—none of these things moved him. He believed it was his Master's will that he should remain where he was, and consummate the plans he had begun, and reap the harvest for which he had expended so generous a seed-labor. But these numerous and unsolicited invitations were unmistakable testimonies to his distinguished worth and ability.

In 1836 he accepted the Professorship extraordinary of Biblical History in the Union Thelogical Seminary, New York City, and retained his connection with it for about four years. He was one of the founders and original directors of this Seminary of sacred learning. He felt a deep interest in its prosperity, and watched its growing importance and usefulness with any thing but a jealous feeling. While the unfortunate division of the Presbyterian Church, or rather the tendencies of things growing out of it, and other considerations of a more personal nature, finally induced him to withdraw from any active part in its directorship, and alienated in part his sympathies from it, he still appreciated and spoke kindly of the service it was rendering to the cause of Christ. In the last conversation but one we 'had with him—a few months only before his death—alluding to his call from East Windsor Seminary, and "wishing that he were ten years younger, that he might take hold of it," he expressed his views freely, and at length, in regard to Ministerial Education, in graphic terms characterizing what he thought were the several defects and excellences of our leading Theological Schools. And in the course of this conversation, in language most emphatic, and far stronger than we care to put it, he commended the Seminary at New York, adding that he had carefully watched its workings and results; had assisted in the examination for licensure of quite a large number of its students; and many of them he knew made practical, working men, who understood their business. Knowing that some of its friends regarded him as hostile to this Seminary, we have ventured to give the substance of his remarks, to wipe away this reproach. Whatever may have been the ground of his personal alienation, he carried no resentment with him to the grave. And he had no bigotry to blind his eyes.

Perhaps there is no more fitting place than this, to allude to his ministerial position in Brooklyn, and to his ecclesiastical relations. The dismemberment of the Presbyterian Church occurred a few years after his removal to that city. This was a severe trial to his feelings, and greatly embarrassed his situation. From the well-known character of his theology, and from his antecedents, it could not be expected that he would sympathize with such a wrong, as he viewed it, much less take an active part in perpetrating, or perpetuating it. He never did. He never gave it his countenance. He felt that it was a high-handed procedure, unwarranted by the state of the Church, and greatly injurious to the cause of truth, and the interests of the Presbyterian Church. And in his own place ecclesiastically, and to individuals on both sides, he never hesitated to speak of it thus. We have heard him repeatedly, and with that fearlessness and emphasis which characterized him, condemn the whole movement and its instruments, and deplore its evil effects.

While he could not justify the side of Power, he could not conscientiously join the "New School" Assembly. He condemned, as unwise and uncalled for, in his judgment, the action of the brethren which resulted in a separate General Assembly. He maintained the opinion to the last, that, had the aggrieved party firmly planted themselves on the Constitution, and bided their time, the unity and integrity of the Presbyterian Church would have been speedily restored. His views of this matter shaped his own course. He gave in his adhesion to the "Old School" Assembly on constitutional grounds. And yet his theology and religious sympathies were quite as much in harmony with a large portion of his "New School" brethren. The fact is, however, no school could claim him but the school of Christ. He drew his theology *directly* from the Bible, and preached it, to a great extent, in Bible language, purposely avoiding, as far as might be, the technical language and partisan aspect of the Schools.—The result of this state of things was, that he could not be made to sympathize with the spirit or measures of this division on *either* side. He loved the brethren in both Assemblies, and thought there was not sufficient reason why they should separate. He was perfectly friendly in his feelings toward, and had confidence in both, and yet he could not act decidedly with either. And consequently he was suspected, at least to a considerable extent, by both parties. He stood, as he often remarked, "between two fires. One side is angry with me because I will not fight their battles; and the other will have nothing to do with me because I will not go with them." And, in few places, owing to peculiar and painful circumstances, which we have no wish to revive in the recollection of a solitary reader, did the feeling connected with this division assume a more personal and bitter form than in Brooklyn. And its natural and actual tendency was to isolate, to a great degree, this excellent man, for years, from his ministerial brethren of the Presbyterian Church. He stood aloof from the unhallowed strife. He washed his hands clean of the guilt of it. He frequently absented himself from ecclesiastical meetings, we have heard him say, because he could not give countenance to things that were there said and done, in relation to this matter, and could not have his feelings tried by exhibitions of a party or unchristian spirit. He mourned in secret over the sad breach, and gave himself up wholly to his people.

And Dr. Spencer was the last man to be charged with indifference or laxity in relation to sound orthodoxy. No man, as these Sermons will show, in his place, contended more earnestly for the faith; or held the preachers of error in more hearty abhorrence; or denounced them with greater boldness and emphasis, when he thought fundamental doctrine was at stake. Indeed, his denunciations of religious error, and his exposures and rebukes of those, who, under the specious names of Philosophy, Reform, Liberal Christianity, Science, or Improved Theology, preach *another gospel*, were at times perfectly withering. He reminded one of the faithfulness and severity of the old Hebrew Prophets, or of the boldness and thunder-tones of Paul and Peter. His pulpit never gave an "uncertain sound." His "orthodoxy" was never called in question. No man loved and embraced more cordially the system of doctrines taught in the standards of the Presbyterian Church; or vindicated that system with more thoroughness, discrimination, and ability. Still he was any thing but an illiberal or narrow-minded man. Nay, his soul abhorred every thing that bordered on bigotry. While often suspected, and even charged by those who did not know him, as being a man of "excessive dogmatic tendencies, excessive aversion to the aggressive efforts of his brethren, and of narrow prejudices"—we quote the language of a distinguished divine, addressed to Dr. S. quite recently—few men really possessed more largeness of soul, more true Christian liberality of views, a deeper and heartier sympathy in every effort that Scripture and experience warrant, to advance religion. He held all human authority indeed in comparatively light esteem. His mind and heart were unshackled. We never saw a finer exhibition of true independence of character. Often has he invited to officiate in his pulpit men that some of his brethren had seen fit to brand as "heretical." He was in the habit of exchanging with the pastors of the various evangelical churches in Brooklyn; and all denominations loved and confided in him, and mourned his death. Many of his most intimate ministerial friends—those in whom he confided most, and whose judgment and opinion had most weight with him—were out of his own immediate ecclesiastical connection. And we know that his feelings toward his ministerial brethren generally, in the city where he spent the most of his ministry, were of the kindest character. He had the misfortune, mainly owing to the peculiarities of his position, to be *misunderstood* by some of them. His real feelings toward them were not known, and hence not fully appreciated. But there beat all the while in his bosom a heart warm and true, regulated by Christian feeling and Christian principle. We have heard him speak of brethren in the kindest spirit and with praise, who he had reason to believe were suspicious of him, or believed him unfraternal, if not alienated in feeling.

IN HIS STUDY

Dr. Spencer was a model, in most particulars. His industry was remarkable. Not a moment was spent in idleness, or thrown away on frivolous or useless occupations. He improved every talent, and turned it to the best advantage. He studied early and late; gave his whole mind and soul to the preparation of his sermons, and the duties pertaining directly to his pastorate. He devoted very little time to newspaper reading, or to our current literature, although he had a cultivated taste, believing that this sort of mental dissipation is greatly injuring the minds of many preachers. Speculation he was never fond of. His Bible, a few standard authors, and books that would give him *real information*, enlarge the stock of his actual knowledge—and they carefully studied and mastered—occupied him mainly in the study, while not writing. Few men, in the same number of years, have spent more hours in hard study; and yet, who ever found more time for pastoral labor? The secret was his industry; seizing on and fully occupying each passing moment. He acquired a knowledge of the French language at a time when he could spare but five minutes a day for it. His first volume of "A Pastor's Sketches," was written out and fitted for the press before breakfast in the morning. Until his health failed, he allowed himself but little time for sleep; at work till past midnight very commonly, and up and at it again at a very early hour in the morning. His mind was active; and blessed with a sound and vigorous constitution, he gave more time and application to study than most men could have done.

He had, too, a *system* in every thing. In his studies, his reading, his pastoral labors, and even in his preaching, he worked according to a settled plan; left as little as possible to contingency or impulse. He had a time for every thing, and a place; and when the time came he went about the assigned work without delay, and in sober earnest. Hence he was never hurried or fretted by pressing engagements, or thrust into his pulpit with a hasty preparation. And hence too he accomplished an amount of labor, which, without exaggeration, almost exceeds belief.

As a part of the results of his intellectual labor, he has left nearly one thousand sermons in manuscript, fully written out, and with great nicety; and many of them rewritten and made as perfect as his unwearied industry and application could make them. We give, in these volumes, a few specimens only from this large collection of sermons: no better than a large proportion of the remainder. Such an amount of study-labor as the preparation of so many sermons must have cost; and especially when their superior character is taken into view, and the time and strength given to the other parts of his ministry, is really a matter of surprise. All these the productions of one mind in five-and-twenty years! All this divinity, so thoroughly studied and elaborated, so skillfully arranged and ably discussed and vigorously set forth, and so filled with spirit and life as it passed through his heart and was baptized into the spirit of the Cross, and clothed in a style so varied and attractive—uniting the charms of a brilliant and hallowed imagination with the vigor and depth of the highest order of the reasoning faculty—truly it is an extraordinary practical evidence of the capabilities and resources of the human mind!

In the *thoroughness* of his pulpit preparations, Dr. Spencer deserves to be held up for imitation. With his mental resources, his large experience, and his extemporaneous gifts, he could have preached well without the trouble of such careful writing, and such severe and constant study. But from his first preparation to his last, he aimed to be thorough: he would not serve God with that which cost him nothing; the oil he carried into the sanctuary was well beaten. Habitually did he come forth to his people without having to apologize for an old sermon or a hasty effort; strong in the armor which he had been at pains to burnish and learn how to use skillfully; his mind having mastered his subject; the plan of his sermon well arranged and every word chosen, and even hints scattered along in the manuscript to aid him in the delivery of it. Seldom, we think, was he heard to preach a sermon which betrayed the lack of study and careful preparation. "Few spake like him habitually in discourses of such instructiveness," such varied and singular ability; and so adapted, at the same time, both to convince the understandings and affect the hearts of a Christian auditory.

No characteristic of his mind was more marked than his *reliance on his own resources* in all his intellectual efforts. In this respect he had not many equals. He placed very little reliance on books, on the thoughts or labors of others. He was never a *learned* man, in the broad sense of that term. At least he was not an extensively read man, by any means; he laid no claim to this distinction. His library was small, comparatively, select, characteristic of the man, and in itself a proof of his self-reliance. His own mental resources seemed well-nigh inexhaustible. He worked out his numerous discourses with little beside his Bible and Concordance to aid him. *In all the sermons of his which we have examined, we have found but two or three brief quotations from any uninspired author*, except from our religious poets, whose language he occasionally introduced with good judgment and a most delicate taste. His sermons owe as little to any human aids as any sermons to be found. They bear on every page the impress of his own mind and characteristics. And hence their freshness, their originality, their eminently scriptural character. The lack of this independence; the undue reliance on books and other aids—is it not a marked fault of much of the preaching of our day? Do not the majority of modern sermons evince more *reading* than *study?* the cultivation of general literature rather than painstaking investigation and original deep thinking?

IN THE PULPIT.

As multitudes have read his "Sketches," and will doubtless read his "Sermons," who never saw or heard him preach, we would fain convey, in this "Sketch" of Dr. Spencer, some impression of his *pulpit manner*. His sermons owed not a little to something peculiar and excellent even here. He was himself and nobody else, in the Pulpit as well as out of it. The steel engraving accompanying this volume, will give the reader a truthful life-likeness of Dr. Spencer. His presence was far from being any thing common. There was an iron sinew, and a compactness and vigor of structure about his "earthly tabernacle" which made it a fitting abode for a mind so active and strong. His eye was the most piercing and penetrating that we ever encountered, and seemed to read your very heart. His voice, low at first, rose as he advanced with his subject, and now broke in thunder on the ear, as he reached the climax of his argument, or when rebuking some bold sin, or giving utterance to some impassioned appeal; and then sunk away into the sweet and subdued tones of tenderness, as he expatiated on the love of God, or the freedom of the Gospel, or the scenes of the crucifixion. His look, manner, and voice, all indicated that he habitually felt that the Christian Pulpit is a most sacred and responsible place, and that

> "'Tis not a cause of small import
> The pastor's care demands;
> But what might fill an angel's heart,
> And filled a Saviour's hands."

He was grave, solemn, always in earnest—unlike the portrait

which Cowper in "The Task" has sketched, and which, it is to be feared, finds too many counterparts in our own day:

> "He that negotiates between God and man,
> As God's embassador, the grand concerns
> Of judgment and of mercy, should beware
> Of lightness in his speech. 'Tis pitiful
> To court a grin when you should woo a soul;
> To break a jest when pity would inspire
> Pathetic exhortation; and to address
> The skittish fancy with facetious tales
> When sent with God's commission to the heart!
> So did not Paul. * * * * *
> * * * * * * *
> No: he was serious in a serious cause,
> And understood too well the weighty terms
> That he had taken in charge. He would not stoop
> To conquer those, by jocular exploits,
> Whom truth and soberness assailed in vain."

Spencer resembled Paul in this. We have seen his people weep, but never saw them laugh, while he stood up to deliver God's messages to them. We doubt if Paul or Christ ever provoked a smile while preaching the Gospel to dying sinners.

His general manner was not attractive to strangers. There were some infelicities in it which showed that he had not practiced in the school of human art. Still there was a naturalness, an unaffected simplicity, a variety and earnestness, and often an affectionate tenderness about it, which made it far from displeasing to those who heard him statedly. Many casual hearers thought him "dogmatical" in the pulpit; there was occasionally the appearance of this. But there was no dogmatism in his heart—it was all in his manner. And this arose from the characteristics of his mind—the strength of his own convictions of truth; and from the fact, that he was not preaching *a cunningly-devised fable*, or the speculations of the Schools, or the wisdom of this world; but simply declaring God's message; giving utterance to revealed and authoritative Truth, which could not be gainsayed, and which no man was at liberty to cavil at or reject. He *did* handle God's Word as one who felt that he stood on solid rock—who dealt only in the eternal verities of religion—and who had himself so profound an insight into and experience of the things of God, like Melancthon after his conversion, that it seemed to him no mind could or ought to withstand the truth a moment; every weapon drawn to oppose it looked contemptible; and it stood forth to the preacher's view in the majesty of its own greatness, and bid defiance to unbelief and to all the devils in hell. But his confidence was never in himself—never in his own reasonings—only and always in the Scriptures, on which he grounded, and with which he filled every sermon. In matters of *opinion* he was not positive. He asked no man to receive his *ipse dixit.* But he did demand for *God's truth*, which he demonstrated to their understandings, and applied to their hearts and consciences, immediate and unqualified acceptance; an unquestioning faith and obedience. He verily thought that the preacher of the Gospel has a decided vantage-ground in the nature of the truths he preaches, and in the moral nature of man to which he appeals; and one which ought never to be relinquished by him. He believed that the modern pulpit has lost some of its legitimate power, because the Gospel is too often preached as we would preach philosophy, or literature, or science, or a system of truth based simply on human reason and speculation: with a timidity or misgiving which amounts to moral cowardice; not with becoming *authority*, as the divinely constituted embassadors of Jesus Christ were expected to declare it. And such a view we believe to be in accordance with sound philosophy, and the teachings of experience.

In the gift of *prayer* he eminently excelled. There was no formality, no repetition, no stereotyped forms of thought or expression in his devotional exercises, such as are so painfully common. His prayers, though usually long, were a fitting preparation for his sermon; always appropriate, warm from the heart, new in form, and beautifully and often touchingly expressed. It is said that the preaching of Dr. Payson owed not a little to his extraordinary devotional gift; and the same is unquestionably true of Dr. Spencer. His people have enjoyed and profited by these devotional excellences in the pulpit, as much almost as by his sermons. And yet, not even here did the peculiar richness and fullness of this gift show itself. His prayers in the cottages of the poor, the chamber of sickness, by the bedside of the dying, in the dwelling of affliction—amid such scenes of affecting interest as his graphic pen has sketched in his volumes—will never be forgotten by those who heard them. There his heart dissolved in sympathy and tenderness; he seemed to commune with God face to face, and his whole soul to go forth on the wings of a sublime devotion, and bring God and eternal things affectingly nigh. Never seemed he so truly great and good as amid those scenes of poverty and suffering, sorrow and death; lifting up his tearful eyes to God, and pleading with such fervor for his fellow sinners.

The *uniformity* of his pulpit efforts was not a little remarkable. Unlike many preachers he never laid out all his strength on occasional efforts. He strove, on the contrary, to make every sermon his best, as good as he could make it. He had no " great sermons" with which he aimed to make a grand impression and achieve a reputation. One had to hear him statedly in his own pulpit, Sabbath after Sabbath, year after year, to appreciate fully his ability. We have enjoyed this privilege to a considerable extent, and the more and the longer we heard him, the more were our admiration and surprise excited. The *first* sermon we ever heard from him— he was an entire stranger to us then, and not in his own pulpit— made an impression never to be forgotten; we wept through the most of it and rejoiced; it seemed almost as if we were listening to a new Gospel. The theme was his favorite one—CHRIST, his love, the freedom and sufficiency of his salvation, and the blessedness of reposing in him. We scarcely knew which to admire most, the imagination which spread a hallowed charm over the whole, the ability with which the theme was treated, or the tenderness and Christian sympathy which the preacher threw into it. We thought, and so expressed it then to the friends with whom we were staying, that we had never before heard such a preacher. Every subsequent hearing but deepened that first impression. We have *never* heard from him what we have heard from many of our most distinguished preachers, a poor or even commonplace sermon. *Always* have we gone from his preaching wondering how he could command the time, amid his pressing calls, to make so able and so instructive a preparation for his usual Sabbath labors.

His presence and manner being what they were; his devotional spirit and exercises so elevated and impressive; and his sermons uniformly characterized by so high a degree of excellence; and, superadded to this, the testimony of a blameless life and indefatigable pastoral devotion—it is not surprising that his pulpit was a strong tower; and his ministry rich and instructive to those who were favored to attend statedly upon it.

AS A PASTOR.

Let us follow him from the pulpit into *Pastoral life*. Considering the character and extent of his labors in the Study and in the Pulpit, and the numerous pressing engagements connected with so large a city charge, one might think he would have little time for visitation among his parishioners, and indeed would feel himself excused from attempting much in that way. A diversity of opinion exists among pastors, we are aware, as to how much time it is best to devote to this kind of ministerial work. We suspect men's judgments on this point are very much influenced by their temperament and practice. Pastors not fond of such labor, and not particularly adapted to it, are not apt to lay much stress upon it, and find a ready excuse for not giving much attention to it. It is undeniably the most self-denying part of ministerial duty. Dr. Spencer excelled in this as much as in the pulpit. He never neglected study, and yet he gave much time to visitation. He was qualified by nature and by grace for such

AS A PASTOR. 57

work. He had a love for it. He laid out his strength upon it. He cultivated his vineyard, in this private way, as assiduously and as faithfully as he did from his pulpit on the Sabbath. The amount and variety of his pastoral work almost exceed belief. His people, his brethren, his most intimate friends, could have had no adequate conception of it. Among all his "remains," there are none so affecting as the *dozen closely-written volumes* which contain the evidence of this.

He was thoroughly *systematic* in this. He carried with him always a book, containing a full directory of his Congregation; and in it the date of each visit was registered opposite to the name. It was his *rule* to call on each family, who attended on his ministry, once every year, and as much oftener as circumstances seemed to render it desirable. None were passed by in making these visits. The poor, the obscure, the lonely widow, were as sure to receive the pastor's call as the rich and the distinguished. We never heard it said of him, as it is sometimes said of good ministers, "My pastor never calls to see me."—And he did not confine his visits to his own people. He had a heart for suffering and ignorance, wherever he found them, and a word for souls whenever he could catch their ear. Through the lanes and alleys of the city he often went, exploring the neglected fields of misery and moral degradation; and many an interesting memorial of his kindness and care might be gathered thence. The sun never beat too fiercely, nor the storm raged too severely. Seldom was he away during the hot and sickly month of summer; preferring to wait until his brethren had returned from their annual recreation: keeping his Church open, and ready for any service which might be demanded of him. He had, too, a wonderful faculty of *knowing* people: a person could not attend his Church many Sabbaths and fail to make his acquaintance: he would inquire him out; find where he lived; know something of his history, and interest himself in him.

And he was as *faithful* as he was laborious in this kind of labor. When he found a case of sickness, or affliction, or awakening, or of decided interest of any kind, he followed it up; nothing could induce him to neglect it. And the *fidelity* with which he dealt with all classes of people, whom he was wont to encounter in these visits, is so fully and so affectingly brought to light in those *Sketches*, drawn by him from real life, that we need not add a word on this point. To this unusual fidelity he owed much of his power and success in dealing with souls.

His *tact* seemed almost an inspiration. His perception of character was very remarkable. His knowledge of men and things was extensive and thorough. He was a close observer. He looked into the human heart with a steadiness and power of vision, aided by the daily study of God's Word, which almost laid it bare to his inspection. He studied *particular* characters, that he might know how to approach them and gain an influence over them. And when a sinner once found him on his track, pursuing hard after him, it was vain to flee, and hard to get away from his grasp. He resembled the excellent *Nettleton*, in some of these things, more nearly than any man we have known. And his fearless manner, "bold as a lion," in any place, in any presence; his skill and force in argument; and his sweet and affectionate manner, when his sympathies were touched, gave him great advantage. And he was careful to *use* it. He was restrained by no false delicacy. He would not shrink where others might faint. He *cultivated* this talent, as we think few men do, by study, by meditation, by prayer, and by daily practice; and it *gained other five talents*. He watched for opportunities to put it to good use; and if they did not readily occur, he would go out and create them—challenge Providence. Many instances of this kind will occur to one familiar with his *Sketches*. Did we oftener *do likewise*, should we have such frequent occasion to complain of a barren ministry and a dull heart?

In the *young* of his charge he took a deep interest. He had an unusual facility for adapting himself to their feelings and states of mind. Familiar and affectionate, like a father, he very generally secured their confidence; and by the tender interest he felt in them, and the power of his persuasions, won many of them to the Saviour. Seldom was one of his years more tenderly loved by the younger portion of his flock: and yet he never sacrificed in the least the dignity or proprieties of the sacred profession. He did not forget even those who were temporarily away from his ministry, but followed them with his counsels and entreaties. Many scores of letters has he written to such while at school, or on visits from home, full of ministerial love and solicitude, pleading with them for Christ and heaven.

His sympathy with those in *trouble* or *distress*—with the suffering poor, the sick, the bereaved, the tried, the desponding—was profound and active. He was *charitable*, giving largely in proportion to his means, but always in an unobtrusive way; in his visits of mercy ministering to the body as well as the soul—and never refusing even the door-beggars, so many and generally so unworthy in the city, justifying it by saying, "I had rather be imposed upon fifty times than deny one really deserving person." The poor of Brooklyn will miss him as much as any other class. And so will those who need the balm of the Gospel poured into their bleeding hearts. Dr. Spencer, by nature and grace, and by his own experience, was peculiarly fitted to administer the *consolations* of religion. He had a reputation among those who did not know him personally, for severity, harshness; but we appeal to the thousands of sick and dying persons on whom he attended as the minister of religion—to the afflicted and bereaved whom he endeavored to console, by letter and by word of mouth—and to the many anxious souls who sought his instruction. He had the heart of a woman, pitiful, tender, exquisitely sensitive. His spirit was the spirit of Christ, when he looked on a suffering creature, or on a penitent sinner. He had imbibed the precious life of that Scripture, prophetic of the Messiah, *A bruised reed shall he not break, and the smoking flax shall he not quench.* Who that knew his real heart, or his habits, will doubt for a moment his own words, so modestly expressed in the Preface to the second series of *Sketches:* "He has always been unwilling to utter a single sentence which could wound the feelings of an anxious inquirer after truth, aiming to find his way up to the Cross, and perplexed and harassed with the doubts, and difficulties, and darknesses of his own troubled mind. * * * Christianity, certainly, is kindness, and good manners, and good taste; and the author is confident that he never uttered an unkind expression upon the ears of any inquirer, and never unnecessarily wounded the feelings of any one, who ever did him the favor to come to him."

His correspondence presents him in an exceedingly amiable and lovely light, on this point. We regret that our space will allow only a single brief extract. A dear friend was in deep affliction. At such a time his sympathies were identified with the sufferer. He did not talk or write *about* but *to* the grief. "You will cling closer to Jesus. You will feel how vanishing the world is. You will realize more and more how all the good there is in it, is melting away into heaven. Your thoughts will more and more wander off into that other country where your Father has gone to reside, and the wisdom of paternal lips will now seem to call you to prepare with speed, to go home to the scenes and society that have welcomed him. This event will make an impression on the characteristics of your piety. It ought to do so. It will make you more solemn, but more sweet and cheerful. It will lift your heart more from the world. It will make you more contemplative, humble, dependent, active, and if it should for a time draw you away somewhat from the society of Christians, it will draw you more into the society of Christ. You will go from Damascus to Jerusalem. You will breathe free in the gales of Palestine. You will climb to the hill-tops of Judea in the loneliness of your heart's sorrow and pensiveness; and you will come back again to the scenes of your earthly duties like an exiled spirit, in the temper of another world, to do good for a little while in this."

To give the reader some idea of the extent and character of

Dr. Spencer's pastoral labors, take the aggregate of them for *one year*, so far as figures can express the truth. We copy from his new-year sermon for 1852. If *he* had occasion to mourn and accuse himself, while passing such a year's labors in review, alas for the most of us!

"Looking back now upon the ministry I have exercised for another year, I confess that I am ashamed, and ought to be ashamed, of the feebleness of my ministrations, and that they have been performed with no more faith, and no higher spirituality. On this account I would be ashamed and abased before God. But I am *not* ashamed of the affection which I have ever borne to my people, of my desires for their good, nor of the amount of labor and industry which I have employed. In the year 1851, I preached two hundred and nine sermons.

"I visited all the families of the congregation once, and in special instances more than once. The number of these calls was four hundred and twenty-one.

"I visited sick people and dying ones in one hundred and twenty-one different instances.

"I aimed to find opportunity for conversation with those who were not members of the Church, that, conversing with them alone, I might, if possible, persuade them to seek the Lord. And as they seldom came to me, for the most part I went to them. Such private conversations, and some of them protracted, numbered two hundred and fifty-nine.

"I attended prayer-meeting forty-six times; and other religious meetings sixty-two times; and officiated at thirty-four funerals.

"I did not neglect the poor: I aimed to search them out and, according to my ability, give them pecuniary relief. I am sorry the relief was so small, but I am sure it was given with good will in seventy-two instances." Over *eight hundred* "visits" and "conversations" in a single year, to say nothing of all the other items!

His brethren have wondered where he obtained so much remarkable material as he has drawn upon in his *Sketches;* and some have almost believed that he indulged in a little exaggeration or coloring of incidents—so many affecting and extraordinary cases occurring under the eye of a single pastor. But in view of the character of the man and of his ministry: in view of labors such as above stated, crowded into a single year, and then such aggregates multiplied by twenty-five, we may cease to wonder—cease all unbelief. What a world of opportunity was his! What need had he to draw on fancy or fiction, with such an experience—such an actual life spread out before his mind's eye, and all the materials gathered on such a field not merely garnered in his memory, but committed to paper? His habits in this particular are not common. Nothing escaped his eye. Every person, every incident, every scene, every conversation was daguerreotyped by his memory and pen, and laid up for future use. No writer of *fiction*—Warren, Scott, Bulwer, Dickens, or Sue—ever had a more extensive experience and observation of real life, in its ordinary and extraordinary phases, to draw upon. And his two volumes of sketchings from life, contain only a *selection* from this mass of interesting material: much more remains: and the author kept adding to the stock till his tongue and pen could no longer perform their office. His own language respecting his habit—a habit which imparted such tact, ability and thoroughness to his labors on this field—is worthy of being pondered by every one whose position calls him to deal with the souls of men. "Whenever it was practicable, he studied the subjects beforehand. Having met an individual once, and expecting to meet him again, he carefully considered his case, aimed to anticipate his difficulties, studied the whole subject intensely, and, in many cases, wrote sermons upon it, the substance of which afterward came out, to a greater or less extent, in the conversation. Thus the conversations aided the sermons, and the sermons aided the conversations. If he might be permitted to do so, the author would commend this mode of ministerial action to younger ministers of the Gospel."

RESULTS OF HIS MINISTRY.

These can never be fully known until the disclosures of eternity are made. Still Dr. Spencer was not of the number who sow and reap not; who plant and water the seed of the kingdom, and yet gather no visible harvest. He was permitted, on the contrary, to see of the travail of his soul even in this world. Although he often complained, with tears, of the barrenness of his ministry, and remarked that he had mistaken his calling; yet was that ministry visibly productive of great and glorious results. Few men, as we have seen, were more industrious and laborious in the sacred calling; few *sow beside all waters* more of the seed of the Word; few expend more real strength and energy of life with the single aim of saving souls; and few, consequently, have more abundant occasion to rejoice. God was not unfaithful to forget his work and labor of love. Many were the seals of his ministry while he wept and toiled. The Holy Ghost wrought by him, from the beginning of his ministerial life in Northampton to the close of it in Brooklyn.

The following facts will convey some idea of his general labors, with their immediate known results in the hopeful conversion of men. He made a record of the number of sermons he preached each year; the *whole* number being a fraction short of *five thousand*: the largest number in any one year was two hundred and thirty-eight: or an average of nearly *four a week* during the entire period of his active ministry! He received into the Church, in connection with his ministry, in all, thirteen hundred and ninety-seven souls—two hundred and thirty-three in Northampton, and eleven hundred and sixty-four in Brooklyn. Out of this large number, six hundred and eighty-two were received on profession of their faith—two hundred and one in Northampton in a period of *three and a half years;* and four hundred and eighty-one in Brooklyn, during an active ministry of *twenty-two years*. As a rebuke and an encouragement to his brethren, we are induced to copy from his memoranda the following:

"Admissions to the Church on profession in each year of my ministry, after my ordination [September 11, 1828]:

1828,.......1	1837,......18	1846,.......9
1829,......10	1838,......64	1847,......17
1830,......22	1839,......21	1848,......26
1831,.....144	1840,......23	1849,......44
1832,......34	1841,......20	1850,.......9
1833,......11	1842,......22	1851,......10
1834,......20	1843,......46	1852,......23
1835,......22	1844,......15	1853,......12
1836,......18	1845,.......9	1854,......12."

It will be seen that the lowest number is *nine*, and the highest *one hundred and forty-four*: AN AVERAGE OF MORE THAN TWENTY-SIX, during the period of the same number of years!! Few ministries, confined to two fields of labor, can show larger and more precious results.

It is known too that a large number of souls were hopefully converted under his ministry, who did not connect with his own Church. Thus in the revival at Northampton, there were two hundred and fifty-three individuals that came under his personal observation, who he believed were the subjects of saving grace. In Brooklyn the number belonging to this class was large. Add to this the fact, that he was always ready to assist his brethren; that he labored frequently and quite extensively in revivals in various places, and was the instrument of a powerful work of grace in more places than one. In the earlier part of his ministry, meetings for "continuous days" were common throughout New England, and many other portions of the Church; and few pastors labored more efficiently and successfully on these occasions than did Dr. Spencer. His labors are held in grateful remembrance in several churches in connection with seasons of awakening and rejoicing; by none more so than by the churches of Hartford and Wethersfield, Connecticut. One of the sermons accompanying this Sketch, ("Help in God for Sinners"), possesses a sacred interest, aside from its intrinsic value, from the fact, that it was preached by its author in no less than twenty-five important churches, and in fifteen instances during the progress of a work of grace: and such items as follow are appended in connection with the places where it was preached: "thirty remained for prayer—fifty remained—one hundred and eighty remained [Wethersfield, Ct., March 7, 1841]. The sermon shows too, what *kind of doctrine* this eminently successful revivalist preached to "anxious inquirers." Had such a style of preaching generally prevailed, and such men as Dr. S. been found to conduct revivals, so many good men would not have come to fear them. The Church would not have suffered so much from the abuse of them. And so wide-spread an apathy, as has prevailed for some years past in relation to them, would not give occasion for so much alarm to the friends of an evangelical and aggressive Christianity.

Much of Dr. Spencer's usefulness was connected with revivals. He loved them and labored heartily to promote them. He would not be driven from them because some good men abused them and others were suspicious of them. His character and ministry took their peculiar type from them. But for them *A Pastor's Sketches* had never been drawn. "The most of the instances here mentioned" (see Preface to first series) " occurred in revivals of religion. * * * He would not undervalue revivals of religion because abuses have crept into the churches under that name; nor would he dare to think of choosing the mode in which the Holy Spirit shall do his own blessed work." He had independence enough to judge for himself, and to carry out his own convictions; while his experience gave him confidence in these extraordinary manifestations.

Add to the direct fruits of his ministry in the conversion of souls, the number of Christians so well trained by him for service and for heaven; the incidental and collateral good he accomplished; and the mission of instruction and salvation which his pen has begun and which the press will perpetuate and make world-wide, and it will be admitted that few men comparatively, have achieved more for their Master and for mankind. Entering the ministry quite advanced, and dying in the midst of his days, his ministerial life was not a long one. But that life possessed the highest of all gifts—the gift of eminent *usefulness.* His ministry received the highest of all testimonies to its excellence and Divine authority—inquirers flocking to him—sinners converted to God—Christ's sheep fed, instructed, and helped on in their pilgrimage. *Thousands,* we believe, will call him blessed, in *the day of the Lord ;* will hail him as their spiritual father; and make bright with exceeding glory that crown which he shall wear in the everlasting kingdom. *Let him know, that he which converteth the sinner from the error of his way, shall save a soul from death, and shall hide a multitude of sins.* Yes, Brother, this motive ever weighed on thy soul. Thou didst run a noble race—far outstripping most of thy companions—and being dead thou yet speakest. May the memory of thy bright example—*always abounding in the work of the Lord*—always watching for souls—never so happy as when guiding them in the way of life, stimulate us who remain to greater earnestness and fidelity in the work of our common Master! How many dying sinners didst thou win to Christ! How many sad hearts cheer! How many afflicted souls minister to! How many perplexed minds relieve! How many inquiring ones direct into the path of salvation! How many poor and suffering children of men befriend and bless! How many dying saints commend to God and help to support while they went down Jordan's rugged bank!

HIS CHARACTERISTICS AS A PREACHER.

We have alluded to some of these, and others might be gathered from these Sermons and from his Sketches. Still we think a sketch of the leading traits of his mind and character as developed in his preaching, grouped together, may contribute to give a truthful and complete impression of the man.

He was remarkable and characteristic as a preacher, as all know who heard him much. His excellences were many, and of no common order. He combined elements of beauty, strength and merit seldom found in one and the same individual. There were no mental eccentricities, such as often disfigure great minds; no over-development of any particular faculty to the injury of others. There was a symmetry, a completeness, a unity in his intellectual being, which, while it lessened the effect of *particular* excellences, made him, as a *whole*, a very superior man. Almost any one of a dozen distinguished elements which he possessed would, of itself, have made him no common preacher; and the combination, the harmonious development and skillful blending of them all in one person, made him greatly to excel; made him indeed one of the brightest ornaments of the American Pulpit. We may be partial; our judgment may mislead us. Yet have we heard many of our most distinguished preachers, and are familiar somewhat with the Pulpit Literature of the world. And it is our deliberate judgment, long since formed and often before expressed, that, judged of by the true standard of Gospel preaching, Dr. Spencer scarcely had his superior among his cotemporaries. Others excelled him in *particular* gifts and excellences. He aimed not at display, or a polished eloquence. He despised the wisdom of words, and the tricks of the finical orator. His sermons were not formed strictly after the nice rules of human art, nor it may be always according to the demands of rigid esthetics. Yet as a whole—trying him by the higher standard of real merit and power, true homiletic science— we know not where to look for his superior. There was a vigor and manliness, a depth and comprehensiveness of thought, a skill and power of demonstration, a freshness and originality of form, an independence, fearlessness and force of manner; the reasoning of a man of God, all of whose utterances were in manifest sympathy with the cross of Jesus Christ and came through the realizations of his own experience; the grappling of a masterly mind with its subject and with the understandings and consciences of his hearers, which made it an intellectual and religious feast to listen to him as he came before his people, Sabbath after Sabbath, *holding forth the Word of life—reasoning of righteousness, temperance and a judgment to come*—and bringing out from the inexhaustible treasury of the Gospel, *things both new and old.* His preaching was always elevated and highly intellectual, so that the most cultivated minds enjoyed it. And yet it was so characterized by simplicity and good sense; by broad, thorough and just views of man and of actual life; it was so pervaded with the language and spirit of the Bible; and it was so full of real sensibility, and affectionate concern and tenderness, as he contemplated the love of God and the death of Christ and the ruin of man, and plead with the sinner to turn and live, that *the common people heard him gladly.* Never we believe was the complaint made by one of his people, rich or poor, cultivated or uneducated—which is made so frequently in these days of intellectual and ambitious sort of preaching, " We do not understand our minister ;" or, " We are not fed with the sincere milk of the Word." He *would be* understood. He would not bring abstruse speculation into the pulpit, or philosophy. His aim was to *enlighten, instruct.* And he wasted no words. He found no place for fine sentiment. He made his way straight to the comprehension of his hearers, and lodged the Word of God, clearly demonstrated, in their convictions.

Naturally Dr. Spencer had a mind of the very first order. It was massive, and of Doric strength and simplicity. He was an original, independent and vigorous thinker. He had the elements of true greatness and power. His mind was well trained and disciplined; not by books—not in the schools of art or human learning—but by patient, severe and persevering self-exercise; by the earnest study of the Word of God and the best ways and means of giving it effect on mankind. He was " a *self-made* man." And the BIBLE—the grand and sublime truths of Revelation, pondered, investigated, drank in daily and expounded, had not a little influence in developing and giving character to his gifted mind. His *preaching* naturally partook of this cast of mind. His sermons, intellectually considered, were characterized by freshness and ability, by vigor and depth of thought, often

CHARACTERISTICS AS A PREACHER. 69

rising into real magnificence and almost startling his hearers by the splendor of his conceptions, or by the originality and power of his utterances. They were never filled with common-place remarks, or stereotyped forms of sermonizing, or high-sounding words. There was real, vigorous, weighty *thought* in them—thought that bore the impress of a great mind—requiring attention, reflection in the hearer, to feel its full force and appreciate all its beauty and worth, yet never failing to reward when given. Considered as his ordinary Sabbath efforts, the Sermons contained in these volumes, judged of intellectually, will rank, we think, among the best. His statement and vindication of Gospel doctrines, were often as ably and thoroughly done as in our standard systems of Divinity. Few men have done more than Dr. Spencer to sustain the intellectual ability of the Evangelical Pulpit in these, in some respects, degenerate times. And the contrast between his sermons, in this particular, and those of many of our popular preachers and sermon authors, is great and instructive. The Sermons now given to the Public from his pen, will, we have no doubt, command general admiration and an extensive reading, simply as exhibitions of a remarkably gifted mind.

His mind was truly *original*. He thought for himself. He copied no man. He followed no authority save one, and to that he bowed with the meekness and docility of a child. He relied mainly on his own resources. He was always himself—independent in his investigations, unfettered by human dogmas or customs—fearless in proclaiming what he found to be in the Bible, unpopular or contrary to the received opinions of men, as that truth might be—following in all things his own convictions, even if such a course arrayed him against all the world. He may have carried this too far. Some thought him opinionated, dictatorial, overbearing. But in him it arose from the *original* cast of his mind. It was the testimony of his nature to his love of truth and his determination to obey its convictions at whatever cost. No man, after all, was more easily influenced and won, when once you convinced his judgment.

But this cast of mind and character lent interest to his preaching. It was peculiar. There was a novelty and freshness, an idiosyncrasy about it, which greatly commended it. The Gospel at times was almost made to appear like a new system of doctrines and duties, so original was the form and manner of his setting it forth. His style, his mode of sermonizing, his illustrations, his manner of reasoning, the way in which he set forth the *doctrines* of the Gospel, all were characteristic, and tended to enhance the effect of his preaching. And this originality was not the originality of an erratic genius, which pains while it dazzles. Nor the originality of an ambitious mind, straining after novelty or startling forms of thought or language; which is characteristic of not a little of our modern pulpit originality. It was the originality of a clear, independent, comprehensive, creative and well-balanced mind, strongly grasping its subject, thoroughly investigating it for himself, looking at it from his own chosen point of observation, and able to shed upon it the light and freshness that beamed on his own mind and feelings on the mount of contemplation.—These sermons will, we think, sustain this remark, and commend the Gospel to a class of minds not always reached by ordinary pulpit teaching. The reader will recognize on almost every page the pen which drew such vivid portraitures of human nature; wrought such masterly arguments (as in the instance of the *Young Irishman*); sketched such original definitions and clear outlines of Theology; and gave such proofs of a deep insight into human nature and Christian experience, as are to be found in *A Pastor's Sketches.*

Dr. Spencer's preaching was eminently *doctrinal.* Few men preached the fundamental doctrines of the Bible more than he. While experimental and practical, he grounded all his teaching on inspired doctrine. He was never more at home, or evinced a higher order of ability or skill in handling the Word of God, than when he grappled with some great doctrine of the Christian system, explaining, vindicating, demonstrating, and applying it. He *loved* the doctrines of the Gospel. He loved to preach them.

He made them his frequent themes. He laid out all his strength upon them. He thoroughly indoctrinated his people, giving them the *strong meat* as well as the *sincere milk of the Word*. And he was peculiarly *happy* in doing this. We have never known a preacher to throw so much Scripture doctrine into his sermons—doing it ample justice too—and yet secure the fixed, interested, and often tearful attention of a popular auditory during nearly an hour. It were well for his Brethren to study him and follow his example in this. Often would he preach on Election, Divine Sovereignty, Atonement, Depravity; or on the Character or some of the Attributes of God, and do it so skillfully and with such ability; free from technicality and adapted to the popular mind; give it such practical bearings, and shed over it or mingle with it such touches of sacred feeling and hallowed imagination, that, instead of thinking that such preaching was dry and uninteresting, his people felt that it was the best, the most profitable and highly-enjoyed of his pulpit exhibitions. Some of these sermons, (particularly in the second volume), will show how much doctrine he was accustomed to throw into his discourses, and with what tact and ability he handled such subjects.

His preaching was unusually *demonstrative*. Few have copied *Paul* more closely than he, in this particular. His uniform habit was, to deduce from his text some particular doctrine, or proposition; define and state it carefully; lay his sermon off into formal divisions, which he was careful to announce before entering upon the discussion; and then address himself earnestly to the work of elucidating, vindicating, or demonstrating that doctrine or proposition—keeping it constantly before the minds of his hearers and aiming steadily at one definite point; calling to his aid all his reasoning powers, all the sources of illustration at his command, and all the light of an extensive and varied experience. And when he had fairly got the doctrine or principle before the mind, or secure in the convictions of his auditory, then followed the application in closing up. And, generally, he carried the minds of his hearers with him. He made them comprehend his subject. He poured convincing light on their understandings. He arrayed conscience on the side of truth. If he could not carry the *hearts* of sinners and compel obedience to the truth, he brought them in guilty and left them without excuse; wrung from them the reluctant acknowledgment that it *was* the truth of God and they refused it on peril of damnation! No preacher habitually made a stronger appeal to the *reasoning* faculty of man. He honored this Divine gift in the human soul, and brought the sublime truths of Infinite Reason and all the urgencies of religion, to solicit its submission and allegiance to God. Gifted, as few preachers are, with the power of a brilliant imagination, of eloquent declamation, and of tender and effective appeal to feeling and sympathy; he still held all these gifts in rigid subordination, and gave to MIND, to REASON, that prominence which God gives it in his Revelation, and which experience has proved to be the most effective in accomplishing a great and permanent influence on mankind. His sermons may be deficient, in the judgment of some, in rhetorical polish and finish; in some of the niceties of human accomplishment. They will not be likely to please a fastidious taste or hyper-critic, who is incapable of discerning the higher order of merit. But there is a power of reason, a gift of the Divine faculty in them, the bone and sinew of intellectual strength and exercise, which will commend them to the men of mind; to the thinkers; to those who put their understandings above their tastes, prejudices and passions. They are greatly superior in this respect to the mass of sermons preached and published.

His preaching seldom failed in point of *fidelity*. Most jealous was he of the honor of his Divine Master. He shunned not to declare the whole counsel of God, *whether men would hear or whether they would forbear.* He used great plainness of speech. He addressed himself directly to the sinful and immortal beings who sat under his ministry. He was bold and pointed in rebukeing sin. He feared the face of no man. He courted not popularity. The fact that any doctrine was unpopular; that he might give offense to some of his hearers if faithful, never seemed to influence him in the least. He was among the number of prophets *who cry aloud, spare not.* He warned the wicked often like a son of "Thunder." No one escaped. If there was a *David* among his hearers, and he knew it, a voice would ring out from that pulpit and pierce his ears in prophet tones, *Thou art the man.* He would not let the sinner go away unconvinced, self-complacent, if truth and honest dealing could reach his mind and convict his heart. He seemed habitually to preach with his eye on God and eternity; conscious of his responsibility, and mainly anxious to quit himself of the blood of souls. And yet was he a man of *tears.* His heart often melted into tenderness. Words of inexpressible sweetness and gentleness and affectionate persuasion would often drop from his lips. His appeals to the impenitent were not unfrequently the outbursts of a heart touched with the profoundest grief and pity for them. *With weeping and supplication* did he beseech men to be reconciled to God. After he had warned them in vain to flee from the wrath to come, like his Master, he would go on the mount of Olives and weep out his compassion before God; or as Isaiah did, to borrow his own idea, after reproving Israel in vain, go up on the mountain cliff, and wrapping his mantle round him, complain in the ear of the Merciful One, *Who hath believed our report? and to whom is the arm of the Lord revealed?* Seldom have these opposite elements and characteristics—the iron nerve and the tearful eye—the majesty of righteousness and the heart *touched with the feeling of our infirmity*—the stern, God-fearing reprover and the weeping suppliant—been so perfectly united in the same preacher.

Nothing surprised one more than the *variety* of his preaching. He confined himself strictly to the Bible. He never traveled beyond the inspired record, or introduced topics out of place in a Christian pulpit. And he indulged in no curious speculations or fancies in handling his chosen subjects. And still he always had something *new* as well as old; he was not confined to a few thread-bare subjects. Familiar with every part of the Bible and daily pondering its Divine truths, he was never at a loss for a theme or matter, interesting, weighty and instructive. The compass of his mind, the breadth of his views, the originality of his investigations, and the depth of his experience, gave a richness and fullness, and a variety and freshness to his sermons beyond what is common. During the period of twenty-two years he exercised his ministry in the Second Church of Brooklyn, not only without any abatement of interest and power, but manifestly with growing richness and ability to the last. We might fill a small volume with the bare titles of his sermons—the themes of his pulpit discourses—no two of them alike—not one out of place—all serious and weighty themes—proving that the topics and materials which the Scriptures furnish are varied and ample enough to occupy fully and exhaust the most capacious and well-furnished mind, and leaving that class of preachers without excuse, (not small we fear in this day,) whom Cowper so well describes in that couplet—

> "How oft when Paul has served us with a text,
> Has Epictetus, Plato, Tully, preached!"

But one of the most prominent characteristics of Dr. Spencer's preaching was its *Scriptural* character. He emphatically preached the Bible, the whole Bible, and nothing but the Bible. He drew every subject from it. He grounded every sermon upon the plain import of God's revealed Word. He made that Word his sole authority in all his teaching. The Bible was the staple of all his sermons. They were full of it; and drew their inspiration from it. It was the simple power of Scripture truth that he wielded with so much effect. He had no confidence in any other kind of teaching. He believed that his sole business in the pulpit was to unfold and vindicate, enforce and apply the meaning or truths of God's revelation. Hence he aimed steadily to exalt the Divine Word. He bowed always and most reverently to its authority.

His views on this point were very decided—his feelings strong—his habit uniform and marked throughout his ministry.

Greatly did he deplore the style of preaching which is becoming we fear common and popular—the philosophical, or literary; that which exalts human reason, or deals in unwarranted speculation, or trusts in accomplishments and graces to convert men. He strenuously opposed to this tendency all the weight of his example. And there are scattered through his sermons many severe rebukes of it. Take an example or two. In a sermon preached to a large number of his ministerial brethren not long before his death, he says:

"Be on your guard against a style of reasoning on moral and religious subjects, which is fast creeping into our literature and lectures, and, I am compelled to say, into many of our sermons. Every thing is coming to be *philosophized*. Many a minister in the pulpit—shame on him—betrays his trust to the Bible and his God, by teaching religion very much as if it were a mere matter of reason, and human progress, and human discovery, instead of taking God's Word as his authority and instructor, and uttering in the ears of the people, like the old prophets, *Thus saith the Lord God*. Beware of such proceedings. They tend to infidelity. Learn duty from God. The Bible is safe. Philosophy is blind.

"Be attached to the great distinctive *doctrines* of the Bible. These old doctrines are now sneered at in some quarters and slided over in others. But they are foundations. For true religion, indeed for a decent morality, you can find no other. Such doctrines as the depravity of man, the sovereignty of God, the necessity of the Holy Spirit, the need of faith in the atonement, of repentance, not simply because sin is against nature, and society, but more especially because it is against God—in one word, those doctrines which begin with God, and, unfolding his character and high sovereignty, place every thing beneath the infinity of his attributes—these doctrines, old-fashioned and unchangeable, and these only, will teach you your right place and guide you to truth and eternal life. In his own Word God has revealed his mercy and the mode for our securing it. It admits of no innovations, no new developments. Woe to us, if we heed not his revelation! Woe to us, if we refuse to *bring every thought into captivity to the obedience of Christ!* Woe to us, if, forsaking these *fountains of living waters*, we attempt to *hew out for ourselves broken cisterns* of speculation and *the wisdom of this world!* Our philosophy can teach us nothing to solace or save. It can not know God. It can not learn duty. It can not gild with a single ray of light the bed of death. It can not write a promise upon the grave. It can not bridge the gulf that yawns betwixt this world and another, and furnish light and a landing-place on the shores of eternity."

And on teaching Philosophy, to comfort souls in trouble, he says:

"In the early part of my ministry, I used to aim very often to soothe the afflicted and encourage the darkened and depressed by a reference to natural principles, such as the courses of this world, the common lot of life, the uselessness of repining, the mercies still left, or some such thing. I have done with all that. I do it no more. It never did any good. It only dammed up the currents of grief for a little while, to become the more deep and dreadful, when they burst away the frail barrier. It never carried healing to the grief-spot of the heart. It only smothered the fires of trial, to burn the more fiercely and more deeply too, when, in a little while, the heart should find they were only smothered. I hope I have done with all that. I have learnt its inefficacy. If I can not lead to the exercises of faith, I can not do a smitten heart any permanent good. If I can make an inactive faith active—or a weak faith strong—or a trembling faith confirmed—or bring a wandering faith back, then I can make an unhappy man a happy one. His tears may flow; but they have lost their bitterness—they will not burn and blister as they did. His heart may not cease to bleed; but it loves the bleeding—all that is left after the balm of Gilead has been applied to the gash. I only aim, therefore, in some way, to bring in faith, and let its exercises do the comforting. I only stand by and look on."

He appreciated philosophy. "wisdom" learning, as much as

most men: but he could not endure an exhibition of these things in the pulpit. As much as he honored the power of human Reason in all his preaching, he was careful beyond most men to mark and define its *limits;* and he would not suffer it to open its mouth in the sacred desk on points on which God had not spoken, or to question for an instant a *thus saith the Lord.* He was never ashamed to confess his ignorance where Revelation had failed to enlighten mankind! He strictly followed that Divine injunction: *The prophet that hath a dream, let him tell a dream; and he that hath my word let him speak my word faithfully.* What he says of *Paul* on this point is applicable to himself. "This is characteristic of him. I do not recollect a single instance in all his Epistles, wherein he attempts to speculate. He explains—he reasons like a giant, to demonstrate the great doctrines of Christianity; he embarks all his severe logic to convict men of sin and persuade them to fly to Christ; but in reference to any of the matters which he discusses, I recollect no instance wherein he ventures a conjecture, or attempts a single step of unfolding, by any reasoning powers of his own—a single step beyond the revelation which was given to him. He knew the peculiarity of Christianity, and was willing to let it remain peculiar: he did not aim to level it down to the reason, the sciences, the philosophy of men."

He was careful to select a text which *fairly and fully* expressed the doctrine of his sermon. He usually devoted a considerable space, often the first head of his discourse, to an explanation of the passage, in its connections and expressions, that he might get out its exact meaning. And if the composition of his sermons are *faulty* at all, they are so just on this point—the length of the introductory part. And yet the fault (if indeed it *be* a fault) arose out of his extreme anxiety to ground every sermon on the sure Word of God, rightly interpreted and applied. All his trains of thought, and his arguments, many of his illustrations, and a large portion of his language, it will be observed, are drawn from the Holy Scriptures.

He followed uniformly the *textual* mode of sermonizing. And few men did it so happily. Often are the plans of his sermons very striking and suggestive. See, for a specimen, the sermon entitled *Sketch of the Plan of Salvation.* Indeed few preachers attain to such proficiency and skill in the science of sacred hermeneutics. And yet the plans of his sermons were uniformly natural and simple. He was accustomed to quote freely the very *language* of Scripture. He did this with unusual *accuracy*, seldom trusting his memory; and with great aptness and appropriateness. He wove the language of the Bible into his discourses with admirable tact, never forcing it in; never wresting it from its true meaning. Indeed such was the cast, the genius of his habitual preaching, that not only the sentiment but the very language of the Bible came in *naturally*, and helped to give point and richness, instruction and solidity to his sermons. Not since the days of President Edwards have we found a preacher whose sermons have in them habitually more of the inspired thoughts, the reasonings, the imagery, the language, and the life and spirit of God's own Word. And we have consulted the lamented Author's own taste in these published sermons, by putting the Scripture language into *italics.* This feature of these pages—too rare in modern sermon literature—will not be the least attraction which they will possess to his numerous friends and readers.

Nor did he preach simply the *letter* of God's Word; but also its *spirit and life.* His preaching was, much of it, experimental in a very high degree. No Christian could hear him long and doubt that his own heart was profoundly exercised and affected by the truths which he preached to others. There was too a depth and breadth to his religious experience which made his preaching eminently rich and instructive to God's people. If he was argumentative, rousing and powerful, in his addresses to the unconverted, he knew how to comfort and build up Christians. His *personal* experience was of a very decided and thorough character. He knew what trials, temptations and buffetings were, for he had endured them all. The flow of his religious feelings was far from being even and peaceful. He was familiar with all the states and conditions both of the unrenewed, and of the sanctified heart. He preached the religion of the *heart;* not a negative, theoretical, doctrinal Gospel merely, but a Gospel of spirituality and inward life—one which is *the power of God unto salvation.* His piety was not of a doubtful kind; it was deep-toned; and it gave character to much of his preaching. He reminded one in this particular of the best preachers of a former age, when a contemplative, experimental religion was more common than it is in this more active and practical age. Is there not at the present time a deficiency, in the general cast of much of the preaching of the evangelical Pulpit? The negative and practical parts of Christianity are dwelt upon much and earnestly. But is the experimental, the positive side, exhibited as fully, as thoroughly, as frequently as it should be? Is not the popular cast of preaching wanting in the elements of real piety? in that which is distinctive and positive in the religion of Jesus Christ? in that which really nourishes "the life of God in the soul," and pertains strictly to the spiritualities of our faith? The preacher must himself drink into the spirit of the Bible—enter its inmost sanctuary—understand it both experimentally and critically, and have his intellectual and spiritual being in the Bible—must experience the power of God in his soul and know the experimental side of Christianity; he must love to study and pry into the Bible, and dwell in that world of spiritual light and wonders, before he can truly and effectively *preach* the Bible. And the more intelligent piety there is in the preacher; the more familiar he is with the inner life of the Scriptures; and the more he comes under the baptism of that same Holy Spirit which indited and dwells in the Word, the more truly and powerfully will he be likely to preach it.

So felt the subject of this memoir, and so he preached. While he labored with unwearied effort to convert *the sinner from the error of his way,* and to develop an active practical piety in the

Church; he strove to have Christians grow in all the graces of the Spirit. Like a faithful shepherd, he *made his people to lie down in green pastures: he led them beside the still waters* . . . . *in the paths of righteousness.*

But the crowning excellence of his preaching, after all—that which gave it such distinguished power, and secured for it so high a degree of usefulness—was its *thoroughly evangelical character*. No one since the days of the apostles, we believe, surpassed him in this.

If ever a man preached "Christ and him crucified," Dr. Spencer did. As a preacher he gloried in nothing *save the Cross of our Lord Jesus Christ*. His sentiments had drank deep at the Gospel fountain, and been formed amid "profound contemplations of the infinite atonement of the Son of God." The doctrines he dwelt upon most, were the peculiar doctrines of the Christian system. These he loved. These were the themes, and the matter of his preaching. These he aimed steadily to exalt. He was never ashamed to preach them. He was never weary of exhibiting them. He expatiated upon them with a heart in full sympathy with them;—with a mind bathed ever in the light of the central truth of the Gospel—of the Son of Righteousness—and with a faith in their power which nothing could move. There was something affecting, really sublime, in some of his exhibitions of personal sympathy with the Cross of Christ. Who ever had more exalted views of the love and grace of God! or of the freedom and all-sufficiency of salvation! Who was ever penetrated with a deeper sense of man's depravity, moral inability, and utter ruin! and at the same time of Christ's infinite readiness and ability to save him! Who ever plead with guilty and perishing sinners with greater earnestness, sincerity, and importunity, to accept at once of the salvation provided for them! arguing the freedom and urgency of the offer, the needlessness of any Gospel sinners dying—the sufficiency of Christ's blood—the utter groundlessness of the excuses and reasons plead for delaying or rejecting religion, in a manner at times deeply affecting, and well-nigh irresistible! The sermons on "The Mercy of God," and on "God no pleasure in the death of the Wicked," are fine illustrations of these remarks. And it was doubtless this thoroughly evangelical spirit pervading all his sermons—living and breathing in all his thoughts, and shedding the sweet and hallowed influence of the Cross on all his ministry, which contributed most of all to his distinguished power and usefulness.

The combination of so many excellences, and in so high a degree, made Dr. Spencer a most *instructive* preacher. Few will doubt this, who have read his Sketches, and will examine his published sermons. He *aimed* to be instructive. He aimed steadily at this end, and in every sermon. He lent all the powers of his mind and gave the most unwearied and laborious application, to build his people up in Christian knowledge and experience. He strove to inculcate an *intelligent* piety: so to instruct them that they might be able to give a *reason of the hope that is in them.* Hence the Bible was the treasure-house whence he drew all his thoughts and arguments, motives and appeals, and not a little of the very language of his sermons and prayers. He wore no armor but the simple armor of the Gospel; and he became most expert and a master in the use of that. No man more than he abhorred ignorance, pedantry, superficiality, fine-spun speculation, sounding words, *clouds which carry no water*, the mere prettinesses of style or oratory or sentiment. He despised, nay he religiously *hated*, all such things; he could not allude to them without a feeling of shame and indignation mantling his cheek. It was the *substance* he cared for mainly. He seemed to realize that immortal souls were before him, not to be "amused" or entertained, or have their fastidious tastes catered to by the man of God; but to be *instructed*—instructed in truths of grave and eternal moment—*fed*—fed with the pure and simple Word of God, faithfully explained and enforced. His preaching was a beautiful commentary on that Scripture: *Sanctify them through thy truth, thy Word is truth.* If his people failed to *grow in grace;* to become *rooted and grounded* in doctrine and experience; if they did not make intelligent, stable and superior Bible Christians, the fault was not their pastor's. To this feature of his preaching we attribute the fact, that Dr. Spencer's Church in Brooklyn, during the period of nearly a quarter of a century—a period marked by unusual excitements and changes in the social and religious world—and notwithstanding all the strong currents and counter-currents which beat against it—has stood firm and unshaken, anchored to a rock—holding on the even tenor of its way, and quietly prosecuting its useful mission, undisturbed by inward commotions, and unaffected comparatively by the strifes and changes without. Few churches have been more favored in this particular.

Such was Dr. Spencer as a preacher. We have tried not to exaggerate: we have rather qualified the expression of our personal conviction through fear of seeming to do it, to those not knowing him well. Truly might the venerable Dr. Spring say, as he did in the discourse preached at the funeral of our Brother, in the hearing of many of his ministerial brethren and of the assembled multitude among whom he had spent most of his ministry: "The Church of God has not many such ministers of the Gospel to lose as Dr. Spencer. His brethren in the ministry have rarely, if ever, been called to mourn a heavier loss."

TRAITS OF CHARACTER.

Character has quite as much to do as intellect and mental training, in making a man and in gauging his usefulness. It is not always, alas, that mind and character go together. Many a splendid intellect has been associated with moral imbecility, or moral deformity. The history of genius, talent, learning, gifts, is, in this respect, a sad history! Many an intellectual giant has proved a Samson shorn of his locks. He might bear away the gates of Gaza, and not be able to resist the smallest of the weaknesses of fallen human nature. The loftiest intellect is of little use united with a morally weak nature. It is a curse and not a blessing, to its possessor and to the world, when, like the mind of Lucifer or Voltaire, Hume or Byron, its guiding spirit is the genius of evil. It is only mind *sanctified by the Spirit of God*, controlled by religious principle, and subordinated to the ends and purposes of the Gospel, that fulfills the condition of its being and really benefits mankind. But even many *good* men, from lack of *character*, are mere ciphers in the world; weak and inefficient, almost a disgrace to human nature, and any thing but helps to religion.

The *character* of the Brother to whose memory we render this humble tribute, was as decidedly strong and superior as were his intellectual gifts: it was a fitting counterpart to such a mind. Not perfect—not faultless by any means—but combining more of the excellences of goodness and greatness than commonly meet in a single man. And it was the peculiar stamp, the energy and weight of his character, which gave so much force, such a moral charm and attraction to his preaching, to his pastoral life, and to his social intercourse with mankind.

His natural qualities were undoubtedly superior. Nature did more for him than for most men. His training too was just adapted to such a nature. Like the mountains he was nurtured among, his development was massive, and broad and lofty as they; and discipline and culture beautified it even like the green carpet that creeps up their sides. Trained on the "rough fields of life;" thrown at eighteen upon his own resources; fitted for service amid trials and struggles severe; and borne on to victory by his indomitable energy and resolution, his habits of self-reliance and self-tuition made him independent, bold, free—a hard student, an original thinker, and an earnest worker—and gave to his character some of the ruggedness, the iron firmness, the unflinching courage, and the towering grandeur which were characteristic of him physically and mentally.

He was a man of very *decided opinions*. He had a mind of his own on most subjects, and he was never afraid to speak it, and emphatically too, when the occasion called for it. His *manner* of doing this was somewhat peculiar, and at times did his real sentiments and feelings injustice, unfavorably impressing strangers, and possibly wounding the feelings of friends. But it was his manner *only;* that positive, decided element in his nature which sought an unequivocal and understood expression of his sentiments and feelings. He detested that weakness which has no opinion of its own, and readily adapts itself to every company, or to the popular mind. This decision of character, amounting at times almost to rudeness and sternness and to a contempt of men, but in itself a virtue and an element of great power, impressed itself upon his preaching, his public life, and his ministerial and social intercourse.

As a kindred element he was endowed with *fearlessness.* This was natural to him. He had the courage of a hero. No danger could intimidate him; no threats deter him; no difficulties discourage him; no weaknesses of any kind dampen his spirits; no fear of unpopularity or regard for men's opinions shut his mouth, or dictate to him how he should preach or act. Grace too aided him in this. No man scarcely had the fear of God more vividly and habitually before his mind. He *was afraid*—but he was only afraid to offend God. Man, the world, the littleness of time and of all earthly interests and questions, weighed not heavily on a mind that dwelt in its daily meditations and communings on the Eternal One, the judgment, and the momentous issues of probation and immortality! He was often heard to say: "I never knew what it was to be insnared or embarrassed in preaching God's truth, and the thought of being afraid to utter it because it was unpopular, never once entered my mind." This trait of character not only made him a faithful preacher, a bold defender of the faith, and a reprover of sin, not unlike some of the Prophets of old; but it gave him great influence and usefulness in the spheres in which the timid and shrinking are sure to fail. He was never afraid to encounter opposition, come from what source it might. He carried the Gospel into the mansion of the rich, into the office of the professional man, into the counting-room of the merchant who had no time to attend to religion, into the circles of thoughtless gayety and heartless fashion and hardened impenitence—to the bed-side of "The Dying Universalist"—and into the streets of Northampton and Brooklyn—wherever indeed he could catch the ear of dying mortals, and urge upon them the claims of God and the interests of another world. This also it was that gave him a steady hand while he probed to the core the festering wounds of pride, self-righteousness and sin, in those who sought his skillful aid as a physician of souls. You see this trait on almost every page of his *Sketches*. Those who knew him not, might think him destitute of feeling, so thoroughly did he perform the painful task. But it was only the nerve and fearlessness of the man of God, anxious lest he should heal slightly the deadly wounds of sin.

We have already alluded to his *independence and self-reliance*. These were traits of character as really as they were of mental habitudes. Knowing the position he would fill, Providence, by nature and grace and training, fitted him for it. He was to stand for many years almost alone; in a great measure deprived of that ministerial and ecclesiastical sympathy and support which most men have. He was to take rank also among the very first of modern preachers, in a day when there is a sad lack of independence, originality, and profundity, in the matter of thinking, of character, and of position. He was likewise raised up to do a difficult, delicate, and great work in instructing "Anxious Inquirers respecting the way of salvation"—a work needing, preëminently, the skill and wisdom of one taught simply and thoroughly in the school of Christ, flinging from him all human "helps" and "guides," and applying the touchstone of God's unerring Word, mastered by a life-long study, by much prayer, and by a heartfelt experience. We never knew a character that was indebted so little to this world—to men's opinions and tastes—to books and reading: a character so assured of its own strength and so reliant on its own resources, and yet really so free from pride and arrogance. We never encountered a *piety* that seemed to have in it less of an earthly element. Its life was from God. It dwelt in the very light of the Throne. It was nourished by the study of the Bible, and by much meditation and prayer. It took its impressions, drew all its inspirations, from eternal things. The motives which moved and ruled it were drawn from religion. In his closet, in his study, on the mount of sacred contemplation, looking up into heaven, dead to the world, filled with the weighty thoughts of God, and pondering the scene of probation and the wonders and mysteries of redemption; there it was, amid such realities and solemn musings, that he girded on his strength, wrote his sermons, replenished his quiver, took his views of man's littleness and God's greatness, earth's vanity and eternity's grandeur—and thence came down to his people and to the world, to proclaim the Everlasting Gospel.

Sincerity and *candor* distinguished him. Never was he guilty of double-dealing, of concealment, of any thing that bordered on flattery, or of the sin of *speaking smooth things, prophesying deceits,* through fear of wounding feelings, or giving offense. If he disliked a man, a doctrine, a habit, any thing, he took no pains to disguise his dislike. If he believed a man in error, deceived, mistaken, in danger of losing his soul, no false delicacy, no consideration of selfish expediency, would prevent him from expressing his honest and candid judgment, when the opportunity demanded it. He could not suppress the truth any more than he could preach contrary to it. He could not tolerate any thing that looked like compromising the claims of God. He often condemned, in language of just severity, the position and the course of men, who, in order to conciliate the opponents of the evangelical orthodox faith, were ready to meet them half way—fritter away the boundaries, or remove the "land-marks" of Gospel truth: and also the preaching and conduct of brethren who trimmed their sails to the popular breeze; or aimed to adapt religion to the tastes, prejudices and likings of an ungodly world; or to conciliate and court philosophy, science, fashion, rank, station, or wealth. If he was at times a *blunt*-spoken, he was always an *honest*-spoken man. His judgment was candidly given. His position was well-defined. The tones of his clarion-trumpet were not apt to be mistaken. He was free from worldly policy, from all artifice. He met the world and his brethren always, openly, in a manly way. His sentiments, his feelings, his position, his principles, were well understood. Dr. Spencer never had the misfortune which so many men complain of, to be *misunderstood*. He would make himself to be understood. He was "read and known" by all who attended on his ministry, or encountered him in any of the relations of life.

He was also *self-sacrificing* to a degree that is seldom equaled. He was so habitually, and in every relation. Ease, enjoyment, popularity, personal interest, seemed to be always subordinated to the claims of his Master and the welfare of souls. In health and sickness—at home and abroad—in the pulpit and in the parlor, mingling with his flock or with his friends, or associating with the world—self seemed to be almost out of sight, and his wish and steady aim to make himself useful to them in some way. We have seen how he labored: what sacrifices he made: what efforts he put forth with unwearied zeal: how entirely he gave himself to the ministry and to his people: how ready he was to respond to every call: seldom seeking relaxation: never complaining, except of his own short-comings: taxing his mind and bodily strength to the utmost point of human endurance. The reason was, grace had in him wonderfully subdued the strongest principle of human nature: he was not his own but Jesus Christ's, and he felt it: the spirit of his Master was infused into his heart. He could say with Paul: *Ye are in our hearts to die and live with you. Always bearing about in the body the dying of the Lord Jesus, that the life also of Jesus might be made manifest in our body.* His ministry was one unbroken career of self-sacrifice. The martyr at the stake seldom made the sacrifice which such a devoted and laborious pastor makes, on the altar of love. How little does the world, or even the Church, appreciate such a toilsome life, such a self-sacrificing service and ministry for human well-being! Spent on any *other* field—for any interest save man's eternal interest, and how the world would ring with his fame, and unite to honor his memory; and competence reward his exertions! As it is, the minister toils on till he sinks into the grave. Piety sheds a few tears over him. His family usually are left dependent. And quickly he is forgotten, except it be by those doubly-bereaved ones, and in the memories of those whom he guided into the way of life! But his reward is on high. This world would be a poor compensation for services and sacrifices like his! It may be sufficient to reward an earthly ambition. Our brother, we doubt not, wears a crown amid the hierarchies of heaven, bright with a Saviour's glory; rich with thousands of priceless gems.

Our departed friend was penetrated with the spirit of Christian *humility*. He was *meek and lowly in heart; poor in spirit*. No one ever saw any thing like spiritual pride in him. His views of himself were very humbling. A sense of sin, of unworthiness, of unfitness for the sacred office, was ever present with him, and it was deep and all-pervading. His expressions of this kind of feeling were often strong and really distressing. Again and again has he remarked of himself to intimate friends: "I do not believe there is another such sinner on earth as I am! I seem to myself to be the vilest of creatures! I have mistaken my calling! I was never fit for a minister of the Gospel!" And the confessions which he at times threw into his *sermons*, respecting his short-comings, his faults, or the unfaithfulness and little fruit of his ministry, were touching and expressive to the highest degree: "I declare to you that if salvation were not published to me as thus gratuitous, thus gracious—God loving the sinner where he might most righteously have sent him to perdition—I should often find all the light of my hope going out under the oppression of the fear that I had sinned beyond the reach of all the mercy of God! In my heart what ingratitude! what forgetfulness of God! what pride! what coldness! what vanity! what hardness after all the mercies he has shown me!" There are many stronger far than this. And this was not affected. He spake as he felt. No man ever suspected Dr. Spencer of saying any thing for effect: he was incapable of it. He seldom spoke of his own feelings or efforts, in the pulpit or elsewhere; and when he did it was plain to see that he put a very *low estimate* upon his talents, piety, preaching, services of every kind. His heart was a *contrite* one. He sympathized deeply with Isaiah when he said: *Woe is me . . . because I am a man of unclean lips, and I dwell in the midst of a people of unclean lips.* With Job when he confessed: *Behold I am vile; what shall I answer thee? I will lay my hand upon my mouth.* And with Paul in his expression of weakness: *Who is sufficient for these things?* How unlike was this eminent servant of God in this particular, to many who are his inferiors in every thing!

This profound humility evidently arose from his intimate and frequent contemplations of God, and his appreciation of the sanctities of religion; and from his decided convictions and strong feelings respecting the sinfulness and wickedness of human nature. Few men have more thorough and abiding convictions than he on this subject. The way in which he preached human depravity—exhibited man's desperate sinfulness by nature—the workings of the unregenerate heart—his absolute dependence on grace for all goodness—and the trials, temptations and difficulties of the Christian life—abundantly prove that his humility was the legitimate fruit of Bible and experimental knowledge. He had seen God in the glory of his holiness, and therefore he abhorred himself and repented in dust and ashes. He had studied the character of sin, and he knew his own heart; and therefore he had no confidence in any creature wisdom or goodness, and was ready to write bitter things against his own soul. He appreciated, as few do, the sacredness of the ministerial office, and therefore was distressed at his personal unfitness for it.

It was this very humility, contrasting so greatly with many others, that often clothed his ministrations with affectionate tenderness; which gave him access to the inner hearts of Christians; and won him the confidence of all classes. It *is* a charm, an element of no little power in any man; and above all in a minister of the Gospel; and especially when united to commanding talents, a high position, and a sphere of extensive usefulness.

This lowly spirit exercised him not only as a Christian and a minister, but in other matters. It made him shrink from public observation. He had an extreme aversion to any thing like notoriety. The publicity which his Sermon on "Obedience to Law" gave him in certain quarters, and especially when he saw how ready men in place and power were to use his name to answer their own political or party ends, was any thing but pleasing to him—nay, it was painful. *He was very reluctant to become an author.* Nothing but the earnest solicitations of those who were so fortunate as to see the first series of *A Pastor's Sketches* in manuscript, and in whose "judgment and taste he placed great confidence," overcame his reluctance, and secured that highly useful work to the public. Notwithstanding their remarkable interest and power for usefulness, their author thought them "hardly fit to print." Not soon shall we forget a little incident connected with their first appearance, illustrative of the modesty and humility of the man. As the Editor of the *Biblical Repository*, we reviewed the work in the October issue for 1850, while it was yet passing through the press, and in our simplicity, confident of its wonderful merits, we commended it in very strong terms, and predicted for it an extensive sale. The good Doctor, when he saw what was said of *it* and of *him*, was greatly concerned. He said playfully, yet with an air of earnestness: "You are a fool! You have entirely overshot the mark! The result will prove you a false prophet! The public will be quite willing to let me die a natural death." And in the Preface to the second series he says: "The former one has a thousand-fold more than realized every expectation that was ever entertained by the author respecting it." Great as was the success of his first effort, and numerous as were the testimonials of its usefulness; and although often urged to publish another volume, it was a long time before he could bring his mind to do it. And when it did appear it was prefaced with the remark:

"What is here presented to the public, has been submitted to the inspection of some of the author's ministerial brethren, in whose judgment and taste he has great confidence; and, without their approval, these pages would never have been printed."

Such modesty, such humility, is as rare in these times as it is beautiful.

With all his nerve and masculine strength, and notwithstanding appearances at times to the contrary, Dr. Spencer was a man of unusually deep and tender *feelings*. He had a heart as well as mind—a heart too, of great sensibility—fresh, warm, confiding—strong and true in its affections. The world could never have known the delicacy, the sensitiveness and tenderness of his feelings. None but his family and most intimate friends knew him fully in this respect. In his *preaching* he was often tender even to weeping. There were frequent exhibitions of yearning affection for his people; frequent outbursts of sacred passion, when pleading with souls to turn and live, that few could withstand; and which reminded one of the compassionate Saviour's lament over Jerusalem. In his *correspondence* with friends, the depth and delicacy of his feelings, the strength and unchanging character of his attachments, clearly appear. There were a few friends who had his heart's entire confidence; with whom he corresponded for years; and his letters to them breathe the spirit of a tender interest in them and an affection for them, which seems almost heavenly. There are passages in this correspondence, equal, in delicate sensibility, and tenderness and sweetness of soul, to any thing that ever met our eye. Confiding himself, and inspiring confidence, he writes with the utmost freedom; pours out his heart without reserve; imparts all the sympathy of his nature, and challenges the love and sympathy of his friends in return. Never was there a warmer or truer friend, when once his confidence had been gained. And yet his manner did not always indicate this, especially to *strangers*, and in his general intercourse with the world. Some indeed thought him distant, reserved, austere. But they did not know him fully. We are thoroughly convinced that he often put on this reserved manner in his intercourse with mankind, as a shield to his feelings. He could not trust his heart, it was so pitiful and weak. But in his family this flow of inward feeling was unrestrained. There he was all affection and sweetness. His heart there freely and habitually indulged its love and tenderness.

None but a heart of deep affection, and intensely longing after social sympathy and love, could indite such touching passages as are scattered through his sermons. Take one as a specimen: "My salvation commenced in *love*. Not in might, not in majesty, not in any of those attributes of grandeur which fling such fearfulness and awe around the throne of God's almightiness! No, no. It began in *love*. This is what my heart wants—just what it wants. It wants *God* to *love* me. Nothing else will do. In a few days I am going to be cut off from all the endearments and sympathies of life. My friends, my wife, my children—if they live, I must die! I haste to the end. The grave is ready to receive me, and I sink into its bosom! Neither in that cold spot nor in the country beyond it can the loves of the world reach me! In that country I shall possess these same sensibilities, my spirit will be such that I shall want something to love, and want some being to love me. Earthly loves may do very well for me here. They may still the throbbings of many an anxious hour, smooth the pillow for my dying head, and let me know that the clay I am forsaking shall have a decent burial. But for my eternity no love but God's will do for me. If he can love me, sinner as I am, and I can know and love him, then I am perfectly assured that nothing shall ever arise in the mighty roll of eternal ages that shall dash my joys, and make me a miserable creature. This is enough. To have my God love me is enough. The Gospel assures me that he *has* loved me, and loved me though a sinner; and has given an infinite and bloody demonstration of that love; *the* demonstration—the *only* demonstration which could ever satisfy my heart in respect to his love; namely, that his love has made a precious SACRIFICE for me. And, now, if my faith embraces that love, I can look for the sympathies, and kindness, and tenderness of my God and Maker, in all the exigencies which may betide me, from the death-bed where earthly loves forsake me, onward to the remotest ages of eternity. This attaches me to God by the right bond and right demonstration. It satisfies my hopes and my heart when I know the *great love wherewith my God loved me.*"

Dr. Spencer was a man of *peace*. He disliked strife. He would not quarrel with any man. He could differ with his brethren and still respect and love them. His heart was sore pained within him by the spirit of controversy and bitterness which rent in twain the denomination he loved, and separated brethren holding to the same essentials of faith, and so long walking and working together; and by the alienations and recriminations consequent on the division. We have remarked that he took no part in this matter. He tried, as did other men, good and true, to prevent it. And when it was done and there was no help for it, he gave himself with renewed diligence to his own people, cultivating among them the graces of forbearance and love, *endeavoring to keep the unity of the Spirit in the bond of peace.* He mingled as freely with his brethren from whom he had ecclesiastically separated himself, as before, and was always ready to exchange with them, or help them when they solicited his services. He was also kind and courteous towards all evangelical denominations. He was free from a sectarian spirit. He made no war upon the peculiarities of the different branches of Christ's family. His habit was to preach *the truth*, and leave that to counteract and root out error where it existed. There was as little of sectarian zeal, or even denominational zeal, embodied in his sermons, as could be found any where beside. He preached the fundamentals of Christianity mainly, in which all Christians are agreed. He was careful—more so than is usual in one so decided in his views—to utter nothing in disparagement of sister denominations. He respected the religious views of individuals, even when he knew them to be greatly erroneous; and would reason fairly and kindly to convince them of the fact. He was fully established himself in the doctrines of the Word of God, and he preached those doctrines unhesitatingly and plainly; but not in a manner to give just offense to those who differed from him. We think he was somewhat *peculiar* in this. While aiming to exhibit the true view, as he believed, of any doctrine, he sought to magnify differences with those who held the substance of the truth as little as possible; and was anxious not to identify himself with any "School" of theology, that the truth might not be prejudiced thereby, or the minds of his hearers biased. See the Sermon on "Atonement," in the second volume, as an illustration of this remark, and of his general spirit and manner in this matter.

And we know personally that he was most anxious that nothing should appear in his *Sketches* to wound the Christian sentiment or feeling of any part of *the household of faith:* and it grieved him that an incident connected with one of the experiences related by him did give offense to a large and respectable evangelical denomination. It was not so *meant* by him. And it is among the excellences of those useful volumes, we think, that while they contain a good deal of practical theology—as much as can be found any where almost in the same space—it is presented in such a Bible light and manner, so free from the spirit and language of merely human systems, as to commend his "conversations" and "experiences" to the Christian sentiment and feeling of nearly the entire Christian world. And still no man ever contended more *earnestly for the faith* than he. He was not indifferent to the cause of sound orthodoxy; nor to the distinctive interests of the Presbyterian Church. He was not a little alarmed by the inroads of Error, and by the boldness with which it is every where lifting up its head. And his trumpet gave no faint or uncertain sound on this subject. He thoroughly instructed his own people in all the fundamentals of Bible doctrine. He took unusual pains to instill into their minds, choosing his time and manner, the principles of the Gospel so admirably set forth in the Shorter Catechism. He was in this a model pastor.

We can not close this imperfect Sketch of this Christian Brother's character without alluding to another trait. We do it reluctantly. It gives us pain to trace his life from this point of view. And yet he could never be fully understood, if the knowledge of it were withheld. For it influenced much of his preaching; it greatly affected his spirits; and had much to do with his religious development. His *religious despondency* was frequent, and, at times, very distressing. It was the Lord's will that he should pass a considerable part of his religious life in fear and doubt respecting his own acceptance; under a cloud; almost without hope, and shut up to a naked *trust in God*. Indeed he knew for a brief season what absolute despair was. No discriminating person could hear him *preach* for any length of time, and fail to discover that his soul was often in deep travail; not discover the action of a mind walking in darkness and feeling its way along; peculiarly alive to the profound mysteries of Providence and Redemption, and grappling with them and longing to clear them up: a heart not wanting in sympathy with the dying Saviour when he uttered that startling death-wail: *My God, my God, why hast thou forsaken me?* and yet a heart schooled by a severe experience to lie in the dust, and, lifting up its weeping eye to Heaven, say: *Though he slay me yet will I trust in him.* But this very state of mind, distressing as it was to him, gave additional interest and power to his ministrations. It imparted a chastened and subdued feeling to much of his preaching, that was indescribably touching. It enabled him to preach Christian experience itself, not *about* it, and with a thoroughness and vividness seldom equaled. It led him to explore the recesses of the human heart; to watch its varied workings; study its manifold deceitful forms; and to search into the foundation and evidence of Christian hope, as few Christians and ministers do. It constrained him to give such *prominence* to *Faith*, which must have struck all who ever heard him, or have read the productions of his pen: and such a view of the simplicity and efficacy of this grace. And it was this state of mind which made him such a master in handling that class of subjects which involve the darknesses of Providence, the mysteries of Revelation, and the trials of Christian experience. Where, beside, can be found such a scope of argumentation; such varied, abundant and comforting light; such a breadth and depth of Christian feeling and faith under trials! God overruled this very darkness to shed fresh light on many a page of his Word and Providence as read by others; to lift the cloud from many a troubled soul; and carry the comforts of hope and the evidences of faith into thousands of disconsolate hearts. He sometimes complained of this feeling to his friends, and accounted for it by questioning his own piety. But no one save himself ever doubted that. His expressions on this point were at times very strong, and came direct from an anguished and bleeding heart. He thus pours out his troubled feelings into the bosom of friendship, and closes by begging for prayer in his behalf. "I thought you would bear with me kindly, and appreciate justly the feelings which oppress me. May I hope you will pray for me? I have need of more grace, (if indeed I have any at all,) and I beseech you, my very dear friend, offer to God one prayer for me." And again: "Live nigh to God. Live in the sunshine of his countenance. I have tried dejection and find it does no good. The Lord keep you from it. Pray for me. My own prayers are not answered, and clouds and darkness thicken around me. They are *God's* clouds. I will try to let him manage them." And this despondency continued until he had well-nigh reached the gate of glory. During much of his last severe illness, as we shall see hereafter, his mind struggled with darkness, and his heart was sad and heavy, while his body was tortured with pain. But he never ceased to trust. Never for a moment, even in the darkest hour, if we except a single instance, did he cast away his integrity or abandon faith. In his extremity he often said, "I can do nothing *but* trust." And *that* he did. And all the while he was a humble, active, devoted Christian; careful in all minor points of duty, and yet neglecting not *the weightier matters of the law.*

"His preaching much, but more his practice wrought,
A living sermon of the truths he taught."

Yes; and all the while he was ripening for heaven. Piety will thrive amid darkness and storm, quite as well and as rapidly, as in the sunlight of peace and prosperity. Indeed the piety nurtured in darkness, in the furnace of affliction, in the school of a severe discipline, is sometimes the strongest, the sweetest and most heavenly in its type.

"In climes full of sunshine, though splendid their dyes,
  Yet faint is the odor the flowers shed about,
'Tis the clouds and the mists of our own weeping skies
  That call their full spirit of fragrancy out.
So the wild-flower of passion may kindle from mirth,
  But 'tis only in *grief* true affection appears;
To the magic of smiles it may owe its first birth,
  But the soul of its sweetness is drawn out by tears."

His intimate friend, Dr. Spring, bears this testimony of him: "He was a sufferer for years, and his sufferings sometimes oppressed his heart, because they unfitted him for active labor; yet I have seen him more depressed when the sunlight of prosperity shone upon him, than in the dark night of his affliction. His graces grew under the sharpest trials; and amid all the outward darkness with which he was so long enveloped, his path shone brighter and brighter unto the perfect day."

It is not our province to explain the cause of this despondency. It was doubtless partly constitutional. But it was thus ordered by the Lord. We know how he himself resolved all such questions: *Even so Father, for so it seemed good in thy sight.* Many of the most eminently pious and devoted men, like Martyn and Brainard, and even Payson, have gone "mourning all their days." Not even the Son of God, who *was made perfect through sufferings,* was spared the bitterness of this trial. The climax of his mission of suffering, was the hiding of his Father's love from his soul while he endured the agony of crucifixion.

But it is all light with thee now, Brother. The sky which now canopies thy spirit holds no cloud or tempest. Thou hast attained to that for which thou didst here sigh and strive—assured and perfect knowledge of the truth—the eternal demonstration of God in Christ—and the full reign of peace. And sweeter is the light and rest of Heaven to thee, by reason of the darkness and trial of thy earthly pilgrimage. Oft did thy oppressed spirit, even while comforting others, force thy lips, while here, to utter the pilgrim's song:

> "It is a weary way, and I am faint;
> I pant for purer air and fresher springs;
> Oh, Father! take me home: there is a taint,
> A shadow on earth's purest, brightest things.
> This world is but a wilderness to me;
> There is no rest, my God! no peace apart from thee."

But infer not that this *heavy laden* Christian was a gloomy misanthrope, and his life shaded with habitual melancholy. It was not so. He was generally cheerful. He had much to enjoy and he had a heart to enjoy it. He seemed to forget himself in duty, and in unwearied toils to benefit others. He was often lively and playful. In his family, especially, his spirits were buoyant; the burden of care and anxiety was laid off; and the cheerful smile and hearty laugh, and the lively interest he took in all family enjoyments, showed that his heart was no stranger to the sweets and joys of life. The language of gratitude was often on his lips. Frequently would he say: "I do not think any one has so much cause for gratitude as I have; and when I feel well, and am at home with my dear wife and children, I am so happy! Do let us be grateful."

He appreciated innocent wit and humor as not every man does. His heart was susceptible, in no common degree, to the beauties of nature wheresoever they bloomed; to the genial influences of social life, to the pleasures of refined sentiment and feeling, and to the attractions of goodness in every form. He loved children and would play and frolic with them. His intercourse with ministerial brethren, who were at all congenial, was enjoyed by him, and he was ready to contribute his full share to the "feast of reason and the flow of soul." He seemed sometimes to take a mischievous pleasure in saying some severe or sweeping thing with apparent meaning, and when he saw it was taken in earnest, his hearty laugh would ring out and dispel the impression. Many of his letters also are exceedingly playful, sometimes facetious, breathing a healthy, buoyant feeling.

There were times too, when the cloud of despondency, which cast its shadow on a considerable part of his religious experience, was dissipated; or when, at least, through the rent darkness light streamed down from the throne on his heart. He could, he did sometimes magnify the Lord, and rejoice in the God of his salvation. From lamenting he went to praising. From "the Valley of the Shadow of Death," he came out "into the country of Beulah." He took down his harp from the willow, and sweetly did the strains of Christian joy go forth. There is a beautiful hymn of Cowper's, which was a favorite of his, the last two stanza particularly. Often would he softly sing them to himself, walking about his study, as the evening shades fell around, seemingly meditating on heaven.

> "Lord! I believe thou hast prepared,
> Unworthy though I be,
> For me a blood-bought free reward,
> A golden harp for me!
>
> "'Tis strung and tuned for endless years,
> And formed by power divine,
> To pour on God the Father's ears,
> None other name than thine."

At the communion-table, often, did this feeling break forth. His addresses on these occasions were frequently characterized by a tenderness, and a sweetness and elevation of Christian sentiment and feeling, that excelled even himself. Never was he so truly eloquent, and so effective, as when he spoke over the memorials of our Saviour's death. His communion *sermons* were remarkable. Few preachers ever wrote so *many* strictly communion sermons; or so laid out their utmost strength on sermons of this character. They are among the ablest and most richly instructive of all his efforts. He had thought during his life, as appears from memoranda, of publishing a volume of "Communion Sermons." Would that he had! We have given a few of these as specimens of his power and interest, when he directly contemplated the death of the Cross, and aimed to prepare his people to come into the banqueting-house of the Prince of Love.

One of these communion seasons (the last Sabbath in June, 1852) will not soon be forgotten by those who were present. He seemed now to stand on the mount of transfiguration, and see the Saviour in his glory; or, rather, like Paul, to have been caught up into Heaven where he had experienced unutterable things. A coal from the heavenly sanctuary touched his lips. And such views of Christ; such an apprehension of eternal glories; such rejoicings of spirit and enjoyment of infinite love;—and such yearning tenderness toward those who bore the image of Christ, are not given to many believers without the gates of the "New Jerusalem." There were circumstances connected with this communion season naturally calculated to excite his feelings more than usual. The affection of the father, the love of the Christian, and the rejoicing of the spiritual husbandman met in the scene, and made it tender and solemn. He thus speaks of the occasion in a letter to a friend, after stating the circumstances above alluded to: "That day was indeed a memorable communion day in our church. Never before did Christians look so—never before did they commune so. This is not any mere fancy of mine; scores of them mentioned it with amazement and gratitude. As I made the communion address, it seemed to me that I could carry up to the gates of the New Jerusalem, the soul of every child of God, and could persuade any sinner on this side of hell, to praise and love Jesus Christ. I never expect another day like that on earth."

During the last two or three years of his life, his family particularly remarked an increasing sweetness and gentleness of temper in him. He seemed daily to grow in heavenly-mindedness. The more rugged features of his character were softened. The furnace of suffering did its work, and the remaining dross of earthliness and sin consumed away, and the likeness of his Divine Master became more perfect and more visible. This is seen in the *retouching* which he gave to quite a number of his sermons, in preparing them for the press, or for his pulpit during this period.

An instance occurs in that beautiful and suggestive sermon found in this volume, entitled "Mingled Light and Darkness," where, in the revision, he gives more delicacy and tenderness to the thought expressed, showing a greatly chastened spirit and a most exquisite sense of moral loveliness! " Such vicissitudes used to seem strange to me—the most strange of all the inexplicable things in nature or religion. They seem strange still. Even yet, *the light is not clear* to me, though not all *dark*. I remember now, that the comforts of a Christian are the gentle, tender, sensitive matters of affection—the heart's delicacies as well as delights—and can not bear the rude touch they often meet with. If they could bear it, they would lose their character —just as the rose would lose its character and be rose no longer, if it could bear the tread of the wild beast's hoof uninjured."

IN HIS FAMILY.

We scarcely dare to lift the curtain and enter the sanctuary of his domestic affections. Yet it is impossible to do justice to his character without viewing him in the relations of a husband and father, the head of a Christian household. Few appreciated home and the bosom of the family, more than he. And few possessed more of those qualities of mind and heart which fit one for home duties and enjoyments. We have spoken of the tenderness of his nature, and the warmth and devotedness of his affections. And in his every-day life and intercourse among those whom he tenderly loved and cherished, these were continually gushing forth with perennial freshness, and in every form of loveliness and endearment. As a Husband he felt a deep and sacred love, and with almost unearthly tenderness watched over and cherished the object of it. And no other earthly feeling had so much influence on his character and life; no other earthly feeling was so deep in his heart, so abiding, so closely identified with all the thoughts and states and interests of his being. From home even for a brief season, his mind and heart turned to it; and his frequent letters to his wife and children, were full of conjugal and fatherly tenderness. "There is very little happiness for me away from home, away from you all:" "I can not enjoy any thing without you:" "I feel more and more every day that home is the only spot on earth where I can be happy:" "Your love is every thing to me:" "I am never half myself when away from you:" such were the expressions contained in every letter. His daughter says: "I never received a letter from him—none of us ever did—that did not contain some passage commending our *Mother* particularly to our attention and affection." But his own parting words to her, spoken amid the grief and solemnity of a dying hour, only can do justice to this deep and sacred feeling of his soul: "My wife, you have been a *precious wife* to me. You have been my support in hours of darkness. You have held me up when I should otherwise have sunk. You have cheered and consoled and advised with me with unfailing love. I commit you to God. I know he will take care of you. *My best earthly friend, farewell!*" And then he commended her to the care and affection of his children in a manner which can not be described. I dare not trust my pen further on this field. Perhaps I have already violated the sanctity of private feeling. Yet such was the *heart* of our brother; such the influence that helped to mold and develop his character. Such the man where the eye of the world seldom saw him.

As a Father he was kind and indulgent. His eldest daughter bears this testimony: "To us his children he was a most indulgent father. He delighted in planning gratifications for us, and promoting in every way our pleasures. He scarcely ever denied us any thing. Any happiness coming to us pleased him as much as if it were his own—it *was* his own. Even in the midst of his thousand pressing duties and heavy weight of cares, he found time to interest himself in our pursuits, however trifling. We took delight in referring every thing to him. Our purchases were no satisfaction to us unless he approved them. The books we read—the visits we paid—the acquaintances we made—the pleasant sights we saw—even the gossip of the day—we went to him with every thing. We never received any thing but tenderness and sympathy from him. He was never too busy to attend to us. He seldom reproved us. I have heard more reproofs in one day from parents who were considered kind, than I heard from him in years. But we always knew that when we had done wrong he felt sorry, and one grieved look of his had more effect than long lectures from any one else. We were always perfectly happy when he had time to spend an hour with us in the evening. It was enough just to look at him and listen to him. I do really believe there never were children who idolized a father so. To his fatherless children he has left the rich legacy of a high and spotless name, and a burden of gratitude to God, that they have had such a father. Oh! the days seem weary till we can join him again! Our loss grows heavier every day." We can add nothing to this touching tribute of filial regard. We know that it is not exaggerated. And we know the sorrow and desolation of that circle where, day and night, in silence and sadness, fall the widow's tears, and is heaved the orphan's sigh!

Dr. Spencer was not selfish in the exercise of these home affections. He was a *Christian* parent; and he aimed steadily and prayerfully to train his children for the service of God. He early consecrated them to him. He taught and counseled them faithfully. He neglected no duty, no means, that Christian love and authority might use. He sought in every way to *win* them to Christ. His daily example was blameless. His prayers for their early conversion, in the family and in the closet, were abundant and fervent. And may we not believe that his recorded prayers and bottled tears, and the memory of his virtues and teachings will prevail, and they make an unbroken, happy family in heaven! May the mantle of the ascended father fall on them!

AS AN AUTHOR

Dr. Spencer's relations were wide, and of an unusually interesting character. Few authors, considering the limited extent in which he used his pen for the press, and the late period in life at which he became known in this sphere, have been more extensively read by religious people, or are held by their readers in higher respect, and regarded with a feeling so near akin to personal affection, as he. It is fitting that we should briefly sketch him in this character, and field of usefulness. Although last occupied by him, and reluctantly entered, it is now, alas, the only one on which his commanding influence and abilities can be felt. And we have no hesitancy in believing, that, great and precious as was the harvest gathered by him in the pulpit and in pastoral labor, the souls garnered in glory in the final day, by means of his authorship, will outnumber the fruits of his personal ministry. We bless God for endowing our brother with a gift so remarkable, and so useful; and for constraining him, by a sense of duty, to exercise it in a public and permanent form, before he was called to rest. So that *being dead he yet speaketh*, and *will* speak through a world-diffused agency, to guide "Anxious Inquirers into the Way of Salvation," and to demonstrate and commend the great facts and doctrines of Redemption. Wonderful gift! Wonderful agency! The Church can afford to lose the personal presence of her chieftans; may consign them to the grave almost without a tear; now that a sanctified press may catch their glowing thoughts and holy utterances; the testimony of their life and death, and with a power which never dies, multiply truthful impressions of them, and scatter them over all the world!

Dr. Spencer had employed the press perhaps as little as any man ever did possessed of such abilities, previous to the issue of the first series of "A Pastor's Sketches." A little fugitive poetry, always anonymous, and an occasional sermon in the *National Preacher*, or on subjects of particular interest to his people, published at their solicitation, are all that we know of his efforts in this direction. He seldom if ever wrote for any periodical; or so much as penned a newspaper article. His shrinking diffidence and modesty were remarkable in a man who could not have been unconscious of his own powers. His literary taste and judgment too were such as to make him a severe critic. There were but few of all the books of the day that he could read through patiently; comparatively few that he thought *paid* to read. And his occasional criticisms on those he did read, showed a high standard of judgment, no mean literary taste and skill, and a mind that grasped and comprehended a subject almost intuitively. It was this appreciation of decided merit only, that made him so slow to give his own thoughts public life. He judged *himself* quite as severely as he judged others. "It is n't fit to *print*," was his emphatic and almost certain decision. We care not to repeat remarks we have heard him make respecting *authors* of not a little celebrity in the religious world, condemnatory of the practice of casting so many hasty, and of course superficial and crude, and often unwise productions upon the world. He believed that the press is greatly abused and sinned against in this day, even by good men; and not a little imperfect, erroneous, and hurtful teaching inculcated thereby, by writers professedly religious. Much of the modern literature of the Church, that especially prepared for the *young*, he strongly condemned, as wanting in many essential elements of such a literature. And not a few of the books commonly found in Sabbath-School and other similar libraries, which are forming the minds and tastes and guiding the piety of the rising generation, he repudiated as worthless or even injurious. He was at great pains to *inform* himself on this last point; and it was his conviction that Christian pastors, parents and teachers, were greatly at fault in not instituting a more careful and thorough examination into this matter.

The only published *Sermon* that we need allude to, save that on *Obedience to Law*, is one entitled *The Comparative Claims of Home and Foreign Missions*. It was preached to his own people on the occasion of their annual collection in behalf of Home Missions, and shortly after published by the American Home Missionary Society, we believe, and circulated to some extent. A few years after it was revised by the Author, and republished by us in a permanent form, in the *National Preacher* for May, 1849. It is not too much to say of this effort, that as a Plea for Home Missions it has not often been excelled; many and able as have been the efforts of others on this field. Its breadth of view, grasp of thought, power of argumentation, condensation of facts, and weight and urgency of appeal, make it, in our judgment, equal in interest and value to any of the productions of his gifted pen.

In October, 1850, his first series of *A Pastor's Sketches: or Conversations with Anxious Inquirers respecting the Way of Salvation*, made its appearance. The peculiar character and merit of this work, (and the same is true of the volume which followed it some time afterward,) are too extensively known and appreciated to need any extended remark in this Sketch. It at once attracted no little attention. It was noticed with universal favor by the religious, and even the secular press. It has already run through many editions; having had a larger sale than almost any other strictly religious book which has ever been issued in this country. It has been republished in England, and on the Continent, and portions of it ("The Young Irishman" for instance) at some of our Missions in Asia,* and is now known and

---

* A specimen of it, from the mission press of Bombay, with a letter of thanks from the Brethren of that Mission to the Author, was received just after his death.

highly valued in almost every part of the Christian world. Nor has the demand for it at all lessened. Several editions of the *second* series have also been scattered far and wide. And we have no doubt that the death of the Author, and the interesting Sermons which accompany this Memoir, will serve to awaken fresh interest in, and greatly to extend these first efforts of his gifted and sanctified pen. The *four* volumes will scarcely be surpassed, we think, in point of real interest and excellence, by any four volumes which American talent and piety have given to the religious world.

No one familiar with "A Pastor's Sketches," wonders at their popularity. They combine the graphic and pathetic interest of the productions of the best class of novelists, with the instruction of a great mind and of an extensive experience on the highest and most solemn of all themes. None but a genius of the first order, a wisdom imbibed at the feet of the Great Teacher, a thorough knowledge of the human heart in its most subtle forms of deception and in all its casuistries and varied developments, and a personal observation of singular scope on this field of labor, could have produced such deeply interesting and life-speaking sketchings. Some of them evince a reasoning power of no mean order. The sketch of the "Young Irishman," argues the existence of spirit, and of God the Infinite Spirit, in a manner at once original and admirable. There is not in the English language an abler or more satisfactory specimen of argumentation on this doctrine. This is the judgment of many more competent than ourselves to express an opinion on such a point. The work as a whole is an invaluable contribution to our doctrinal and practical literature. It has aided not a few pastors in some of the most difficult and perplexing cases which officially claim their attention and skill. It has relieved, guided, and comforted, many souls. Christian liberality and activity have pressed it into the service of Christ in numberless instances. And the Author before his death, was made acquainted with many testimonies to the blessing of God attending the reading of it. He received letters almost daily, from his brethren in the ministry, and from laymen, in all professions and from every part of the Union, expressing their deep interest in the work and their gratitude to the Author for the service he had done to the cause of Christ. We might make an interesting chapter with extracts from this wide-spread and voluminous correspondence; but we must be content to give one only. It is contained in a letter from one of the most distinguished pastors of New England, received soon after the issue of the first series. We select this both to show the *false* impression which some had respecting the character and position of Dr. Spencer, and the kind of responses he received from his brethren, and others distinguished in other walks of life. The Christian ingenuousness of the writer, too, is highly commendable.

"DEAR BROTHER SPENCER—I have for some time hesitated between writing a newspaper-notice of your Sketches, and a fraternal note. You see I have decided upon the latter. When a man removes a prejudice from my mind, he adds a new star to my firmament. You have done so. I have always regarded you as a man of excessive dogmatic tendencies, excessive aversion to the aggressive efforts of your brethren, and of narrow prejudices. My soul, with humble acknowledgment of my fault, and a request for your forgiveness, acquits you of all this, and hails you with joy as a chosen workman, 'that need not be ashamed; rightly dividing the word of truth.' I can not tell you with what delight I have read about half of your book; for I read it only by cases; two or three in a week. I want to write to you two or three sheets, to express my satisfaction; finding however all the fault my present good humor will allow. But I will trouble you only with a sketch of my impressions. When I read 'The Young Irishman,' I was enchanted with the intellectual and courteous character of your interviews with him. It revived some of the finest impressions received in my intercourse with polished Europeans. The gladiatorship is magnificent. The faithfulness, tenderness, judgment and skill of the pastor are passports to my inmost heart. On finishing it, I sat down and sketched a review.

But that was thrown aside, because I got an unfounded view of your intention from the peculiar type of that story. After remarking on the modesty, soberness and good sense characterizing the preface, I was going to commend it as one of the most admirable popular treatises on Theology I had ever met. I do not know however that one man's experience would furnish the material for such a volume. But I got the thought from your first sketch; how admirable it would be, to reason out every great doctrine in that form, with people who in reality object to them! You could do this better than any man whose writings I have seen. The terseness, clearness, promptness, soundness, fullness, fairness, faithfulness, wisdom and tenderness of your replies, I assure you, dear brother, are to me professionally, and as a Christian, a delicious entertainment. Why may you not follow out this suggestion? The narrative form will induce many to read it, who would not read a formal discussion in Theology; while it will give them all the advantage of consecutive thought. Your book has the vivacity and variety of ordinary life. No graphic pen of a Scott, no thrilling touches of a Bulwer, no pathetic scenes from Dickens can give a more rich or a more profitable entertainment than 'The Young Irishman,' and 'The Welsh Woman,' &c. * * * I congratulate you on this highest human testimony to your ministry; the earnest send for you, though they have no direct claims on you. God bless you."

"The favorable reception which the first volume met with from the public—the numerous testimonials of its usefulness to private individuals, which were received from many different parts of the country—and more especially the similar testimonials received from many of his ministerial brethren, induced the author to believe it was his *duty*" to issue a second series. "And although this volume may be less interesting in tender and affecting incidents, it is believed there are some reasons to hope it will not prove less useful." So wrote the Author in the Preface to it. It has been received with equal favor. Many think it superior to the first. While it has no single sketch to match "The Young Irishman," in ability of execution, or "The Welsh Woman and her Tenant," or "The Dying Universalist," in graphic power and affecting incident; yet its *average* interest and instructive merit, is, we judge, nearly equal to the former series. They are fit companions. And safe guides to the kingdom of heaven, whither, with God's blessing, they will guide many an anxious pilgrim.

The publication of these volumes, making him widely known as a skillful and experienced solver of "questions of conscience," laid upon him an additional responsibility and delicate service. Very many persons in religious trouble, from all parts of the country, addressed letters to him, stating their difficulties and soliciting light or relief. Very many strangers also called upon him in person, for the same purpose. And it required no little time, patience, wisdom and application, to attend to so many calls of this peculiar and special kind, and administer according to their varied circumstances. He alludes to this *care of all the churches* which had come upon him, in a letter to a friend : " I have been a very imprudent man in my publications, for they have brought upon me more labor than I could describe—a correspondence of a most delicate and difficult nature, extending from Canada to Florida, and conversations without number and without end, with multitudes of people in religious trouble. A gentleman from Montreal has just left my study after two hours of conversation upon his terrible gloom. A young theological student from Connecticut spent last Sunday evening with me till midnight. I have some of the most wonderful religious histories, I am sure, that ever existed, which I will tell you about when I see you; but I shall never print them. In some cases my *patients* have wonderfully recovered, and in others they are as hopeless as ever. Nerves are strange things. Never get nervous. Have faith. Obey these two commands and you will be happy." And again : " I am overwhelmed with labor, not an hour of leisure, and at times my brain reels under the burden of a thousand perplexing affairs." "This is not our rest. I have a very vivid idea of that description of Heaven which makes it a *rest*."

His Sermon on *Obedience to Law* obtained a very unexpected notoriety. Circumstances beyond his control made it very widely known, and the occasion of not a little warm and even angry discussion. He was not a little censured for it by many of his real friends, and denounced in no measured terms by a portion of the Northern press and pulpit; while he was as warmly praised and his sentiments as thoroughly indorsed by other portions of the press and pulpit, and by multitudes of good and wise men, to say nothing of the highly commendatory expressions from many of the first statesmen in the land.

In judging of this effort the reader must bear in mind the highly excited state of the national feeling at the time, growing out of the recent passage of the law in Congress known as the Fugitive Slave Law, and the conflicting opinions and counsels strongly expressed in every quarter in canvassing its provisions and principles, and in regard to the measures to be adopted in relation to it. Some Northern journals advocated a forcible resistance to the execution of the law. Ministers from their pulpits, and ecclesiastical bodies in various branches of the Church, in their hasty zeal, gave utterance to sentiments which few sober and conservative men, now that the excitement has mainly subsided, would justify. His position; the relations of his people to the all-engrossing question, and the alarming state of the country, led the Pastor of the Second Presbyterian Church of Brooklyn, in his place, to lift up his voice and denounce a spirit which he believed had been for years growing and strengthening in this land, subversive in its tendencies of all law: and to rebuke sentiments which shocked alike his patriotism and his piety. In vindication of this trumpet-sound at this perilous juncture, his own words shall speak: " Think of the anti-rentism and its murders—nullification of law in South Carolina, in Vermont, in Connecticut—anti-Sabbathism—anti-parental authority—and the thousand rills of evil, all swelling that 'Gulf Stream' of wickedness, on the curl of whose topmost billow was the floating ———. And then, when the religious world was still, and no minister dared or thought best to lift up his voice to rebuke this 'spiritual wickedness in high places,' will you be severe on me, if I have uttered my feeble words in a clumsy manner, against the fanatical *heart* of these abominations—the idea that a man is accountable only to himself, and may innocently do whatever his conscience can be persuaded to let him, if he will only set up the shout, 'Higher Law'?"

The Sermon happened to be written in rather more than his usual haste, and was published with slight revision, under a pressing call from his people. The natural consequences were, that certain points discussed in it were left somewhat ambiguous; the *limitations* of his main doctrine were not stated with sufficient fullness and exactness; and omissions of points essential to a comprehensive view of the subject occurred, which marred the perfection of the effort. It did his own real sentiments as a whole a little injustice. The teaching he *meant* to inculcate was partly misapprehended. Conclusions were drawn from his reasonings which he utterly repudiated. And the whole thing was prostituted by a party spirit, and a political machinery, to purposes from which his whole soul revolted. He was honest and fearless in his utterance; and, correctly understood, his position was, substantially, the position of Northern conservative men generally. He never regretted the publication of the Sermon, we have authority for saying, but he did regret a few unguarded or ambiguous expressions in it, and the imperfect, or, as he expressed it, "awkward" manner of defining and limiting the main doctrine of it. We happened to be the medium of a lengthy and able correspondence in relation to this Sermon, between its author and a brother, in the neighboring city, who had also published a sermon on the same subject, containing somewhat different views. For this brother he cherished a very unusual regard, and it grieved him to differ from him publicly on so serious a matter. There was much gladiatorial skill and prowess shown by both in this paper combat—keen thrusts and hard hits; but the *spirit* of the whole was most lovely. It is the only war of any kind that we ever *enjoyed;* for we were favored with the position of chief spectator. It gave one a higher opinion of the Christian temper of both. And we know the effect of it on Dr. Spencer's mind, was to draw that respected combatant nearer to his heart, and make of him a warmer friend, and induce him to confide greatly in his judgment and counsel. We trust that nothing we have penned will be construed into a wish, either to excuse or condemn the Sermon alluded to. It has been both blamed and praised sufficiently perhaps already. We only wish it to be judged of from a favorable point, in the spirit of *truth and soberness.*

SICKNESS AND TRIALS.

Having sketched the life, character and ministry of Dr. Spencer, we draw toward the end of his earthly career. If human wisdom had had the ordering of it, such a highly useful and singularly self-sacrificing life and ministry, would have closed in peace and unclouded sunlight. The toil-worn veteran would have passed straight from the field of his public conflicts and achievements to the bed of death, and laying off his armor, and wrapping his mantle around him, have gently fallen asleep, "like the warrior taking his rest." But no : it had been ordained in Heaven that that noble career should close in storm and darkness; amid trials sharp and heavy, and sufferings protracted and peculiarly severe. But they were " *God's* clouds," and he was " willing that *He* should manage them." We are to view him now on a new field—on a field on which he confesses he has had " no training"—and on which many a good man, and many a valiant soldier before him, has fainted and fallen. And although we shall find him much depressed and almost overwhelmed; writing bitter things against himself; enduring excruciating mental and physical suffering; and like his Master, in the garden and on the cross, lifting his heart-piercing cries to Heaven for succor and patience—yet shall we find that he held fast his integrity to the end; *troubled on every side, yet not distressed; perplexed, but not in despair; cast down, but not destroyed;* always saying, *Thy will be done;* triumphing in all his sufferings as wonderfully as ever martyr triumphed at the stake; and in his experience, at the last, verifying that beautiful and expressive promise: *It shall come to pass that at* EVENING-TIME *it shall be* LIGHT. Willingly had he fellowshiped the toils and self-sacrificing spirit of the Gospel, exercising nobly the active graces of religion. And it pleased the Lord that he should finish his testimony on earth in the furnace of personal affliction, and that furnace heated seven times, that the passive graces also might be exercised by him and making brighter thereby his eternal crown; treading thus in the footsteps of the *Captain of their salvation, who was made perfect through sufferings.*

His ministry was very little interrupted by sickness. He has made a record of each Sabbath that he was unable to preach, and the number is small indeed, till the last year or two of his life. Still was he a sufferer for a considerable part of the time. He bore up under a most distressing disease for years, until heart and flesh finally failed, and the strong man had to bow. He was very unwilling to be laid aside, even for a single Sabbath; and often preached and wrote, in the closing part of his life, in great pain. He says of himself, when disease had prostrated him and was fast wearing away the foundations of his robust frame: "I am such a fool I can not *play* for more than a week at a time." In the Spring of 1852, after "struggling against disease all winter like a rebel," his people became alarmed about the state of his health, and proposed that he should cease his labors for a season, and make a voyage to Europe in order to recruit himself. But instead of this he took a trip, of a few weeks, to Savannah, seeing and characteristically describing many things at the South, both with praise and blame, and suffering greatly. "I could keep from crying out," he writes; "I could keep my face straight and good-natured by the power of my will; but I could not hinder the tears from gushing out of my eyes. Pain would compel them, and my poor will was obliged to knock under." Returned by way of Washington, and "preached in the House of Representatives:" "inquired into two queer affairs, the morals of the members of Congress," (which, together with the character of his audience, he speaks of in terms any thing but flattering,) "and the works of art in and about the Capitol"—"some of which," he thought "execrable and some exquisite; could look on Daniel Boone and the Indian for hours unwearied:" stopping at Philadelphia, "had the pleasure of being assured, at a consultation of surgeons, that nothing but a surgical operation would do him any good"—"would have submitted to it on the spot, but wife was at home and could not be consulted:" in eight weeks after reaching home "was entirely restored." "Then I went to work again." The relief however was only temporary. Yet he continued his active labors till the close of the following year—as long as it was possible for him to bear up against the inroads of a disease which baffled all the skill of medical science.

His last and fatal attack occurred early in January, 1854. It was very severe and alarming from the first. His resolute will was constrained to yield, and all labor was suspended. He lost in a few weeks, he writes, "twenty-five pounds in weight, and found this *invalidity* no joke." But the violence of the attack at length abated, and on the last Sabbath in March he was able to visit the Sanctuary of God. And in May, "after frequent and distressing relapses," he had so far recovered as to take a journey to the White Sulphur Springs of Virginia, accompanied by Mrs. S. and his eldest son, who was also an invalid. He returned, after six weeks, so much improved as to preach again to his people, until the closing of his church in August; for the last time on the 30th of July. It was about this time that I was favored with my last interview with him. We accidentally met in Wall Street, New York, and amid the crowd, the bustle and anxieties of that mart of business, held sweet converse for an hour on heart themes and holy things. He appeared much better than when I had seen him last, but was still very feeble. His people, he said, were determined to shut his mouth, and so had resolved to close his church for awhile. He hoped however to do "a little service yet." I never saw him so gentle, so affectionate and confiding in his manner. He spoke very freely of personal and family matters, and of his hopes and fears respecting the future; and mentioned the several afflictive dealings of God with him in a manner which plainly showed that his heart was very heavy, and his soul in deep distress. I saw him on to the ferry-boat at the foot of the street, and we parted! I was not to see again in the flesh one whose bright example had given me new views of ministerial faithfulness; whose pulpit instructions had seemed to me, ever since I had known him, to be eminently superior, and to which I confess a deep debt of gratitude; and the memory of whose friendship and intercourse will be sacredly cherished while life and being last.

During the summer he visited Sharon Springs, Saratoga, and other places, seeking health, and leaving no means untried which promised relief from his depressing and torturing malady. It was a summer of "Mingled Light and Darkness." There were the alternations of hope and fear—abatements of the disease and revived expectations; relapses, and the gloom of despair as to any cure, continually agitating his mind, and, very naturally his religious feelings. In August he experienced a very violent paroxysm of his complaint; and about the middle of October returned to his home from the last of his health-pursuing journeys, feeble and cast down. On Saturday, the 28th of the same month, he joined the family circle below for the last time: that evening he went up to that chamber and bed where he was to glorify God by sufferings prolonged through four long weeks, and which he was not to leave till the agony of the conflict finally brought release to the sufferer.

SICKNESS AND TRIALS.

> "The chamber where the good man meets his fate
> Is privileged beyond the common walks
> Of virtuous life—quite on the verge of heaven."

But before we enter that chamber, made sacred and memorable by triumphant suffering and dying, let us pause a moment and know the state of mind and the exercises of our brother at this moment, under the long baptism of darkness and suffering, against which he had so manfully striven. Ten months of excruciating pain had now, without interruption and with only occasional abatement, been borne by him in patience. Nor was this all! There were "*two* rods" with which his heavenly Father was scourging his faithful servant at the same time. It was indeed a dark day. The trial was greater than we can set forth by any power of language. And why marvel, if we see the good man at first fainting under the double load, and even crushed to the earth; perplexed at the ways of God; and in his extremity driven where we have oft found him before in his desponding hours, to *trust*—"just to trust in God"—whose throne is above the clouds, and whose *faithfulness* he had so often preached to others! There was an hour when even the Son of God fainted, and prostrated himself at midnight on the cold earth, in the weakness and sorrow of suffering manhood, and tremblingly prayed that the cup might pass from him. And like him, our brother came out of this midnight travail of soul strengthened, and, made *perfect through sufferings*, entered the open gate of glory, bearing away the victor's crown.

Under date of September 23d he thus writes: "My weakness is extreme. One faculty after another gives way, and I am only the wreck of what I was. If body only was a wreck and mind was left to its integrity, I should not be so wretched. Then a shattered frame might lean upon a sound mind and find some support. It is not so now. Both body and mind are in ruins. Ah! God *will* teach me that I can lean only upon him. Hard lesson to learn! I have had so many props, so many friends, and other comforts to lean upon—and more especially I have such a slow and doubting heart, that I find it no easy thing now (when friends can not reach me and when nothing but a heart of faith will do) to lay myself down helpless, hoping, happy in the hands of a trusted God. Yet I trust. Or, if it is too much to say that, I *try* to trust. *Though he slay me, yet will I trust in him.* I have little hope of ever being well. But I wish to live—much wish to. My family seem to need me, at least a little longer; and I am very sure that I need more grace to die with than I have got now. Pray for me."

Again he writes to this same friend, in language highly suggestive and with a heart still agonizing in grief: "The troubles of life thicken around me. I am afraid I know not how to meet them. More and more I see the necessity of the *passive* graces. Such a grace, for example, as patience—how much better is it than courage, and how much more difficult to exercise. To plan, to act, to persevere, to combat difficulties and fight enemies, all appears easy to me, trained as I have been on the rough fields of life. But now I am called to a field on which I have had no training, and on which I am a poor scholar and learn slowly, or not at all. I have only to submit and endure. Dreadful lot! dreadful lesson! I am not happy. Yea, I am miserable. I did not expect this. The morning of my life was somewhat obscured by clouds, but hope gilded their edges; my noon was brilliant—but now clouds and darkness rest heavy upon the evening of my days! How different from my expectations. I had hoped to throw a kind of security around the decline of life, by energy and industry in the middle of it. But I find there was little *faith* in that, and God will be *trusted* at every step. Very well; I will trust him; though he slay me, yet will I trust him: for I can do nothing *but* trust him." And yet, in this hour of trial and extreme depression, when, like David, this afflicted soul cried, "All thy waves and thy billows are gone over me," the anchor which he had cast within the vail, held him fast to his mooring; and feeling that he was safe even amid the storm and the deep, he closes this same epistle of touching sadness and grief, with the triumphant testimony: "One thing, however, I can say to you, that *faith* is the most precious of all things on earth."

But it was not *all dark*, while heart and flesh were failing him, and a double rod was sorely chastising him: "However, I have had some views of time, and eternity, and God," he writes, "in my season of trial, which I hope have not been lost upon me. I have long known (theoretically) that God knows what rod of chastisement to lay upon me, and now I see it more clearly. He has employed upon me the *two* rods which cut most deep! No, no. I do wrong to say so. I don't know that. But yet it seems to me that I could have borne something else better. But it is well for us that we have not to choose our own sorrows. 'Two rods?' Yes, my dear friend *two*. The severest of which must be nameless till I see you."

How true it is—

"'Mid glimm'ring hopes and gloomy fears
We trace the sacred road:
Through dismal deeps and dang'rous snares
We make our way to God."

It was his earnest wish to recover, and many and affecting were his supplications to be spared a little longer to his family and people. These were the strong ties which bound him to life. "Oh, my wife and children, how can I leave them!" was his frequent exclamation. Even amid the agonies which were rending his strong frame, his prayer often was: "Send thy blessing upon my people." But his petitions for recovery always ended with, "Thy will be done!"

It was no ordinary trial for such a man to surrender life. Life is sweet to all, and especially to such a husband and father, *now* it would seem doubly needed by his family: to such a pastor, surrounded by an affectionate and numerous flock, for whom he had toiled so long, and sacrificed so much, now weeping at the thought of a separation; still also, in the midst of a daily widening sphere of Christian usefulness; *his bow abiding in strength; his eye not dim, nor his natural force abated.* Providence could scarcely have arranged the circumstances of the case so as to make the surrender of this life a greater trial to him. Hence, when he found his *strength weakened in the way,* and his *days shortened,* like the Psalmist, with impassioned earnestness he prayed: *O my God, take me not away in the midst of my days.*

His illness, after his confinement, was of such a nature, and his sufferings for the most of the time so terribly severe, as to prevent much conversation, and constrain the use of opiates. Few sufferers probably ever endured more intense bodily pain than he for so long a time. His physicians remarked, that they had never seen, and scarcely ever heard of a case of such protracted agony. Only his iron constitution enabled him to bear it. There was scarcely a moment's cessation. And yet patience had its perfect work. "It is all right." "*It is all right.*" Even when agony forced the screams from his lips, the next words would be, "I do not murmur! Jesus, Master, help me to bear it!" In the brief intervals of suffering, he seemed conscious of the danger of his situation, and then in murmuring prayer he was heard committing himself and those dear to him on earth, unreservedly and confidently to the God of all grace. On the Monday preceding his death, the violence of the disease having spent itself, and feeling that his end was drawing nigh, he gathered his family about his bed, and in a clear, strong voice, and with a manner tender and solemn as such a scene could impart, addressed to each his parting words of advice and affection. He expressed his own firm reliance on Jesus Christ, and his humble expectation of shortly going to be with him for ever. And he charged them all to meet him there. With words of undying affection and full of wisdom, he alluded to his absent son. And then, one by one, he gave them his parting embrace, and consigned them to the care of the widow's God, and the Father of the fatherless. His intimate friend and highly esteemed brother, Dr. Gardiner Spring, called soon after. But let his own pen describe this last solemn interview:

"It was just after this affecting scene [the one described above] that I knocked at his door. And never was I more kindly directed than in making this fraternal visit. I had some fears, from what I knew of his self-scrutinizing spirit, that I might find him in a depressed state of mind. But as he drew near the close of his struggles, God was kind, and gave him sweet indications of his paternal love. There he tossed, day after day, and night after night, upon that couch of racking pain, with a mind as clear as Newton's, and a heart as peaceful as a child in its mother's bosom. The great peculiarity of his Christian character was his shrinking humility and self-diffidence. More than once, in the days of his unbroken vigor, I have heard him say, 'I have mistaken my calling; I never was fit for a minister of the Gospel.' No one else thought so; yet he retained this self-diffidence to the last. I said to him, 'Brother Spencer, I am afraid you are about to leave us.' He replied, 'I think so.' I took his hand, and he said, 'You see I am strong; I may rally, but it is more than probable that I shall leave you by to-morrow morning.' 'Is it *peace* with you, brother?' His body was in agony; he tossed his head on the pillow, and replied, '*It is all peace!*' He paused, and, fixing his piercing eye upon me, said, 'I am afraid *it is too much peace.* I can not discover in myself those evidences of personal godliness which justify me in enjoying *such abundant peace.*' I could not repress a smile at these sweet words, and then reminded him of those words of the Lord Jesus, when he said, 'I am come that they might have life, and that they might have it *more abundantly.*' He simply replied, 'Pray with me;' and then called his family around his bed, where we knelt and prayed together for the last time."

In the afternoon of the same day, to his intimate friend, Mr. Jasper Corning, he said, "All is peace—All is peace." In answer to his inquiry, if he could cheerfully submit to the will of God in causing him to suffer so much, he replied: "Now no chastening for the present seemeth to be joyous, but grievous; nevertheless, afterward it yieldeth the peaceable fruit of righteousness unto them which are exercised thereby." A brief prayer was offered by Mr. C. and an affecting farewell taken. During Tuesday night, an Elder of his Church who watched by his side, heard him ejaculating his trust and joy. He repeated many times, as if his soul overflowed with peace : " Glory be to God! Glory to God in the highest! no more pain—no more sin—no more temptation." On Wednesday morning when he was thought to be unconscious, a friend sitting by him, repeated the first line of the Hymn, " Jesus, lover of my soul," to which he instantly responded, " Let me to thy bosom fly," in accents that seemed to say, the bitterness of death was already past. In the afternoon of the same day, another Elder of his Church who was standing at the foot of the bed, was suddenly and tenderly recognized by him. The only person that he seemed to notice, after this, was his highly valued friend and family physician, DOCTOR WENDELL, whose tender and self-sacrificing ministries, beside his professional skill, had greatly endeared him to the dying sufferer. With the affectionate manner of a child he exclaimed, " My dear doctor Wendell—my *dear* doctor!"

After this, he lay partly in a stupor, and partly in a sleep, which at one time seemed so sweet and peaceful as to attract the anxious attendants to his bedside. On Thursday evening, November 23d, at a little past eight, he closed his eyes on this world of suffering and sin, as gently as the infant falls to sleep, to open them in that heavenly kingdom where *there shall be no more pain*, and no sin, nor death. And no sooner had the scene of mortal agony closed than his countenance put on the look of perfect peace and serenity, as if the triumphant spirit had left its impress even on that mortal part which death had vanquished.

" What a triumphant chamber was that! and what an hour of triumph, when that creature of suffering, poor in spirit but rich in faith and heavenly hopes, was released from the bondage in which he had so long struggled, dismissed from this sinning and weeping world, and winged his way to his appointed and prepared place near the Eternal Throne!"

It was *all light* with him at *evening-time*. He, while living, had thus discoursed and testified to his people: "Take the believer on the bed of death. He has struggled along through his dim day of life, lighted a little sometimes, and sometimes walking in darkness, and through *fear of death, all his life-time subject to bondage,* till the *evening-time* has come. At this *evening-time it shall be light.* I have often noticed it in the dying members of this Church. They have died in a blaze of light—died more happy than they had lived, and wondering at their own composure and faith. The hour they most feared has become more light than any before it, and old Simeon exclaims: *Lord now lettest thou thy servant depart in peace, for mine eyes have seen thy salvation.*" Yes: and so wast thou to depart, our Brother! So was the faithful shepherd to testify from his death-chamber to all the world! He who had been so safe and strong a light to guide many of God's mourning saints through life's dark and treacherous pilgrimage; who had instrumentally given comfort and courage to so many fearful hearts as they went down the rugged banks into the river of death, and had with a joyful soul heard their triumphant shout as they passed safely over—was not himself to be left to darkness and trembling in his last hour.—" Oh, if we could have that hold on God," which this eminent saint had, to use his own strong language, "we could die a thousand deaths, after wiping the death-sweat from the brow of our last friend."—He died at the age of fifty-six years and nine months— by a singular coincidence, the exact age of his father at the time of his death.

The public funeral services occurred on the Sabbath following, from the Church in which he had officiated for so many years. It was a solemn and deeply affecting occasion. Most of the evangelical pastors of the city, and many from other places, were present, and mingled their tears with the assembled multitudes.

The large Church was crowded to its utmost capacity, and thousands were unable to gain an entrance; so universal was the respect felt for his memory, and so great the anxiety to mingle in the melancholy scenes of his burial. The services were conducted by Drs. Cox, Dwight, and Spring. The venerable Dr. Spring, of New York, preached an appropriate Sermon from the words of the Apostle (Rom. vii. 18): For I reckon that the sufferings of this present time are not worthy to be compared with the glory which shall be revealed in us. The theme of the Discourse was triumph in suffering, suggested no doubt by the experience of his lamented Friend and Brother, during his last illness. Beautifully and feelingly did he expatiate on the chosen subject, and apply it for the purpose of instruction and consolation, under the deeply afflictive Providence which had bereft his family and people and the Church of so good and useful and great a man. And he closed the Discourse with a touching tribute to the memory of the departed. It was a scene of solemn and tender interest which no words can paint. Writes an eye-witness: "My eye has never rested on a more sublime spectacle than was presented by that house of God, clothed in its gloomy drapery, and crowded with that sea of faces; now turned upward to listen to the venerable preacher, as he expatiated on the glories of that land where there is no more sickness, nor crying, neither any more pain; and now bowed down to weep when reminded that the body of him who had so long been the light of that sanctuary, was coffined before its altars." Not often is it that so many pious tears consecrate the burial-service of the dead. The death of this saint was *precious* not only *in the sight of the Lord*, but in the sight of his whole Church, and of the city in which his light had shone so long and so conspicuously.

The interesting Sermon preached on the occasion, has been published: we have taken an extract or two from it to enrich this Sketch; and would have drawn more liberally from it had our space allowed.

The next morning his relatives and immediate friends, including a large portion of his bereaved congregation, attended his remains to Greenwood, where, without show or ceremony, they were committed to the grave in certain hope of a glorious resurrection.

> "Not with the roll of the stirring drum,
> And the trumpet that sings of fame,"

but with the chastened and solemn feeling of Christian sentiment, and the low and trembling words of Christian faith and prayer. His place of burial seemed appropriately chosen—on "Ocean Hill"—commanding a magnificent ocean view—the breaking waves seen in the distance dashing high on the Rockaway beach—and the deep anthem of the Atlantic's eternal roar falling on the ear—the symbol of grandeur, of power, of eternity.

And I heard a voice from heaven, saying unto me, Write, Blessed are the dead which die in the Lord from henceforth: Yea, saith the Spirit, that they may rest from their labors; and their works do follow them. It is a profoundly mysterious providence that calls such a laborer away from the harvest-field, and especially in this evil day, when characters such as his are rare, and from a position where his presence and influence, to the eye of man, seem more and more necessary. But such a providence, as our Brother would reason, assorts with many of God's other dealings. He has always sustained his people by appealing to their *faith*, not to reason. He has made his Church strong by tearing away her earthly props. He has overruled her seeming reverses for her real advancement. Baptisms of darkness and trial are made the tokens of covenant love, and the heralds of deliverance and enlargement. The tears of mourning and sadness bring forth a harvest of gladness and rejoicing. The *dead bones of the prophet* are sometimes the Lord's chosen instrument of life. He oftentimes, doubtless, accomplishes more good by taking a godly man out of the world than by continuing him in it. While the hearts of many thousands of Christians are made to bleed and mourn over the death of such a man, and such a preacher, in the full measure of his strength and usefulness, and to lift up to Heaven the prayer of the smitten : *Help Lord, for the godly man ceaseth*—we would be comforted, nay encouraged to redouble our diligence, assured that *The Lord reigneth ; let the earth rejoice.*

Dr. Spencer is among the number of those sainted ones, whose influence will go down to posterity, gathering fragrance, and volume, and fresh memorials of its usefulness, from age to age.

We commend this humble endeavor to make a little better known a great and a good man; and these volumes, through which he will yet preach the Gospel of salvation, to the blessing of Him whose providence and grace alone can make them of use to the world.

Sermons.

A Devotional Spirit.

It is good for me to draw near to God.—Psalms, lxxiii. 28.

THE devotional spirit manifestly was prevailing in the heart of *Asaph* when he uttered these words. In the former part of the Psalm, he rehearses what *had been* some of his experiences, at a time when, it would seem, such a spirit of devotion did not prevail with him. At that time speculation prevailed. It had very much taken the place of devotional feelings. It did him no good. He *found* it did him no good. *His steps had well-nigh slipped.* Says he, *He was envious at the foolish, when he saw the prosperity of the wicked.* He could not so understand God as to be happy and satisfied. The impenetrable shade of a dark cloud hung over his allotments; and all his sagacity in study could not lead him to such an understanding of God as to bring peace to his heart. But now, done with speculation, and animated with the spirit of devotion, he was more happy. He was satisfied with God. He was satisfied also with himself. The exercises of his devotional soul were soothing and pleasant to him: *It is good for me to draw near to God.*

The text itself, therefore, taken in its connection, shows us that the author was now in a devotional frame of mind.

There are different means of grace, and there are different exercises of piety. None of them are to be undervalued. In their place they may all be beneficial. But there are some reasons for supposing that those exercises of religion which are more purely of a devotional nature, are not, comparatively, justly valued among Christians, and much less are they justly valued among unbelievers. Be this as it may, the devotional parts of religion are of much moment to us. We ought to know this. We ought to give to them their just weight. We propose, therefore,

I. To explain what is meant by this devotional spirit.

II. To demonstrate its importance and commend it to your cultivation.

I. The explanation.

A devotional spirit is a thing susceptible of an intelligible explanation. The accuracy of the *understanding* of the explanation will always depend far more upon the justness of the heart's temper, than upon any mere clearness of intellectual ideas.

But it is easy for any one to perceive that there is a vast difference between that state of mind which merely delights to contemplate religious truth as a matter of observation or intellectual apprehension, and that state of mind which contemplates it in the way of a personal and ready application for the soul's use. Study is one thing, and obedience is quite another. To know is one thing, and to feel is quite another.

It would be impossible to sketch all the exercises of a devotional spirit. They are infinitely various. Such a spirit has its peculiarities of exercise in all the means of religion, in all its ideas, and all its affections.

A DEVOTIONAL SPIRIT. 131

You will have sufficient understanding of it by attention to these three ideas: its *means*, its *refuge*, and its *exercises*.

1. *Its means.* Such a spirit finds, at once, delight and improvement, especially in such things as prayer, meditation, contemplations of God and heaven, remembrance of God's dealings with the soul, and thankfulness and praise, amid both recollections of the past and anticipations of the future. *Private* prayer and private meditation, in especial manner, are the means of good to which a devotional spirit turns. Such a spirit is the poetry of religion. It delights in song. It breathes in song. It lives in song. Its soul—its whole soul—can blend with the harp of *David*, or the lyre of *Asaph*. A believer of such a spirit delights in, and is improved by, the Psalms and Hymns of religion, as well as the mere argumentative or didactic truths of religion. It is not so much the *study* of truth, as the use of it—the taste and enjoyment of it. And hence its resort is, in especial manner, to such means of grace as we have just mentioned.

2. *Its refuge.* A devotional spirit is a spirit which has direct reference very much to God himself. *To draw near to God* is its aim and delight. His character, his law, his love, his dispensations, and his presence, are not mere matters of a speculative understanding to a devotional soul, but they are matters of taste and experience—of delight and strength. God is sought. And hence, all those religious exercises which have more immediate or direct respect to God himself, become the choice of the soul: *Whom have I in heaven but thee, and there is none upon the earth that I desire beside thee. My soul thirsteth for God, for the* LIVING *God. As the hart panteth for the water-brooks, so panteth my soul after thee, O God.*

And hence it is easy for us to understand that those great doctrines of truth which unfold the character of God, his sovereignty, government, and grace, are the very matters which kindle the devotions of a truly pious soul. God's independence, his majesty, his holiness, his eternal election, his redemption by the great atonement, his efficacious grace and everlasting faithfulness, the truths which make God himself familiar to the soul, in all the solemn holiness and majesty of his nature, are the things which true devotion loves best and clings to longest. *Solid doctrine* feeds devotion. It fills the soul, because it is full of God. Aside from such doctrine, true devotion dies.

3. *Its exercises.* With a devotional spirit the *religious affections* are particularly exercised—not merely religious mind, or religious conscience, but religious affections. Heart takes the lead in a devotional spirit. Principle is not undervalued indeed; but principle is not every thing, nor the main thing, with a believer in his devotional frame. Instruction has more immediate respect to the understanding, the will, the conscience. Devotion exercises the affections. And consequently a devotional spirit is ordinarily a more happy spirit; indeed, happy it will be, with a species of happiness it would not willingly dispense with, even amid its occasional pensiveness in seasons of the twilight of the soul. Such graces *of the Spirit, as love, joy, peace, long-suffering, gentleness, goodness, faith, meekness, temperance*—the dependence of the spirit upon God, and hope in him, are the common exercises of a devotional spirit.

These are some of the marks of such a spirit. You may find examples of its exercise in such places as the Psalms, in Job, in many passages of the Prophets and of the New Testament. You may find examples of it, too, wherever you can find believers having peculiar attachment to prayer, private and social; to meditation, habitual and sweet; to contemplations of heaven, and remembrance of God's mercies; and having habits of walking with God, and habits of exercise in the affections of piety as the delights of the heart.

II. We pass, as we proposed, TO DEMONSTRATE THE IMPORTANCE OF A DEVOTIONAL SPIRIT, AND COMMEND IT TO YOUR CULTIVATION. We name to you nine different ideas.

1. The devotional spirit, in a very special manner, tends to improve a believer in the most important parts of his piety. There are sentiments as well as principles in religion. In some respects, the piety of sentiment wherein the ardor and strength of the affections are brought into exercise, is superior to the piety of mere principle wherein reason and conscience take the whole control.

The affections, more peculiarly than either reason or conscience, constitute the life-blood of a vital religion. If the affections were right, the conscience would seldom be wrong; and reason would seldom be jostled from her throne by the deceptions of sin. Sin itself, in the deep home of its existence, is to be found rather among those *diverse lusts* that take up their abode in the heart, than among imperfections of knowledge or primary pollution of the moral principle. While it is true that the sinfulness of man certainly includes the "corruption of his whole nature," it is at the same time true also, that the fountain-head of corruption is to be found in the heart. And the employment of argumentation, of principles, of conscience and reason, on the subject of religion, is a matter which has its aim, not so much to drive deception from the judgment, as to dethrone sin from its empire-seat in the heart. Reason and the moral principle are brought into exercise, in order to have all the thunder of their artillery directed against the citadel of sin, and make the sinner know in mind, and feel in conscience, that a *new heart* is indispensable to his peace with God.

And in the exercises of a positive religion, a believer will be very signally defective, unless he has to aid him the impulses and delights of affection, as well as the purity and strength of principle. A devotional spirit is just the thing to reinstate the affections into their own place, and gift them with power. It is this which will lead one to that part of piety which is most directly opposed to the very essence of sin. It is this which will lead a believer to serve God from love, and not from mere principle—from delight in his character, and not from a cold respect to the magnitude of obligation. In devotion the soul is fed; it gains its strength and satisfaction.

Devotion is not study—it is not labor—it is not mind grappling with the severities of knowledge; it is just heart breathing its wants into the ear of God in prayer, meditating in delightful complacency upon his character and love, or singing its joyful songs of delight. It is *heart* entering into the great doctrines, feeding on the bread of life. It is, therefore, just an indulgence of the heart's affections, satisfied with God, and hoping in his loving-kindness. By a devotional spirit the heart becomes better. It becomes more tender, more humble, more happy. It breathes freer. It rises above the cloudy atmosphere of this world, where mists and fogs obscure, and storms beat;

and, in the light of eternity and God, takes its own chosen course in the exercise of affections, bland as they are strong.

A devotional spirit, exercised in the love of God, in the faith of Christ, in Divine fellowship, in prayer, in song, will wear away that sternness and severity of character, and all that coldness of a calculating spirit which sometimes distinguish a man of principle without love. It is this devotional spirit which we need to make us affectionate Christians—to cultivate and adorn that part of piety which tends as much to make men love us, as purity of principle does to command their esteem.

2. A devotional spirit is of no small moment for us, even in reference to a just apprehension of Divine truth. Because the truth is the instrument of sanctification, it does not therefore follow that mind alone has business with it, or alone can understand it rightly. The heart has much to do with it. Indeed, there will always be a real and practical defect in the religious intelligence of the mere scholar. He may learn his lesson intellectually; and then it is only half learnt. He needs to learn it devotionally. His heart needs its impulse quite as much as his head needs its light or its logic. Divine truth will have quite a different aspect when a soul comes to employ it in intercourse with God, from what it will have in the eye of a mere beholder who only examines it by itself. An affectionate Christian, full of sentiments of piety which delight in prayer, in meditation, in praise, in the exercises of trust and love and hope, is just the soul to see Divine truth in its proper dimensions and aspects, and to take its proper direction. It is speculation which bewilders. Love, tenderness, faith, delight in God, never bewilder. A frame of mind

which does God the homage that belongs to him, which delights to draw near to him, and depend upon him, will ordinarily give to different Divine truths their just relative importance. And those great and deep doctrines, which trouble so many minds with perplexity and doubt, will lose all their power to trouble when received with the solemnity, homage, and affection, which are exercised and nurtured by habits of devotion.

Such doctrines, like the majesty and mysteries of the thunder, were not given to be understood, so much as to awe and humble. *Impression* was more the purpose of them, than comprehension. Like the self-existence of God, and the eternity of God, we may grapple with them for ever in vain, if we only design to sit in judgment upon their dimensions, and not to be awed and influenced by matters we can not fathom. Much in God, and therefore much in religion, is unfathomable to us. And those deep things which a mere speculator might dig at for ever without profit, are the very things which a devout spirit contemplates most delightfully and understands the best. These deep doctrines are most like God, unfathomable and peculiar; in many things beyond mind, but in all things such as the heart loves to lean upon, sensible of imperfection and sin here, and hasting to a deep and unseen eternity. The sovereignty of God, his eternal decrees, his blended justice and mercy in the atonement made for sinners by the sacrifice of Christ; these are just the rock of repose for a devotional man, and just the wilderness of perplexity for one of an opposite spirit. The frame of devotion is the fit frame of study. You will not be likely to misunderstand God on your knees.

3. A devotional spirit greatly contributes to the pro-

motion of holiness in the soul; because it employs the influences of beneficial and powerful habitudes of mind. Devotion is not like study. There is a wide difference betwixt them. You can not take it up when you will. You need something more than an act of volition to enter upon it really, and therefore profitably. It belongs to the *heart*, its frames, temper, and hopes—its delights, tenderness and faith—more than to the *mind:* and the heart will not yield its frames and impressions to your command, in the same manner as you can command your thoughts to what subject of study you will. A devotional spirit is a *habitude* of the soul; it is a cast of character flung over it, and woven into it. It is more of a frame than a mere fact—more of an abiding spirit carried along with it than a mere exercise taken up for the occasion. Human character, good or bad, worldly or religious, is very much formed by the subtle and plastic influence of habits—and habits too, in all ordinary cases, in very little things. To cultivate a devotional spirit, therefore, has the advantage of arraying the full influence of habit on the side of sanctification. Such a spirit not only keeps the mind in such a frame, that the *occasions* of devotion are not barren, but in such a frame that its ordinary exercises amid the business of the world are more just and peaceful. A devotional man has his spirit arrayed in the panoply of God. He brings all things to the examination of a mind tempered with piety. He receives more profit from devotional privileges, because he goes into his closet, or to the place of social prayer, or to the house of God, with a soul ready for their duties; and he departs, carrying the same spirit along with him, a help, a habit, and a delight. The devotional *habit* lends its influence amid the thousand thoughts and emotions of life, to promote the holiness of his soul. It spreads over all of them. It tempers every emotion—touches every thought—tunes every passion; because it lives and bears the sway of habit in the life-spring of them all.

4. The devotional spirit is one of the strongest safeguards, therefore, against the subtlety of temptation. Temptations are ordinarily addressed to two things.

First, to an unguarded *heart*. They seldom assail principle directly. They assail it only through the medium of affections, of passions. The power of truth is always superior to the power of error, when the two principles assail an unbiased mind. Temptations to sin prevail when the mind has received a bias, and principle has become weak through sinful affections. Passion is a foe to principle. It biases mind. It creates prejudice, or some other mental deception; and truth is obscured and principle sacrificed, not because the argumentation of sin is superior to the argumentation of holiness, but because their argumentations are addressed to feelings, not to reason.

Now, it is only a devotional spirit, occupying the heart, which can prevent its bias of the mind, and its giving efficacy to temptation. An unoccupied heart is a source of danger. An engaged one is a source of security. And mere conscience, mere truth ever so clear, mere principle ever so pure, do not lie in the soul on the side where temptation assails. There is nothing which can secure, but a *heart* accustomed to something more than doctrine, more than truth in the abstract. The heart needs precisely that frame of devotion which spreads over it all, which forms its habitudes of affection, and which says to the solicitations of the evil, *Depart from me*, *ye evil-doers, for I will keep the commandments of my God.* Not the most instructed, the most enlightened believers, are the most secure, but the most habitually devotional.

All the high places of our Zion are wet with the blood of the slain; while the foot of the altar, where the humble kneel, has never yet been reached by the sword of the enemy.

The second thing which temptation addresses is a *lacking* of enjoyment. Some painted delight is held up before a wanting heart. And the arguments which may impose silence upon the passions are not always powerful enough to eradicate them. The arguments may be conclusive enough in the sermon, in the book, in the hours of abstraction and study, and yet they may fail entirely, their strength be turned into weakness, before the attractions of pleasure, or the wild tide of solicited passions. Now it is the piety of devotion, just the piety of affection and taste, just the piety which is more than principle and truth, and has become habit and happiness, which can secure a tempted believer. The delight of a devotional spirit needs to be put in opposition to the proffered delights of sin; joy in God must be opposed to joy in sin; and the pleasures of a devotional indulgence opposed to the pleasures of indulgence in forbidden delights. Then, feeling in religion will be opposed to feeling in sin; the security will be just where temptation assaults; joy will be opposed to joy; pleasure to pleasure; the pleasure of converse with heaven to the pleasure of converse with the world; and the delights of the place of prayer to the delights of the place where prayer is never breathed. With a heart whose frame of habitual devotion can say, *It is* GOOD *for me to draw near to God*, temptations of sinful pleasure will seldom prevail.

5. Let it be remembered that a devotional spirit cultivates *all* the Christian graces. If truth and instruction lay the foundation of them, it is devotion that adorns them with their loveliness. Faith is nurtured by devotion. So is love. So is peace of mind. So is humility. In meditation, in prayer, in retirement from the world for the purposes of fellowship with the Holy Ghost and contemplation of the saints' everlasting rest, those Christian affections which are denominated the *fruits of the Spirit* receive more of the vivacity and strength and delight of life, than by any other means. All the Christian graces are *exercised* in devotion. Faith is exercised in prayer, in praise, in anticipations of heaven, in communion with God. Hope is exercised. Joy in God is exercised. The whole heart is unloosed from the bonds of the world, and the labors of study, to act its chosen part in the enjoyment of God, in all the felicities of a foretaste of heaven. Hence,

6. One advantage of a devotional spirit arises from its independence. There is such a thing as leaning upon others for aid, and doing nothing in the style of independence and personal strength. Such a one always remains feeble. His powers are only half developed. He can not have much manliness of character. All men can not become accomplished theologians, and, by extent of knowledge and chains of logic, become firm and secure in opinions of truth. But all men can be men of love and men of prayer. All believers can attain a piety, whose taste and sentiment, whose delight in God and ardor of love may do more for them than all possible stores of knowledge. You will never find a man of prayer less firm, less independent, less manly, than a man of knowledge. One whose devotional heart

has its affections habitually exercised in religion; one whose piety is his delight as well as his duty; one who can say to his God and Father, *I remember thee upon my bed, when I awake I am still with thee;* such a man will have an independence, a manliness of religion, which mere principle, mere knowledge and moral obligation can never attain. His piety is woven round his affections. His heart will be firm. Love has taught him. Prayer has taught him. Praise, meditation, contemplations of heaven, and walking with God, have taught him. He judges of all things for himself, for he judges of all things not by the human book, not by the beauty and tastefulness of the sermon, but by the Book of God and the great doctrines which feed the powers of life within him, a life which breathes in prayer and lives on God. He can tell what feeds him, aids him, comforts him. He can judge for himself, because he judges by his heart. Hence,

7. The spirit of devotion tends to cultivate a different kind of piety from the piety of mere knowledge, and a kind, perhaps, not a little wanted. The piety of devotion, of taste and sentiment, is tender, child-like, habitual, and humble. It is patient, forbearing, forgiving. If it is not qualified for attack, it is qualified for defense. If it can not make display, it can be diligent in duty. And it will be found like the flower of the rock, green and flourishing when all around is wilted and barren.

8. The spirit of devotion we commend to you is the spirit which will make increase of holiness from means which, without it, would be barren of benefit. A devotional spirit is its own instructor. It does much of its own preaching. It is self-tuition, self-rebuke, self-monition. A man of this taste for walking with God learns

and grows on his knees, in the closet, in meditation, in society. Means of good profit him which are barren to others. Take a single example. The works of creation and ordinary providence are full of benefit to him. If he can not have a sermon in the sanctuary, he can find one in the field. The heavens preach to him. The earth preaches. The beasts and birds teach him.

O Lord my God, thou art very great; thou art clothed with honor and majesty: who coverest thyself with light as with a garment: who stretchest out the heavens like a curtain: who layeth the beams of his chambers in the waters: who maketh the clouds his chariot: who walketh upon the wings of the wind. . . . . He sendeth the springs into the valleys, which run among the hills. They give drink to every beast of the field: the wild asses quench their thirst. By them shall the fowls of heaven have their habitation, which sing among the branches. He watereth the hills from his chambers: the earth is satisfied with the fruit of thy works. He causeth the grass to grow for the cattle, and herb for the service of man. . . . . The trees of the Lord are full of sap; cedars of Lebanon, which he hath planted; where the birds make their nests: as for the stork, the fir-trees are her house. The high hills are a refuge for the goats; and the rocks for the conies. He appointed the moon for seasons, and the sun knoweth his going down. Thou makest darkness and it is night. . . . . The earth is full of thy riches: so is the great and wide sea. . . . . The glory of the Lord shall endure for ever: the Lord shall rejoice in his works. He looketh on the earth, and it trembleth. He toucheth the hills, and they smoke. I will sing unto the Lord as long as I live: I will sing praise to my God while I have my being. My meditation of him shall be sweet: I will be glad in the Lord. It is good for me to draw nigh unto God.—(Psalm civ.)

Thus a taste for devotion and piety can not be at a loss for materials to work with. They are every where, because to such a spirit God is every where visible. It is the Lord who *clothes the grass of the field, which to-day is, and to-morrow is cast into the oven.* He gives the touches of their *beauty to the lilies of the field which toil not.*

9. Finally, that spirit of devotion which we commend, very much hangs round the very essentials of religion. It is familiar with *Christ;* and familiar with him, not as a mere king, but as a friend. His love prevails in its songs; his tenderness, his sacrifice, and compassion. A man of this sort of piety loves the communion-table, the closet, the prayer-meeting. He is familiar with *sin:* he knows who has lifted off from his soul the burden of its guilt; and he often has occasion to mourn its power as it clips the wings of an affection which would soar to God. He is familiar with *God.* Prayer, praise, and fellowship with him; joy, peace, and hope, which bathe now in his light, and drink from his rivers of love, do not leave God a stranger to the soul. He is familiar with the *promises:* he gathers up the history of their verification from the saints who have gone before him, and takes their safe-conduct to lead his willing spirit to that unseen abode:

> "Apostles, martyrs, prophets there
> Around my Saviour stand,
> And soon my friends in Christ below
> Will join that heavenly band."

He is familiar with that iron fortitude and tender love which took Jesus Christ through all the scenes of an earthly humiliation and death. He sings of Gethsemane. He plucks the flower that blooms in the garden of Arimathea, and lifts his longing eyes from the top of Mount

Olivet, as the ascending Saviour cleaves the clouds of heaven back into the bosom of his Father. He is familiar with *death*. He has often contemplated it, feared it, prayed about it, and, amid the crosses of the world and hopes of a final rest, sometimes even longed for it. He is familiar with *heaven*. It is his home. His hope is there. His heart is there. Sweetly he hopes, while tossed amid the storms of sin and the world here, and sometimes driven to despair by the buffetings of Satan, that he shall yet be at rest, where sin and Satan can not reach him. Says he:

> "It is a weary way, and I am faint;
> I pant for purer air and fresher springs;
> Oh, Father! take me home: there is a taint,
> A shadow on earth's purest, brightest things.
> This world is but a wilderness to me;
> There is no rest, my God! no peace apart from thee."

Thus a devotional spirit lives, and moves, and has its being among the very essentials of religion. Its frame is peaceful, though sometimes pensive; it is happy; it is heavenly. It hushes to rest the commotions of passion, and gives some solid good amid the tears and turmoil of the world. Happy frame! it wafts the spirit toward its home. God and hope and heaven are the solid materials for its joy; and, though pained and barren every where else, such a devotional believer can always say, *It is good for me to draw near to God.*

Sorrow for the Death of Friends.

But I would not have you to be ignorant, brethren, concerning them which are asleep, that ye sorrow not even as others which have no hope.—1 THESSALONIANS, iv. 13.

THE particular explanation which the Apostle himself gives of the meaning of these words, immediately follows them. It extends down to the end of the chapter: *For if we believe that Jesus died and rose again, even so them also which sleep in Jesus shall God bring with him. For this we say unto you by the word of the Lord, that we which are alive and remain unto the coming of the Lord, shall not prevent them which are asleep. For the Lord himself shall descend from heaven with a shout, with the voice of the archangel, and the trump of God; and the dead in Christ shall rise first: then we which are alive and remain shall be caught up together with them in the clouds to meet the Lord in the air; and so shall we ever be with the Lord. Therefore, comfort one another with these words.* This is the Apostle's own explanation of his particular meaning in the text. It would take us too long and open too wide a field of discussion, if we were to attempt a minute examination of all this passage. Its general significance every body understands. A few remarks, therefore, will be all we need upon the passage in general, before we return to the text we read to you, as the foundation of this discourse.

It is probable that the Apostle had recently heard of the death, perhaps the martyrdom, of some of the members of the Thessalonian church. While writing to them he adverts to it. Christianity never diminishes human sympathies. It makes them more wise, more judicious and tender; it sanctifies them, but it never represses them. The inspired Apostle himself poured forth the *comforts* of Christianity on the bleeding hearts of his smitten brethren.

It is nothing but Christianity which can bring comfort to the desolated heart of those who are called to part with their dying friends. *I would not have you to be ignorant*, says the Apostle; and every idea he expresses is taken from the peculiar religion of Christ. What a tribute of respect the unconverted world are compelled to pay to our religion, when their pious relatives die in their arms! Even without faith in Jesus Christ, how often do we hear them attempting to moderate their grief by the faith of their departed friends! Hear them, amid their bursts of sorrow: "My sister, my mother, was a good, a pious woman, and I know she is happy—she is happy!" What a tribute to Jesus Christ! What a glorious tribute! Even the unconverted soul is obliged to resort to him in afflictions which none but Jesus can reach!

There is a difference betwixt the sorrow of the world and the sorrow which is proper for believers in such cases. Believers are not to sorrow as those which have no hope.

It is faith, it is a Christian faith, which should guide the sorrows of the afflicted. *If we believe*, says the Apostle.

This faith should be very simple and very extensive.

Its rock is the word of God—its reach is all redemption. This faith should embrace, then, the death, and resurrection, and glory of our Lord, as an example and pledge of our own, and of all those that die in Christ. Jesus died and rose and revived again; *even so them which sleep in Jesus will God bring with him.*

Which sleep. Christianity turns death into a sleep. In these verses it is called so. The Pagans called death a sleep, for a very bad purpose: Christianity calls it so for a good one. Death was so cheerless and horrid to the Pagans, that they wished to forget it—to avoid the idea—to obscure it—to cover it up with a figure. They contrived methods for banishing the fear of death, and one method was, they avoided pronouncing the word even. Instead of saying any one was *dead*, they would say, "he was," intimating that he is now no more. The poet borrows this foolish yet touching figure, and puts it into the lips of one saddened over the ruin of his beloved and proud city. "Ilium fuit," Troy was, is the delicate and touching mode of affirming that Troy is no more—blotted out—gone! The Pagans sometimes called death *an exit;* sometimes *a departure;* sometimes *a destiny;* sometimes *a submission;* sometimes *a sleep.* But what was with them only a deceptive figure for a bad purpose, becomes, with Christianity, a glorious and consoling fact. The Apostle adopts their language. He calls death *a sleep.* He can do it with truth. Grace turns a Pagan figure into a Christian fact. "These dead bodies shall rise." The sleep of death shall be broken. And henceforth we are allowed to have, by certainty, more than all that the hearts of the heathen *could* have, by their attempted deception: *Blessed are the dead which die in the Lord, for they* REST *from their labors.*

It has been mentioned by some as a principle of the human mind (whether justly or erroneously I will not decide, I need not) that the human mind requires greatness of evidence, according to the greatness or wonderful nature of the facts which it is called on to believe. Be it so. And let this resurrection of the dead be the most stupendous and wonderful thing that can be conceived—the most difficult of belief. Here is the evidence: *I say unto you by the word of the Lord.* The word of God is the greatest and best of all possible proofs. No demonstration can go beyond this or add any thing to it.

When our relatives and friends are passing away out of the world, it is natural for us, and it is wise, to look down to the end of all sublunary things, and anticipate the final winding up of this earthly scene. This is what the Apostle means by the coming of the Lord: *The Lord himself shall descend from heaven with a shout, with the voice of the archangel and the trump of God* (every eye shall see him): *the dead in Christ shall rise first.* That day is coming. The trumpet-summons shall break open graves and echo along the cold, damp vaults of death; and the obedient *sea shall give up the dead that are in it;* then, they *which are alive and remaining* on the earth *shall not prevent* (not go before) *them that sleep. They shall be changed in the twinkling of an eye, and shall be caught up together* WITH THEM *to meet the Lord in the air;* and *so shall we ever be with the Lord.* Well may the Apostle add: *Comfort one another with these words.*

From this general view we return to the particular text we read: *We would not have you to be ignorant, brethren, concerning them which are asleep, that ye sorrow not even as others which have no hope.* Here the Apostle expresses the idea of a *difference* between the sorrow of those who have hope and those who have not. He desires that the Thessalonians, under the bereavement of relatives or friends, shall *not sorrow as those do who have no hope.*

There is an ambiguity about this last clause—about the object of hope. It may possibly mean no hope in respect to them who are dead. Surely, to think of those whom we have loved, and who have just died in our arms, and left us no reason to suppose they have gone to rest in heaven, may very well penetrate our hearts with the deepest and most dreadful sorrow! This is the worst of all the ills we could mourn over on their account! In such a case the mind shrinks from the very idea of their destiny. The thought is too horrible! To think of the friend whose eyes we have just closed and whose corpse still lies before us as having already entered into hell; and while we are attending to the solemnities of the coffin, the shroud, the funeral and the grave—to think of him as an outcast *for ever* from God, and now *suffering the vengeance of eternal fire*—this is too much for the human mind! The heart sinks under it! All nature recoils from it! Possibly the Apostle has reference to such a kind of sorrow when he speaks of the sorrow of those *who have no hope,* and reminds his brethren they were not called to sorrow like this. Those they had buried were the friends of Jesus, and they could have hope for them; and, instead of following them with their sorrowful thoughts to the dark doom of hell, they could think of them with a very different kind of sorrow, as already passed into glory, and their dead bodies awaiting in the grave the trumpet-summons that shall call them *to meet their Lord in the air.*

But I do not think this was exactly the idea of the Apostle. Beyond all doubt, he was speaking of the death and resurrection of the just—the whole context shows this. But if he had been speaking to mitigate the sorrow of the Thessalonians by contrasting the grounds of it with the grounds of sorrow when the unbelieving die, probably he would at least have mentioned the dismal condition of such. The mention of their dreadful doom would have been natural in such a case, and would have tended to comfort the Thessalonians more strongly, by bringing them to think how different their sorrow would have been if they had buried their friends while they could have *no hope* for them.

But I have not time fully to explain why I do not receive this interpretation. The meaning (I think) of the phrase, *others who have no hope*, is this: those who have *themselves* no hope—who are not believers—not Christians. When such persons bury their friends, they have sorrow; believers should not sorrow *like them.* In the case before us, the sorrow rose from the death of pious friends only; none others are alluded to. Both those who have hope—hope in God, hope for themselves—and those who have no hope, will have sorrow in such a case, and will mingle their sympathies and tears together around the coffins and graves of their pious friends. At the death of the pious, Christians should not sorrow *as* those do who are not Christians. This, I suppose, is the meaning of the text, and this the single thought which solicits your attention during the remainder of this sermon.

I. We will restrict the application of this principle.

Some sorrows of the irreligious are not to be condemned or shunned. We will maintain that part of the sorrow of those who have no hope is not improper for a believer.

II. We will apply the principle, and show what *kind* of sorrow common among unbelievers, is improper for pious people.

When unbelievers are called to part with Christian friends by death, their hearts are affected with grief; and *some* of their sorrow is not to be considered as improper for those who have hope in Christ. Let us see: we name three particular ideas.

1. There is a sorrow arising from the recollection of past *endearments*.

Persons without piety are affected with it when their friends die: and the text would not forbid this sorrow to them or to believers. On such an occasion, how natural it is for the mind to turn back upon the past! We recall the benefits of our departed friend. Our mind wanders back upon the years we have lived together. We remember the instances of kindness, the days of intimacy, the times in which the cares and counsels of our friend aided us. We recall the seasons of fear, of perplexity and discouragement, when our friend took us to his bosom, and we learnt to know there was one spot on earth where we could weep and be comforted. We recollect how our distresses melted away under the soothings that fell from those lips, and the kindness that beamed on us from those eyes. But that bosom is cold, those lips are silent, those eyes are sealed up in death! One for whom our labors were endured, and round whom our hearts hung, is gone—he will meet us no more! And now we turn our thoughts down to the future, and are sadly reminded that we have met with a loss never to be retrieved! We are to go abroad: and amid trouble, toil, and unkindness, our heart can not turn back for its solace to the friend who used to cheer us when we came home! We are to come home: there is a voice wanting in the circle! there is a seat vacant at the table! there is a heart that once opened to us, now gone—gone for ever! We are compelled to have sorrowful recollections of the changes that have passed upon our lot! Midnight has settled down upon our soul!

This is a kind of sorrow which belongs to those *which have no hope*, and this sorrow is not to be censured in a Christian. It is proper to dwell on the endearments of the past; to remember the fidelity of our friend; the counsels he gave us, the conversations of frankness, and the hints of delicacy so tenderly flung out, lest our sensibilities should be wounded. It is right to remember the language of the death-bed—those tears, those prayers, those anxieties of expiring nature! Yes, Jesus may weep at the grave of Lazarus: her friends may weep when they *show the coats and garments which Dorcas made while she was with them*. David may go up to his chamber, weeping as he goes: *Oh! my son Absalom! my son, my son Absalom! would God I had died for thee, oh, Absalom, my son, my son!* This is one kind of sorrow which the text would not censure.

2. There is a sorrow arising from the recollection of our past *failures*. It is sometimes a very bitter sorrow. When we are parting with our friends we are prone to think how little we prized them, and how very improperly we requited their kindnesses while they were living. Even if we did not blame ourselves for lack of ten-

derness and affection while they were alive, we are very apt to find good reasons for doing it when they are dead. Then, how every unkind word, every ungracious look, every emotion of indulged resentment, will come thronging over our memory, and deepening the poignancy of our anguish! Oh! how we wish we could live those days over again, when our ingratitude or unkindness wounded the heart which will bleed for us no more! Oh! if we could put hearing into the ears of the dead, how we would confess our faults, and beg forgiveness for the errors which our thoughtlessness committed! This is a kind of sorrow which children often feel when they lose their parents. They bitterly remember their disobedience, their petulance, their unkindness, and the lack of gratitude for those favors and that love which flowed out in such numerous instances of tenderness from the *heart* of the parent that never will bleed at their unkindness again! That heart has ceased to beat! It is cold and dead! Ah! if they could bring back its love, and put its wonted sensibility into it for a single hour, what tears of penitence they would shed! how fondly they would ask forgiveness! and with what diminished sorrow they would resign again to insensibility in death the heart that had forgiven them!

This kind of sorrow is common with those *who have no hope*, and it is allowable for believers. It is nothing more than a tender and affectionate justice. It is due to the dead. It is not one of the deceptions of grief, but it arises from mournful deficiencies which affliction brings to our mind, and compels us to weep over, and weep the more bitterly because now we can do nothing else! the dead are beyond our confessions and our unkindness for ever! This sorrow arises from the honesty of grief. It is profitable for the living. It tends to humble us, and tends to make us more careful and affectionate to our surviving friends, when our heart bleeds at the remembrance of our cruelty to those who are now dead.

3. There is a sorrow concerning them which are asleep, connected with the consideration of *our loss*. You will excuse me for not attempting to sketch it. I can not describe it. I remember my father! And I am sure no words could give any idea of the feelings of desolation that came over me, when I came back from his funeral and found myself fatherless, young, unbefriended, and poor! Oh! what a dark wilderness the world was! Who should take care of me? Who should defend me against the injustice of a cold world? Who should educate me, and fit me for the conflicts of life? Who should soothe me when I should be sick? who should gently counsel me any longer, and let me pour my young sorrows into his bosom? No, no! language has no terms to tell the sorrows that came on my heart! There is something that can not be described, when we realize the loss we have met with by the death of our friends. Some of you do not need any description. The wounds are fresh and bleeding in the hearts of not a few who are here.

And if you have any doubt whether religion allows of sorrow on account of such a loss, look at bereaved families, and you will doubt it no more. You shall see little children fatherless! stripped! But here again I must stop! I can not speak of it! Let the *facts* preach to you.

These considerations (and we might add to them) are enough to show that there is a kind of sorrow for the death of friends which affects those who *have no hope*, and which is not disallowed to those who have hope in God. This is the *restriction* in the application of the text.

II. We proposed, in the second place, to show what kind of sorrow, very common with them who *have no hope*, is improper for believers. *Five* items will include all we mean.

1. With those *who have no hope, sorrow concerning them which are asleep* sometimes becomes *unsubmissive*. In the freshness of our affections it is very difficult for us to tell (and no one can tell for us) whether our sorrow is tinctured with rebellion or not. Certainly, no one in such sorrow *intends* to be rebellious. But when the full sense of trial comes over the heart, we are exposed to feel that God is dealing hardly with us. Persons without faith do sometimes feel so. The text reproves *them*, and admonishes *you* that ye sorrow not like them.

Submission under such strokes may be a most difficult thing, but it is a Christian duty. Sorrow and submission should go together; not that we should be willing to be miserable, but that we should be willing that God should reign; and if his dispensations cause us sorrow, we should be willing that our tears should flow. Two considerations especially ought to restrain us from a murmuring and unsubmissive sorrow. One is the righteous sovereignty of God. We are his, and our friends are his. We live by his sufferance, and die at his bidding. *The Lord killeth and maketh alive, he bringeth down to the grave and bringeth up.* The other consideration is, that we are unable to penetrate his designs; and the things which seem to us most severe are often to be numbered among our most remarkable mercies. Let us take them submissively at his hand. If there is goodness any where, it is to be found in God. Let us trust him. Let us trust him in the dark. Let us resign up our friends to death like old Eli, and say over their coffins and their graves: *It is the Lord, let him do what seemeth him good.* Let us receive the cup of bitterness out of his hand like Jesus Christ: *The cup which my Father giveth me, shall I not drink it?*

I am not going to undervalue the sentiments of grief or the feelings of submission which often dwell in unsanctified hearts when friends die. I am sure, that in such cases there are sensibilities and sentiments deserving of all respect. And it would be contrary alike to the tenderness of humanity and of God to insult the wretchedness of the weeping unbeliever in such cases. But we must honor religion. It deserves honor. Here, not less than on every other point, it surpasses any ordinary measure of humanity. We must not undervalue the sentiments which grace implants. And it is a truth—it is a blessed truth—that faith in God produces a *kind* of submission which unbelief knows nothing about. Unbelief submits at best *because it must.* The time has come. An inexorable destiny has taken away a friend; and the power, the right, the wisdom of God in doing it, are not to be called in question. The heart bows before the majesty of a throne which the eyes can not gaze upon, and which the arms can not embrace. But it may—it ought to be different with a believer. While his heart bleeds under the stroke, he looks up to the God that smote him: *Though he slay me, yet will I trust in him.* He turns from the fresh grave of his parents: *When my father and my mother forsake me, the Lord will take me up.* He submits, not merely because he *must,* not because it is *right,* but because he *loves* to submit; and never does he cling to the throne of God with such a willing and submissive embrace as when his dearest friends have dropped from his arms.

Sometimes it takes repeated bereavements to bring a believer to this sweet submission. A Christian of Florida, of whom I have some knowledge, once said: "After my husband died, and I had mourned bitterly and long, my heart turned to my children. When my first child died, all my grief came back upon me. The second died, and I murmured! The third died, and I was entirely rebellious; I thought God was cruelly and improperly severe upon me! But now, the fourth and *last one* is taken away, and I am satisfied. I *know* that the rod with which my heavenly Father hath smitten me was cut from the tree of life." Grief ought to be submissive. To make it so, sometimes stroke follows stroke.

At the funeral of President Davies, just as the people were about to take up the coffin to remove it to the burial, his mother, an aged widow, came to take the last look of her son. She gazed intently upon him—the tears fell upon the face of the corpse as she bent over it, and then, retiring a single step as she still gazed upon him, she exclaimed: "There lies my only son; my only earthly comfort and earthly support. But there lies the will of God, and I am satisfied." Sorrow, tearful though it be, ought to be submissive.

2. Under such afflictions as the text mentions, those *who have no hope* are sometimes inconsolable. They feel their loss. They can not but feel it. The heart is robbed and desolate. Indeed, they seem to think it due to their departed friend to resemble Rachel, and *refuse to be comforted*. And their consolation comes only from the fact that the lapse of time wears out the traces of grief.

It would be easy to apologize for this, and justify it too, if we had no Bible and no Christ. Situated as we are in this world, all our blessings seem to be wrapped up in a single point. That point is—the father of a family—is an only child—or the wife of one's bosom. On this point we rest. We have nothing earthly without it. We are compelled to feel so. And when we have seen surviving parents committing their only child to its little grave; or seen the mother bedewing with her tears the coffin of a mature daughter, who had become companion as well as child; or seen the strong man robbed of the wife of his bosom; or seen the widow and her children turn away from the grave where they had just buried their father and their friend; who has not felt, that if Heaven could excuse any sin, it must be the sin of that heart which should refuse to be comforted?

But after all, the believer ought not to mourn as those *who have no hope.* His sorrow ought not to be inconsolable. Child, wife, and father, should not be such heart-idols to us that we can not give them up. God, the blessed God, should be the object of our warmest attachment and our firmest confidence. We ought to have only a submissive attachment to the objects of earthly and transient good. They that *use this world ought to be as though they used it not, for the fashion of this world passeth away. Put not your trust in princes, nor in great men, in whom there is no help: his soul goeth forth, he returneth to the earth, and in that very day his thoughts perish.* A believer may be consoled. He ought not to sorrow as those *who have no hope.* His best friend can never be taken from him; his firmest support can never be laid in the grave. His God liveth, and he may pour his sorrows into his bosom and be comforted.

3. The sorrow of those *who have no hope* has a character and depth which arise from their own unbelief and the false estimates they put upon the world. They judge of the happiness of others very much as they judge of their own. And since their own felicity is found in the world, they sorrow for those who are taken out of it as if they were deprived at once of all their enjoyments. They think of the dead very much as if stripped of every comfort and consigned to the dark and cheerless tomb. This is common. Go out with me and I will lead you to a desolated habitation, where the widow weeps with her fatherless children, and bemoans the lot which has taken the husband and father away from the comforts of life. Draw near. Listen. What is she saying? Alas, says she, that dear companion of my life has gone! That friend on whom I leaned, that father of my children, that tender husband who sought to do me good, has gone from all the enjoyments I hoped he would have shared with me! He sleeps in the cold grave! No comfort can reach him! no voice of friendship breaks the eternal silence of the tomb! Turn again to another habitation. Here is a mother, but she is childless! Fresh tears flow unbidden at the recollection of her babe! Poor babe, (she is saying,) he sleeps in his little grave! No mother's kindness can reach him! I can never do him good! he has gone to his cheerless and lonely tomb!

Sorrow like this is the sorrow of those *who have no hope*. In such cases the Christian should not be like them. He need not: no, he need *not*. That little babe is in heaven. That pious husband would gladly have remained to comfort the partner of his life, support her children, and aim to lead them all to salvation; but grace has taken him to glory. As Christians we are extremely liable to forget that which, as Christians, we rejoice to believe. We believe the immortality of the soul. We believe at the moment of death the soul of the Christian takes its flight to heaven. To die is gain. Jesus Christ verifies his promise, *I will come again and receive you to myself, that where I am there ye may be also.* The departed babe and the departed believer have gone to the bosom of God. We ought not to sorrow as those *who have no hope.* We ought rather to rejoice that our pious friends have died on earth to live in heaven. Death has done that for them which our affection tried in vain to do. Many, many times we saw them *tossed with tempest and not comforted.* But now they have entered into a haven of rest. Would we wish them back again to be lashed with the storms of life? Many times we were unable to dry up their tears and make them happy, but now God hath wiped all tears from their faces. While they were with us we heard them often lamenting their sin, and expressing many a bitter fear that they should never reach heaven. But now they are afflicted no more. Now they fear hell no more. Now they see God face to face. *They are come unto Mount Zion, and unto the city of the living God, the heavenly Jerusalem, and to an innumerable company of angels, to the general assembly and church of the first-born, which are written in heaven.* They are now like God in perfect holiness; the measure of their bliss is full. *Blessed be the dead that die in the Lord, for they rest from their labors.*

Our feelings do dishonor our faith when we think of death as a loss to the pious. It is gain. It may be loss to us; but it is gain, it is all gain to them.

4. Those who have no hope, yield up their friends to death, with—(I am sorry to be compelled to say this, but

it is true, it is greatly true; I must say it)—they yield up their friends to death, with the sorrow of an *eternal separation*. It is so commonly—not always, perhaps, but ordinarily it is just this. Unbelievers seldom joyfully think of meeting their pious friends in heaven. Dearly as they prized them, they think little of meeting them again. They do sometimes rejoice that their departed friend has left behind him evidences of piety, and is now happy in heaven. But they have no pious hopes of their own which assure them that they shall yet meet them and be united with them for ever in bonds more endearing and tender than any which death has broken. At the mouth of the tomb they give up their friend *for ever!* They resign the parent, the brother, the child, in the sadness of an eternal separation! Their sorrow is not assuaged with the assurance that that parent shall own them in heaven—that that brother shall take them by the hand on the hills of the heavenly city—that that child, with more than an angel's bliss and glory, shall come back to their bosom in the eternal kingdom of God.

But believers sorrow not so over the death of saints. They look forward to a happy meeting. Their friend is "not lost, but gone before." When *they* shall be released from the body and take their flight, that friend perhaps will rush to welcome them into heaven, and lead them up to the embrace of the blood-stained Redeemer that brought them there. Heart shall again open to heart, and love mingle with love in the bliss and glory of the city of God. And when the scenes of this earth shall be no more, and the time of the resurrection of the dead shall be sounded by the voice of the archangel and the trump of God; these blessed souls shall come back again to enter into spiritual bodies *made like unto Christ's own glorious body, not having spot or wrinkle or any such thing.* Communicants, friends separated by death, shall see one another again. Pious ministers and pious people shall meet at the mouth of the opened tomb. Pious parents shall see their pious children. Friend shall greet friend, and brother shall greet brother, as grave-yards are broken up in the day of the resurrection. They *shall be caught up* TOGETHER *in the clouds to meet their Lord in the air; so shall they* EVER *be with the Lord. Comfort one another with these words.* Sorrow not as those who have no hope.

Death and the grave are dreadful realities. We shudder at dissolution. We fear the judgment of the Most High God, and are overwhelmed when we stand just on the entrance of eternity! We know the world is little to us. We shall soon leave it! Covered with crape we are traveling toward the resting-place of the dust of our fathers! Our sins, our deathless souls, our God—oh, what amazing anxieties crowd on our aching hearts! But in the Gospel we see every thing provided for us that sin, and death, and the grave, and the judgment, and eternity can make us need. If we are to die, Jesus Christ can sympathize with us: he has died *before* us; he has died *for* us. O Death, where is thy sting? Death may be a terror to nature; but death is the servant of the Christian. *Death is yours.* Ye are not death's. He shall not hurt you. All he can do is to take up the trembling believer, and put him into the arms of Jesus Christ, when he *comes again to receive him to himself.* If we are to give our bodies to the grave, we know who owns it, who has conquered it, and robbed it of its victory. Ah, more: we know *how* he robbed it. Our best

Friend, our Almighty Saviour has been down into its bosom. He has softened, sweetened, sanctified that bed of sleep! Oh! if I am a Christian, I would rather go by that dark path to heaven, than go like Elijah with his *chariot and horses of fire!* It will be more like Christ. I shall lie where he lay. I shall prove his love. I shall experience his power. This dead body shall rise; and in heaven, sinner saved, redeemed, loved, raised from the dead and taken into the family of God—in heaven, I shall love to tell what Jesus Christ hath done for me! Angels shall hear it! I will tell it to the old prophets! I will hunt up my fathers who got there before me, and tell it to them! I will wait for my children to die, and as they come there, I will tell it to them! Oh! my God, my God! this is enough! I will praise thee for it for ever! Oh! I am comforted now. I can bury my friends, my minister, my father, my daughter; I can set my foot upon the grave; and, with a heart filled with comfort from the God of heaven, I can wait the day when that stilled heart shall beat again, and those dumb lips shall speak from the opened coffin, and we *shall be caught up together in the air. For our conversation is in heaven, whence also we look for the Saviour, the Lord Jesus Christ, who shall change our vile body, that it may be fashioned like unto his glorious body, according to the working whereby he is able to subdue all things unto himself.*

5. Those who have no hope are exercised in such cases of affliction (I am *ashamed* to say it as much as I was sorry to say the other, but it is true; I am compelled to say it)—those without hope are exercised with a very *ineffectual* sorrow. How few of them make any good use of the affliction. We see them *afflicted* often. Where is the sinner without hope who has lived in the world

twenty years and not had his heart torn and forced to bleed at the death of some loved and valued friend? But what is the result? We see those without hope, then downcast and troubled. We go to the funeral of their friends; we bear them to the tomb; we come to sympathize with them and beseech them to *lay it to heart*, for such is *the end of all flesh*. But such persons—these same persons so afflicted, so tender and heart-stricken—do not come at the next communion to the Lord's supper! They mourned their friends; they remembered for a little while that the way he had gone was the way of all the earth. And they believed, too, that such an affliction would not be lost upon them—that the counsels and entreaties of the dying would not be to them a vain lesson. But they do not come to repentance. And while their happy friend is in the bosom of God, they continue the same rejection which gave the last and the deepest pang to the heart of that friend in his hour of death! The grass has not sprung green upon the turf that covers him before they are embarked again in the world as eager as ever, dishonoring his memory by their transient impressions, and his anxiety by forgetfulness of God!

Christians ought not to sorrow like them. Such sorrow dishonors the dead! It pours contempt upon the anxieties and prayers of the dying, and insults by neglect the grace of God which enabled them to die in peace! No, no! let your afflictions make you better. If you are Christians, let your sorrows lead you to mourn the sin which brought death into world, and trust more firmly in Christ who vanquished death for you. Make due improvement of your afflictions—solemn improvement. God means something by it when he afflicts

SORROW FOR THE DEATH OF FRIENDS. 165

you. Ask him what he means. Let not the affliction sit lightly upon you, and for a mere transient week. You do not sorrow in a proper manner if your sorrows do not make you better Christians. They ought to make you better. They ought to make you love prayer more, love Christ more, love one another more. They ought to bring you to the communion-table on next Lord's day in a more tender, and holy, and happy frame. Death is doing up his work in this communion! And, my brethren, my dear brethren, shall we not make haste and get ready to die? Where the next blow shall fall, God only knows! This father, this mother, this child, this minister may fall next! Oh, God! take none of us away unprepared! Plunge none of us into hell! Lead us by our warnings to our Saviour; and then come—come when thou wilt—and take us from the pains of our death-bed home to the bosom of our God. Amen.

Reasons for Affliction.

For the Lord will not cast off for ever; but though he cause grief, yet will he have compassion according to the multitude of his mercies, for he doth not afflict willingly, nor grieve the children of men.—LAM. iii. 31-33.

TO whatever special affliction or peculiar providence these words may have originally been designed to apply, there is a great prevailing principle which makes them universally applicable. They speak of God, and God is uniform. He is invariably like himself—invariably consistent—and his analogies are to be found every where. Just because he is unchangeable we can trust him and reason about him. What he was once, he is still. With him is *no variableness, neither shadow of turning*. And what he *did* once, we may expect him to do again under similar circumstances. Hence, if the text announces a principle about him on which he acted in relation to men in sorrow and trouble, when Jeremiah wrote his Lamentations; men in affliction *now* may rest assured that the same principle holds good. God is *the same yesterday, to-day, and for ever. I am the Lord, I change not.*

The last clause of the passage before us contains the thought to which we desire to confine your attention. It affirms that God *does not afflict willingly, nor grieve the children of men.*

We understand this expression to embrace all earthly afflictions—all griefs, all trials of whatever kind or name. We take it to have been penned on the implied principle that God's governmental control extends over every thing; and that, therefore, the afflictions of life come from him.

We understand, too, that the text designs to assure us of the unwillingness of God to inflict pain upon us— his reluctance to order any of those dispensations which may justly be regarded as afflictive or grievous. In this sense we take the text to accord with the benevolence of the Divine character; and probably the idea of that benevolence gave rise to the affirmations it makes. Not that idea alone, however. It is probable that there was another idea which lay back of this. Probably Jeremiah's mind was in precisely that state in which the minds of good men before him and after him have often been found in the times of distress. In such times there *seems* to the mind to be something in the distresses which are experienced incompatible with the idea that they are sent in love. And good men have often felt this so deeply that they have been compelled to look away from every thing else but God—compelled to look away from their afflictions, from the nature of them, from the results of them, and from the gathering gloom of their own minds, and have tried to school down their hearts to submission, by saying, "God is good—after all, God is good." The mind in such cases just takes refuge in God's well-known character, and by that character gives solace to the heart, and hope for it, when neither hope nor solace could come from any other quarter. On this principle, as we suppose, Jeremiah had recourse to the benevolence of God. He says, amid his lamentations, *The Lord will not cast off for ever; but though he cause grief, yet will he have compassion according to the multitude of his mercies; for* (it is a great principle of his nature) *he doth not afflict willingly, nor grieve the children of men.*

This refuge of Jeremiah is ever open to us, as God is ever the same. May we all have Jeremiah's faith to resort to it.

Still, afflictions are common. The world is full of them. No man is exempt. And since they are of God, and since he *does not afflict willingly*, it may both instruct our understandings and improve our hearts if we examine into the reasons why he gives us so many afflictions here.

This matter occupies us. The chastenings of God are *for our profit.* They do not come from his pleasure. He has no delight in them. Let us see, if we can, the manner in which they are designed or tend to our good.

Afflictions probably profit God's people in more ways than *we* can tell, or *they* would believe if we could tell. We can not pretend to exhaust this subject. We only name a few of the particulars. We mention only *six:*

I. Afflictions are peculiarly *instructive.*

There is a tendency in deep trials to bring the justice of the Almighty to mind. Griefs and pains are very unacceptable. No man loves them. Most men find it difficult to bear them with commendable patience. And as the mind is troubled under them, nothing is more natural than to inquire whence they come and why they are sent. And thus the mind is led away to God, and reminded of the justice of his character. He does the sufferer no injustice. The sufferer may sigh and be dissatisfied, but he can not accuse him. He may long for relief, and be impatient, but he can not convict God of injustice. And the sufferings that are abroad in the world constitute one great chapter of demonstrations, that the justice of the Almighty is in operation—that he is an angry God—that he is bending the frowns of his anger upon the world, a world of sinners! Were it not for this great chapter of ills, there is many a man who would never believe at all what the Bible says about the sin and guilt of our race, and about the anger and justice of God. There is a strong tendency in the human heart toward an unbelief about the punitive justice of God; and were it not for this great chapter of earthly afflictions, it is impossible for us to tell to how wide an extent infidelity would have insnared the human mind. If there had been no suffering here, if all around us was fair, and bright, and bland, and happy, every face dressed in smiles, and every heart bounded with joy, men would have asked where is there any proof of God's anger? of his aroused and operative justice? of his great displeasure against sinners, if you will call men sinners? And by such courses of thought, the natural atheism of the human heart would have fortified itself against the truth. It would have pointed to a world of felicity as an unanswerable demonstration that the world was basking under the smiles of its Governor, instead of lying under his frowns. But when the man sees all around him a suffering world, his infidelity is silenced, or driven for its support to some other deception. He *does* see such a world. He feels it, too. Miseries are every where. Hearts bleed every where. Sighs load the air he breathes. At home he finds a sick-room. He goes abroad, and stumbles over a grave! Old age trembles beside him! Hungry, houseless beggars solicit him!

And if he is tempted to attribute the miseries of age to the course of nature merely, and of want to indolence, his deceptive thoughts are compelled to abandon their argument, for infancy cries, and infants die! There is a vast amount of instruction in the afflictions of life.

It may not be owing entirely to the deteriorations of sin, perhaps, but there is a strong desire in man to have some visible, sensible proofs, some demonstrations by matter, to substantiate the abstract and spiritual ideas of religion—to *teach* the truths of religion. The miseries of this life do much to answer the purpose. The argument is easy. Here is a man that is miserable. How comes it about? Does he suffer wrongfully? If not, then he is a *sinner*. Who makes him miserable? Has God any hand in it? If so, then he is angry with this sinner. Is God righteous? If so, then this man deserves to suffer. And by the power of such common-sense thinking, there comes up from the afflictions of this life an amazing amount of instruction, which can neither be misunderstood nor gainsayed, and which never could have reached the human mind (so much it recoils from truth) had not "thorns and thistles" sprung up from the earth "cursed" by its Maker, and did not the voice of the grave reach every mortal ear, *dust thou art and unto dust thou shalt return*. As it is, men are instructed by the very materials of the world. Earthquakes teach them. The invisible pestilence becomes an instructor. Famines teach. Storms and hurricanes teach. Lessons according with the Gospel and enforcing it are chiseled upon the tomb-stones of even infancy! If faith could spare these lessons, unbelief can not.

God *does not afflict willingly;* but he afflicts in order to furnish important instruction, which the folly and hardihood of sin are not prepared to receive in any other way.

II. God sends afflictions upon men for the sake of their influence as they bear upon *the passions and purposes of life.*

You can scarcely choose any example amiss. Our griefs address themselves more eloquently to our hearts than to our minds.

Amid the prosperities of life, when pains, disappointments, and distress are strangers, *pride* is very apt to be strong and influential. Prosperity is very favorable to it. It does not implant it, indeed—it is an implantation of the fall—but prosperity fosters and strengthens it, and gives it the larger opportunity for its bad work. And many a man has been led into insolence, and haughtiness, and tyranny by the influences of prosperity upon him. The miseries of this life are sent to repress this pride. They rebuke it. They check it. They stand in its way and hinder its influences. Pain and pride do not thrive well together. Far from it. There is little manifest arrogance and haughtiness, or even ambition, on *Cæsar's* bed of sickness. When amid the burnings of his fever he cries: "Give me some drink, Titanius," like a sick girl, he is a very different man and different example from what he was at the head of his legions, his strong hand upon his sword. He cares very little *now* for his eagles—very little for glory. Fame has lost her charms. And the influence of his fever may last upon him also, and when he goes out again to the field of battle, he may carry along with him at least some faint remembrance that there *is* something which shall yet lay Cæsar himself in the dust. To what an extent pride would rise, and how far it would undermine all the amiable affections of nature, if there were no miseries to reprove and check it, no man can tell. God sends the miseries for this office—*not willingly.*

These afflictions of life also repress *worldliness of spirit.* Men are naturally worldly; just as naturally as they are sinful. The nature of sin, indeed, is such that its aims all lie beneath the moon. It has not one to overpass the grave. But when the ambitious spirit of worldliness finds nothing beneath the sun which can constitute a secure and sufficient portion, or can avail as a shield to ward off the arrows of affliction, its zeal is damped—its career is checked—its heart appalled—it may be only for a moment, indeed, and while the pain of affliction stings —but yet the power of worldliness is diminished by it. Amid unbroken felicity and successes, the worldly spirit increases in power. It becomes strong, absorbing of mind and heart, far-reaching, rancorous, and unsatisfied. Then there is no end to its ambition—no limit to its hopes —no boundary to its aims; it would engross the whole soul, and would gain the whole world. There never was a more blind and stupid spirit. It aims after what it does not need and can not use. It longs to attain that which has no other tendency than to prove a burden. And this stupidity and blindness are not to be cured by moral lectures. Lecture to rock as soon. There is a necessity for affliction to come in to hush down the clamor of worldly affections before the man will hear you. Trial must open his eyes or he will see nothing but *the world*—a world that dazzles and blinds him. Make him miserable and you may cure his stupidity. And were it not for the miseries all around the worldly, and so often coming in at their windows, the evils of worldliness would become far worse than they are. A worldly spirit has strong influences to check it. What a lecture a fever gives to it! or a funeral! What a lesson the grave-yard reads in its ears! What a rebuke when the man bears to the tomb the son for whom he thought he was hoarding his thousands! The miseries we suffer are sent to repress a spirit of worldliness which might ruin us without them.

These miseries, too, have an influence upon *disappointed ambition, envy,* and such like. The *heaviest* of them are seen to be impartial. They go every where, and every where alike. The *heaviest* of them reach the palace as soon and as often as the cottage—they press upon the rich as sadly as upon the poor. Pain, sickness, bereavements, death, are seen to do their dreadful work upon royalty just as readily as upon the veriest slave. The high and mighty, the proud and prosperous, (so often envied, and therefore so often hated by those in an opposite condition,) however they may be free from some of the minor afflictions of life, are compelled to feel the *heaviest ones* as severely as the most unenvied beggar that lives. No gold can soothe pain. No power can battle death. And when the disappointed, the obscure, the poor, behold all this—behold those whom they are apt to envy as poor and helpless as themselves, as much needing of pity and consolation, the sight awakens another species of affection. Instead of envying, they pity; instead of hating, they sympathize; instead of discontent with their own lot, they see it to be about equal, after all, to any other; entirely equal except in the minor miseries of life. The sight awakens compassion, and represses envy, and corrects error. They are led to say of those whose condition they would otherwise covet,

They spend their days in wealth, and in a moment go down to the grave. One dieth in his full strength, being wholly at ease and quiet; another dieth in the bitterness of his soul, and never eateth with pleasure. They shall lie down alike in the dust, and the worms shall cover them. Lo, their good is not in their hand. Where is the house of the prince? No man can tell into what ranklings of wickedness envy would run, or into what depths of despair disappointment would plunge, if miseries and affliction were not abroad upon the earth, to level men down to the same grade and sink their distinctions in the dust. There is a stern equity in sorrow. It treats all men very much alike. The history of human afflictions is so even, uniform, impartial, that its influence upon the evil passions is of momentous importance. How often alienated friends are reconciled again by sorrow. Mourners seldom quarrel. Tenderness and love are often cultured by the grave.

Our miseries, too, affect our *purposes.* Indeed there are very few of our *best* purposes that are formed without them. Vice forms *her* plans amid pleasure. Virtue is more apt to form hers amid pain. Not among the successes of life, but in the midst of its reverses and fears, is the vanity of the world seen, and the determination formed to aim after some better portion. Good resolves are often made at the funeral; bad ones never. Earthly misery gives birth to *more* good resolutions than spring from earthly felicity, and thus bears powerfully against the depravity of the human heart. This, perhaps, constitutes another reason why God afflicts us—*not willingly.*

The tendencies of our earthly misery appear to be *all* against the indulgence of evil passions and purposes.

It can think of few exceptions, or none. A wretched heart is not apt to become by its wretchedness more ambitious, more proud, more covetous, more unjust, more revengeful, more unsocial, more haughty, or more hard. Afflictions often bring estranged hearts together again, and disputes cease when the tomb speaks.

Our afflictions tend strangely to impress us with a *sense of our dependence on God*. We are not so apt to feel it in times of felicity. Misery *compels* us to feel it. We have many trials which we are unable to refer to any source but God, and in which we can turn to no other relief. Our real dependence upon the Deity amid our brightest prosperities may be as easily demonstrated as amid our deepest griefs; but it is no slander upon our hearts to say that prosperity is not apt to impress them with a sense of helpless dependence. If we had nothing to do but to enjoy good here, and had it to enjoy to the full, it is more than probable that few of us would ever realize our dependence, or be led to be truly grateful for our mercies, or led to seek that *holiness without which no man shall see the Lord.* Amid our enjoyments, if they were uninterrupted and full, it is extremely likely that our hearts would be too much absorbed by them to admit of much serious reflection; and it is extremely probable, also, that our hearts would become more and more insensible to our littleness, dependence, and necessity of renewal by God's Holy Spirit. Not unfrequently have we heard the declaration made in evident sincerity and truth—(have not some of you here made it?)—"The first time that I ever really prayed was in the time of my affliction." So it is with man. If there were no afflictions he would seldom be driven to prayer. Afflictions make man feel his dependence on God, a feeling which constitutes certainly a necessary ground for any true piety.

And beyond this, the miseries of this world often constitute the rod of iron to dash into pieces wicked hopes and drive men to seek in another life what they can not find in this—a resting-place and rock for their souls. For this purpose God sends these miseries—*not willingly*. He spreads them all over the world. He makes them various, multiplied, severe. He repeats them. It seems as if he would compel the worldling of every name to let go of this world, and reach forth to eternity his aims. God has not left a single spot, or object, or preference without the print and the poison of misery upon it. They begin in the cradle, and they cease only in the grave. And since we behold the wicked every where *like the troubled sea when it can not rest, whose waters cast up mire and dirt*, shall we not entertain a more enlarged idea of the benevolence of God, because he has sent so many urgent and tearful influences to drive men off from the world, and make them lean on him? And since, after all earthly afflictions, we see so many men still as worldly as ever—as unfit for death and all there is beyond it, shall we venture to think for a moment that God has made the miseries of this life too many or too deep? Deep and many as they are, hearts are still proof against them. Men will still go from the funeral to the frolic—from the coffin to the club, as if worldly enjoyments were all they were made for; as if death were a bugbear and the judgment of the Most High God a dream! And to what excesses they would run, and to what a pitch of hardihood they would rise, if there were no sorrows to sober their mad career, it is impossible for man to conceive.

Not willingly, but to teach man his dependence, and

save him from excesses of indulgence which might render him incapable of religion, has God sent him so many miseries. There is, perhaps, no more common failure of true wisdom, and yet, certainly, there is none greater, than to think of this world by itself, and this life by itself. The grave links us with another. And the grave is God's beacon, built up in the path of every man that lives, and not far before him, to teach him that here he is a dependent worm, a child of the dust, and induce him to secure interests untarnished with sin, and pain, and shame, and eternal as his immortal soul.

> "The grave has eloquence; its lectures teach
> In silence louder than divines can preach;
> Hear what it says—ye sons of folly, hear;
> It speaks to you—lend an attentive ear."

III. The afflictions experienced by the people of God furnish opportunity and means for the *cultivation of the highest and most difficult virtues.* There are excellences of character unattainable without trials and distresses. If there were no instances of distress, we should have nothing to excite our pity. If there were no instances of want, there would be nothing to call forth our charity. If nobody injured or offended us, we should have nobody to forgive. We could pray for no enemy if we had none. Aside from something to distress or annoy us, the virtue of patience would not be called into action and cultivated. Our fortitude, if not much of our faith, could never be exercised at all, if there were no burdens to bear, no distresses to endure, no furnaces of trial to burn upon us. This piety, this charity and forgiveness, this fortitude, patience, meekness and depending faith, are among our most difficult virtues, and they constitute our highest excellences of character. The idea is not mine. It is the Apostle's. If he has not plainly expressed it, it lurks in that remarkable passage wherein he makes an exhortation to one of these graces: *Let* PATIENCE *have her perfect work, that ye may be perfect and entire, wanting nothing.* Just as if *patience* were the crowning grace of all—just as if this gave the last touchings and finishings to a perfect character—*that ye may be perfect, wanting nothing.* He says *patience.* He does not say *courage*—he does not say *peace*—he does not say *gentleness, brotherly kindness, charity,* or even *faith.* He says simply *patience.* And he certainly can not mean less than to select one as an example, from a class of excellences which lie far on in the work of a believer's sanctification. When graces like patience have their perfect work, there is not much more to gain. Even the great Captain of our salvation *was made perfect by sufferings.*

Expand this idea for yourselves, and you will see its justice and strength. Remove all afflictions from the world. Suppose there are none here—suppose paradise again in bloom and wide as the world. Then discriminate. Form two classes of duties which are incumbent upon you now, but which you would not be called upon to discharge in this paradise world. Let the one class have respect to yourself, and the other to your neighbors. Then see. As to yourself—unafflicted, not a want, not a sorrow; you can exercise no patience, no fortitude, no forgiveness—you can not endure, for there is nothing to be endured—you can not forbear, for no enemy injures you—you can not be grateful for relief, for you never needed any—you can not cling to a friend who stood by you in trouble, for you never had any trouble—you can not trust God in darkness and storms, for the sun of your paradise is ever unclouded, and storms never beat upon your head. One very extensive class of virtues lies beyond your reach—a class to be exercised only when afflictions visit you.

And not one class only. As to other people in your paradise world, they are as unafflicted as yourself. You can not feed the hungry or clothe the naked, for there are none. You can not exercise that sympathy with sorrow whereby you now take half the sufferer's anguish from his heart to lay it upon your own. You can not take your stand by your friend in danger, and tell him if he must sink you will go down with him. Though you may be kind, you can not be generous. Though you may be benevolent, you can pray for no enemy, nor *do good* to them who *despitefully use you and persecute you.* Another very extensive class of virtues lies beyond your reach—a class to be exercised only when afflictions are around you.

IV. How could you, *then,* judge whether you were a child of God or not?

The temper we have and the demeanor we exhibit *in* afflictions, and toward the afflicted, constitute more just criterions of our character than any other. If there were no afflictions here, we should have no "good Samaritan" to copy, and no "priest and Levite," whose irreligious example to shun. God may have sent us trials and filled his world with sorrows, *not willingly*, but to furnish us opportunity to test our faith and find whether we are on the way to heaven, following that Christ who *endured such contradiction of sinners against himself,* and *suffered the just for the unjust that he might bring us to God.*

And here, if I might, I would attempt to elucidate to you the idea that the field of sorrow is the very field which conspires with *all* Christianity. I would ask you, when does a mortal most feel that he needs Christ? and *you* would answer, when he knows that he needs comfort. I would ask you again, when does a man most feel that he is a pilgrim here? and you would answer, when here he can find no rest. Again I would ask you, when does a man most feel that he is a stranger here? and you would answer, when he stands amid the graves of his companions and buried kindred. And I would ask you again, when does God seem most precious? and you would reply, when he puts his everlasting arms around the wretched, falling mortal, and whispers to him, *It is I, be not afraid.* Again still I would ask, when does heaven appear most sweet to you? and you would answer, when here I am tossed with tempest and not comforted; when my heart is sad, my limbs are weary, and my feet bleed along the rugged paths of life—and when I should die in despair, if I could not lift my eyes to heaven and sing,

"Blessed seats, through rude and stormy scenes
I onward press to you."

Surely, afflictions conspire with *all* Christianity; but we have not time for the demonstration. You may just remember when it is, that you feel you are a *reed shaken with the wind*—a *vapor that vanisheth away*—a *flower of the grass*, in the morning green, in the evening *cut down and withered*—a *worm*—a *shadow*—a *breath*—a *nothing* but dust and ashes—aside from Christ and the heaven for which he has redeemed you. Our sorrows conspire peculiarly with Christianity, and to make us Christians God sends them—*not willingly.* Hence,

V. Afflictions make *demonstrations* of men, proofs, exhibits to the world, of the power and divinity of faith. The world needs such demonstrations. The wicked are not to be convinced by principles merely. Unbelievers are not likely to be fully convinced and to have even any tolerable ideas of the Divine efficacy of religion till they behold some examples of it. And where shall we look for examples that will answer the purpose?—examples which will confound skepticism and make unbelievers feel to their very heart's core that these Christians are something more than mere common men, that they are aided and sustained by something within them which can be explained by nothing but the presence of God the Holy Ghost in their souls? You must look among the *tried* for such examples—among the poor—among the widows, giving their *two mites*, and finding exhaustless *the cruse of oil and the barrel of meal*. In trial grace brightens—it shines—it demonstrates. For this reason God sends trials. Mark his manner of distributing them. He does not send many of them to *us* weak Christians who could not endure them; but he sends them upon some who can stand the furnace when its flames kindle, and its heat is terrible!—*not willingly*, but because he will have examples of righteousness and enduring which shall demonstrate to men and devils, that *God is with his people of a truth.* Hence,

VI. Finally, if I might, I would finish the subject by showing that it is just in times and by means of afflictions, that God bestows upon you his most precious gifts. If I had time, I would make your own hearts preach to you on this point—and make them demand of you an answer to the question, Where had you been now had your heart never bled or been torn with anguish? I would summon your closet of prayer, the *stone should speak out of the wall, and the beam out of the timber should answer,* if that sacred spot was not *most* sweet and *most* precious, and your own covenant God *most* near, just when you went there to meet him, a poor, stricken mortal who could do nothing but cry. You would own that his best gifts have been sent in sad times, and that you love him *most* for what he has done for you, when sorrows lay heavy upon your soul. They were put there by God, *not willingly*, but to teach you the best lessons and lead you to the best comforts your soul ever had.

Your reflections must compensate for my deficiencies. God grant they may. Amen.

Chastisements Disciplinary.

My son, despise not the chastening of the Lord, neither be weary of his correction: for whom the Lord loveth he correcteth; even as a father the son in whom he delighteth.—PROVERBS, iii. 11, 12.

THE very nature of proverbs gives them a general character, and makes them susceptible of a very general application. This is their beauty, and in this lies most of their utility. But this renders them in some measure obscure. They can not have the freshness and vivacity which distinguish a more extensive detail, a more graphic delineation. We must arrive at that vivacity and freshness (if we reach it at all) by the application of them on the field of subjects which lie within their compass.

The text before us, though in the form of advice, has the significance of a proverbial saying, and is justly placed under the title of the book that contains it. It is of a general nature, a kind of condensation of practical wisdom for the direction of life.

It has reference to those dealings of God with men which have a stern and severe aspect, which are in themselves painful and unwelcome, and under which the human soul can not well be satified or sustained, aside from the two considerations, *first*, that they are the appointments of God, and *second*, that they are designed to be instrumental of our good.

One of the most striking and unusual marks of human destiny is to be found in the afflictive dispensations which trouble us. It is these dispensations which the text calls the *chastening of the Lord*—his *correction*. In the other part of the text, the application is referred to the benevolence of God: *Whom the Lord loveth he correcteth;* and the expression implies that the affliction or trial is designed for personal direction and amendment, and therefore for personal benefit.

The general counsel of the text is aimed at one of the common errors of men; an error into which human nature is very apt to fall. We are such beings of passion and darkness, of haste, impatience, and limited thought, that one of our most common failures is to be found in our *not* being affected by our trials in a wise and beneficial manner. We are prone to *despise the chastening of the Lord; i. e.,* to take it as no chastening, or rebel at its deemed severity; and we are almost equally prone to be weary, impatient, or discouraged, under trials designed for our correction. Against this tendency the counsel of the text is aimed. This is the general sense of the passage before us.

I. Let us consider the afflictions we meet with in the character the text assigns to them. They are *chastenings;* they are *corrections*. Let us see what reasons we have for viewing them in this light.

1. They are *of God*, and God takes no pleasure in the miseries of his creatures. He does not afflict *willingly*, nor *grieve the children of men*. Such are his own declarations, and they entirely comport with all that we know of his character and perfections. His entire benevolence is not incompatible with all the earthly sufferings which

so often afflict us to behold, and sometimes almost crush us to bear. How it is that his infinite power should not be wielded by his infinite benevolence to shield us from harm, that he should so often and so deeply embitter our cup, since his benevolence is infinite and pure, must ever remain to us here as one of those deep and dark things of God which no human wisdom can penetrate. As we gaze at the darkness of the cloud that covers us, nothing will answer our purpose but that childlike faith which recognizes it as God's cloud, and thinks of the light which beams in our Father's house beyond it. By some other demonstrations than the dark demonstrations of the storms of sorrow, we know the benevolence of God; and as afflictive dispensations do *not spring from the dust*, but are appointed of God, we have reason to deem them disciplinary—a part of the discipline of his love. And it may further reconcile us to this idea, and enforce it upon us, if we reflect that his benevolence to such creatures as we are, is in itself an inexplicable mystery, apparently contradictory to his infinite justice, and to all the conclusions of an analogy which would judge of God by the fate of the fallen angels; and therefore we can well afford to have that inexplicable benevolence maintain the mystery and magnitude of its own character, *in* the darkness of its strange and astounding operations; wonderful in *itself*, we can afford to have it wonderful in its workings. It is a wonder that God should love us at all; no less a wonder than that, loving, he should afflict us.

2. The *rule* or *order* of human afflictions indicates their corrective intent. All of them do not come under this principle indeed, but many of them do. Because it is a manifest truth, that, in respect to a vast portion of human

ills, God pursues, in the dispensation of them, a steady and unvarying law. He has appointed a rule for himself, and he follows it in his afflictive providence. He makes the miseries of life follow close and visible the sins and crimes of life to a very wide extent. They follow the sins of individuals and of nations. The man of intemperance soon becomes a man of misery. His misery results from his sin as manifestly and indisputably as any effect from its cause. And thus there is a continued demonstration that the misery is just designed as a correction. It both comes and goes, as vice comes and goes; and if the man is not twice a fool, he will confess, amid the miseries of himself, his wife, children, and friends, that the rod of God is upon him for his correction. The idler is another example. Misery creeps on in the path of his indolence. He loses gain and he loses character among men, and he fails to acquire habits and capacity for business; and he will be twice a fool if he charges his misfortunes more upon his condition and circumstances in life than upon his indolence in youth, which has produced poverty, and contempt, and incapacity in manhood and old age.

A nation plunged in unnecessary war, as often nations are, for some contemptible trifle, some despicable dream about a point of national honor, must be doomed to suffer for its sin. The evil of suffering will come. Its cry will come up from the ground—the voice of a brother's blood. Bereaved families, mutilated limbs, mangled bodies doomed to drag out a miserable existence, vast expenses to be met, and a beggared and vitiated soldiery to feed upon the community when the contest is over, and to scatter immorality and defilement through the nation, are some of the afflictions which tread upon the heels of war, and tread so close and constant, that they are manifestly the chastisements of God to teach nations a corrective lesson.

Just so of a very vast portion of earthly evils. These evils have a rule and order about them ordained of God, and they so stand connected with their visible causes that a rational mind can not fail to regard them as disciplinary and corrective.

We can not rank all miseries under this rule. Some of them lie beyond it. Some of them are unavoidable. Some of them are not the direct effects of actual transgression, of vice and crime. But if we could see further than we now see, if we could trace all connections, if we could know as God knows all the secondary causes which he employs, it is extremely probable that we should attribute many human miseries to human sin which he now attribute to the just and naked sovereignty of God. All misery flows from sin in one sense, and is a dispensation of Divine sovereignty and justice to show to every one that the frown of God bends darkly upon this sinful world. But in the rule and order of which we speak, we are permitted to behold the connection between misery and sin, and see *how* the former flows from the latter, and see that the misery is an avoidable thing. Death is not an avoidable thing. Much of grief, much of pain, mental and physical, are not avoidable. And this simple fact goes far to demonstrate to a reflective mind that the curse of sin extends much beyond the human will, because the disposition most ready to receive correction can not by any possibility *so* turn from sin as to avoid the strokes of the rod. If there were no miseries of sin but those avoidable by amendment, we might be led to believe, perhaps, that the *will of the flesh, the will of man,* unaided by the Holy Ghost, has a sufficiency in itself; and that, under the dispensation of discipline, God was leaving man to his own powers and choice. But when there are miseries which we can not avoid, and grief will go every where, and death will keep on doing up his work every where, it seems to us that we have before us an admonition that sin has gone beyond the reach of the human will, needs an atonement, and needs for its eradication from the soul the power of the Holy Spirit. But yet, it is likely that more of our miseries are linked with second causes than we are accustomed to suppose; and *so* linked with them, that our amendment would avoid our miseries. At any rate, whenever we can *see* the connection, and trace our unhappiness to a fault, we can not but perceive at once that our unhappiness is the blow of a rod of discipline; it is the *chastening of the Lord,* designed for our amendment.

3. There is every reason to believe that a state of entire innocence would have kept the world from *all* suffering. It would have been entirely exempt from every kind of evil, physical and mental, if moral evil, *sin,* had not entered into the world. That species of philosophy, so called, which would refer our afflictions to our mental errors, or to the imperfection or derangement of the natural causes which affect us, is rebuked by the fact that the most of our mental errors which lead to unhappiness are *themselves* the result of a moral obliquity; and rebuked also by the fact that the mental error, aside from such moral connection (if there could be any), can be considered as nothing but an injustice done unto us; and rebuked still further by the fact that there are many, and some of the deepest, of our afflictions not avoidable at all here by any mental or moral

amendment. Such a philosophy is not merely superficial, it is false. And in respect to the imperfection or derangement of the natural causes which affect us unhappily, it is visible every where before our eyes that true virtue, holiness, the obedience and love of God, would turn most of these causes instantly in our favor; the defect or derangement, therefore, is in *us* and not in *them*. Moreover, the supposition of their derangement leaves the derangement to be accounted for; and if that derangement is not a thing for our discipline or our deserved punishment, it will go far to cast an imputation upon the benevolence—yea, even upon the justice of God. Why suffer the east wind to shake our nerves—the lightning to strike us down—the storm to beat upon our head—death to come in at our windows on the wings of the pestilence—and, *before* it comes, our timidity to be such that the *sound of a shaken leaf shall chase us*, if God is good, and if he has the power to control his world? No, no! natural causes are not their own—not afflicting us arbitrarily. The world is deranged because sin is here. The second causes which bring evil are the rods of a Divine chastisement. And the evils which extend so far, or are of such a nature that our reformation could not shun them, are instructive monitions to us that the evil of sin strikes deep, and requires for its cure the Hand that rules the world.

The consideration that innocence unstained never suffers, and that all the afflictions here that we know any thing about are referable to the anger of God against sin, furnishes good reason to refer all our afflictions to a corrective and merciful system.

4. The nature of our afflictions has in it something very remarkable. They are not so heavy as to crush us.

They have many accompanying alleviations. If our evils were intended as a mere punishment, they would have been made more destructive. Vengeance would have made them ruinous to us. For the most part, heavy and repeated, varied and multiplied as are our ills, we are able to bear up under them. This does not look as if they were dispensed in vengeance, but in discipline —not so much in anger as in love. Mere justice inflicting punishment would, beyond all question, have made the miseries of life far heavier, if not destructive to us in every case. God has not treated us as if cast off and given over for ever. He has made our miseries here deep enough to let us know that he is offended; and has made them extend far enough (along every path that man can travel, and into every palace that man can build) to demonstrate to us that the world is not our home, and that there is no perfection in holiness on this side of the tomb. But he has not allowed our miseries to become destructive, and ruin us entirely. They are, therefore, manifestly disciplinary, and designed for our good.

5. Consider the *manner* in which our afflictions ordinarily come upon us. Certainly they are very varied in both kind and history. Certainly it does not lie within the compass of our ability to make any full classification of them, or point out any respect wherein there is a resemblance among all the evils which afflict us. But yet we venture to say that no small portion of human ills have their manifest rule of dispensation; that is, they commence gently, and if the chastised do not amend, they are increased. Stroke follows stroke. One ill treads upon the heels of another, and heavier blows follow lighter ones, if the discipline does not lead to re-

formation. This is the manner of God's chastisement, to a very great extent. This seems to be the manner of all of them which aim at correction in any particular sins. In such cases misery does not rush on at once like a torrent. It creeps on little by little. Its increase is gradual, as if reluctant, and waiting for some reason to be dispensed with altogether.

The examples of this are all around us. The man of excess does not ruin his health or his reputation irrecoverably all at once, nor all at once blast his sensibilities, and utterly unfit his mind for its service. His health, his mind, his reputation, his sensibilities forsake him little by little. His excess is undermining them all. It is becoming worse and worse with him. Every day the ill grows heavier—the stroke of discipline more severe.

The young man who wastes the precious hours and opportunities of his youth when he ought to be gaining knowledge, and acquiring capacity and skill, and forming habits and working up a character which shall do him good, does not find all the evils of his folly rushing upon him at once like a flood. They come one after another. At first his name is no commendation to him; but yet (not in business) he does not need capacity nor the benefits of just habits of attention and care. Soon he needs them both, but he has not got them; and thus another evil is upon him—he has not capacity now for the business which engages him nor the habits it demands. And now, too, comes another evil—he has not the *character* he needs. His bad reputation, which did not afflict him so heavily when it was known only among a few, and those few his friends, disposed to favor him, now afflicts him most deeply just when he needs a good name most for trusty business, and among a cold world which will not respect him unless he compels it to do so. He might have compelled it if he had reformed under the first light rebuke which met him in his earlier years, when his *mother* besought him to waste time no more, but acquire the capacity, and knowledge, and character of a man. He might compel it still, if he would; and by an entire amendment wring from it the benefits of a good name. But here comes another evil—his *habits* are like chains of iron to him—to break off from idleness and inattention is a thousand-fold more afflictive to him than it would have been to form just habits in the earlier days of his youth. And now he is *discouraged;* he says he can not, it is too late; and certainly, as he continually says so, it is a grave case with him—he will be good for nothing for ever.

You may apply every one of these ideas to morals and religion. It is the same there. Afflictions, trouble, misery, do not come in all their strength at once. Despair in religion, one of the most dark and dreadful evils certainly that the world holds, and one of the most unnecessary, does not come at once. *Before* it comes, one affliction after another has been upon the heart and has done no good; one affliction after another has been upon the mind; one burden of anguish after another has been upon the conscience; and they have been growing heavier and heavier. This is the *manner* of afflictions here, to a very wide extent. And this we deem a sufficient and visible reason for deeming all such afflictions as designed, not for judgment, but for correction—and *sent*, not in God's anger, but in his love. If he was afflicting in anger he would have taken a different method, and would not have left the severest rod for the last. And that very *despair* in religion which we just mentioned comes under this rule. *That* is not the *last*. God is *waiting* even *there to be gracious*. If he were *not*, his Spirit would not be in that harrowed conscience and grief-torn heart: the conscience would be *seared as with a hot iron*, and the heart *hard as the nether mill-stone*. Let even the child of despair listen to the voice which comes to his ears from above: *My son* DESPISE *not the* CHASTENING *of the Lord; neither be* WEARY *of his correction*.

6. The alleviations which accompany earthly afflictions are so extensive, so many, so precious in themselves, and many of them so connected *with* the afflictions, as to furnish almost a demonstration that the afflictions are designed for amendment. Miserable as the world is, we have many solaces. God's goodness is certainly visible here. He gives us not only *rain from heaven, and fruitful seasons*, as a *witness of himself, filling our hearts with food and gladness;* but, beyond the measure of our mere necessities, he has made arrangements for many a happy hour. The fragrance and beauty of the flower that pleases us seem to be things separate from mere necessity and utility—utility in its ordinary sense. They are just delights and luxuries to us. They are the overflowings of Divine bounty. They are tokens of God's love—just those little testimonials to make us happy, not by their necessity, their intrinsic value, so much as by their tastefulness and their suggestions. As if he would convince us that he has not forsaken us altogether, he compels the *thorn* that sprang from the curse to scent the breeze of the evening, and compels the *thistle* to clothe its blossoms with beauty.

All the ordinary purposes of hearing might have been answered, if God had never implanted a musical taste, and made us susceptible of the delights and solaces of song. Some of our solaces spring directly out of our trials. If labor is an affliction, and man, as a part of his chastisement, must *eat his bread by the sweat of his face*, he eats it with a keener relish, he sleeps the more sweetly, his blood flows in more healthful and joyful currents, his fancy is more free, and his mind is happy in the contemplation that he has done his duty and can lie down in peace. Some of our sweetest solaces never could have been known but for the afflictions which bring them. What tender friendships gather around us when we are sick! What hearts beat for us and sympathize with us, and would, if they could, take themselves the pain that racks us! We should never *know* what tenderness and pity and kindness there is in the world, if our trials did not bring them out. Many of our calamities attach us more to our fellow-men, and make us think better of the world than we did before.

> "In the morning of life, when its cares are unknown,
>   And its pleasures in all their new luster begin,
>   When we live in a bright, beaming world of our own,
>   And the light that surrounds us is all from within;
>   Oh, 'tis not, believe me, in that happy time
>   We can *love* as in hours of less transport we may;
>   Of our smiles, of our hopes, 'tis the gay summer prime,
>   But affection is warmest when these fade away.
>
> "When we see the first dawn of our youth pass us by,
>   Like a leaf on the stream that ne'er will return,
>   When our cup which had sparkled with pleasure so high
>   Now tastes of the other, the dark flowing urn;
>   Then, then is the moment affection can sway
>   With a depth and a tenderness joy never knew;
>   Love nursed amid pleasures is faithless as they,
>   But the love born of sorrow, like sorrow is true.

CHASTISEMENTS DISCIPLINARY. 195

> "In climes full of sunshine, though splendid their dyes,
> Yet faint is the odor the flowers shed about,
> 'Tis the clouds and the mists of our own weeping skies
> That call their full spirit of fragrancy out.
> So the wild-flower of passion may kindle from mirth,
> But 'tis only in *grief* true affection appears;
> To the magic of smiles it may owe its first birth,
> But the soul of its sweetness is drawn out by tears."

There is an extensive system of delights and solaces which spreads all over this dark and miserable world, which God has arranged for our support and comfort amid sufferings, and which certainly could never be accounted for if we did not believe that our sufferings were designed for our amendment and improvement. As it is, we see that God has not forsaken us—nor is he dealing with us in mere anger. Every where he teaches us the contrary by some solace or some support. On every hill-top and in every valley he holds out the signals of his good-will. He makes the birds sing it—and the winds sing it—and it comes echoed back to us in the deep anthem of the ocean's eternal roar. He makes the tears of tenderness tell of it as they fall upon the drapery of the sick bed, or upon the marble of the tomb. God's good will, if it is not the *first*, certainly is the *second* lesson of his universe. If sufferings here betoken his displeasure, solaces here betoken as clearly that he is *waiting to be gracious*, and frowns and afflicts only for our good.

The improvement which you will make of this subject you can yourselves best tell. But surely it becomes you, who have so many distresses to bear, to consider well their design. The world you live in, with its mingled chastisements and mercies, perfectly accords with the declarations of the Gospel, that God is displeased, but waits to be gracious. His earthly discipline and the Gospel doctrines go hand in hand. And I beseech you to remember, if you are yet unreconciled to God, that all your trials are only sermons on repentance and reformation. God makes his world preach to you. And all your solaces are only sermons on faith. God makes his world preach to you. Will you be deaf? Will you not fear the anger of God, who brings on you so many distresses in such a warning manner, making them all spring from sin, and often grow deeper and deeper, darker and darker, as you continue to disobey him? Will you not trust in the love of God, who, amid his frowns, furnishes you so many solaces—and solaces in such an instructive manner, making them sweeter and sweeter, brighter and brighter, the more you love and obey him? Shall God smite in vain? Shall he hush the thunders of Mount Sinai where the law puts on its dress of lightning, and give you silence for a time to hear the *Father forgive them* of Mount Calvary, where Love did its finishing work; and yet will you go on in this world of warnings and tokens unterrified by justice and not won by God's good-will?

You will soon have done with this system of disciplinary affliction for ever. Now you may seek God, you may flee to Christ for pardon and peace, you may pray for the Holy Ghost, you may put under your feet a withering and temporary world, and may gain by grace a title to that better world which affliction never touches, and where your life and joy shall be eternal. But soon it will be too late for this. Your last mercy-token will soon have wilted, as your eye swims in the mists of death, and you will go out of the world condemned by its *two most significant lessons*, both unheeded in your life—*first*, that God is offended with you, and *second*, that he is placable. A disobeyer of the law and a despiser of Christ can never appear in eternity in peace!

Enduring Temptations.

Blessed is the man that endureth temptation; for when he is tried, he shall receive the crown of life which the Lord hath promised to them that love him.—JAMES, i. 12.

NOTHING can exceed the diversity which characterizes the lot of men in this life. Looking abroad on the surface of human society we behold constant and most wonderful mutations. Changes, which no sagacity could foresee, are occurring with such wonderful rapidity that the history of human life seems little less than some vision of fancy—some reverie of a lawless imagination! The rich, one day in delightful security flattering themselves that want shall never reach *them*, the next day are compelled to tremble—they see want staring them in the face! The poor now rise to opulence—and now feel more deeply the stings of poverty, till death or some other overturning presents a new aspect. The ambitious, some of them have reached the pinnacle to which they aspired—some of them have plunged headlong from the dizzy hights they were attempting to climb! Thrones crumble! Scepters are shivered into pieces! And kings are refugees in the land of strangers! Mourners, at one time we see them comforted; at another, forced to drink still deeper from that chalice of wormwood and gall they have lifted to their lips! No *anticipation* has ever contemplated what fact makes true in the world. You do not see around you *now* such a state of things as you ever expected. Some whom you hoped to see in honor are covered with infamy—others are covered in the dust! Some, whose character once forbade hope, are now the objects of wonder, and perhaps of envy. And as you attempt to look forward to the future, you are forced to anticipate such a rapidity and strangeness of changes, as if some magic were at play and sporting itself with the destinies of the world. As you look, the view changes—it is gone! new objects arise, and new changes fill you with wonder!

In the midst of just such a world we are living, my hearers; and in a little while we shall die and depart out of it. We can not tell what shall overtake us here. A dark cloud hangs over the future; and as we attempt to enter into it, our eyes fail us, and even the objects by which we would feel our way, suddenly vanish while our hand is on them.

There is something unpleasant to such beings as we are, in this strange uncertainty and fluctuating state. We meet with much to try us. We have disappointments, afflictions, fears, reverses; tears fall from our eyes, and even the very hope that enters into our heart may cause its most bitter bleeding when it is torn away!

And there is no course or character that can secure us. As dieth the rich man so dieth the poor. Piety is not proof against disappointment, and the grave of the graceless is dug just beside the grave of the man of God.

Let us look over and beyond these changes. Let us anticipate that state when change shall be no more. Let us neither despair nor murmur at what meets us in this world. Let us remember, *Blessed is the man that endureth temptation, for when he is tried he shall receive the crown of life which the Lord hath promised to them that love him.*

This is the direction that the Holy Spirit gives us, to furnish us for our changeful and trying situation. *My brethren,* says James in the second verse, *count it all joy when ye fall into divers temptations;* and then he tells the reason why: *Knowing this, that the trying of your faith worketh patience.* Again, in the fifth verse: *If any man lack wisdom, let him ask of God.* Nothing tends more to convince us of our lack of wisdom than the trials and changes to which we are subjected here. Who has not felt, amid the fluctuations of life, that he did not know what to do? and felt it to his very heart's core? Who has not experienced trials and temptations, difficulties, embarrassments, perplexities, which seemed to sport themselves with his sagacity, and turn all his wisdom into mockery? *Let him ask of God*—ask, *without wavering,* and *in faith.* Again, in the ninth verse: *Let the brother of low degree rejoice in that he is exalted, but the rich in that he is made low.* The *first* of these rejoicings needs no enforcement, and therefore the writer adds none. But the *second* one is more difficult, and therefore the writer tells *why* the rich man should rejoice *when he is made low; because, as the flower of the grass, he shall pass away.* He is to have the same end in this world as if he were not rich; and therefore his poverty ought not to afflict him. And that end will come soon—come like the withering of the grass! *The sun is no sooner risen with a burning heat, but it withereth the grass, and the flower thereof falleth, and the grace of the fashion of it perisheth; so also shall the rich man fade away in his ways.* Rich as he may be, he shall die! gold can not save him. The most it can do for him is to furnish him a splendid sepulcher: for he *brought nothing into this world, and it is certain he can carry nothing out.* And therefore, when he is brought to poverty, there is no real occasion for mourning—for any thing but *joy;* because, (and this is the idea which the Holy Spirit would impress upon our minds from all the mutations of human life,) *Blessed is the man that endureth temptation, for when he is tried he shall receive the crown of life, which the Lord hath promised to them that love him.*

The ideas, therefore, which it seems to me the Holy Spirit would fix in our minds by these words, are the following:

I. That trials and temptations are to be expected in this life.

II. That the purpose or object of them is our trial.

III. That our duty and interest require us to endure to the end, and not yield to temptation, or sink under trial. And,

IV. That our only wise method of resistance is this—to be led by the promises of God to anticipate felicity in *another* world, as the inheritance of those whose *love* to *him* here enables them to endure to the end.

Let us attend to these ideas, in the fear of God and with prayer for his grace.

I. Trials and temptations are in this life to be expected.

We often flatter ourselves that we shall pass smoothly through the world; and either by our sagacity to shun evil, our vigor to resist it, or by the favor of Heaven, shall never be placed in those terrifying circumstances where we shall be in danger of yielding to the assaults of the Devil. We are very much prone to flatter ourselves; and our delusive flattery extends itself to both our character and our prospects. It is sweet for us to anticipate good, but the anticipation of evil is bitter. And that strange vanity which often exercises the mind of childhood and youth in painting future eminence and distinction, does not entirely fail of its influence, even when sober, Christian instruction and thoughtfulness have taken the place of the vain visions of our childish fancy. From some ardor of temperament, from some vanity of self-esteem, from some inadequate idea of the station in which religion places us in this world, or some inadequate idea of the duties it requires, we are prone to flatter ourselves that we are going to find it not a very difficult thing, and a thing not very severe to the flesh, to walk in the way of Christianity and preserve the integrity of a Christian's virtue. But this is a dangerous delusion. We will not say that the life of the most afflicted believer is *less* happy than if he were a man of the world. We know there are consolations furnished to Christian constancy which do much to diminish the miseries which Christians sometimes feel. But we *do* say, that in this life believers should expect temptations, and be on their guard. They will not find it easy to be always faithful to their Master. And no dream of security ought to lull them into a dangerous repose. For,

1. There is nothing said in the Scriptures which gives us any reason to suppose that it is an easy thing to be faithful and sincere Christians. We have no promise against trial and temptation. Provision is made for us to resist and vanquish assaults; but the security and peace of heaven do not belong to us here. The promises of the Holy Ghost even, are, most of them, not for support and strength *under* temptation, but like that of our text,

for a gracious reward *after* our love to God has brought us off victorious. It is true, we have some promises for our cross, but we have more for our crown. Some provision and sufficient is offered to us to enable us to *resist the devil*, and overcome the enticements to sin; but you can scarcely have failed to notice, in reading your Bible, how the most full and clear and frequent of its promises are occupied about the triumphs of heaven, and not the temptations of earth. So far is the Holy Spirit from assuring us that, as Christians, we shall have nothing to tempt our fidelity; he does not seem disposed, by promise, to dissipate our fears of falling when we *are* tempted. He promises *every thing* to fidelity when we get to another world, but he promises sparingly while we stay in this. Heaven he holds up on our view to encourage and animate us while we are *passing* through the furnace; but even sustaining, cheering grace for the passage he has not *so* promised, that we ought ever to believe he intends our trials shall be small.

2. The express declarations of the Holy Scriptures assure us that believers will, in this life, have very much to tempt them and try their fidelity. The believer is engaged in a warfare. Enemies are before him. The battle is to be fought: *Fight* (say the Scriptures) *the good fight of faith: put on the whole armor of God, that ye may be able to stand against the wiles of the devil. Your adversary, the devil, as a roaring lion, goeth about seeking whom he may devour.* The believer is a *pilgrim*—he is a *stranger* and *sojourner* upon the earth. He can not be faithful if he forgets it, and, surrounded with enough to make him comfortable here, takes up with his present blessings and makes this world his home. He will never reach Canaan in this way. The desert must be trodden. Its wastes, its

wilds, its barren sands must be traveled over. Through those regions where he feels that nothing but bread from heaven can feed him, and nothing but light from heaven be his guide, he must direct his footsteps. And when on the borders of his possession new difficulties rise to meet him, no towering son of Anak must force him to turn back.

3. The *character* of the believer is such, that it is impossible he should be free from temptation. He is sanctified only in part. Folly herself never dreamt a wilder dream than that there is perfection of holiness on this side of heaven. There is no perfection here. The sons of God have not, in this life, the whole character nor the whole inheritance to which they were born. In the bosom of every man on earth there are feelings not wholly sanctified. Like Paul, the holiest have reason to say: *I count not myself to have apprehended; one thing I do, I keep under my body and bring it into subjection, lest, after having preached to others, I myself should be a castaway.* Now every feeling and every principle of the believer which are not wholly sanctified, are so many weak points at which he is exposed to injury. More than this; they are so many living, active enemies exerting their energies to drive him into sin. If there is one feeling of sinful ambition unmortified, every eminence, every dazzling honor that meets the eye, will solicit that ambition toward unholy action. If there is one feeling of condemned covetousness unsubdued, every golden stream that rolls its treasures will become a temptation to sin. If grace has not quenched for ever the fires of improper anger, every slight provocation even will be a temptation to unholy resentment. And so of every other sinful propensity. Just so far as man is unsanctified, just

so far he is peculiarly exposed. Temptation is diminished by holiness and increased by sin. This fact forms one of the most consolatory arguments for increasing grace, and one of the most terrible warnings to continued impiety. It is proper for the struggling believer to know that every item of his progress in holiness renders him less assailable by the temptations of the Devil: and surely, it is proper for the unbeliever to reflect that every step he takes in his impiety is putting him more and more into the power of his enemies. But there is not a just man on earth that *doeth good and sinneth not: if we say we have no sin, we deceive ourselves and the truth is not in us.* And because we are of this character, (not perfect in holiness, but retaining in our hearts much of the principles and seeds of sin,) we can not but be exposed to a thousand temptations. We shall find it difficult to *endure.* When we little think it, some propensity to evil will solicit gratification. There is almost an infinite variety in those ways in which corruption operates. The heart is the fountain of a thousand streams. One of them turned from its channel will often seek out another, and flow onward with accelerated speed. Another, checked in its course, will often accumulate its energies for a more terrible rush. We ought not to feel secure. Just as certain as sin dwelleth in us, sin will easily beset us. It is difficult to be faithful. And our difficulty is as great and as varied as the deceitfulness and corruption of our hearts.

4. Whatever we may hope, there is *no situation* in this world which places us beyond danger. Almost every Christian is prone to be looking after something in worldly condition which shall diminish his difficulties and make it more easy for him to serve God with a

Christian's fidelity. He wishes to save his soul from the curse of God and the contamination of sin; and when he is wearied with difficulties which surround him, he longs for some other situation in which he might find repose. But he longs in vain. The very condition he covets is not what he thinks it to be. There is *no* condition in which a Christian can ever place himself where he will *not* find that tribulation is in the pathway to heaven. Take any example you will.

There are temptations of *adversity*. It is extremely difficult for those who have nothing in this world and can expect to have nothing, to avoid envying the lot of more favored mortals, and avoid that anxiety about worldly subsistence which the clamorous calls of our nature seem to demand. The hungry man will find it difficult, by faith, to live upon the precept, when he reads in his Bible, *Take no thought for to-morrow, what ye shall eat or what ye shall drink.* The desolate man, stripped of those who were the joy and solace of his life, will find it difficult to say over the tombs of his wife and children, *The Lord gave and the Lord hath taken away, blessed be the name of the Lord.* The friendless child of misery, whom adversity drives into the wilderness like David, will find it no easy matter to exclaim: *When my father and my mother forsake me, then the Lord will take me up.* Our confidence is apt to be shaken by reverses. It is a hard matter to think that God loves us, and have faith enough to be satisfied with his allotments, when our hearts are bleeding under his strokes. In such cases we shall be tempted to distrust his goodness, or deny him our *faith* if we do not our *love*. While we suffer under his hand we shall be tempted to think, "Surely if we were his beloved, he who feeds the fowls of the air, and clothes the lilies of the field, and tempers the breeze to the shorn lamb, would not leave us to nakedness and famine." Oh! how few are the Christians of whom it would be said under such trial, *In all this Job sinned not, nor cursed God in his heart.*

There are temptations of *prosperity.* Perhaps it is *more* difficult for the believer to be faithful when the world smiles upon him than when it frowns. Prosperity places the means of sinful indulgence within our reach. We are very apt to think better of ourselves when prospered, as if Divine Providence would not thus distinguish us were we not more deserving than others. There are also correspondent duties which prosperity imposes; and there is no little danger that we shall fail to serve God in proportion to the ability he puts into our hands. I wish I could write this sentence in letters of eternity before the eye of the church in the present day. There is no little danger that we shall fail to serve God IN PROPORTION TO THE ABILITY HE PUTS INTO OUR HANDS! How many rich men are extremely tempted to cherish ideas of pride and independence, and forget their reliance upon God! How many of them are in danger of being unfaithful in their stewardship, using their possessions as if God had *not* given them! It is no small matter to resist the temptations of prosperity. Many a tempted and tried professor of piety is manifesting to us *how hard it is for a rich man to enter into the kingdom of heaven.*

There are temptations of *youth.* When life is young, when the blood flows in healthful currents, when the spirits prompt us to seize on enjoyment, when the world is smiling on us, when the sun of life is rising unclouded in the heavens, it is extremely difficult to look on this world only as a *tabernacle in the wilderness, and seek first the kingdom of God.*

There are temptations of *middle life.* The business, in preparation for which youth has expended so many of its hours and its energies, is apt to claim an undue importance. How many men, full of this world's business and hopes, are putting off the service of God and preparation for eternity till old age shall furnish them with leisure! When their best days have been spent upon the world—when their energies are gone—when, trembling with age, they are standing upon the borders of the grave, worn out and good for nothing, they intend to offer themselves for the service of God, and abandon their worldliness! Oh, what an offering! giving to God what the world will not have!

There are temptations of *old age.* How difficult for the man of years to give up the world! It is woven round his heart! He clings to it from habit. The feeble knees—the failing mind—the dimmed eye, already dusky with the shades of death, are not demonstrations strong enough to turn the whole soul forward to that *house not made with hands.*

There are temptations of *health.* How easy it is to flatter ourselves that our tabernacle stands strong! We do not live as if we were mortal. We imagine that we have many energies to spend upon the world, and that when the pains of illness shall come upon us, it will be time enough to prepare for our latter end. Even the finger of God in the pestilence, when many a man rises in the morning in health and slumbers before sunset beneath the sod—even this is not sufficient to impress a due sense of danger.

There are temptations of *sickness.* The sufferer will

hope against hope that he shall recover. His distressed body is his apology for *not* thinking of his sinful soul! How can he pray, how repent, how seek God, while his anguish and his remedies demand all his thoughts? Indeed there is no situation between our cradle and our coffin, where there are not temptations to try us, difficulties to be endured and overcome, if we would enter into the kingdom of heaven.

5. If we look at the course in which God *has led his own people*, we shall find that they have been *tried so as by fire*. Can we find among the biographies of the saints any one that entered into his rest by a smooth path? Behold Moses. His journey is in the wilderness; his station that—(no uncommon thing, I assure you, with men of God)—his station that for which he feels himself by nature disqualified. Hunger, and thirst, and the accusations of those who feared he was leading them to ruin, and more than all, his own impatience under difficulty when the unsanctified will rebel, present alarming obstacles to his fidelity, and make it hard for him to serve God rather than sin against him. Behold Job. The possessions of the rich man are swept away; the health of the vigorous is gone; his children, over whom the heart of the father yearned, are dead. In the dust, sick, bereaved, abandoned, and hearing from the lips of his wife even the impious counsel: *Curse God and die*, was there nothing of difficulty in having grace enough to say: *Shall we receive good at the hand of the Lord, and shall we not receive evil also?* Behold Abraham. His home must be abandoned; its delights sacrificed. Not knowing whither he went, he must leave possession and live on promise, and, after all, not be accepted if he refuses to sacrifice his own son upon the altar at the command

of God. Behold David. At one time in the wilderness, pressed by famine, and hunted by his foe like a partridge upon the mountains—at another time upon the throne, tempted to every indulgence, it could not be easy to resist evil or find grace amid royal pleasures to repent of sin. Behold Samuel, Elisha, Daniel, Jeremiah, Paul, Silas—who of them ever found a way into heaven not beset with most perilous snares? Temptation ought to be expected by God's people. Wherever we look we find no indication that the heart of the believer will be left free.

II. Now the *object* of all these is our *trial: When he is tried*, is the language of our text. There may be some obscurity lingering around this idea which it belongs not to us to explain. At any rate we will not at present attempt it. Certainly our God does not try us for the same purposes that men make trials. He knows perfectly what we are and what we shall do in every situation, and needs not the evidence of a trial to enlighten him or confirm his knowledge. Still Christians must be *tried;* and this is the object of all our difficulties and our temptations to sin. Without pretending to *discuss* this matter, we will mention *two* ideas in relation to it.

1. The trial may be designed for *our improvement.* For aught we know the economy of grace is such, and the nature of our hearts is such, that without enduring temptation we never could be fitted for the kingdom of heaven. Surely, those who have had the most mature fitness (so far as we can judge) for entering into the *assembly of the first-born*, have been indebted for it, under God, to those times and circumstances of difficulty which

"tried men's souls." Grace is a gift, but it is the nature of grace to improve by action. No man can be of strong body whose muscles have not been used to hard work. No mind can attain much vigor without much severe exercise. And the temptation which tries grace may be necessary for that perfection of grace which fits for heaven.

2. The trial may be designed *as a proof* to the creatures of God. The day is coming when crowns of life are going to be distributed in heaven. Angels, men and devils shall witness it! And then they shall see that those who receive them have only a proper though a a gracious reward; for they *have been tried and found faithful. They shall walk with Christ in white, for they are worthy.* But,

III. Whatever may be our trials or the design of them, both duty and interest demand our unshaken fidelity. God is a righteous rewarder. And while he bestows the *crowns of life* upon those who have *endured temptation* and been faithful *unto death, the fearful and unbelieving, and the abominable, and murderers, and whoremongers, and sorcerers, and idolaters, and all liars, shall have their part in the lake which burneth with fire and brimstone, which is the second death.* There is no difficulty or temptation which will excuse us for unfaithfulness. There is no want of gracious resource in God. *Let no man say when he is tempted, I am tempted of God; for God can not be tempted with evil, neither tempteth he any man. Drawn away of his own lust and enticed,* is the manner in which the unbelieving sin.

Amid the strange overturnings of the world and the stranger wickedness that is in it, no doubt every man will meet with many things that oppose his fidelity to Christ. But his heaven is at stake! Just as valuable as that is, just so important is his faithfulness in the midst of temptations: *He that endureth to the end, the same shall be saved.*

IV. What shall we do? What shall be our resource amid the temptations that beset us—these *outward fightings* and *inward fears?* The text tells us (it is the last idea I mentioned): it holds up a *crown of life* upon our view; it points to the *promise* and speaks of the *love of God.* Listen to *three* ideas on this point.

1. You will find but little, my fellow sinners, to fortify your souls by hope against temptation, if you do not look *beyond time.* Here few joys will you have. Your peace will be often interrupted—your pleasures vanish—tears flow from your eyes and many a poisoned arrow enter into your hearts! But there is another and a better world. Look forward to it. Prepare for it. *There* is your home. There is your crown. There is your Saviour, scarred with wounds and bloody, waiting to welcome you to his rest. He was once tempted. *He endured the cross, despising the shame;* and you may *consider him, lest ye be weary and faint in your minds.* He was tempted for you; he endured for you; he died for you; and now in heaven he reigns and waits for you. You shall soon go up to him, and rush into his arms. Oh! how little would the trials of this world be, if we would only bring heaven down upon our hearts! Endure temptation then by remembering your home is in heaven—your seat ready—your crown woven, and the hand of Christ holding it, when death has done with you, to drop it upon your brow!

2. And remember, the *gift is certain*. The text mentions *a promise*. It is the promise of Him who can not lie. Resort, then, to the promises of God when temptation assails you. Do not be afraid of doing it as if the promise were not *for you*. It *is* for you. Learn to live upon it. Be comforted by it. Learn to oppose the promise of heaven to the prospects of the world. Contrast the *crown of life* with the richest diadem that ever glittered with the diamonds of earth. Look forward to that city which *hath foundations, whose gates are of pearl, whose foundations are precious stones, and whose walls are of jasper;* and let the prospect throw all the glory of the world into contempt! Oh, if men would remember their souls and the high birthright that God has prepared, we should not have in the Church so many mournful instances of worldly conformity and failure under trial!

3. But hope and faith need assistance. *Things* unseen and eternal are not, always, as living realities to such creatures as we. And amid the difficulties that meet us, faith may not be able, always, to *embrace the promises that are afar off.* Hence the text says, *To them that love him.* You ought to have no hope, my brethren, that you are going to *endure to the end* if you have not the *love of God* in your heart. You may muster resolution, array arguments, multiply resolves, and do whatever else you will for your security; but the love of God is worth more than all. Christians often resort to vain contrivances. Religion, and fidelity in it, are very simple things. *Draw nigh to God and he will draw nigh to you.* Let the love of God be *shed abroad in our hearts* and it will vanquish the love of the world. But if the love of God be not in you, inevitably you must fail! To the eye of man you

may seem to endure, but the eye of God will behold your emptiness, and when you are judged you will be *cast out from the presence of God*—no *crown of life* for you.

My hearers, ought you not to apply these truths with the utmost candor to your own souls? Is it not true that some of you, who at times attempt to seek God, have very little idea of encountering difficulty? Do you not stop and turn back when some unwelcome doctrine, opposed to pride, or some severe duty opposed to carnality, meets you? You can never become Christians in this way. You may be deceived, but you can not be saved! If you think to get to heaven without trouble, you are mistaken! It will cost you many a struggle! That depraved heart will *bleed* before it will relinquish sin! It must *break* before it will be bound up and healed by the balm of Gilead! Salvation is indeed free; the blood that bought it flowed freely from the offered heart of the Son of God. Pardon is easy, but the repentance and faith that embrace it must surmount many obstacles. *Never* was *striving* more requisite than in a sinner with a wicked heart and in a wicked world, endeavoring to lay hold on eternal life!

And are there not those who bear the name of Christian whose course is very unlike that we have been contemplating? In these days not a few seem to imagine that it is easy to follow Christ. Their religion gives them little trouble. What *trial* means—what enduring means, they can not tell! There is no spot in all their experience where they can say they were tried! There is no leaf in all their history which tells the tale of their endurance! When religion does not form a most distinct and important business with us—when we do not find it demanding effort—when it makes no calls but such as are easy to answer—when it leaves our whole heart sound and our whole life untouched with trouble—when it permits us to flow on with the world, like them to gather its possessions, and like them to prize and enjoy them—where shall be our evidence that we are *enduring trial*, to be proved for the day of Christ? When I behold the easy life and untroubled mind of many who hope they shall be saved, I can not but tremble for what is before them! So much like the world, and their hearts so much on it, can it be that they are the sons of God and their hearts on heaven? In Scripture times believers found difficulties. Temptations assailed them, hard to be overcome. Their eye was cheered with nothing in this world. They were only comforted by the promises, and promises which they could not inherit till they were dead and gone! And *has* religion changed its nature—or the heart its sin—or Heaven its mercy? It does seem to me that some of us find so little trouble in being Christians that we have need to tremble! What *temptation* has tried us? What *endurance* has demonstrated our faith? What furnace has kindled upon us, to burn up the dross, and brighten the spirit for its heaven?

But if you *are enduring* temptation, take the consolation of the promise. You shall not endure in vain. The day dawneth. Its light breaks upon your eye *afar off*. It shall light your pilgrim steps till it has lighted you down into the sepulcher—nor be extinguished there! It shall brighten up the *dark valley*—for the grave is Christ's. Fear not, then. If you do love God and live upon his promises, and *by* doing so, are held above the world and enabled to endure temptation, go on—go and prosper—go, *mortify the flesh*—go, *resist the devil*—go, vanquish the world—go, *endure temptation*, and, *when you are* tried, go and receive *the crown of life which the Lord hath promised to them that love him.* Oh God, grant it to us all, through Jesus Christ our Lord. *Amen.*

The Depression of Believers.

Make me to hear joy and gladness, that the bones which thou hast broken may rejoice. Hide thy face from my sins, and blot out all mine iniquities. Create in me a clean heart, O God, and renew a right spirit within me.—PSALM, li. 8-10.

THIS is the language of David at a period of trouble. His soul was depressed. He was fully conscious of his sins, but he was not conscious of forgiveness. He pleads with God for pardon, and, sensible of his indwelling sin, he pleads for deliverance from its dreadful power.

David was unquestionably a child of God at the period of this depression. But he could not realize clearly his condition as such. His comforts were few, if any. His hopes were dimmed. His communion with God was interrupted. A cloud hung over his soul; and in the struggles of his prayer he was aiming to catch something of the light which he still believed lingered beyond. He was not happy; and, in his present moral condition, he felt that he never could be.

True religion, in the experiences of it, is as much beyond an ordinary understanding as it is in its foundation, or in the great truths which constitute the substance of the system. It no more belongs to the human mind, as a mere mind of thought and reason, to understand God in his personal dealings with souls, than to understand him in the infinitude of his awful perfections. In his leading the souls of individual believers to heaven, he will be as strange and mysterious to us—as much beyond our reason—as he is in the government of the world.

To us it may seem very strange that God should ever deal with a believer as he sometimes does. Such a believer is his child—God loves him. He has chosen him out of the world. He has uttered the cheering of his promises to him. And, therefore, that he should ever leave him to darkness and depression, unsolaced, as sometimes he is, with a single ray of light, appears to an ordinary understanding as a thing which never could have been expected, if not unreasonable and severe. And if the idea comes up that such an abandonment to doubts and darkness never takes place unless some sin committed—some more than ordinarily offensive sin—has provoked God to inflict this distress, the idea does not remove the difficulty, it only enhances it. Another question instantly arises: How can God suffer a child of his love to perpetrate such a sin?

Besides, if we may judge at all by what lies within the compass of our knowledge, it is not true that doubts, darkness and depression of mind among believers exactly correspond with the unfaithfulness and sins of believers. God will do no injustice, no unkindness; but he will be a sovereign, and will lead his people through just such wildernesses as he pleases. Almost every believer on earth, conscious at all of any increased measure of holiness, is conscious also that his attainments have come to him very much by such modes of discipline as he never expected. What he feared and deprecated has done him good, while his failures have resulted from things he expected to be profitable to him. A Divine sovereignty is inscrutable in many of the experiences of the soul. To this sovereignty alone we must refer much that is mysterious in the doubts and depressions of tried hearts.

We can readily perceive some reasons why such depressions of mind should sometimes exist.

First, There are many instances of great *unfaithfulness* in the love and service of God. In such instances, doubts and difficulties of mind arise on both gracious and natural principles. It is a principle of grace, in God's dispensation of it, to withdraw his Spirit from those who forsake him. He frowns upon them. He puts out their light. He leaves them to wander in the darkness of a spiritual abandonment, as an act of discipline, sometimes as intolerable to the soul as it is deserved. It is a principle which lies also in the nature of the case, that an unfaithful believer must, more or less, part with his peace of mind and comforts of hope. This hope and peace are not mere casual or arbitrary gifts. They result from the two matters of exercise and evidence. Both these matters are necessary to them. It is in gracious exercises—in such exercises as love to God, humility, dependence, thankfulness, and heavenly-mindedness—that both peace and hope take up their abode in the believer's heart. God can not be enjoyed afar off. He must be near. And all that belongs to the peace of religion will lie for ever beyond the reach of the soul, unless the soul is exercised—itself exercised—in the affections and duties of religion. In such exercises, also, there arise evidences of religion. All gracious exercises are evidences. And hence hope has something to originate it and sustain it as long as such exercises continue and no longer. So that a believer's peace of mind and comforts of hope have a most intimate connection, both gracious and natural, with his spiritual condition, and must be impaired or lost utterly by his unfaithfulness. Depression and gloom, therefore, may be expected on this ground.

Second, They may be expected also from the difficulties of determining his character. One of the most embarrassing and perplexing of all studies is the study of one's own heart. Almost any thing else can be more satisfactorily answered than the question of character in the sight of God. There is a deceitfulness and a changeableness about the heart; there are minglings of its affections and contrarieties of affection which render it an extremely difficult thing for us to be certain of the correctness of our conclusions. No believer that lives is perfect in holiness. A struggle is going on between opposing principles within him at every step of his religious advancement; and not only so, but the struggle becomes the more hard, very often, in proportion as grace becomes more triumphant. A man of but little determination against sin will find but little difficulty with it; while a man of more fixed resolution, determined to go on in his Christian progress, will very often find himself beset and baffled and disheartened; and while in this troubled state he will not be ready to believe that he is making more gain, and furnishing more evidence of his real piety, than his brother by the side of him who finds little difficulty. If there were no home-bred depravity in the believer to contend against—if feelings of good and evil were not mixed together in his heart—he could more readily determine his spiritual condition, and would not, therefore, be so often beset with the glooms and depressions of doubt. But since his imperfection is so great, and the heart so deceitful, and the opposition of indwelling sin so much the more real and desperate, and therefore more sensible in proportion to the believer's determination against it, it is no wonder that he should sometimes doubt, and sometimes be driven to despair.

The one thing which embodies in itself to a great extent all that a depressed soul longs for, is just this: to know whether he is a child of God or not. Oh, how much he wishes to know this! Let him be assured of his adoption, and he could rest. Then he would pray differently, hope differently, fear and aim differently. Then he would take courage in dark days, and would walk cheerfully in rough places. And now we lay down this principle: We affirm that there is a difference between the religious doubting, darkness, and depression of mind which sometimes assail a true believer, and the doubting, darkness, and depression which would belong to him if he were not a true believer: we affirm that there are *peculiarities* of grief, and fear, and anxiety in the dark soul-troubles of a child of God.

I. Let us give some brief proof of this; and
II. Let us state some of the peculiarities.

I. It is evident that a true believer will be unlike an unbeliever in his doubts and depression, because he is unlike him all around. He is not what he once was. He is a new creature. He has a new nature. He is born of God. All things have become new to him. Old things have passed away. And though, (since sin still remains in him, and holiness in him is only in its infancy), he will have, and must have, some resemblances to a mere ordinary man; yet, because he is *not* a mere ordinary man, but a child of God, in the very nature of the case he must have his own and peculiar marks upon him—his own and peculiar exercises and characteristics of all things which religion touches. Were it not so, regeneration would mean nothing. It would be only a name—a fancy. It is a thing not to be rationally conceived of that one should be renewed by the Holy Ghost—should have such a renewal as to lay the foundation for salvation from sin and death eternal, and for salvation in entire holiness, in a few brief years—should be turned from supreme love of the world to supreme love to God—from all hope on the ground of his own righteousness to hope in the blood of atonement or hope nowhere—should repent, should believe, should love God, and take up his line of march with the soldiers of the cross toward the kingdom of heaven; and after all this, find in the times of trial, doubt and depression, no difference betwixt himself and one to whom all this is unexperienced and unknown.

It is not possible to give a blind man eyes, and let him see the light, and let him use it, and let him know the value of it and rejoice in it, and let him look out upon the garniture of this magnificent creation smiling in the blended hues of its loveliness, and see the sun in his car of glory, and see the leap of the lightning, and count the hues of the rainbow, and muse over the lilies of the field as they put on their dress of beauty, and, after all this, put out his eyes, even, and leave him just what he was before. You can not make him what he was. Made *twice* blind, again he would be a different creature. You can not put out of his soul the poetry which the vision of only a few days put into it. He will think about the light, and feel and talk about the light, and all that the light made visible to him, not like a man that never had any eyes, but like one who once had. And if it were so, (as blessed be God it is not), that a believer, by some mishap of sin, or by some mysterious design of God, could lose all the spiritual organism which regeneration gave him, and could become again as fully dead in sin, and as fixedly an enemy of God, as he was before he was born of the Spirit, still even this would not reinstate him into all the experiences of his old existence. He would take along with him recollections and marks upon his mind, upon his heart, upon his conscience, and his character, of which even his fall could not rob him.

There are no transformations of character to be compared to that which comes by the regenerating power of the Holy Spirit. There are no such moulding experiences as those of a sinner repenting of sin and fleeing to take refuge in Christ. These transformations, these experiences have not, indeed, so much to do with the surface of character—they lie down deep in its depths—they work in the inside of the hidden spirit—they leave there an impress which time, and sin, and Satan, can not remove, and which the God of grace *will* not; and, therefore, under the religions exercises of the soul afterward, in its doubts and depressions, as well as in every thing else, a believer will not be affected like an unbeliever; he will carry along with him the marks of his religion. He may not be able to see them. He ought to be able. We propose, therefore,

II. To aid him as far as we can. We name some of the peculiarities accompanying a true believer's depression of mind, and which distinguish him, *as* a believer, in his times of doubt and darkness and spiritual abandonment. We mention some different particulars. Let *eight* be treasured in your memory.

1. In his depression of mind, when he doubts some-

times of his piety and fears final ruin, or mourns because he has no more evidence of his adoption ; a true believer finds his soul uneasy and troubled more *constantly* than it would be if he were not a true believer, but were only a Christian in mere name. The uneasiness and concern of mind which belong to hypocrites and deceived persons resemble the uneasiness of all other unconverted sinners. Their concern is *occasional*. It comes and goes. It has not fixedness about it. It does not *stay* in the mind as if it originated in some active cause working within, as indeed, it does not; it only flits over the mind and is gone; returns again and is gone again, fitfully, capriciously, accidentally. It comes from some cause or occasion without.

When a *believer* is in depression, his sadness is more fixed and less fitful. It clings to him. He can not fling it off, if he tries, and he deems it almost a wickedness to try at all. He feels bound to be sad, and deems himself forbidden to hope. A gloom rises upon him with the sun, and when he lies down at night he says mournfully to God, like David, *I water my couch with tears.* His depression has this constancy and fixedness about it because it arises not from external occasions, but from a cause that lies deep within. He has lost the light of God's countenance. His wounds are deep, not mere external or on the surface. Hear him cry : *Make me to hear joy and gladness that the* BONES *which thou hast broken may rejoice.*

2. Christian depression of mind has a kind of *supremacy* about it. The matter of thought and grief, then, is a supreme matter. It rises above all other things. All other things are trifles, contemptible and mean. They would not weigh a feather—the *world* would not,

and all that is in it, balanced against the sense of God's favor. This favor is the *one thing* wanted—the only thing. It is the *one thing* valued and sought for. In an entire supremacy it rises above all things else. *Enter not into judgment with thy servant, for in thy sight shall no man living be justified. . . . My spirit is overwhelmed within me; my heart within me is desolate. I remember the days of old; I stretch forth my hands unto thee: my soul thirsteth after thee as a thirsty land. Hear me speedily, O Lord; my spirit faileth. Quicken me, O Lord, for thy name's sake: for thy righteousness' sake bring my soul out of trouble.* (Psalm cxliii.)

A believer in his trouble is not tempted by the world. An unbeliever may be. He would renounce *any thing* to attain that for which his soul longeth. It is supreme with him. Hence,

3. There is a deeper *sensibility*, and a greater degree of anguish with a believer in his spiritual abandonment, than an unbeliever knows any thing about. He does not feel like the orphan that never knew a father; he feels like a disowned and outcast child. He has no more a father, no more a home or a hope. There is nothing for him to turn to, and no friend for him to hope in. If he had never known any thing of peace with God, and had *never* rested in the calmness of faith, he would not be so miserable and downcast as he is. His affliction is the affliction not of mere want, but of bitter bereavement. He resembles Rachel when her children were dead, and Jacob when Joseph was lost. If she had always been childless—if Joseph had never been born, Rachel and Jacob would have been very differently affected. And of just that kind is the difference between the depression of an impenitent sinner and that of a child

of God. There is a depth and tenderness of anguish—a keenness of anguish that reaches the heart's core, when a true believer loses his hope. *He* thinks, that because his heart is cut *so* deeply, he *can not* be a Christian; and for that very reason we think he is. His grief is the grief of a child; his tears are the testimony of an affectionate heart.

4. In the seasons of his sadness, a true Christian will be looking very much *to God* for relief. The Psalm before us is an example. If one is only a hypocrite, or deceived into a *name to live while dead*, the attention will be very much turned for relief, in times of doubt and depression, toward one's own self, or services, or purposes, or some such thing. But a *believer*, in trial of soul, carries along with him the impression that none but God can help him. He knows his own feebleness. He knows it well. He knows that by no bidding of his own his chains of bondage will fall off. And though compelled by his sense of want, and his fears—it may be of hell itself, he is driven from one trial to another, and one device to another, (for it is not possible that a believer, in such darkness and abandonment, should rest); yet it is very noticeable that he holds on to prayer more than to any thing else. His hope, if he has any, is simply in God; his despair, if despair he must, can not drive him from God. Hence,

5. Notice the resort to this means of grace which always marks the course of a troubled Christian. Pray he will. He will pray when he does not believe in its efficacy: *Thou hast covered thyself with a cloud that our prayers can not pass through.* He will pray when, from his dark and unsoothed experiences of anguish, he finds and knows that prayer does him no good. Praying thus

is not a matter of reason with him, of judgment or understanding. It is just one of the promptings of his new nature—one of the instincts of a child of God. If he were *not* a child of God, he would abandon prayer after the painful experience of its inefficacy; he would sit down silent in his gloom, or resort to some other means for relief. But on the ground of his new nature—on a principle which he can not himself explain or understand—he holds on to prayer. He seldom abandons it, and only for short periods. To pray is just one of the instincts and strugglings of the nature within him. An unconverted sinner, anxious for his salvation, having prayed for a time, and not having realized an answer, will often cease from it. So will one who has rested upon a false hope, when that hope is shaken, and his soul is depressed. It is a thing very much worthy of our notice, that almost the *entire sum* of all that the Bible teaches us about religious depression, doubt, and gloom, is taught in the very language of prayer. The Divine writer does not tell his troubles to *us*, he tells them to God. It was so with David. It was so with Asaph. And if Job has recorded it differently, and Paul like him, the record still shows us that prayer was the very breathing of their depression and doubt. The text is, all of it, an example in point.

6. Amid the dark glooms of a believer's trouble there will be *occasional flashes of light*. The cloud will sometimes break away. The sun will appear, if not in its glory, at least in its glimpses. And, accordingly, you find in the prayers of depression and doubt recorded in the Bible, such a mingling together of complaint and complacency—of gloom and gladness—of trial and triumph, as makes them appear to an unwise mind like in-

consistencies and absurdities. Job was compelled to make one of the bitterest of all possible lamentations. He was abandoned to despondency and fruitless searching of spirit. *My complaint is bitter,* says he, *my stroke is heavier than my groaning. O, that I knew where I might find him! I would order my cause before him, and fill my mouth with arguments. I would know the words which he would answer me, and understand what he would say unto me. . . . Behold I go forward, but he is not there; and backward, but I cannot perceive him; on the left hand where he doth work, but I can not behold him. He hideth himself on the right hand, but I can not see him.* All this is depression and darkness. Then comes a flash of light: *But he knoweth the way I take: when he hath tried me, I shall come forth as gold.* The relief which a true believer finds in his sadness comes from these sudden and partial gleams of light which seem to struggle through the darkness of his midnight. If he were an unbeliever his relief would come by forgetfulness and inattention—from turning back on the world—or turning his eye away from the dark cloud that hangs over him. A *believer's* light comes to him right through the cloud, and while his tear-dimmed eye is fixed upon its gloom. *To the upright there ariseth light in darkness.*

7. The state of those who are really irreligious is described in the Bible, by saying they are *without God in the world.* Whatever else this description may mean, it certainly means that they are greatly unconscious of God's particular dealings with them. This is their ordinary condition of mind. They are very slow to see God in any of his external providences. They can see *nature* as they call it but they can not see God. At most they see him only acting on a general system, which

they suppose has no special application or significance for them. God may do what he pleases to them in his providence; may send sickness or health, poverty or riches, trial or triumph; they are slow to believe he means any thing in particular by it. Just so in respect to any of their internal affections, of grief or joy, of hope or despair. They do not recognize *God*. They are as slow to recognize him within them as without them.

Now, you may apply this principle to the matter before us. There is a strong contrast between the consciousness of a man with a good hope and a man with a bad one, in the times of their mental depression and doubt and fear. The man with a false hope recognizes only such things as reason, and truth, and evidences, and affections, and conscience, and sin, and duty. He thinks himself in trouble simply on the ground of such things. He fears God's anger, fears condemnation, fears hell, as *he* supposes, simply because, with the common powers of a man, he has been examining religion and his own heart, and has found no evidences of religion within him. With a true believer in his difficulties of soul it is quite different. He is not *without God in the world*. He is *not* slow to believe that God's spirit is dealing with him; and that his fears, his troubled conscience, his dark mind and desolate heart, as he is *tossed with tempest and not comforted*, have some deep and special significance wrapped up in them which he is bound to heed. With him it will not be circumstances, or nature, or even truth and evidences. It will be *God*. He will recognize *God* at every stage of his trouble. Hear him: *I am the man that hath seen affliction from the rod of his wrath. He hath led me and brought me into darkness and not unto light. Surely against me is he turned: he turneth his hand against me all the day. My flesh and my skin hath he made old; he hath broken my bones. He hath builded against me and compassed me with gall and travail. He hath set me in dark places; as they that be dead of old. He hath hedged me about that I can not get out; he hath made my chain heavy. Also, when I cry and shout he shutteth out my prayer. He hath inclosed my ways with hewn stone; he hath made my paths crooked. He was unto me as a bear lying in wait, and as a lion in secret places. He hath turned aside my ways and pulled me in pieces; he hath made me desolate. He hath bent his bow, and set me as a mark for the arrow. He hath caused the arrows of his quiver to enter into my reins. He hath filled me with bitterness and made me drunken with wormwood. He hath also broken my teeth with gravel stones, he hath covered me with ashes. . . . I said, my strength and my* HOPE *is perished from the Lord.*

Finally. In all the depression and gloom of a believer, there are very few ideas of darkness and trouble which have their origin in any uncertainty of mind in respect to the realities of religion, in respect to God or any of the truths of Christianity. Very seldom has he any doubt about any of these things. So far from being troubled, because he feels uncertain about them, his troubles arise from the very certainty he feels. He *knows* the reality of religion. He knows the security of it. He knows the blessedness of its experience. His trouble, his very trouble is, that he can not get at such blessed realities *for himself.* He would be less troubled if he had any doubt about the good he longs for, and if he did not set upon it such an indescribable value. If he were not a Christian, there would be some doubtings of mind about religion itself, its doctrines, its realities, its experiences, or some such thing. The *matter itself* would appear dark to him, and the trouble of that darkness would be mingled with the troubles about his own state; he would be distressed about the nature of religion itself, and its certainties, and about his own experience in it; a cloud would hang over the subject as well as over his heart; over the subject as a matter of reality, of certainty, and not merely as a matter of experience with him. When the distressed mind of a true believer can not see God; when God hideth his face from him, he is troubled. But his trouble ordinarily is not that he doubts of God's existence, of his grace, or of his mercy, or of the reality of religious experience. His trouble is, that he can not find in himself the evidences of an experience which he so firmly believes in and so tearfully longs for.

Make me to HEAR JOY AND GLADNESS, is the very distress of his cry. He knows they are truths. He knows *joy and gladness* in experience are no fictions. On such points as depravity, guilt in sin, the sovereignty of God, the efficacious aids of the Holy Spirit, the presence of God with his people, a true believer in his glooms is seldom troubled. If ever there comes up a believer toward the Lord's table in this house with trembling heart and staggered steps, scarcely daring to approach lest he should *eat and drink unworthily*, and feeling a mountain weight upon him ready to crush his heart, he does not tremble and stagger and bear along that heavy heart within him because he has any doubt about the efficacy of Christ's atonement, or the freeness of Christ's invitations, or the willingness of the Master to meet him there in the communion of forgiveness and love. Doubt the atonement? No! He could as soon doubt his own distresses of soul!

His distress exists because he believes in and values so highly the atoning efficacy of the blood of Christ, and can not feel that it is sprinkled upon his sad heart to mark him as a guest for heaven. His *heart* is dark; not God, not Christ, not the Holy Spirit, not Divine pardon, or Divine love. His very darkness is an evidence of his adoption; his distress and tears are the tears and distress of a child of God.

If we have *none* of these burdens of spirit, we have reasons for a deep and solid thankfulness. Let us be grateful if we can approach the table of the Lord, seeing light and glory, love and welcome, spread over the whole moral scenery of the crucifixion. Blessed for the communicant who can say, Christ died, I live; I love him here, and shall soon pass from the table of memorial to his presence in glory.

If any of us are sad and uncomforted, and yet *want* what our sacrament symbolizes, and know its truth, and are sad only because our heart is dark while God is light, let us aim to triumph over unbelief and the temptations of the Devil; let us be as free to take, as we know God is free to give, and while we lift the cup bid defiance to guilt and unworthiness, to sin and death and hell; *because* HE *lives I shall live also.*

The Woman of Canaan in Prayer.

Jesus answered and said unto her, O woman, great is thy faith; be it unto thee even as thou wilt.—MATTHEW, xv. 28.

THE woman to whom Jesus Christ gave this answer appears to have been entirely a stranger to him. In what manner she had heard of him we are not informed. But it is not improbable that she had never heard of him at all until about the period referred to in the text. Jesus Christ seems to have been accustomed after he entered upon the work of his ministy, wherever he went, to carry along with him in all his habits some signal mark of his high character. By miraculous healing of the diseased, or some other ministration of mercy, or by conversation and preaching on the great objects of his mission, a manifestation was made of the power and wisdom which attended him. His acts and his instructions circulated from lip to lip among the people; and through the rumors about him, which went abroad over the land, probably this woman had heard of him.

Man was made for religion. His conscience, his mind, heart and hopes, as well as his fears, naturally prompt him toward religious endeavors. This is an impulse of his nature. The influence of it does not cease till he learns the sad fact that he is a sinner in the very bent and preferences of his heart; and then, too often, by the law of sin which truth demands of him to mortify, he is induced to forego all his attempts. On this principle that man has impulses, capacities and wants which demand religion, the people in the time of Christ conversed much about him; and in this mode the woman who approached him so earnestly may have heard much of him.

We know little of her. She was not a Jewess. She appears to have been born and educated in a heathen country. She was a *Canaanite*. She belonged to that doomed race with whom the patience of God seems to have been exhausted on account of their wickedness. Probably she was herself like the rest of her blood—not only a sinner, but one of aggravated guilt. But she had heard of Christ, and now when he was on the coasts of Tyre and Sidon she came out and cried unto him, saying, *Have mercy on me.* The doom which hung upon her nation, the evil character of her people, and the vileness of her own sin, did not hinder her from applying to Christ in her time of trouble; and *he* did not fail to do that which assorted with his character and his commission—the Redeemer of lost sinners. *O woman, great is thy faith; be it unto thee even as thou wilt.* The story shows us at once what Christ is, and what needy sinners ought to be. His grace is unlimited, inexhaustible and ready; and sinners who need it ought to copy the example of the Syro-Phœnician woman.

She was in *deep affliction.* At the period of affliction is the very time to apply to Christ. Her daughter was in trouble, and, it would seem, a hopeless trouble, unless some hitherto unknown power should aid her. This affliction gave point and pathos to her entreaty: *Have mercy on me, O Lord, thou son of David, my daughter is grievously vexed with a devil.* Affliction has a rhetoric of its own. It makes no prefaces and preludes—it passes no compliments—and seldom employs any argument save one. Absorbed itself in the one matter of its troubles, it can not wait to arrange considerations taken from any other quarter; and it can not but feel that the sadness it breathes must find its way to the spot of pity in any heart that beats. Hence the agitated woman at once, nature acting out nature both in matter and manner, breaks over all the forms of society, and without introduction or hesitancy, and just with the propriety of grief, lays down her plea of affliction at the door of her Saviour's heart: *Have mercy on me; my daughter is grievously vexed with a devil.*

There is an eloquence in grief which no dramatist can imitate, and no insincerity can counterfeit, but which every heart can feel.

This woman's *parental love* has here a fine and striking manifestation. It is the true love of a mother. No other heart would love so. She took all the torment upon herself. She does not pray for her daughter. That is not the form of her speech. *Have mercy on* ME, *O Lord.* This is woman; this is mother. If any thing touches her child, it touches *her.* The affliction becomes her own. She has adopted it; and it would lose more than half its anguish if she could take it all upon herself and let her child go free. Somewhat on this ground it was, perhaps, that this woman, so much of a stranger to Christ, would almost go counter to the very modesty of her sex, and uninvited, yea, almost repulsed, would break through the crowds which attended Christ, and amid the gaze of the multitude come up to the very presence of her Master. She did not send. A messenger would not do. No message could carry along a mother's heart, or offer a mother's prayer. Grief has a law of its own; and no matter what the conventional rules of society may say, where it acts in its own sincerity it will act rightly, and human nature will respect it. But be it remembered, it did not rely upon self; it did not despond. It just prompted the heart-stricken mother to pray. Fit model for parental love to copy. There is the same Christ to pray to still.

The *solicitude and determined earnestness* of this woman were very remarkable. See how she perseveres. Nothing can stop her or still her. She *will* keep on. When she first came to Christ, it is said *she cried*. Nature, woman, mother, was acting; and though a loud and earnest female voice might sound strange amid such a throng crowding the house and around it the highway, and men might aim to stop her as they did; yet all that was a mere trifle to her. She would not stop—she could not—nature, woman, mother, was at work. But she seems to have gained no attention in the very quarter to which her maternal grief and solicitude had directed her. Even Jesus *answered her not a word*. What ice is this! How strange! *Not a word!* And what then! Nothing is so tender as grief. It seems to dissolve the heart. It needs sympathy; and when even a little word of kindness is uttered to it, such a word falls on the heart like a smile of Heaven and puts new courage into it. If Jesus had but spoken one kind word to her we should not be astonished that she persevered; and it would at first sight appear to be more like himself. But he had higher ends in view.

Not a word: still she kept on praying. She would not *take* discouragement. She would not take it from even the quarter whence, if it should come, there would seem to be no ground for the utterance of another syllable. She kept on. Maternal solicitude and affection are not to be measured or weighed by any thing else. At length the disciples became weary with her importunity; or deemed it indecorous toward Jesus Christ, since he had not answered her a word; or perhaps their hearts were touched with some tender compassion for her, and they could not bear to hear the poor creature's cry; and thinking that Christ did not deign to regard her, they did not wish to have their feelings harrowed up by the pitiful wail of her misery any longer. So they besought him: *Send her away, for she crieth after us.* Here was another obstacle. She had a right to expect that her misery would have found at least some seconding to its plea among men, mortals and sinners like herself, exposed *themselves* to have their hearts torn with anguish; and when she only found the contrary, what a new wave of trouble must have come darkly and dreadfully over her heart! Christ did *not answer her a word;* and now even his disciples would not pray for her but pray against her: *send her away!*

And when Christ makes his answer to them, *I am not sent but unto the lost sheep of the house of Israel,* another item of discouragement would seem to have come up, sufficient to take away the last gleam of hope, and plunge her into the depths of dark and desponding affliction. She was not a woman of Israel. She was a Canaanite —of a cursed and outcast race. She knows it very well. Her ancestors had been driven from their country generations ago. She and her people had been sunk into the dissoluteness of morals, such as their idolatry promoted; and now, when Jesus Christ speaks of the *Israel* to whose *lost sheep* he *was sent* exclusively, the woman would have stopped, if any thing could stop her. But she rises with the occasion. Her prayers keep pace with the difficulties as they come up before her. Instead of turning back in despair to her home, she approaches Christ as boldly as if he had bidden her welcome. She *falls at his feet, saying, Lord help me.* And there the poor creature lies—at his feet—as much in anguish as ever. And there the eye of the Lord is upon her. She pleads, and he listens. Surely now she must succeed. She has got the Master's ear and his eye. She has made her way through the crowds and the disciples, and flung herself on the ground before him. But he answers: *It is not meet to take the children's bread and cast it to dogs.* What a repulse! Dog was the lowest of all terms of reproach and contempt. How could the afflicted woman endure it? Especially, how could she have any courage or heart to utter another syllable, when she heard this from the very lips of him in whom all her hopes centered. She did not know what *we* know: she was ignorant that Christ intended to put her to the test, and then relieve her. How could she have expected that Jesus Christ would regard her favorably after he had applied to her such an epithet? But this woman does not sink into despair. She does not complain. She does not manifest any dissatisfaction at the rank which Christ seems to assign her. Dog! yes, she'll be a *dog;* she will be *any thing,* if he will heal her daughter. Self is sunk, and forgotten, annihilated, in maternal solicitude, at the feet of Jesus! With the instant quickness of grief, and with the devotion of a mother, she takes up the reproach which Christ appears to have flung upon her, and just turns it into an argument to put back into his own heart. She consents to be a dog, and take the dog's place and portion, and ask for nothing more, and be content with that: *Truth, Lord; yet the dogs eat of the* CRUMBS *which fall from their master's table.*

This was enough. The purpose of Jesus Christ was now answered. The woman had been through a trial, and had manifested an affection, perseverance, prayerfulness, and discouragement, and a humility, which constitute a lesson to all after her. As long as the sun shines, no sinner on earth can ever be found in any such condition of discouragement and ill-desert as ever ought to silence the lip of prayer, or turn back a poor sinner from seeking the favor of Christ.

And now notice the answer of the Lord: *O woman, great is thy faith.* It is not a little remarkable that Jesus Christ takes no notice of the maternal affection, and maternal solicitude, earnestness, perseverance, and humility of this mother. He certainly could admire these qualities, as well as we. There are many demonstrations in his life that he had taste and tenderness, as well as discrimination and perception of what is touching and beautiful; and that herein he never had any equal among men. The taste and tenderness of his teachings are not less remarkable than the truthfulness of them. And when we behold him loving the young man in the Gospel, forgiving the woman taken in adultery, or weeping at the grave of Lazarus, or providing for his mother as he hung upon the cross, we can not but perceive that the sensibilities which adorn human nature were all his own. He must have honored and admired the workings of this woman's heart—her entire devotedness in the midst of her grief—her decision, her indomitable perseverance amid discouragements, her humility, and her fondness which adopted her daughter's affliction as her own, and which could not be damped or repulsed by all the strange treatment it met with. But he does not commend any one of these things. He commends only her faith : *O woman, great is thy faith.* He singles out her faith as if it were the sole matter for any commendation, or any admiring regard. He read her heart, and read it not as you or I would have done, in the mere aspects of its humanity alone; but particularly and the more in the aspects which were cast over it all by a divine principle within her. She had FAITH; and it was faith which started her out from home to find Jesus. It was faith which put the cry for mercy into her trembling lips. It was faith which urged her on through the throngs of stranger men who encircled Jesus Christ. It was her faith which would not sink at the silence of Christ, at the complaints of the disciples, or at the seeming rebuke of her Lord, when he ranked her among dogs. It was faith which made her take the dog's place—any place and any portion he would assign her. Faith stood as the origin and prompter of all her other virtues. It gave her courage. It increased her maternal tenderness, and wisely directed it. She applied to *Christ* in her affliction. Faith made her open to him all the sacredness of a mother's grief, and trust her bleeding heart to him, to touch the sacredness of sorrow even just as he pleased. When he himself seemed to be against her, silent to her cries, or speaking to his disciples, or standing over her as she lay at his feet, willing to be any thing for her daughter's sake, she would not believe that Christ would cast her off. She believed he would hear her; and by faith she looked through and beyond all the dark and discouraging signals which hung around her, and seemed to block up her way to any expectancy of relief. This faith was really the moving principle of the woman all along, from the time that she left her sad home, to hunt up Jesus, down to the moment that she left him to return to her gladdened home, a grateful and happy mother.

It is quite probable, if not quite certain, that both her maternal tenderness and her grief would have failed her, and left her heart to sink within her amid her discouragements, had it not been borne up by the power of her faith. Tenderness and grief, as they are by nature, are very touching, and may be very useful; but they are not strong. They are easily discouraged. They can not bear unkindness and ill-treatment. Such unkindness drives off grief to hunt after relief in some other quarter —some heart-quarter. Tenderness and grief demand sympathy, and can not well bear repulse. So they are by nature. But as they are by the commingling influences of faith, while they lose none of their tenderness they put on the power of perseverance—while they lose none of their sweetness they put on strength. By faith they refuse to despair, and refuse to be repulsed. The woman would not believe *that* to be in the heart of Jesus which appeared to be indicated by his own treatment of her. Be she Canaanite, or be she dog, she would believe that Christ had mercy for her, and this faith, by doing him justice, did him the highest honor.

Hers was great faith. Christ called it such. And I do not think we are to regard the greatness of it as being proved by her making her way through the outward obstacles we have mentioned, and persevering in her entreaties amidst all these discouragements, so much as in another thing. This woman had received no assurances of acceptance. No conditions or offers had been made to her on the ground of which she proceeded. She did not regard herself as a child of God. If any one can entertain *such a regard*, it does not require a great amount of faith to make one's way to Christ determinedly and commit one's case or cause into his hands. A weak faith might do it, on the ground that one is a child of God, and that Christ, after all, will act accordingly. How often, how very often, amid the miserable hearts of this world, do we find persons extremely desirous to feel that they *are* the children of God, before they venture a single word of prayer! Because they do *not* feel so, they are afraid to pray—afraid to hope—afraid to commit themselves to any perseverance—afraid to take a low place at Christ's feet, like this woman, and lie there and plead. This woman ventured all this without a word or a thought that she was a child of God. The greatness of her faith appears in this, that she just acted faith, instead of hunting around her heart first, to see if she had got any. Herein she was a good example for many a sinner that resorts to this sanctuary. If they would but *go* to Christ as they are, as sinners, as undone sinners, *believing* that he would accept such, many a dark day would be turned into a bright one—many a heavy and hesitating heart would make this woman's proof of Christ, and get this woman's answer: *O woman, great is thy faith: be it unto thee even as thou wilt.*

Jesus Christ had marvelously delayed to answer her. He often does this by his own people—even those whom he loves the best, and even those who best love him. It does not belong to us to fathom the depths of his wisdom; and therefore we can not tell all the reasons he may have for such delaying. It tries their faith. That is one thing. And an untried faith is not commonly a very constant and comfortable one. We are such creatures that we have a sort of necessity for something to look back upon amid many of our glooms and doubts, which shall be a sort of argument to prove our piety. If we can look back upon such seasons as show that our faith has been tried and has not given way in the trial, then a little gleam from the past lights up the gloom of the present and sends on its ray into the darkness of the future. Moreover, a good sailor is trained among storms; a good soldier has heard the shots rattle; and few Christians have been qualified for either great service or great comfort who have not parted with much of their dross in the crucible of trial. Hence we find *David* complaining of the Lord's delay: *I am weary of my crying; my throat is dried; mine eyes fail while I wait for my God.* Hence we find the sad-hearted *Jeremiah* exclaiming: *When I cry and shout, he shutteth out my prayer.* Habakkuk complains: *O Lord, how long shall I cry and thou wilt not hear?* And the Church even, the very bride of Christ, his love and his glory, after representing him as inviting her requests, strangely represents him as retiring from her: *I opened to my beloved, but my beloved had withdrawn himself and was gone. I sought him, but I could not find him; I called, but he gave me no answer.*

God is not to be judged of by man's wisdom. He has a way of his own. But one thing is certain, delay of answer is no denial; and the woman who lies at Christ's feet in tears, where faith put her, shall yet be glad that she lay there. If you can not rejoice in the answer as you seek God, keep seeking, and the answer is sure; it may be swelling in sweetness and magnitude as it delays. The woman's power to persevere in prayer was itself part of her answer. It was grace which Christ bestowed upon her, while he did not appear to be bestowing any thing. Consequently her prayer becomes the more earnest and humble as she waits and pleads for an answer. Sometimes when a desired blessing comes at once the soul is rather injured than benefited by it. Prayer languishes, and the sense of dependence melts away, and the soul wanders off from God. At other times the answer is delayed, and then faith is stirred up in the soul, and the individual cries like the Psalmist: *My soul followeth hard after thee. As the hart panteth for the water-brooks, so panteth my soul after thee, O God.* It is one of the marks of true prayer where the heart is quickened, and will not be discouraged or dispirited by a delayed answer. While this heart-stricken woman was holding on to her purpose and refusing to give back, perhaps, indeed probably, it never entered into her heart that her Lord was strengthening her just to pray. She probably felt just as any of you would, or as many of you *have*, when in the time of your trouble you have not obtained your request, but have not ceased to solicit. You felt unanswered—not satisfied—not happy. Oh, you did not know that the grace to persevere in that prayer was the very richest answer you could have. You knew it only afterward. And you could remember it *then* with such a vividness and belief in the power of prayer as you never could have had, if your answer had come as soon as you opened your lips to supplicate.

There is a light in the inner sanctuary which does not shine in the exterior courts of God's house. There is a spirit of intimacy and communion, of solemnity and satisfaction in God, which no man can reach without mustering all the powers within him, and embarking all his soul in his supplication. God delays to answer in order to draw the sinner. He is too far off for one of God's children. God wants him nearer. And he lets them go unanswered till he comes nearer and nearer, and gets into the presence of God, and is filled with the sacredness and sweetness of the secrets of God's tabernacle. The delay just leads him up to God's heart and makes him acquainted with it.

In the experience of this woman we remark, therefore, beyond all this, that there was an enhanced felicity. She got near to Christ through her discouraging delay. He did not treat all sinners so. He did not treat the centurion so when he prayed for his servant, sick with the palsy at home. But I ask you, would you not rather be this poor Canaanite woman, hoping against hope, and struggling up into the presence of Christ, and lying at his feet, and having faith enough to turn his repulse into an argument and aim it back at his own heart—would you not rather be this poor creature, and have her experience, than to be the Roman centurion, answered almost before he began to ask? Christ had tried her. She stood the trial. And evidently he admired and loved her. *O woman, great is thy faith; be it unto thee even as thou wilt.* Never distrust him. And you need not misunderstand him as long you have faith to pray like this woman, while not answered. The answer will come if the prayer does not cease. All she asks he gives her. He lays down his own omnipotence at the door of her will—*even as thou wilt.* Till this moment he had been trying her. He had concealed from her his intent. There was that in his heart which she could not read, and which she would certainly have misread if she had attempted to read it from his actions. He had heard her cry and did not answer her a word. He had replied to his disciples as if he did not intend to do any thing for her. He had seen at her at his feet prostrate on the ground, and all but called her a *dog*. She bore it all. Oh, if she had known what was in his heart toward herself, and how he was making an example of her which should encourage ten thousand mothers in prayer long after she was dead and gone, and help them on to Christ and glory after her, how her heart would have leaped for joy! And now the time has come, and the Saviour's heart indulges itself. BE *it unto thee even as thou* WILT.

Happy woman! return to thy happy home. Thy faith has met its reward. Thy daughter is free, and thy faith has led thee to such a knowledge of Christ and his love as shall shine bright and cheering in thy soul to the end.

Happy woman! Such an experience as thine shall raise thee above the gloom of dark Providences in days to come. Thou wilt never distrust the heart of thy Redeemer, let him call thee dog or treat thee as such.

Happy woman! Thou hast learnt the value and the power of prayer. Never wilt thou forget the hour when, low in the dust, thy motherly lips would *not* be still, and then thy admiring Lord let out his heart to thee, *O, woman, great is thy faith; be it unto thee even as thou wilt.* The recollection of that hour shall never fade from thy memory, nor the love of prayer from thy heart. The recollection shall gild thine hour of death, and beyond it sweeten the bliss of thine eternal heaven.

Happy, happy woman! who would not pray like thee; and then, like thee, on the wings of death soar to thy reward? *Be it unto thee even as thou wilt.*

The Blind led in a Way they Knew Not.

I will lead the blind by a way that they knew not; I will lead them in paths that they have not known. I will make darkness light before them, and crooked things straight. These things will I do unto them, and not forsake them.—ISAIAH, xlii. 16.

I WILL *lead them in paths that they have not known*, is a single expression of the text that embodies the idea to which we solicit your attention.

This is the language and promise of the Lord. He here speaks of himself and tells what he will do. The things which he promises to do are things strange and unknown beforehand, and perhaps unanticipated even by the most enlightened. Those for whom the promises are made he will lead, blind as they are, *in a way that they knew not, in paths that they have not known; will make darkness light before them and crooked things straight.* His acts will be superior to all human foresight and calculation, even if faith may have sometimes anticipated their final results. In the particulars in the ways of his providence and grace, God will rise above all previous expectancy. However the result may come within the scope of faith's anticipation, the mode in which that result is reached will always be one of the matters of an unfathomable wisdom.

It is impossible to have a just view of this text without adverting with some minuteness to its original application.

If you recur to the commencement of the chapter, you will at once perceive that it is prophetical of Jesus Christ. *Behold my servant whom I uphold; mine elect in whom my soul delighteth; I have put my spirit upon him; he shall bring forth judgment to the Gentiles;*—*i.e.*, give them a just judgment of God and his salvation, in place of their former errors and idolatries. *He shall not cry, nor lift up, nor cause his voice to be heard in the street. A bruised reed shall he not break and the smoking flax shall he not quench: he shall bring forth judgment unto truth.* If there could be any doubt in reference to this passage as prophetical of Jesus Christ, considered by itself, that doubt could exist no longer after the application of it to him which Matthew has made in the seventeenth verse of his twelfth chapter and onward to the twenty-first. He quotes the whole passage, and interprets it as a prophecy relating to Christ.

The particular matter of the prophecy has respect to the extension of God's kingdom among the Gentiles. Whatever may have caused it—whether it were national pride or spiritual pride, or limited and selfish views which commonly attend a weak faith, or an excusable ignorance—it is unquestionably true that the Jews were prone to consider themselves in their very blood exclusively the people of God and heirs of all the promises, and were extremely slow to believe that the promised Messiah should be the Saviour for any blood or nation except their own. They carried this infirmity along with them from generation to generation. Children inherited it from their fathers, and again transmitted it to their children, to be again transmitted. It was brought down to the times of Jesus Christ; and even after his death had cast light upon the ancient promises, and his resurrection and ascension into heaven had become bold indications that *his kingdom is not of this world;* there lingered even among his disciples a remnant of the ancient prejudice. It was mingled with the very sadness of the crucifixion. They could inquire, *Lord wilt thou at this time restore the kingdom to Israel?* They could lament, *We trusted it had been he which should have redeemed* ISRAEL. *Israel?* There is nothing so monopolizing as a contracted selfishness. It would not only monopolize earth but heaven also. It would limit the Divine benevolence, and in its ignorance make it earthly, expecting only a temporal kingdom for Christ, and that kingdom hemmed in by the narrow limits of Palestine and the veins of the Jewish blood! Poor human nature! How slowly does it let go of pride and earth, and rise to the just conception of the benignity of God! How slowly do even the disciples come to believe that *God has* indeed *granted to the Gentiles repentance unto life!* To correct this Jewish error and expand this contracted selfishness into a brotherly benevolence, and to humble this haughty pride into a humility which should fit the soul for a just acceptance of Gospel mercy, and to put a stop to the power of that worldly disposition which would make Christ's kingdom an earthly kingdom, the prophet was sent to teach that this promised Saviour was the Saviour for all mankind : He shall set *judgment in the* EARTH : *the isles shall wait for his law.* The Father says unto him: *I the Lord have called thee in righteousness and will hold thine hand and keep thee, and give thee for a covenant of the people, for a light of the* GENTILES. A full salvation by Christ for all mankind, provided and proffered, is the burden of the Bible.

Would that all men would accept it. So the prophet

felt. *Hear, ye deaf, and look, ye blind, that ye may see.* So he calls unto them. There is no being so blind as an earthly-minded sinner who wants nothing of God but his temporal benefactions! He misunderstands God, and is ignorant of himself, and misconceives of the way in which God would load him with his precious benefits. In the twenty-first verse the prophet announces, *The Lord is well pleased for his righteousness' sake; he will magnify the law and make it honorable.* Righteousness—salvation from the eternal curse of the law—may be had through the great atonement by every sinner that wants it and will seek it there. If they will *not* seek it, the prophet goes on to say of them: *But this is a people robbed and spoiled; they are all of them snared in holes, and they are hid in prison-houses; they are for a prey, and none delivereth; for a spoil, and none saith, Restore. Who among you will give ear to this? Who will hearken and hear for the time to come?* And then, to convince sinners of the verity of God's threatenings upon the impenitent rejectors of Christ, the prophet appeals to the open and visible acts of God, making his providences here a testimony to what he will do hereafter: *Who gave Jacob for a spoil? and Israel to the robbers? did not the Lord, he against whom ye have sinned? for they would not walk in his ways, neither were they obedient unto his law. Therefore he hath poured upon him the fury of his anger and the strength of battle; and it hath set him on fire round about, yet he knew it not, and it burned him, yet he laid it not to heart.* Even Jacob must become a spoil; even Israel must be swept with the besom of destruction, if they will not obey God and trust in his Son; and the fact—the historical fact—open to the eyes of every body, and known to every historic scholar, that such a calamity has come upon them, and positively forms one of the deepest tragedies of the earth's history, is here appealed to as a motive of dreadfulness to induce sinners not to reject Jesus Christ. If they will reject him, God will reject them in the final judgment, and they shall come to that place where *none delivereth and none saith, Restore.*

But if they will *hear for the time to come,* in the *day of their merciful visitation,* aiming to lay up treasures for a future life, God will bring them, blind though they be, by a way that they knew *not, and will lead them in paths that they have not known.*

This promise, indeed, as we have seen, was originally prophetical of benefit and mercy to the Gentiles through Jesus Christ, but its meaning is no less spiritual than prophetical, and is applicable to every soul as it was to the Gentile nations. This union of prophetical and spiritual meaning forms one of the most striking characteristics, and one of the greatest beauties of the writings of this prophet. The prophetical meaning has been verified by centuries of history; and all that history now is a bold and open evidence that the spiritual meaning shall equally hold good. If the darkened Gentiles have been *led in a way that they knew not,* the darkened sinner, if he will heed God, shall be led so too. God will *make darkness light before him, and crooked things straight, and will not forsake him.*

We propose to give some illustration of this proposition. We propose to show that when God leads men to true religion, he does lead them very differently from any and all of their previous anticipations—*in a way that they knew not.* This is true of every soul, in many respects, and most in the respects which we shall name:

1. The thing, circumstance or truth, whatever it may

be, which first fixes the great matter of salvation upon the mind, and sets out the sinner upon a course of earnest and painstaking inquiry after salvation, is something very different from any thing he has commonly anticipated. There are few of the sober-minded hearers of the Gospel who do not entertain the idea that at some time or other they shall become Christians. They hope for this with a very serious sincerity, if they do not confidently expect it. And it would be something strange, if a busy imagination did not figure the mode in which their anticipation shall begin to be realized. It does figure it. Commonly, if not always, there is some indistinct notion floating over an irreligious man's fancy, that his mind, heart and habits, will undergo yet a religious transformation through the influences of some particular causes which he contemplates. One man has one set of causes, and another, another. The young man—if I may say so—expects time to convert him. He is now, he thinks, at an age for enjoyment. He loves pleasure perhaps; and as his blood leaps in its veins, his muscles are elastic, his bones full of marrow, and his vivid fancy paints the world in beauty before his eye, too attractive and enchanting to be exchanged for any thing else; he has a sort of expectancy, that as years move on they will bring him into a temperament more favorable to religion. They will make him a man—perhaps an old man—and then he thinks religion will be more becoming to him than it is now, and he will be more inclined to it. So he thinks: so he sincerely thinks. But he thinks wrong. He is blind. Can you name any instance—did you ever hear of an instance, of a man who became serious and entered upon the ways of religion, because he had lived up into manhood, or down into the old age when he thought religion would become him, and he would become religious more naturally and easily? Not one. An instance is not to be found. Men are converted sometimes—yea, old men—but not because they have become men, or have grown old. Their youthful expectancy has not been realized, even if they have become Christians. They did not seek God because their anticipated time had come—because they had reached manhood and had become sick of pleasure, or because they had got on further in life, and their knees were stiff, their hands trembling, and their blood chilled with old age. Look around you. You may find such chilled blood and such stiff knees among the hearers of this congregation, and their owners were young once, and *when* they were young, they indulged the same foolish fancy which their juniors indulge now, about their becoming Christians when a few more years should have rolled over their heads. The attention of men is *not* directed to religion, and their efforts embarked to secure it, by the causes which they have anticipated, and sometimes fondly anticipated. If they are led to seek God at all, God *leads them in a way they know not.*

There is no little difficulty, in such a selfish and grasping world as this, in attaining a competency and respectability among men by personal or professional acquisition. And many a man who, at the outset in life, finds he has still these attainments to make, deceitfully but sincerely imagines that this necessary and laborious duty is the only thing which prevents his attention to personal religion. If he shall prosper, if he shall reach, as he hopes he yet shall, the competence he wants, or the skill, or science, or professional standing he wants, and thus no longer have the necessity pressing upon him to devote all his attention and energies to such attainments, he has not a doubt but in that more favorable condition his willing mind will take up the subject of religion in earnest—a subject which he deems important, and of such importance that he is sincerely mournful at finding himself compelled, as he thinks, by worldly urgencies for the present to neglect it. This is common. The picture is no fancy. It is drawn from real life. Society is full of just such men. But look around you again. How do you find it? What do you see? When our young men have got over the pinch and pressure which trouble them so much at the beginning, and have got on a little further in life, and have attained skill, or science, or competence, or character, so that they have no occasion to feel the pinch and pressure so hard upon them, what becomes of their earlier religious anticipations? How is it? Do they become pious? are they any more attentive to religion at sober forty than they were at anxious twenty-one? at established fifty than they were at hoping and busy thirty? No such thing. Their expectancy and purposes have turned out vanity. You know it. You can see them around you. One of the rarest of all religious things is to behold a man betwixt forty and sixty turning his attention to religion. And if you find such an instance at all, his seriousness did not come upon him according to his anticipation (because the world ceased to press him so much). Far from this. I have never yet heard a religious man giving such an account of himself. If one has lent his attention to religion at all, his course has not been according to his calculation, but *God has led him in a way that he knew not.*

It is an unhappy thing that unbelief resorts to deceptive reliances. Many an unconverted sinner, with some conscience and little wisdom, entertains an indistinct hope that in attendance upon the preaching of the Gospel he shall yet hear some such alarming and terrible truth as shall shake him out of his indifference and inattention, and compel him in spite of himself to seek God. He looks for some alarming or persuasive sermon, or some new view of the way of salvation, or some argument better adapted than any he has heard yet to the peculiarites of his mind. His minister has not touched the right chord yet, he says. Such preaching will not move him. Perhaps not; but if this man is ever led to seek the Lord, it will be in a mode much farther off from his own anticipation than from his minister's preaching. It will *not* be by some argument better adapted, nor by some new truth, nor by some more powerful or persuasive sermon. It will be by precisely the same truth which he has heard all his life, aimed at the same chord of his heart, and aimed with the same power and the same persuasions. His calculations will be disappointed. *God will lead him in a way that he knew not;* and he himself will lend his prayerful and earnest attention, if he is ever saved, to those very truths and arguments and persuasions which now he half-mournfully believes can never profit him.

If you were to go round the whole circle of the religious among you and examine the treasured recollections of every heart, you would have another cluster of illustrations about the verity of the text. Not a heart, perhaps, could you find; few at most, if any, which found its seriousness commencing in any way it had ever anticipated. You may find some who carried along with them for years that truth locked up in their own mind which afterward led them to reflection, and all the while they never once thought that that unheeded truth would yet assert its power over them; they were waiting for something else. You may find some who spent years under the entreaties and terrors of God's preached word, and all the time waited for some stronger persuasion, who finally were brought to reflection and led to seek Christ, not by any more tenable or tender persuasion, but because some wise friend or some occurring circumstance induced them *to think*—just to think about duty, destiny, God, and the world to come. You may find multitudes who had never been moved by the most powerful arguments of the ministry, and who, through years of indifference, expected some calamity, some sickness, or the loss of some friend, to lead them to piety, but who buried friend after friend, and were tossed by fever after fever, and yet rose from the bed of illness at one time, and came back from the funeral at another, as unalarmed as ever; but whose attention was finally fixed on religion by some old familiar truth which they had despised a thousand and a thousand times. *God led them in a way they knew not of.*

And it positively does form among Christians one of the most common and most cherished reasons for gratitude to God, that he *did* lead them to reflection, and to conviction, and then to Christ, in a way which still seems strange to them, but good as strange. They recollect it. They love to recollect it. They love to remember it was he who led me to listen to that sermon when I was a careless sinner; it was he who directed my roving eyes to that chapter; it was he who sent me that friend to whisper words of love in mine ears and exhort me to love God in my youth, when the thought had never entered into my heart that that friend would be God's messenger sent to bring me to reflection. *God led me in a way that I knew not of.* Such recollections are common. They are cherished—they are dear to the soul. And they are due to God. He *does* lead us more kindly than we ever anticipated.

The same thing will find illustration in the matter of a sinner's forgiveness. An unforgiven sinner is blind. Unbelief is the most blind of all things. An awakened sinner, who has been told all the truth of the Gospel a thousand times, as plainly as the tongue of man or angel could tell it, does not *see* that his guilt is no barrier against his acceptance in Christ, but, on the contrary, is the very thing which commends him to him, as Christ loves to save sinners just as a merciful and compassionate man loves to relieve the miserable and soothe the sorrowing. Anxious inquirers after salvation are prone to think that they must endure some more painful fears, or attain some righteousness which, somehow, shall be an offset to their guilt, before pardon, God's pardon, can ever reach them. For this they aim. They struggle for deeper convictions. They *go about to establish a righteousness of their own.* They pray even sometimes that the horrors of the pit may get hold upon them, to drive them from sin, and compel them into a holiness which shall secure pardon. All this is in vain. If God leads them they will see it is in vain. *He will lead the blind by a way that they knew not, and they will see that Christ is the end of the law for righteousness to every one that believeth;* that all their own works of penalty or positiveness have nothing to do with their deliverance from the great condemnation, and their justification into life eternal. At the very time when sinners are aiming to work out some righteousness of their own, by reformations, or sacrifices, or the forms of religion, God leads them in an unknown and unexpected way by just showing them that salvation is a gift, that their own works are vanity, and Christ's work is perfect. And that God *has* led them in an unexpected way, their own astonishment is evidence when they have found peace in believing. They did not anticipate finding it so; they did not know that they had only to trust to Christ and live. God showed them this. *He led them in paths that they had not known.*

And here again, to swell and strengthen the evidence, we may remark, that among the sweet and grateful recollections of believers, this leading of God has universally a place. They recognize his hand in turning them to Christ. *He* led me, they say; and they know they say true. He removed my blindness and unbelief, and gave me *faith—such* a faith as my heart never anticipated. *He sent from above; he took me; he drew me out of the deep waters and set me on a Rock.* If the sweetest Christian rememberings are not dreams, God does *lead the blind in a way they knew not.*

The errors of sin are innumerable, and many of them seem to cluster around that period when a sinner would make his peace with God. Even *after* a sinner (according to the language of Paul) has been *slain by the law, i. e.*, perceives he is justly condemned, and perceives, too, that there is proffered pardon for him in the blood of atonement, he still thinks that a demand is made upon his heart which he finds it hard to answer. But he designs to answer it. He hopes that he shall be able yet to offer God a better heart than he can offer him now. For this he struggles and thinks he must.

He supposes that even Christ will not accept him as

he is. Because he perceives his sinfulness of heart, he can not trust, he can not rest, he can not hope. He anticipates a victory over indwelling sin, and when he has gained it he thinks to find a Divine acceptance and enter into peace with God. But if he ever becomes a Christian, God leads him in an unknown way: He makes *darkness light before him, and crooked things straight.* He leads him to despair of any worthiness, and then trust in grace for every thing. And then to his utter astonishment the sinner finds that faith *is itself* the fountain of holiness, and gives rise to the purification from sin, the love of God, the humility, and the victory over the world, which he aimed after in vain without it. He never anticipated this: *God has led him in a way he knew not.*

Perhaps the most remarkable of all illustrations of this truth is to be found in the experiences of Christians. We should naturally expect *them* as being enlightened, and knowing more of God and the ways of God than irreligious men—we should naturally expect *them* to have more correct expectations of God's treatment than other people. But they are slow to learn—they are often disappointed—their anticipations are no foreshadowing of God's treatment of them. Their comforts, their prosperity and strength seldom come to them in the way of their anticipations; yea, *very* seldom, or never. The allotments of Divine Providence which affect them most are such as they little expected. Some of the evils they have suffered were evils which they struggled hard and prayed hard to escape. But God would not let them off. His unseen hand pushed them steadily on right into the cloud and the calamity which they most dreaded. Our Josephs have been sold into Egypt. Our Jobs have been compelled to curse the day in which they were born. Our Davids have been hunted by the foe like a partridge upon the mountains. Our Jeremiahs and Rachels have been compelled to utter moanings of bitterness they never anticipated; and our whole army of Israelites have been turned into the wilderness of sand, and compelled to wander there till they were fit for Canaan. Out of these calamities, out of these griefs and shocks, and shiftings, which they deemed curses, God gave them the most signal of their benefits—teaching them best to know him—to trust him and distrust themselves. *He led them in a way they knew not.* What sinner ought ever to despair?

I wish the converse of this were equally pleasant to contemplate. In some instances it is; but the instances are not common. There are some—yea, there are many with whom God hath dealt more favorable than their fondest expectations. His smiles, his prosperities have attended them all along—and all along their hearts have been overwhelmed, and their souls become more humble and holy, by a sense of the goodness and mercy and bounty of God. They never expected such days of sunshine. They expected storms. They knew—have always known—that no fidelity in them gave them any claim or ground to expect such favors; and now when they contemplate them and look back, and aim to number up their mercies, love, gratitude, faith, fill their hearts—and fill them most of all because God's outward benefits have not led them to forget him. There are some such; yea (let us do religion justice) there are many such. And just like the others, they have been led in paths they never anticipated. Indeed, I believe it is almost universal with Christians when they remember

Divine Providences which have affected them, and especially when they remember how they have been spiritually dealt with—I believe it is almost universal with them to wonder and praise and adore God that he has led them in a way they knew not—*his* way and not their own. Sooner or later he has made darkness light before them, and crooked things *straight; these things has he done unto them, and not forsaken them.*

Some remarks on this subject will close this discourse.

1. God will make himself known as infinitely above us. He outdoes our expectations in good for us, while he worketh in darkness, draweth back the *face of his throne, and spreadeth his cloud upon it.* Be ashamed that you ever distrusted him, ever despaired, ever repined. I summon your whole heart and history as proofs that his way has been better for you than your own.

2. We must have faith. It is indispensable. We cannot walk by sight. His way will be above ours, to us often dark and inscrutable in all its means, but its results will be all that he ever promised, and better than we ever expected.

3. If God is leading us on toward heaven, he will *compel* us to trust him. We are blind. We need him to lead us. Often he confounds our counsels, defeats our purposes, disappoints our hopes, and drives us into difficulties, yea, sometimes into despair, just to bring us to that sweeping and sweet faith which puts every thing into his hands, and trusts him in the dark. By such a faith *darkness becomes light.* It makes us know God better, and Christ better, and grace better. Never point out a way for yourself. Take God's way. Never wait for the circumstances, or sermons, or times which you some-

times think will awaken you. Take God's sermons and God's times as laid down in his Word. Never despond. Despondency is of the Devil. Hope is of God. Trust *him*. Accept his Son, and pillow your aching head upon his promises. Hence,

Finally. This mode of God's leading us is calculated to bring us most near to himself. I appeal to a thousand closets if they have not witnessed the deepest humility and the closest clinging to God, yea, and the sweetest sacredness of communion with him, just when you went there stricken and staggered, helpless, and all but hopeless, and cried your sorrows into your Father's bosom. Go there again. There God waits to meet you. And if you will but leave with him all your difficulties, darknesses and despondencies, your heart whose obstinacy you can not master, and your sins whose malice you can not measure—that is all God wants of you. Trust him. Do nothing but trust him in his Son. He will never forsake you.

Mingled Light and Darkness.[*]

And it shall come to pass in that day, that the light shall not be clear nor dark; but it shall be one day which shall be known to the Lord, not day nor night; but it shall come to pass that at evening time it shall be light.—ZECHARIAH, xiv. 6, 7.

THE first clause of the text is religious. *It shall come to pass in that day that the light shall not be clear nor dark.* It does not refer to the light of the natural heavens. It does not refer to the mere good or evil of the nation. It refers to all there is in the religion of man, and in the things which affect him in the experience of it. His condition is to be one of a mixed character, not wholly good, not wholly evil—not all light, not all dark. This is his state as a religious being, and will be, at least until *there shall be upon the bells of the horses, Holiness unto the Lord.*

This mixture may be seen in several particulars.

1. In the matter of a believer's *holiness.* Therein there is some *light*; but it *is not clear nor dark.* A be-

---

[*] It is due to the Author and perhaps to the reader to note, that the above contains the substance of *two* sermons from this text, leaving out much of the first, which has reference to its prophetical character, and was designed to guard his people against certain false principles of interpreting the prophecies. This will explain the abruptness of the introduction, and any apparent infelicity in opening the subject. In doing this we have done what we know to have been the Author's wish.—EDITOR.

liever has some true conformity to God; but it is not a perfect conformity. He often wonders at himself—at the inconsistencies and contradictions that he finds in his own experience. There are times when it appears to him that his soul never will again be overshadowed with the clouds of doubt and fear which have troubled him, and about which he has shed so many bitter tears in secret, because he could not be more certain that he was a child of God. There are other times when his darkness comes back upon him and he returns to his former doubt, and gropes on in his dismal way of gloom. He does not find within him the established holiness he wants, and which perhaps he once fondly expected. He thought once that if he only had a new heart, so that the impulses of his affections would all conspire with the decisions of reason, the monitions of conscience, and the Word of God, he should not be troubled with sin any more, with a wandering mind any more, with a divided heart any more. But he does not find it so. He *finds a law in his members warring against the law of his mind. The flesh lusteth against the spirit and the spirit against the flesh.* At one moment he can sing, at another he sinks. In his poor soul faith struggles to get the better of unbelief—the love of the world comes up to combat the love of God—impatience assails the submission of his spirit—the love of duty at one time bears sway against avarice, ambition and sensuality; and then again, some of these things come over his spirit, and the love of duty grows cold. There is a strange mixture within him. His heart is inconsistent, his soul unsteady, his way devious, and he can not be ignorant that his holiness is only of an imperfect character. His *light is not clear nor dark.* This is a most accurate description of it; an exact description. He has some light, but then it seems to come to him only as it struggles its way through surrounding darkness. He can not but believe that he loves God some—loves duty some—prizes Christ some—denies self some; but then he can not but perceive some sad deficiencies which hang like a determined darkness over his soul. And what could be a more accurate description of his state than this strange language of the prophet, *the light shall not be clear nor dark?*

I can not affirm it *is* so, but I have reason to entertain such an opinion, that whenever God spares a regenerated sinner upon the earth after the time of his regeneration, such a regenerated sinner will have this checkered experience. His old notions will come back upon him—his old follies and temptations will assail him—his crucified passions will come to life again—his ambition, worldliness, pride, impatience or petulance, will creep into his heart again. He will see that his history is very much made up of instances of falls and recoveries—of departures and returnings—of defeats and victories. If he has none of these diversities, this mingled light and darkness, that is no evidence at all that he is a true Christian. But if he *is* a true Christian, it is probable, it is very probable that the light will grow upon him—that he will come out of his darkness each time more confirmed, and prepared to be more cautious. And it is quite probable, too, that he will know *how* he got out of it, and will look up thankfully toward his God. HE *restoreth my soul. His light shall not be clear nor dark* in respect to the holiness *within him.*

2. This mixture may be seen in a believer's *knowledge.* There is a mixture of clearness and obscurity in the knowledge of God's people which nothing could de-

scribe more perfectly than Zechariah has here described it. They have knowledge, but, in all parts of it, it is limited not only ; but, standing in intimate relation with the things which they know best, there are other things which they do not know at all. You may find examples of this throughout the whole field of religion.

Behold a *disciplined* believer. He is in the furnace. Its fires have long burnt upon him. He *knows* who put him there. He knows, too, that the purpose of it is his purification, that the dross may be separated or burnt up, now when his Lord has come to him and laid his hand upon him and thrust him into the flame, and keeping his eye upon him, *sits as a refiner and purifier of silver*, to mark the time when the work is done, by seeing his own image in the purified soul. All this he knows, and knows, too, that the process will stop when the purpose of it is accomplished, for *God does not afflict willingly*. But *the light is not clear nor dark*. There are other things which he does *not* know. He attempts to know them but he can not find them out. He studies them but they baffle him. He studies them again, but they are as obscure to him as ever. Anxiously he puts the question to his own heart, For what particular sin is it that I am afflicted? What have I done, what have I left undone, for which God is dealing with me? From his heart he carries the question to his God. He asks God to show him for what sin it is that he has plunged him into the furnace. His heart does not tell him—his God does not tell him. He asks again, for he wishes to cast out from his heart whatever sin it may be that keeps the furnace hot upon him But he seldom discovers the particular sin. Sometimes he does, but not often. In error he often hunts for the particular sin. His error is this: he thinks *only* of some particular instance, and thinks *only* of repentance and purification on that point, when he shall be so happy as to discover it. Quite likely he has forgotten how much discipline his heart needs in every part of it, and how God may be disciplining him, not so much for the purification of a particular, as for the purification of the whole.

Consider his case: this man wants to repent of the *particular* sin which has plunged him into the furnace, in order to get out. He wants to find out what part of his heart he has not given to God, and give it. Ah! he has little thought how much his whole heart needs the flame that burns upon it! His *light is not clear nor dark*. He knows he deserves discipline; he does not know for what particular. And when he hunts for the particular he does not know that in the very hunting he is holding back from submission and from God all his heart except that one thing. Let him not suppose it will suffice for him to repent of his avarice, or of his ambition, or his pride, his passion for ostentation, his petulance, his self-conceit, or any other particular, while the general spirit of his soul is all so worldly, and the whole sum of it needs to be purified as by fire. Why does not the man think how, if the whole yields, it carries the particulars along with it, whatever they may be? He can not get off with a few items. God wants the whole. This idea may perhaps make his *light* a little more clear.

Sometimes his obscurity of knowledge lies on another point in the time of affliction. He knows not why God has sent that *particular* affliction on him. Perhaps it is sickness; and why was it not a loss of some property? Perhaps it is a loss of some property; and why was it not sickness? Perhaps the widow has buried her only son; and as she stands and gazes upon his new-made grave, and thinks of the past, and thinks of the future, and thinks of the death-cold heart that would have loved her, and the death-cold hand that would have fed her; there is not a feeling or a principle within her that can tell *why* God has written her childless just after he had made her a widow! Why *this* trial? Why not some other? The light is not clear, if it is not indeed all dark.

Behold a believer, aiming to examine his own heart. He knows something about it. He very well knows its deceitfulness. In his experiences he has found out by many a sad chapter that he can not rely upon it. But it is a wonder to him how its deceitfulness *will* work. It has led him off in a way that he never suspected. The first he knew he had fallen. He did not know that he had wandered from God at all till the season of communion was coming round, and he began to prepare himself to enter again upon those sweet scenes, those covenant solemnities and filial communings with Christ, which have been so delightful to his happy soul. But he can not prepare. God is now a far-off God. He knows him —he believes in him—he wants to love him. Thus he has some *light*, but it is not *clear*. It is not *dark*, for he knows Christ is a full and free Saviour—at any rate, he is so to every body but him. But he seems to be unable now to get near to that far-off God. *Why* does the Saviour hide himself from him? What has his heart done that has displeased his Master? When shall he ever be sure of a heart which has so often wandered? Never, never! His *light shall not be clear nor dark*. Happy he if he can only long and look upward, and, knowing where his security lies, and recollecting past experiences, say, *He restoreth my soul.*

In one word, there is a mixture of clearness and obscurity in almost every part of a believer's knowledge. He *knows in part,* but only in part. He knows God in part, himself in part, sin in part, and heaven in part. But in all his knowledge there is a mingling of clearness and obscurity, and it will remain there till that day comes, *when he shall see as he is seen, and know as he is known.*

We ought, however, to remember that the imperfection of our knowledge results from our creature littleness, and the imperfection of our present state; and that so far as we have any necessity of knowing in order to be saved, our knowledge may be as clear and definite as our capacities will allow. Every man that wishes it may see clearly enough the way to heaven; and it is a strange reason for not going there, because a sinner here can not have all the light of knowledge which he may have there.

3. I name a third particular. The *comforts* of God's people have in them a wonderful mingling of light and darkness—strange vicissitudes of clearness and gloom. It is not all clear day with them. It is not all night. The sun of their joy never shines so brightly but somewhere in their heavens there is some cloud to obscure it; and the night of their sorrow never becomes a night without stars. They may indeed, sometimes—yea often—fail to give the stars any credit, and blame them because they are not the sun; but they never all go out—they are there, if men had eyes.

I scarcely know of any thing in religion which used to seem to me so strange and unaccountable as the fluctuations of a Christian's comforts. He has his comforts, his joys, his bright and happy days. He would not ex change them for all the earth can give. They are most precious. They seem to lift him above earth and time. Happy season, when he can call God his own—Christ his own—heaven his own! The soul seems to have bid adieu to the minor matters of earth, and in a sweep of faith and hope to have compassed the bliss of eternity. Alone sometimes—sometimes at the communion-table—sometimes over God's Word—and in the place of secret meditation and prayer sometimes, when the soul is loosened from the cords of earth and mounts to its home. What an ocean of delight and peace comes into it as the believer hopes and trusts in God, and allows himself to exclaim, *I am my beloved's and my beloved is mine: thy comforts delight my soul.* But how easily are these comforts dashed! how soon gone! The believer has scarcely had time to exclaim, *The Lord is my light and my salvation, whom shall I fear?* has scarcely had time to set his joy to music and sing it to his happy soul,

> "The Lord's my Shepherd—I'll not want,
> He makes me down to lie
> In pastures green; he leadeth me
> The quiet waters by,"

before his song is exchanged for his groaning, *Oh wretched man that I am, who shall deliver me from the body of this death? My grief is heavier than my groaning.* Such vicissitudes used to seem strange to me—the most strange of all inexplicable things in nature or religion. They seem strange still. Even yet *the light is not clear* to me, though not all *dark*. I remember now that the comforts of a Christian are the gentle, tender, sensitive matters of affection—the heart's delicacies as well as delights, and can not bear the rude touch they often meet with. If they could bear it, they would lose their character—just as the rose would lose its character and be rose no longer if it could bear the tread of the wild beast's hoof uninjured. Wounded affection *must* weep. Miserable if it could not. Tears are its solace. More, they are its security, and nurse it into strength. I remember, too, that the blossoms of sweetness and beauty are not the fruit, and when their hues fade and their leaves fall, they may give place to something else as valuable, if not as beautiful as the flowers of the spring-time. Thus I have some *light*, as the text expresses it, which is not all dark—*not day nor night*.

But the alternation of comfort and depression which Christians experience, constitute a chapter of facts which shows the mingled condition of their life, whether we can have *knowledge* of the reasons for it or not. *Weeping may endure for the night; jóy cometh in the morning.* The vicissitudes and changes are great. Sometimes they are sudden. The song of the morning is exchanged for that song of the night whose grief can be depicted by nothing but the night's gloom, and which the pensive and sad-hearted believer will not consent to sing only amid the sympathies of midnight.

4. A fourth particular, and I will leave this clause of the text. I name the *condition of life*. Do not fear that I am going to make too much of it. In my opinion we fail in few things as Christians, more than we fail of fitly noticing the changes we pass through as God is leading us on. However this may be, there are strange minglings of light and darkness in our condition. Our Samsons are shorn of their strength, and the victor of Gaza becomes a prisoner in the lap of Delilah. Our dethroned Davids are hunted like a partridge upon the mountains. Our

Josephs are imprisoned. Our Jobs are stripped. Our Jeremiahs utter doleful lamentations. Our Pauls and Barnabases, having the offer of even Divine worship in one city, are stoned from another. And so fluctuating and uncertain is the condition of life here, that no mortal can be found whose biography has any considerable resemblance to his anticipations; his life has not carried out the plans of his youth. Amid the remarkable changes which affect our condition, nothing seems *more* remarkable than the nearness of our light and darkness to one another. At the very time when one of us is congratulating himself upon his prosperity, darkness comes upon him from some unexpected quarter. " I never once thought that my child could die," said one of the most prosperous and wealthy inhabitants of this city, when his darling lay a corpse in his house.

At the very time when another of us sees nothing in our condition but darkness and gloom, light beams out upon us from a spot where we could not have expected it. The lost child becomes the salvation of the parent. The lost fortune is more than compensated for by ensuing contentment, when the curse of avarice is dismissed from the heart. We are knocked about in the world. We have joys and sorrows. Our condition is shifting, fluctuating, varying: It is not *clear nor dark—not day nor night*. And there is scarcely a believer among us who is not compelled, amid this mingling of light and darkness, to recognize the immediate hand of his God and exclaim, *Thou hast lifted me up and cast me down*. To-day our condition is happy: to-morrow it is miserable. Now Providence smiles upon us: no man can tell how soon it will frown. We sing of mercy in the morning; in the evening we would gladly exchange our sorrow for that of the wretchedest heart that bleeds. Amid all this mixture of good and evil, we can not understand why it is so. Possibly we may understand afterward, but God will not be understood by us at present. *His way is in the sea, and his path in the great waters, and his footsteps are not known.* How needful is faith! What a blessing it is—what a comfort amid such a mixture of noon and midnight in our condition! *The light of our day is not clear nor dark*—and yet it seems to me there could not be much clearness at all in it, if we had no faith.

I leave this clause of the text. For I think the very intent of the next clause is to conduct us to faith. Examine it. *But it shall be one day which shall be known to the Lord, not day nor night.*

Standing amid the mingled, uncertain, strange and apparently contradictory things which affect us here in this life, I can not conceive how any reasonable being can have any satisfaction or rest to his thinking soul only as he carries his world and his condition in it up to his God. Zechariah meant to have him do so. And hence, after he has mentioned to us the mingled clearness and obscurity of our state, he immediately points us to one who can understand it: *It shall be one day which shall be known to the Lord, not day nor night.* Not day nor night in itself—not *day nor night to us*. In itself it is of a mixed character. To us it is mixed. Strange picture to our eyes! Lights and shades blend together on the canvas of human life, run into one another, struggle with one another; light lies where we expected darkness, and darkness spreads on the very spot where we looked for light. We can not understand it. God can. Happy for us to know it. We can now turn over the checkered scene into his hands. It is to him all *one day.* He sees no darkness in it. It is all light to Him. All alike light—all *one*. He has *one* intent in all the dispensations which affect us. All our changes are formed on one plan and have one design, and conspire to the production of one great end. Our checkered state is *one day known unto the Lord*.

In our changeful and mixed condition here, where we have some light and some darkness, it is a high privilege to know that an infinite wisdom has made it thus. Sometimes a believer can not take a single step beyond this knowledge. He has had checkered and mixed experiences. He has *sung of mercies* sometimes, but has been compelled also to *sing of judgment*. He has had inward comforts of soul in exercises of hope and peace and joy sometimes, but his comforts have withered away out of his heart. At one season he thinks God treats him as a child; at another he thinks he treats him as a rebel. This all seems strange to him—his mingled comforts strange—his heart strange—his word strange—his furnace strange, as its fires burn upon him. What shall he do, what *can* he do, but to turn this checkered world and his checkered experience in it over upon the hands of his God? "He knoweth what he is about;" *he knoweth the way I take, and when he hath tried me, I shall come forth as gold.* I think it happens not very unfrequently that a believer gets into such straits and perplexities, into such embarrassments about doctrine, or duty, or circumstances, that it is utterly impossible for him to get along without despair, unless he is enabled to exercise this sweeping and universal faith in God which utters no complaints, and asks no questions. He has not God's eye, nor God's hand. He can not use God's mind, nor *thunder with a voice like him*. And therefore he can not grapple with the strangeness of his circumstances. But when he can have a sweeping and universal faith—and especially when his faith can see the eternal son as acting for him, and suffering for him, and reigning for him, as *all power in heaven and earth are given unto him;* then surely he can see all he wants to see, and his faith shall bring him a light to gild the edges of his clouds in the darkest day that ever was: and *it shall come to pass that at evening time it shall be light.*

This is the last clause of the text: *At evening time it shall be light.*

I do not understand this meaning that the *evening* or night shall be turned into day. However true it may be that the faith we just mentioned has power to gild the darkest night of a believer, my opinion is that the reference of the text is to another thing. The evening is the close of the day. The experience of the day is then past; its hours are gone and its labor done. By the course of nature we should expect the coming on of darkness. By the promise of grace there shall be the coming on of light. And you may apply this interpretation to any item in a believer's mingled experiences of *clearness* and darkness. Light shall come at THE END, *at evening time.*

Take a believer in his mixture of mercies and afflictions. When does it become *light* to him? Does the light come hand and hand with his sorrow? Does it beam upon the first tears he sheds? Does he know God better and rejoice in him the more as soon as the rod of affliction is laid upon him? No. He must go through the scene; he must wear out the hours of his day of discipline; he must endure to the end of it. And if he does endure just at the time when the shades seem to him to be gathering thick around him, and the last ray of his joy and hope seems about to be quenched, at the *evening time it becomes light*. It is *afterward*, when affliction has wrought the *peaceable fruits of righteousness*, that *light arises in darkness*.

Take a believer in his perplexities. Doctrines trouble him. He has some flashes of light, but the *light is neither clear nor dark*. He gropes. His soul staggers. Doubts harass him. Unbelief besets him. Obscurity hangs every where, around God, Christ, election, atonement, accountability, freedom of the will. He must walk in this perplexity till he has gone through the day of his enmity and become a child of God, or gone through the day of his error, and learnt that he can not know every thing, and has become willing to let God be God. At that evening time, just when he seemed to be coming into an entire night, at the *evening time* it becomes light—light in a way he never expected—his very darkness itself becomes his light.

Take a believer in his season of diminished comforts. One after another his joys have gone out. His hope is dimmed. His heart is broken. His God has forsaken him. It has grown darker and darker with him, and, just when his crushed heart is sinking as he has gone through this day of discipline, and he is expecting night to close in upon him, *at the evening time it is light*. He sees it. Hear him: *The bruised reed will he not break; the smoking flax will he not quench*.

Take the believer on the bed of death. He has struggled along through his dim day of life, lighted a little sometimes, and sometimes walking in darkness, and through *fear of death all his life-time subject to bondage*, till the *evening time* has come. At this *evening time it shall be light*. I have often noticed it in the dying members of this church. They have died in a blaze of light—died more happy than they lived, and wondering at their own composure and faith. The hour they most feared has become more light than any before it, and old Simeon exclaims: *Lord, now lettest thou thy servant depart in peace, for mine eyes have seen thy salvation.* God replies to the departing soul: *The sun shall no more be thy light by day, neither for brightness shall the moon give light unto thee; but the Lord shall be unto thee an everlasting light and thy God thy glory. Thy sun shall no more go down, neither shall thy moon withdraw itself; for the Lord shall be thine everlasting light, and the days of thy mourning shall be ended.* Happy spirit! depart to thy happy home: IT HATH *come to pass that* thine *evening time has become light.*

Contentment.

I have learned, in whatsoever state I am, therewith to be content.
PHILIPPIANS, iv. 11.

THIS is an expression of Paul. But we should misconceive the nature of it, if we should deem him speaking in the character of an apostle, rather than in the character of a believer. He utters this expression only as a Christian; and is therefore an example to all Christians who came after him to the end of time. Let us therefore consider this text in a personal and practical manner, and aim to draw lessons from it for our instruction, direction, and comfort.

We name to you three general ideas as the three heads of this sermon.

I. The nature of this contentment.
II. The mode of its acquisition.
III. The reasons which enforce it.

I. The nature of contentment can be apprehended more easily than defined. Every body knows what it means; and yet it is of such a nature that the moment we attempt to explain it, we are in danger of diminishing the impression of its significance. It is not one of the distinct and separate sensibilities of the heart, standing by itself and to be examined and understood *alone*, so much as it is a general sensibility which mingles with and tempers all others—which spreads its cast and character over the whole. It is not the rock on the landscape nor the rill—it is not the distant mountain of fading blue which loses its head in the heavens—it is not the tree, or the flower, or the contrast between light and shade, or that indescribable something which seems to give it life, as if the grass grew, and the flowers breathed, and the winds were singing some song of pleasure or sighing some mournful requiem. It is none of these. These can be more clearly described. But it is rather that softness, that mellow light, which lies over the whole—which sleeps on rock, and river, and tree, on the bosom of the distant mountain, and on the bosom of the humble violet that blushes in the sweetness of its lowly valley.

Content is a general cast of sensibility which lies all over the heart. It has a depth and an extent of significance to which many minds are strangers. We can not spare time for a full examination of its nature. We only mention items enough to give some definitiveness to our apprehensions, and some direction to minds disposed to contemplate the subject more maturely. Suffice it to remark:

1. That contentment is opposed to dissatisfaction, murmuring, complaining, and repining. It is a submissive spirit that yields to the necessities or hardships of life, and *by* submission disarms them of more than half their power. Content is the child of reason, not of fancy. It is the companion of conscience; and if it does sometimes sigh, it will neither complain nor despair. It is united with too much good sense to aim after impossibilities, or to increase the infelicities of life by an unceasing fretful-

ness and dissatisfaction. Its foundation is laid in justice if not in faith. A just mind is necessary to it—a mind that sees things as they are instead of seeing them through the distorting instrumentality of a jaundiced eye; which makes and unmakes facts as if they were fancies, and which works up fancies into stable and melancholy realities. Such a just mind seldom fails to be a contented mind. It is the *in*justice always accompanying an ungodly disposition which originates, and then increases and perpetuates most of the discontent which torments, so unnecessarily, the hearts of the worldly. The injustice of mind accompanying pride, for example, often makes the proud man a peevish man; the injustice accompanying ambition often makes the ambitious man petulant; and so in all the errors of sin. The false notions—the unjust estimations lay the foundation of no small part of the discontent which fills the world. A strict justness of mind, a just judgment, would undo more than half this mischief. And when *faith* fixes the just balances wherein the mind weighs the subjects of its contemplation, then it is that complaining ceases to utter its ill-natured syllables, murmuring learns to be still, and repining exchanges the scowl of gloom for the smile of gladness. Contentment is incompatible with a fixed, and cherished, and unhappy dissatisfaction.

2. It is *not*, however, indifference or stupidity. Indeed, it is very distant from both.

There is a species of indifference among men which often passes for contentment, but which is not even a respectable counterfeit of it. It originates not from seeing things justly, but from *not* seeing them at all. Minds too sluggish to think and hearts too insensible to feel—souls too selfish to do either, become half indifferent to the circumstances of life; and superficial thinkers imagine such persons to be content, while in reality they are merely stupid. All the contentment there is about them consists in a lacking of sense and sensibility; they have neither sensibility nor sense enough to *be* dissatisfied and complain. They are too selfish to be aroused at all. They are incapable of any just appreciation of a better condition, and they are too groveling to have even virtue enough to be discontented and fretful. Discontented and fretful they *would be*, if they were not, at once, little in mind, and incapable of any strong or tender emotion.

True contentment is very different from this. It is not stupidity. It is not a negative but a positive virtue. It can feel, it can hope, and it can sigh. But its feelings are not allowed to run into complaining and fretfulness, and its sighs are often exchanged for smiles more congenial to it. If it can not have what it would, it will not, by cherished dissatisfaction, brooded over and nursed into gloominess, turn all its means of enjoyment into materials of misery; but will the rather brighten their influence by gratitude and a sweet submission. Paul was not a man of indifference; nor was he lacking in sensibility. He was a man of energy and prayer. He had wants and he felt them keenly. His contentment never degenerated into a selfish stupidity, and he could not *be still* as long as there remained a height of holiness yet to be reached or a sinner on earth yet unconverted to Christ. His perceptions were quick, and his sensibilities were keen and strong. He felt his trials *as* trials, and his contentment was something *more* than the schooling of a cold philosophy. It was a glad submission to the Divine will—a submission, in which sensibility lost none of its tenderness, none of its readiness, none of its strength. And his contentment, entirely superior to dullness or apathy, was that exalting and triumphant principle which disarmed affection and made grief a joy. If his trials *were* clouds upon his heavens, his contentment was the deep sun-light in which they bathed; and, just like the clouds of an evening sky, they made the heavens more beautiful than if no clouds were there.

3. Contentment has no kindred with a dark *fatalism* which deems all things fixed, and not to be affected by the energies of determination and faith. There is no such fixedness; and no soul (out of the mad-house) ever yet believed there *was*, except as the half-formed belief fell in with the cherished inclinations of its sinfulness. Nobody's fatalism keeps him from getting out of the way of the wild beast which would devour him, or out of the fire which would consume him. If one *says* that he believes in such a fixedness of destiny, that his contrivances and his energy can avail him nothing, just do him the credit to believe him a liar if you do not wish to think him a fool. His own life, all his plans, and all his actions contradict his declaration.

But when the calls of imperative duty come into conflict with the desires of a cherished sinfulness, it is no uncommon thing for a foolish sinner to aim to excuse himself from the unpleasant duty by a sort of half-formed idea, a sort of foggy and silly notion, that his plans and actions can alter nothing. The real meaning of all this is, that he is too lazy to plan or act at all; or the duty to which he is called is contrary to his sinful inclinations in some other way. And he calls his sinful indulgence by the name of contentment—mis-names his vice a virtue—and neglect his duties simply because he loves his sins. This has no resemblance to contentment. It is directly its opposite. It is *dis*content with duty, with truth, with reality, with God, with all that is good and all that ought to be desirable.

The contentment of Paul was utterly unlike this. It was not a contentment which let the future take care of itself, lest action for it should cost some energy and some hardship. It was a contentment to work, to plan, to pray, to traverse nation after nation, to navigate one sea after another, hunted from one city to fly to another and then another, as duty called him, and wherever he could hear of a sinner that had never listened to the gospel of Christ. And when the event *had* come, and by its occurrence he knew what *was* the will of God (which is the only mode in which human nature can know), then, be the event what it would, or press hard upon him as it might, he submitted to it. He did not submit beforehand because he did not *know* beforehand; and if he had undertaken a submission then, he might have submitted wrong—to the wrong thing. In whatsoever state I AM, says he, in the present tense. He was content to do as God bade him, and then to take what God sent him; and he would *bear* stripes, bonds, imprisonment, scourging, *any thing* when it had come upon him, and he thus knew it *was* the will of God. But he did not court these things, he did not stand still and see them coming and never move a step. I appeal to Cæsar, says he, when, standing before one unjust tribunal, he found himself in danger of getting into the hands of a worse one. Indeed there never *was* a more laborious, energetic, and prayerful man. At least the world has seen few like him. He traversed Asia, and when he wanted to go to Europe it was not that he was disposed to be a fashionable minister, but that he might preach the Gospel in Spain also. I wish he had more followers. (Romans, xv. 28.) His contentment was just with the ascertained will of his Master—with work, with duty—and then, with whatever events might befall him at Jerusalem or at Joppa.

Let nobody think that either indulgence or laziness is contentment. Let nobody call that disposition a virtue, or think it a blessing, which will aim to shelter its meanness under the name of content. Let nobody deceive himself with the idea that he is a contented man because he feels an indisposition to the duties needful to throw a security around the future. Be it remembered, *whatsoever a man soweth*—himself, by his own choice and act—*that shall he also reap*. And let him be *content* with that principle of the Divine administration over both worlds.

II. The second general idea is the mode of its acquisition. Contentment *is* an acquisition. The text implies this: *I have learnt*, says the Apostle. He had learnt something. He did not always know it. It was a lesson, and he learnt it *as* a lesson. He may have learnt it with some difficulty: I believe he did. It may have cost him many a struggle: I believe it did. His deep and strong sensibilities, so often crossed, and so much torn and wounded, could not have been soothed down into a quiet satisfaction without many a heart-ache. And if it were possible to trace his experiences, we should probably find among them such things as the following:

1. A sensibility to the Divine hand. He saw *God* in his trials—in his hunger and stripes, and bonds and im-

prisonments—in his storms and shipwrecks. *Thy will be done*, said he, as any new storm burst upon him.

It is a very different thing to have a submissive heart under the ills of life, through a blessed realization that an infinite wisdom appoints them, from what it is to have a stupid heart or a sullen one. If we have no faith in God, no apprehension of his control, no confidence in his rectitude, truth and faithfulness; our submission will just become sullenness, our fortitude fatalism, and our patience stupidity at best. It was not so with Paul. He saw God in every new disaster that befell him, and in every field and every friend that smiled upon him. Back of the disaster, and guiding its movement, and ordaining where it should fall, he saw the God of all wisdom and all goodness—the God of the promises.

2. He *hoped* in God. Beat as it might, he knew the storm was God's storm, and he would stop it when he pleased. Heave as they might, he knew the surges that swelled on the troubled ocean of life could never heave him from his anchorage; he had that *hope which is an anchor of the soul, sure and steadfast, and which entereth to that within the vail.* Hope is natural to us. Man was made to hope. Hope is no implantation of sin. It belonged in Paradise, and it belongs in heaven now, where souls redeemed, sending forward their contemplations down into the remotest distances of an unmeasured eternity, find them lighted up with the brightness and glory of a yet unattained measure of bliss. No man need think to be contented without hope. He can not be. And no wise man will long be contented without hope in God. We want something to cling to which will not give way, which shall comport with our imperishable nature, and, amid the crosses and disasters of life, bring

a light to gild them from the effulgence of immortality. Paul had this hope. He used it. Says he: *I know whom I have believed, and am persuaded that he is able to keep that which I have committed unto him against that day.* He might well be content.

3. He had his *treasure* in heaven. He perceived that earth was inferior. *None of these things move me,* says he, *so that I might finish my course with joy.* To finish life rightly, to use it justly to the end, was of more moment to him than to enjoy all that earth could heap upon him. With heaven in his eye—a heaven seen more clearly often in dark days than in bright ones—the glooms of earth had but little effect upon him. Indeed, they often appeared to heighten his rapture of faith: *Our light affliction which is but for a moment—light!—a moment!* strange words to a worldly mind! Yet all true. Burdens *are* light—life is a moment when faith penetrates futurity and draws contentment from that ocean life where lies a *far more exceeding and eternal weight of glory.*

It is not to be expected that there will be much contentment amid the distresses of this life, if indeed there will be any amid its richest joys, aside from those exercises of mind which anticipate something better to come. Among all the favored children of pleasure, of prosperity, health, abundance, and honor, you can scarcely discover a contented mind. Something *more* is wanted. Some competitor is to be out-stripped, some favorite point is to be gained, some darling desire is yet to be gratified. *Contentment* is not yet reached. Such is human nature; and such it will ever remain. A defect marks all the earthly attainments. They may amuse for a moment; but they do not satisfy the soul. Something beyond them is needed. And when the eager mortal attempts to make deeper the bowl of his earthly pleasure, or add one pleasure to another, he carries along with him the same eager craving and heart-emptiness which made him discontented at first. Much less can there be much human contentment amid the distresses and disasters of life if the mind is confined to earthly contemplations merely. We need something beyond. We need to be able to carry forward our dark and distressful scenes to another life, and behold them bathed in the sun-light of an expected heaven. Contentment is heaven-born if it lives at all, and it needs to be baptized with waters taken from the river of life. Paul was contented, not as a man of earth, but as a candidate for immortality.

4. He had *experiences* which *tried* him. His content did not all spring from tuition, nor from faith alone, nor from hope alone, nor from heavenly-mindedness alone, nor from all these together. Though he was a Christian and an Apostle, he was still a man, and possessed both the affections and infirmities of our common humanity. And in the first stages of his trials, it is extremely likely that his sorrows weighed heavily upon him and his circumstances cost him many a tear. But when he would not give back from duty, and would not sit down in despair, but just met the waves of trouble as they came, he found he could breast them—he found the dark waves, so terrible in the distance, brightened up as he rushed to meet them—he found the Christ in whom he trusted not only more near but more tender also in the tempest than in the calm; and these *experiences* just gave strength and sweetness at once to the contentment he cultivated. Hence the *second* trial became lighter than the *first*, and he met it more willingly. He learnt where his strength lay, and learnt to know that he might draw

upon the exhaustless fountains of God. He learnt to be more sensible of his weakness; and, standing amid a whole army of difficulties, he could say: *When I am weak, then am I strong: I can do all things through Christ strengthening me.*

There may be some Christian graces which have all their excellences by the direct implantation of God. But if there are any such, contentment is not one of them. It belongs to another class. *Experience* is needful for its excellence, if not for its existence. This experience will accomplish two benefits for every tried believer.

First, It will give *confidence* to faith.

Second, It will give it *extension.*

Faith is itself the fundamental principle on which all true contentment rests. And as experience tries the good and ill of life, it will most assuredly confirm faith because it will find the promises of God *realized* and demonstrated to be true by the successive chapters of a believer's own biography; and thus he will be ready to trust God in the future, more wholly and unreservedly than he trusted him in the past. Experience will come up from the remembered past to rebuke unbelief and fear, to sooth despondency, and encourage the timidity of the staggered heart. The remembrance of the Red Sea will give confidence in the desert, and the recollection of the victory over Amalek will prepare for the conquest of Canaan. And many a David called upon to battle where his faith otherwise would shrink, will move to the unequal contest with the war-cry of experience: *God, who delivered me out of the hands of the lion and the bear, will deliver me out of the hands of this Philistine.* It is one benefit of experience that it confirms faith—that fundamental principle on which all true contentment rests.

But (second) what experience most does for contentment lies more in the particulars than in the sum of life; it lies in those thousand nameless and indescribable annoyances, which are far more apt to awaken discontent than are any of those great calamities which we muster our powers to endure. And the *mode* in which experience fosters content seems to be very much this: it gives a detail and a minuteness to the exercises of faith of which the inexperienced never dreamed. It is experience which expands the light of the promises, and makes it shine just as brightly on the minor annoyances of life as on its heaviest calamities. It is experience which makes us believe that our God will allow us to lean upon him in our *smallest* difficulties—in those little and nameless troubles which have their power over us quite as much from our nerves and our caprice of disposition as from their own magnitude or strength. It is experience which will convince us that whatever affects *us* is regarded by our heavenly Father, and that his ear is as open to the half-formed sigh of a pensive breast as to the shriek of anguish or the deep wail of despair. It is experience which constitutes the field on which we may look back after we have traveled over it, and see at every step the memorial way-mark with the inscription, *Hitherto hath the Lord helped.* And beyond all this, it is experience which makes us know that the manna of the wilderness will more than compensate for the corn of Egypt; that God's deliverances are so precious that it was good for us to have needed them. Hence we shall be content. In straits and difficulties we shall learn to confide. The wilderness of sand will be better than the fertility of Egypt, because, if there were no wilderness there would be no pillar of cloud and no pillar of fire—emblems of a present God. When by experience we have these emblems, and by the recollections of experience have the proofs of the faithfulness which they betoken, contentment rises to its dignity and strength, and what is better, retains all its sweetness and the simplicity of its infant confiding. Then come disaster, come shame, come pain, come what will, nothing *can* come but God will come with it. The thunder of the storm-cloud will be his voice, the lightning will be the opening of his eyelids, he will be enthroned upon the storm and ride upon the wings of the wind. And then if the sea roar, its deep growl shall be an anthem to God; if the conflagration rage, we shall remember that *burning coals go forth at his feet;* if the poisoned arrow of affliction pierces our heart, we shall be content, because, by our own experience, we have learnt that the *balm of Gilead* shall stanch the blood and stop the poison. Yea, *although the fig-tree shall not blossom, neither shall fruit be in the vines, the labor of the olive shall fail and the fields shall yield no meat, the flock shall be cut off from the fold, and there shall be no herd in the stalls*, yet we shall be content, for we shall *rejoice in the Lord and joy in the God of our salvation: The Lord shall be our strength, he will make us walk upon our high places.*

It would be interesting, if we had time, to trace the history of contentment as it has existed in numerous instances among men. In all these instances we should find it feeble at first, but nurtured into strength by the successive lessons of a checkered experience. Amid the results of such an experience we should find an increase of gratitude, of humility, of courage, of fortitude, of patience, of gentleness—in one word, of all the graces of the Spirit; and should find this increase making Christ more near, and prayer more precious, as trials fall to the lot of the people of God. Every one of the experiences of faith, especially amid trials, tends to the acquisition of the spirit of the text: *I have* LEARNT *in whatsoever state I am therewith to be content.*

III. The third idea we proposed upon this theme was the *reasons which enforce* contentment. We will hastily name a few of them—only a few.

One reason for contentment with our state is to be found in the *Power* which has allotted it to us. God reigns. Though the heart of man deviseth his way, the Lord directeth his steps. There is an overruling power which is not to be forgotten. There is an inscrutable wisdom at work which has seen fit to make one man poor and another man rich, one sickly and another strong, one happy in all things to enjoy, another the miserable child of disappointment and sorrows. Aside from this unseen power, no man carves out his own destiny. If he did, he need not thank God for mercies, nor pray to him in his calamities. This unseen power never so rules him, as either to frown upon his virtues, or to excuse his indolence of body or mind. But it does so rule him, that very often his disasters could not have been avoided; and very often his means of an earthly felicity come rather from the bounty of God than from his own wisdom and skill. If man's troubles here have *not* arisen from his own follies and sins, but have been portioned out to him by a wisdom beyond his power of scrutiny, how unreasonable for him to be discontented with a dispensation whose mastery he can not understand, and whose wisdom and goodness he can not impeach! If his troubles here are the legitimate fruit of his own doings, how reasonable for him that he should be willing to reap as he has sown, and not murmur, because that economy of righteousness has not been overthrown, because he himself chose to be unrighteous! It is a privilege to know that a larger wisdom encompasses our own—a superior power rules over us. It is a privilege to be submissive and contented: the Lord reigneth, let the earth rejoice. Amid the night of storms, it is a privilege to realize that the night and the storm are God's, and submissively wait for the returning sunshine of a cloudless noon.

How much more just and more happy we should be, if we fitly felt that we had all from God—if we realized that the sun is God's; the clouds which canopy us, the winds which fan us, the fields which put on their dress of green now, to be exchanged for their dress of gold under the autumnal suns soon—that the strength of our muscles, the sagacity of our mind, our breath, our blood and our bones, are all of God. What are we that we should allow our discontent to criticize his dispensations, and wish to wrench out of his hands the helm of the universe? Discontent is an injustice—an injustice done in high quarters. Take your own place, dependent worm, mortal of a day, the creature and the care of God, whose providence regards *the young lion's roar,* and feeds the *young ravens when they cry,* and paints with the touches of his own pencil *the lilies that toil not, neither do they spin!* Take your own *happy* place, just as happy as it is right, thou dependent worm, thou mortal of a day, thou creature not able to *add one cubit to your stature;* and from the lowly spot of your contentment, do God the justice and yourself the kindness to believe in the wisdom of his dispensations.

2. Most of the things in this life which make contentment a difficult virtue are either the offspring of our own follies, or are sent as acts of discipline for our good. It would be unreasonable to murmur at those infelicities which we have brought upon ourselves, and which often spring up as a warning to keep us from those follies which may be still more ruinous to us. Let us be content that we are warned before we are ruined—that we are pained before we are punished—that we *have* in this life some tokens of God's disapproval of sin, so pointed and so painful, that we are compelled to heed them, before our sins have ruined us for ever. Let us be content, when the narrow limits of an earthly bliss are made thus narrow, on purpose to check the cupidity of our worldliness and turn our eager longings toward the boundless bliss of a world of immortality. Let us be content when the discipline of affliction is sent to fit us for a world that affliction never visits; and especially, when heaven smiles on us brightly, in proportion as the world frowns on us darkly; and while God, visiting our iniquities with stripes, does not take from us his loving kindness, nor suffer his faithfulness to fail. It is a small thing to have some tribulations on earth when the good of them may be eternal.

We are greatly ignorant of ourselves. We can not tell what our virtue could endure. *Lead us not into temptation*, is one of the wisest prayers ever breathed. The very benefactions which our discontent longs for, might be the veriest curses to us. The world is full of examples of such results. Humility in the valley becomes pride on the hill-top; and coolness of judgment is exchanged for the heat of passion and the tumults of indulgence. The steadiness which could stand upon the ship's deck, could *not* stand upon the topmast, when the vessel reels upon the dashing waves of an ocean life. The virtue that has flourished in retirement, has drooped and withered in high station. David fell, *not* when he leaned upon the crook, or fled in the wilderness, or whirled the sling of the shepherd boy: he fell amid the pomp and pride of the royal residence, where his own will was law, and where passion became too powerful for his virtue. It had been well for Solomon, both his character and his conscience as well as his dynasty, if he had never risen to such an eminence as to aspire to connection with the royal family of Egypt. The things which discontent wants are very generally dangers, and when God denies them, it is very generally a discipline for our good. Such things loom largely in the distance—they are ashes as we touch them. If we had them *all*, they would not give us holiness or faith or peace with God. They would expose us to the roughest storms and the hardest thunder, and we should fall as the oak breaks on the hills at the sweep of the tempest, while the violet of the valley sleeps lowly and is safe.

3. It is no small reason for our being content, since content at once enhances our enjoyments and diminishes our miseries. Often, it is not the bitterness of the bitterest cup that gives us so much trouble as the discontent with which we drink it. The *discontent* is the misery, rather than the contents. The discontent is itself the wormwood and the gall. Evils become lighter by bearing them with patience. Discontent poisons our benefits.

4. Discontent tends to defeat the designs of affliction. However benignant may be the disposition which dis-

ciplines us with the rod of sorrow, the discipline will be very much in vain, or worse than vain, by impatience under it. The benefits of afflictive discipline lie very much in such things as humility, submission, lowliness of mind, deadness to the world, deeper sense of sin, and more gratitude for the mercies which discipline has left to us. All these things are incompatible with a discontented spirit. Such a spirit is proud, selfish, worldly, ungrateful. It rebels against the strokes it bleeds under, and the pain of the rebellion added to the pain of the bleeding makes no beneficial impression upon the sufferer. Moses, at the waters of Meribah, was a very different man from Job when calamities were let loose upon him; and it was a very different thing for him to find his grave before he entered into Canaan, from what God gave to Job when his last days were loaded with benefits. It is bad enough to have *mercies* lost upon us; it seems to be still more mournful when discontent robs us of the benefits of tribulation.

5. The miseries of this life are sufficiently deep and extensive. It seems unnecessary to add to them. At any rate the very feeling of a discontented disposition embodies itself in the idea that our troubles are too many. How unreasonable then to add to them! Discontent does not diminish them. It only adds weight to the very burden it deplores. It deepens the midnight of our darkness; it puts out the light of our stars; it makes our mind pour contempt upon the goodness which we have to enjoy, undervaluing it as if it were nothing, simply because some evils afflict us. And not only so, but the discontent, be it remembered, brings that ONE species of affliction which NEVER CAN tend to our good. The discontent must *cease* before the soul can be benefited by trials.

6. Such trials may well be borne contentedly, because then the soul of the sufferer may receive *new lessons about God.* Never, never beneath the skies does God give to our experience, amid our mercies and delights, such precious enjoyments of himself as he furnishes in the night of our trials. Then we can lean upon him only. Other resources are cut off. Other friends can not reach the deep recesses of the heart where grief and pain find their home. But God reaches them. He lays his benefits upon the home of pain. He lets us lean upon him, and loves to have us, and never gives way beneath our burden. He stands by us in the night of trouble, and whispers to our trembling soul, *Fear not, thou worm Jacob; when thou passest through the waters I will be with thee, and through the floods they shall not overflow thee; when thou passest through the fire thou shalt not be burnt.* It is not so much what we learn to know of God in the sunshine as in the storm that attaches us to him. We know his *heart* better in days of calamity. We take a deeper view of his character in times when we can do nothing but trust him. And it is the recollection of what he has done for us in such dark seasons that enables us to say afterward, when we see the clouds gathering in the time of trouble, *he* shall hide me in *his* pavilion, in the secret of his tabernacle shall he hide me. The best and the sweetest views of God are taken in days of trial. We may well be content that they should come.

7. There is a very ordinary discontent among men of the world which does them a very bad service. It *adds to the power of their worldliness of spirit.* It keeps them from attention to the concerns of a future life. Not satisfied, and fixing in their mind no limit where they would be satisfied, they take their discontent as their counsellor,

and devote their minds, time, talents, heart, *every thing*, to attain something of earth which shall content them. Young men who have no interests secured for immortality, con their eager schemes for mortal interests, and devote to them energies enough to have saved a thousand souls, because they can not be content with such things as they have or such as they ought to desire. Their discontent gives the world a new power over them, and they put on its yoke and yield to its lash—the slaves of a dreadful tyranny. Old men, yet unsealed by the Holy Spirit for their immortal life, not yet content, cling to their earthly scheming, and in the very work-shop where their shroud is weaving drive their eager plans to make gain from the manufacture! Horrid plans! Unhappy mortals! Accursed discontent! It cheats heaven! It gives the world dominion! How much better the lesson I have learned, in whatsoever state I am, therewith to be content. Follow Christ, like Paul, and you will be able to adopt his language.

Assurance Attainable.

For I am persuaded, that neither death nor life, nor angels, nor principalities, nor powers, nor things present, nor things to come, nor hight, nor depth, nor any other creature, shall be able to separate us from the love of God, which is in Christ Jesus our Lord.—ROMANS, viii. 38, 39.

THE general sense of this passage is very manifest. It means to set before us a part of the experience and confidence of Paul, in respect to grace and salvation. And thus it teaches the general doctrine that a believer may attain unto such holiness and faith that he shall be assured of his perseverance and his final salvation.

There is no need of any extended explanation of this assurance. It is sufficient to remark that it signifies a state of mind in which confidence predominates; a state of mind above glooms, doubts and fears, in which hope is carried to its full extent, and the believer, no matter what weaknesses lie within him, or foes without him, *is persuaded* that all these difficulties will be overcome, and he shall reach heaven. This is the meaning of assurance. If few believers attain this, then there are few imitators of Paul. He attained it. And his attainment was not an example beyond imitation.

In addition to all we advanced on this point this morning, we propose in this sermon to establish the proposition—That a Christian may attain this assurance; that he may (by Divine aid) *persuade* himself, not merely that the promises of God are true and the faithfulness of God unfailing, but also that he himself is fully and for ever secured by them.

We name several proofs of this.

I. The character and privileges of faith. Separate the two ideas, and after examining, combine them again, and you will have the argument we intend.

The *character* of faith. Faith has a reality in it, and such and so extensive a reality, that its existence is ascertainable. It has its effects and influences. It operates upon the mind, upon the heart, upon the habits of life. *It works by love. It purifies the heart. It overcomes the world.* If it does all this, it accomplishes visible things—prominent and not doubtful things. These things may be known; and, therefore, though the principle itself may lie hidden in the heart, yet by its own and indubitable evidence its existence may be demonstrated. A man's own *mind* is hidden. He can not look directly into his own bosom and see his invisible spirit. How does he know he has a soul? By its effects. That is one way of knowing. He may, indeed, know by its own consciousness; but he knows too by the effects it produces, and knows beyond doubt and beyond the possibility of mistake. Just so he may know of his faith. When it wields *his mind*, giving it a direction counter to that of a natural man, giving it thoughts of himself, thoughts of God, of sin, duty, felicity, time and earth, eternity and heaven, such as an unbeliever has not; he may know that he is not an unbeliever. When it wields *his heart* and, putting a new aspect over two worlds, leads him to exclaim:

> "I give my mortal interest up,
> And make my God my all."

he may know that he chooses and acts by faith—that faith exists within him. It is an ascertainable thing, just as much as the existence of a man's invisible soul.

The Scriptures have not failed to lay down this principle. They lay it down in every possible mode. We find it in *the precepts*. *Examine yourselves whether ye be in the faith; prove your own selves.* The thing is to be tested and known. We find it in *the exhortations: Hold fast the confidence and the rejoicing of hope firm unto the end.* We find it in *the examples: We know that we have passed from death unto life. We know we are of the truth and shall assure our hearts before him.*

This is enough. The Scriptures and the nature of the case demonstrate to us, that faith has such *a character* about it, that if a man *is* a believer, he may be assured that he is a believer; he may know that he has faith.

But this is not enough for our conclusion. How shall he be assured that his faith shall continue? Suppose he does know that he is in a condition of salvation to-day, what shall assure him that he shall be so to-morrow? There is one answer: *The privileges* of faith may assure him. Faith has privileges attached to it. They are as ascertainable as its character. *Forgiveness* is one of them: *the blood of Jesus Christ his Son cleanseth us from all sin.* And if this does not reach far enough, because a believer sins after his first forgiveness, then, *if any man sin, we have an advocate with the Father.*

An interest in this high *advocacy* is another of the believer's privileges,—one which reaches him in his weaknesses, in his sadness, when faith even staggers, and the soul experiences the buffetings of Satan.

Holy Father! keep, through thine own name, those whom thou hast given unto me . . . neither pray I for these alone, but for them also which shall believe on me through their word. I will pray the Father, and he shall give you another Comforter, who shall abide with you for ever. Simon, Simon! behold, Satan hath desired to have you that he may sift you as wheat, but I have prayed for thee that thy faith fail not. Another privilege is, aid: My grace is sufficient for thee. If any man lack wisdom, let him ask of God and it shall be given him. Fear not, thou worm Jacob. Another is, acceptance to even the feeblest sincerity: A bruised reed shall he not break, and the smoking flax shall he not quench. Conscious imperfection, that crushes the heart as the tender herb is bruised under our feet, and makes grace within us seem next door to death, like the dying candle-wick without blaze, has the promise of acceptance.

To embrace all in one, there is a privilege of this very *perseverance* in grace, the fear of failing in which tends so much to hinder assurance: *I will put my Spirit within you, and cause you to walk in my statutes, and ye shall keep my judgments and do them. I will put my law in their inward parts, and write it in their hearts, and will be their God, and they shall be my people. My sheep hear my voice; I know them; they follow me; I give unto them eternal life, and they shall never perish.* This is enough—this crowns the whole.

Here, then, are privileges of faith which reach the believer under all the terrible circumstances which can ever betide him. How is it? shall his faith not embrace these privileges? shall he *be* a believer, and *while* being so, *not* believe God's words? How is it? shall he *be* a believer, and being so, by the character of faith know that he has faith, and yet find it impossible to have faith in a single one of his Christian securities? How is it? as a believer, and knowing he has faith for the present, that he trusts in the blood of Christ for the pardon of past sin, shall he still be forbidden by a dark and strange impossibility to cast his eye down into the future and see any light there? How is it? can he trust God for the past, and not for the future? Must a sense of his frailty plunge him into despair, or make him for ever uncertain? Must the remembrance of his sins, committed all along and now afflicting his heart, forbid him to believe that he shall persevere to the end? Away with all this! These are the reasonings of unbelief, not of faith! Faith rests on God—the God of the future as well as the past; on *Jesus Christ, the same yesterday, to-day, and for ever.* To him, *God over all,* to his high immutability and faithfulness the believer commits his soul. The character of faith is such, that if a man is a believer he may know it; and the privileges of faith are such, that if a man is a believer, he may carry his faith to such an extent as to be *persuaded* that he shall not fall away—that God will keep him. He may, therefore, be assured. He may *be confident in this very thing, that he who has begun a good work in him, will perform it until the day of Jesus Christ.* He may stand in his conscious weakness and sin, and in the midst of a tempting world, and as he looks down the line of his life, not knowing what shall betide him, and sees its end on that bed of trembling where his breath grows shorter, and his blood stops, and the whole tabernacle of the flesh begins to crumble, he may still say, *I know whom I have believed, and am persuaded that he is able to keep that which I have committed to him against that day.* This is assurance. And the character and privileges of faith show that believers may attain it. Hence,

II. The *mode* of this assurance is another proof that

the assurance is not an impossible thing. We mention this article on the principle that success is a thing to be expected when the *mode* of the success is seen to be fit—a principle which all men believe and act upon.

Now the mode of this assurance is most appropriate. Assurance does not come so much by impressions as by evidences—not so much by any direct illapses of the Holy Spirit into the mind as by personal obedience, by repentance, faith, love, a pure conscience, and thus wearing the family-mark of a child of God.

Do not misunderstand me. I am not combating the idea that God dwells with his people to establish and comfort them by his blessed presence; nor am I maintaining that this is not one of the ways of assurance. Not at all. Blessed be the name of God there is an open highway between him and a believer's soul! There are direct heart-consolations, which God bestows upon his children—gifts, benefactions, smiles, the light of his countenance. But we should be greatly ignorant if we did *not* know that these are benefits, with the direct attainment of which a believer has little more to do than just to long after and receive them. They are the smiles of God, when mere smiles are not sought after so much as duty is attended to. They are the supports of God when his creature can not do without them. They come in needy times—in times when the believer can not get along with *means* merely—can not *attain*, but can only *receive*, as a helpless and fainting child. It is a Father spreading his own arms around his loved one! We do not undervalue this. We have too much occasion to remember it with humiliation and shame. Nor are the experiences of it (as we shall see pretty soon) without value, as proofs that assurance may be obtained.

But after all, assurance generally has first to do with something else. What is it to be *persuaded?* Persuasion is not so much a frame, a taste, a sentiment, as it is a judgment. It is *mind* resting on a foundation fit for it—on evidences, arguments, demonstrations. It is a stable condition of mind. It is something beyond impression. Impressions (on which so many erring believers rest, dangerously, I am afraid) more resemble fancies; they come and go, as if without reason and without volition. Persuasion is beyond them. It comes from mind yielding to the evidences and the power of truth.

Now the truths which go to establish the verity of religion are as clear as the sun. Man did not make himself; there must therefore be a Creator, and that Creator is God. That God has a right to rule. Man has conscience. He knows there is such a thing as right and such a thing as wrong. Man is bound to obey his Maker. Man is a sinner; he must therefore repent, just as certainly as God is holy—as certainly as sin is an impropriety leading to misery. Man is a guilty creature; repentance can not atone for the past—it only guides and secures for the present and the future. There must therefore be some atonement for sin rendered somewhere (if the sinner is to be saved), just as certainly as the Divine law means any thing beyond mere advice—just as certainly as God is to be *feared.* But the sinner can not atone for himself, as he can not *do* any thing beyond his duty, or *suffer* any thing beyond his deservings. God demands all his power in love and service; and to suffer the punishment due to his sins would be the eternal loss of his soul. His known condition of helplessness, therefore, ought to *prepare* him to believe, what God tells him so clearly, that Christ died to make *propitiation for his sins;* it ought to lead him, too, to flee to that Saviour and trust him whose *blood cleanseth from all sin.*

There would be no end to the enumeration of truths whose evidence is so full. Man's heart found to be just as the Scriptures tell—his world all vocal for God—his dark grave soon to be filled with his own crumbled bones—his immortal spirit longing after some firm foothold on another world when this shall be burnt up, constitute a cluster of truths which must compel him to take the Bible revelations of mercy, if he is a reasonable man. In these all is clear that he needs to know. Morality is plain. Piety is plain. The promises are plain. Where then is the difficulty of being *persuaded?* Is it not more difficult to believe that all things exist by chance, that the world is an accident, the sun an accident, man an accident, his birth, his winding-sheet an accident, than to believe in a creating and ruling God? Surely every truth that solicits faith has such armies of evidence to support it, that a believer's mind may be fully *persuaded.*

But the old difficulty comes back upon us. You say that this is not what you want. You have no trouble about being *persuaded* of the truths of religion in the abstract; you wish to be assured of your own. Very well. Take precisely the same principle. Faith is not a dream. Repentance is no fancy. Love is no fond vision. The servant of God does not do his work in the dark where eyes can not see him. And Hope does not cast her anchor in an uncertain ocean. Your personal religion, if you have got any, is as susceptible of evidences as are the truths which govern it. Must you remain distressfully uncertain about it? What! can not you tell whether your hope anchors to earth or holds your soul moored to that *within the vail, sure and steadfast?* No? Then you can tell nothing! You can tell *where* it anchors just as well as you can tell that you have any hope at all. What! can not you tell what you love? what you fear? what you aim after? What! is there no difference, visible difference, between supreme worldliness and supreme spirituality? between the service of God and the service of the Devil? Surely faith, religion, piety, is a thing of evidences. If you can not be fully persuaded of your faith, it must be simply because it is very little and very inefficacious. You have only to carry it to a higher degree, to something like a just extent, and its evidences will make you say: *I am persuaded.* And though persuaded for the present, if you can not be satisfactorily persuaded for the future, you have nobody to blame but yourself. You have but to carry your faith to a just extent, to serve God, and lean on God as you ought, and you may lean on him for ever. You have but to try him as a believer's heart ought, and the visible evidences of your piety will dissipate your doubtfulness; you will see the marks of a child of God upon your forehead; you will exclaim: *I am persuaded—nothing shall separate me from the love of God.* The mode of assurance demonstrates its attainableness.

III. Consider those solid convictions of mind which accompany faith. We have already shown that the existence of faith may be known wherever it does exist, and need not repeat the argument. We have now only to show that the believer may be persuaded of his perseverance in holiness. These two complete his assurance. There are solid convictions of mind which accompany faith, and which furnish ground enough for being persuaded of perseverance.

One of them is a conviction of man's ruin by sin. A believer is a man who knows that sin ruined him, so that salvation must be by grace. Another of them is a conviction of helplessness. A believer is a man who knows that without Divine aid he can do nothing in repentance, holiness, and the service of God. Another of them is a conviction of God's amazing patience and faithfulness. A believer is a man who knows that God has wonderfully borne with him, and that, if he has ever made any advance in holiness, he is indebted for it all to continued aid from heaven. These are some of his solid convictions. On the foundation of them the persuasion of his perseverance may safely rest. The argument is short. He may say, That God who redeemed me from ruin, that God who sought me when a stranger and called me to his communion, that God who has borne with so many sins and has so often recovered me when I have so strangely wandered, *I am persuaded* that he will never give me up. If he could ever abandon me, he would have abandoned me long, long ago. I have deserved it a thousand times! If he gave Christ for me, *how shall he not freely give me all things?* He that redeemed me, and called me, and holds me now, *I am persuaded* will hold me to the end.

If every believer is not able to rest on the conclusion of this argument, the fault is his own; it is because he does not justly keep these convictions in his mind, remembering *the rock whence he was hewn, and the hole of the pit whence he was digged.*

IV. Consider the *general actings* of faith. We mean

by this that faith is such a principle that it has some general and sweeping operations which embrace things, *the particulars* of which *itself* does not understand. We mean by this just what you have yourselves done, if you are believers. For example, you know you were guilty sinners. You could enumerate many of your sins; you could clearly perceive the enormity of many. But you did *not* know that you saw the whole or could gauge the dimensions of your guilt before God. And when you trusted in the blood of atonement, your faith went further than your vision could go; you trusted not only for the forgiveness of sins and guilt which you understood, but your faith went further, and by a sweeping generality it trusted God to forgive all the guilt that he himself could see in you with that eye which reads your inmost soul. After you had gone so far as *you* could go, you asked God to go further; you said: *Search me and know my heart, try me, cleanse thou me from secret faults.* These were general actings of faith—actings in the mass, if you please—actings in the dark, trusting God for the deepest midnight that might ever betide your soul.

Faith, therefore, has these general operations. They belong to its nature. The text, we think, was uttered on precisely this principle. It contains a remarkable enumeration of particulars. *Death, life, angels, principalities,* **powers,** *hight, depth.* What a remarkable grouping! What does he mean by it? In my opinion, he means to mention every strange and dark thing which can possibly be **conceived of as** ever attempting *to separate* a believer *from the love of God.* Thus the strangeness of the enumeration constitutes its excellence. Whatever there *may* be *any where*, dying or living, above or below, among angels or devils, here or in eternity, he *is per-*

suaded it shall not dissever a believer from God! At the close of the enumeration, ANY OTHER CREATURE comes out! What does he mean by it? Evidently his mind was taking a universal sweep in the dark. He meant any thing and every thing there could be in the wide universe of God—he cared not what or where!

If faith, therefore, has these general actings, they have only to be put forth in order to an entire assurance. You are afraid you shall not persevere! You do not see how you are going to get along! You are sensible of your weakness, your indwelling sin, your wandering mind even in prayer; sensible, too, of the temptations which come from the world and the worldly, of the subtlety and *fiery darts* of the Devil, of the dreadfulness of death; and you know not what other things you will have to encounter in this uncertain and dark world which may *sift you as wheat!* It seems to you that a midnight lies before you and your path leads directly into it! In what darkness your footsteps shall stagger and where you shall fall, you know not! All this forbids your assurance. It need not. That is God's midnight—and God's death—and God's Devil! If you are his child he will not suffer them to hurt you! *All things shall work for your good.*

The Christ you love owns the world; he made it, and lost it, and the price at which he bought it back again has reddened its soil! He owns the grave! Death and the Devil are his captives! You have only to trust him by a general acting of faith. This you certainly can do if you are a believer. Certainly, if you *are* a believer, you can *trust* where you can not *see.* You have only to carry your faith out to a just extent, trusting God at midnight, and when the storm beats, as well as in the sunshine of a clear day, and you shall soon have such experiences from him and such communion with him, that you shall be able to say, *I am persuaded.* That which tends most to hinder assurance lies in darkness and uncertainty; but we have shown that it belongs to the very nature of faith to trust God even *there*—and therefore Christian assurance is not to be regarded as a miracle, but as within the reach of every ordinary believer. Let him only think faith, and feel faith, and live faith as he ought, and assurance is his. It grows out of those general operations whereby God is trusted in the mass—in the dark.

V. That economy of grace which saves men is a universal one. The first promise of God and the last rest on the same rock. The *bruising of the serpent's head by the seed of the woman* is the substance of them all.

Now, if under this economy men *have* attained assurance, believers may attain it still. And whether or not they have, you may go home and see, (we have not time to make the examination for you.) Go home and ask your Bible about *Paul.* It will give you his words: *I know whom I have believed, and am persuaded he is able to keep that which I have committed unto him. Henceforth there is laid up for me a crown of righteousness, which the Lord, the righteous Judge, shall give me at that day. For me to die is gain.* Ask your Bible about *David.* It will give you his words: *As for me, I will behold thy face in righteousness; I shall be satisfied when I awake with thy likeness.* Ask your Bible about *Job.* It will give you his words: *I know that my Redeemer liveth; and though after my skin, worms destroy this body, yet in my flesh shall I see God, whom I shall see for myself and mine eyes shall behold.* Ask your Bible about *Asaph: It is my joy to draw near* to God. *My flesh and my heart faileth; but God is the strength of my heart and my portion for ever. Thou shalt guide me with thy counsel and afterward receive me to glory.* These are examples. You will find others. You will feel reproved if you can not say, *I am persuaded.*

VI. Assurance may arise from the known and felt tendencies of a believer's renewed heart. A believer's heart, in this world, is never perfect in holiness nor superior to temptation. But it has its own characteristic tendencies, and they furnish an important lesson.

Let a believer be assailed with the subtle arguments of infidels; and though his lips may not be able to answer and his mind may be staggered for a moment, yet there is *that* in his soul which will inevitably lead him back to confidence in the truths which infidelity would overturn. His soul has received the stamp of truth. It tends toward God.

Let a believer be enticed into sinful pleasures, and he may for a time enjoy the delights into which the worldly have betrayed him. But just as certainly as he *is* a believer, and not a hypocrite, he will soon hear a voice from the conscience within him, amid the din of his pleasures, "*What dost thou here, Elijah?*—is this the place for a communicant—are these the delights of a child of God?" He will recollect the enjoyments of peace with God, and gladly turn back to them from the pleasures of sin. His soul tends toward God.

Let a believer be flung into the furnace of affliction, and its fires grow hot upon him: as he stands amid the heat, conscious that the dross is burning up, he will exclaim: *When he hath tried me I shall come forth as gold.* His soul tends toward God.

Let a believer be flung amidst riches, honors, splendor, where he has every thing which the world can give, and every thing which the worldly can enjoy; just as certainly as he *is* a believer, these things will pall upon his heart—they can not satisfy it—it knows there is something better; and looking over all this splendor, and these possessions, with the exclamation, *Vanity and vexation of spirit;* his heart will turn to its chief good: *Thy favor is life, and thy loving-kindness is better than life: thou art my portion, O my God.* His soul tends toward God.

And now when he finds such tendencies within him, and finds earth can not satisfy him, and finds himself at every aberration turning back to his Father's house, *where there is bread enough, and to spare;* how shall he *not* say, *I am persuaded* that . . . . *nothing can separate me from the love of God?*

If he does NOT turn back, instead of having assurance, he ought to have convictions tending to despair! Probably he is no believer at all!!

At this point I am compelled to separate this assembly into two classes. The one class, however well they may have understood me on the other proofs, will not be able to understand me well on this, the last. I mention,

VII. The witnessing of the Holy Spirit. I do not expect you, worldly and unregenerated souls, to understand any thing about it. You can not. *The natural man receiveth not the things of the Spirit of God, for they are foolishness unto him.* I do not ask you to believe me. I am willing you should think I am talking like a fool. *Foolishness unto him*, saith the Bible! But *when* you think so, remember you think just as the Bible foretold! You have one proof of its truth therefore.

ASSURANCE ATTAINABLE. 313

I turn to the other class. You who are Christians indeed, have some knowledge about *the witness of the Spirit.* You have sometimes felt it in your own hearts. It is a thing which philosophy knows nothing about—and *to* which there is no analogy in the universe. Here natural religion and revealed religion must part! Farewell schools! farewell philosophy and reasoning! farewell world—flowers of beauty, birds of song, mountains, oceans, and the light of the sun! God does something for us beyond all you can whisper!

My dear brethren, there is such a thing as *the Spirit of God bearing witness with our spirits, that we are the children of God.* At such times, our God and Father oversteps all means, all instrumentalities, all preaching and hearing; and in the fullness of his kindness comes directly to our hearts. He comes to strengthen, comfort and assure us. There is (as I told you) an open highway between God and a believer's soul. It is God's work to travel in it. He comes down to you in your distresses. And though (as I said) assurance does not depend on this *alone,* yet this is one cause of it, if not necessary to it in every case. God does sometimes come to his children, to convince them that they *are* his children. He meets them as friend meets friend. Without means, aside from all instrumentalities, in a way which nature and philosophy know nothing about, God does come to be his own present witness in the believer's soul. *He* is not satisfied to leave his loved ones to all that means, and promises, and gifts could do for them. He comes himself to assure their hearts. In the exercise of that supreme power which belongs to him, and whereby he is able to excite such emotions of grief or of gladness as he pleases, he himself *bears witness* in the hearts of his people that they are his people. Reason can not explain it, but surely sound reason demands of us to believe it. If we do not believe it, we dishonor God. Indeed is there a mother, or even a father, who would be willing to leave their exposed child to the mere good of all that gifts and benefactions could do for him? If he were sick, would they not fly to his bed of pain, to cheer him in his distresses, and do for him what no stranger could do? And if *he* has the affection he should have, does he not feel that nothing but this will do for him? So God feels toward his children, and so they feel about him. The witness of the Spirit therefore is a reasonable thing, though reason can not explain it. To explain it would spoil it! *I want God* to do for me something beyond my power to tell! I want him to take this undying spirit into his own hands, to make me his, and TELL me I am his. This he does do for his children sometimes, giving them a lively and joyful confidence of salvation.

My brethren, I can not pretend to tell you *how* you attain this witnessing of God's Spirit; nor accompany your thoughts over those sweet and solemn hours when God dwells with you and you with God. I only know that such seasons are. I know that *the love of God is shed abroad in the heart by the Holy Ghost which is given unto you. He which establisheth you in Christ is God, who hath also sealed you, and given you the earnest of the Spirit in your heart. Ye have not received the spirit of bondage again to fear, but ye have received the spirit of adoption whereby we cry, Abba, Father.*

Surely as you are a believer, you have not utterly failed in all this. Times *have* been, if they are not *now*, when you felt the direct comforts of God in your soul, and were constrained *to expect* heaven assuredly. God came to you. He soothed and softened your heart. He encouraged it. He told you you were his. Perhaps you were alone: and down in that track where the struggle of that closet-prayer went up to God, the voice came back: *Be of good cheer, thy sins are forgiven thee.* Perhaps you were in some difficult service, where the temptations of poverty, or of riches, or of the fashions of the world beat so hard upon you that you were afraid your weakness would give way, and you should dishonor Christ and never reach heaven! And as you stood trembling and ready to sink, God said to you, *Fear not, thou worm Jacob, I am with thee.* Perhaps you were sick, nigh unto death; and while God shook your bones over the sepulcher, he taught you to say: *If the earthly house of this tabernacle were dissolved, I have a building of God, a house not made with hands, eternal in the heavens.* Perhaps you were at the communion-table; and, all overwhelmed with a sense of your unworthiness and guilt, you could say with faltering tongue,

> "Here, Lord, I give myself away,
> 'Tis all that I can do."

You drank the cup: and God sent you away singing—

> "'Tis done! the great transaction done!
> I am my Lord's, and he is mine;
> He drew me, and I followed on,
> Glad to obey the call Divine.
>
> "Now rest! my long divided heart,
> Fixed on this blissful center, rest;
> With all things else, I freely part—
> Jesus is mine, and I am blest."

I do not care where you were. Go back there again. The fountains of God are not dry.

And now I appeal to your own past experience, to what the God of all comfort has done for your soul, whether you do not believe that assurance is attainable. Has not your own heart had the proof? If you will live as a Christian ought; if you will serve God and let him take care of you; if you will keep your heart open to him, like an affectionate and helpless child; if you will lie passive in his hands, and receive *from him*, when all creature supports and comforts are good for nothing; do you not believe that he will spread his arms around your unsheltered and storm-beaten head? Do you not believe, from your own past experience, that the *Spirit of God* and your *own spirit* will *bear witness* together that you are a child of God? And then, though you know not what enemies you shall meet, what battles you must fight, what rough paths you shall tread, or how dark shall roll the waves, when you buffet the swellings of Jordan; Christ yours, and the inward witness filling your soul; can you not be able to say: *I am persuaded that neither death, nor life, nor angels, nor principalities, nor powers, nor things present, nor things to come, nor height, nor depth, nor any other creature shall be able to separate me from the love of God, which is in Christ Jesus our Lord?*

God grant it to you. *Amen.*

Sanctification at Death.

Ye are come unto Mount Zion, and unto the city of the living God, the heavenly Jerusalem, and to an innumerable company of angels, to the general assembly and church of the first-born, which are written in heaven, and to God the judge of all, and to the spirits of just men made perfect.—HEBREWS, xii. 22, 23.

THERE was something not a little remarkable in those transactions of Moses and Joshua, recorded in their history, and which took place before the children of Israel had entered into the promised land. They distributed Canaan to the Israelites *before* they had it. Moses had not set his foot upon its soil. He never was going to. He never did. All that the Divine mercy granted to him was to climb to the top of Pisgah, and from its summit look away into the distance, and behold the blue peaks of the mountains of Judea, and catch a glimpse of the sunny vales that lay between them. Canaan was not yet conquered. Every foot of the country was yet in possession of his enemies. *They* held its strong fastnesses. They felt secure amid its munitions of rocks. Their armies were mustered for battle; and, aware of the hostile intent of the foe upon their borders, they were prepared to dispute every inch of ground, burn every blade of grass, maintain every stonghold, make their stand at every narrow defile between the mountains, and give battle to the death, wherever their enemies should meet them! Whoever reflects upon the zeal with which men will contend for their own soil and homes, will perceive the arduous work yet before the armies of Israel. Prowess and numbers may well have doubt, if not trembling, when men are to be met and overthrown whose every blow will be struck with an arm nerved by the awful power of desperation! But Moses and Joshua do not falter. They dispose of the country of Palestine as if they had already conquered it. They distribute its towns and provinces among their people. They select the location for every tribe. They make official appointments for the government of the country. And in all their transactions and promises they never utter a word of doubtfulness, as if any thing yet depended upon the chances of war.

These were strange transactions. But Moses and Joshua were strange chieftains. They did not act on the ordinary principles of men. They acted by faith. By faith the country was at their disposal already, for they believed God.

On precisely the same principle the text before us was uttered. It speaks of heaven as already secured to believers, just as Canaan was secured to the Israelites when they were only on its frontiers. It speaks of believers as if already in the society of heaven—already *come unto Mount Zion, and unto the city of the living God, the heavenly Jerusalem, and to an innumerable company of angels, to the general assembly and church of the first-born which are written in heaven, and to God the judge of all, and to the spirits of just men made perfect.*

The justness of this interpretation, and the taste of this mode of introducing it, will be manifest to you by a brief consultation of the context.

Paul was aiming to attach the Hebrews more and more to Christianity, and, by the power of its doctrines and promises, aiming to train them up for a superiority to the world, to cause them to live as if their first and grand object was to enjoy God and gain his favor. The Hebrews all prized Moses. They remembered his history. They had not forgotten his generalship. They were familiar with the story of the exodus from Egypt, the wanderings in the wilderness, the promises and threatenings at Mount Sinai, and the triumphant entry into the promised land. In writing to them, Paul sympathizes with their recollections. He only wants them to take along the idea that the things recollected were *symbolical*, and learn that the things symbolized were infinitely superior to the symbols which prefigured them. On this principle he composes this Epistle. He never loses sight of the principle. He has it in mind all the way, from the very first sentence in which he says, *God . . . who spake in time past unto the fathers by the prophets, hath in these last days spoken unto us by his Son*, down to the very last sentence in which he speaks of the God of peace that brought again from the dead our Lord Jesus Christ, that great Shepherd of the sheep, through the blood of the everlasting covenant. He never once loses sight of the principle of his argument, that if a man under the ancient dispensation had reason to be a Jew, a man under the present dispensation has altogether more reason to be a Christian. He may have his fightings, but he shall have his victories; he may have his falls but he shall get his Canaan. It *is* his. God gives it to him, as Moses and Joshua disposed, on its frontiers, of the promised land.

Hence we find, just before the text, the Apostle says

to the Christian Hebrews, *Ye are not come unto the mount that might be touched and that burned with fire, nor unto blackness, and darkness, and tempest, and the sound of a trumpet, and the voice of words, which voice they that heard entreated that the word should not be spoken to them any more,* (*for they could not endure that which was commanded. And if so much as a beast touch the mountain, it shall be stoned or thrust through with a dart; and so terrible was the sight that Moses said, I exceedingly fear and quake*). This was *not* their condition. In opposition to a condition so fearful, Paul affirms that they *were* come to the *city of the living God, the heavenly Jerusalem.* They were become owners of it—heaven was now theirs. Before them had gone all those who *died in* faith. Their fathers, their mothers, who believed, were now in heaven (not in an intermediate state, but in heaven). There they awaited their coming. There they were *made perfect.* Happy spirits, free from sin, and care, and toil, they enjoy the vision of God and the Lamb for ever. Christians in this world, with their battles yet to fight, and, it may be, their blood to spill, ought to have the sentiment deep-fixed in their hearts—heaven is mine, my business is, by God's grace, to reach it. They ought to be animated with their privileges and prospects. They are not come to Mount Sinai, but to Mount Zion. The voice of terror is mute, and the voice of infinite love and mercy bids them on to that sinless city of God, where already are congregated the *spirits of just men made perfect.*

How consolatory, how infinitely consolatory is the Gospel! Those dear to us are constantly dropping out of our arms! Our fathers, where are they? and the prophets, do they live for ever? Rachels weep around us, refusing to be comforted! Jacobs shake their gray locks,

"Joseph is not, and Simeon is not, and ye will take Benjamin away also!" At the mouth of the sepulcher we resign our parents and children to the dust, and no voice of kindness reaches afterward "the dull, cold ear of death!" But, *Lazarus sleepeth!* If they died in faith, they are singing in glory. They are gone *home*. They are better off than I. They have done with sorrow. They have done with sin. They have done with fear. They have joined the army of prophets, apostles, and martyrs, and have been welcomed home to the city of God by the *spirits of just men made perfect.* If I believe, I shall be welcomed there, too; I shall meet in glory those I have buried in gloom, and join all the family of God who are now in heaven.

But this consolation is sometimes attended with a difficulty. Some believers, and we will not say they are weak believers, conscious, as they ought to be, of remaining sin, knowing full well that there is a vast distance betwixt them and perfection now, just as they ought to know—some such believers, aiming, as they ought to do, to *make their calling and election sure*, sometimes are flung into darkness and despondency because they are conscious of being now unfit for heaven, and they can not conceive how that death, whose valley is traversed in a few short hours—(and here we enter upon our subject—fix it in your minds)—can not conceive how that death, whose valley is so soon traversed, can purify away their remaining sins, and fit them for that city where nothing can enter *that is unclean or defileth.* They know that "the souls of unbelievers are at their death made perfect in holiness, and do immediately pass into glory; they have nothing to do with that Popish figment, "an intermediate state." They know that nothing sinful enters heaven; and conscious as they are of a thousand imperfections and crimes and sins, and knowing too that there may be only a single step betwixt them and death, they are almost forced back upon the conclusion that they can not be the children of God! If the pestilence should cut them down in a day, if the lightning should strike them dead in an instant, it seems to them almost too much to believe that souls such as theirs could ride on the breath of the pestilence or on the lightning's wing, up to the gates of the holy city of God. If dying took a great while—if months and years must be consumed in the slow process of putting off the body, they would not have so many desponding fears. They would then hope that as the process was going on a gracious process in their souls would keep pace with it, and by the time the spirit should be severed from its clay it would be purified from its sin, and be ready to rush in among the *spirits of just men made perfect.* But that a day, an hour, an instant of dying should be able to robe their still imperfect and polluted spirits in holiness—the dress of heaven—is almost more than they dare to hope.

We have sometimes met with this difficulty: indeed, very often: not, perhaps, very often with well people, but with sick and dying ones. It has planted many a thorn on the pillow of death! My hearers, the best way to die comfortably is to live wisely. If we *live unto the Lord,* we shall *die unto the Lord;* and then it will not matter much if the hours of our dying are partially overspread with gloom.

But still, such gloom is undesirable. And the state of distraction and weakness so often attending those hours forbid that application of mind so necessary to lay hold of the truths calculated to remove the difficulty we mention. Lend us your attention then, now. We will consider this matter. We will explain to you how it comes to pass, that when believers die, (though always imperfect in holiness, always sinful, till they do die), their believing souls do immediately become *the spirits of just men made perfect.*

But—I am ashamed—I am ashamed, through a thought that occurs to me! You ought to be ashamed, too, for it is a shameful fact, that human depravity will often abuse Divine mercy! It will sometimes make an ill use of the promises of the Divine forbearance and kindness; and the very truths of mercy, which ought above all things to attach a sinner to God, will be employed to countenance carelessness, if not some more alarming sin. This idea makes me tremble—it makes me hesitate on the very threshold of the subject. It may be that the very truths I propose to utter, when I show how " believers at death are made perfect in holiness and do immediately pass into glory," will cause some to be more indifferent about cultivating holiness before they come to die! My brethren, I solemnly assure you that, in my opinion, a person could hardly have a more decisive evidence that he is not a Christian at all, than he *will* have, if the truths about the perfecting influences which accompany dying, diminish at all his aims after present holiness. Let us warn you to beware on this point. Let us caution you not to take the truths designed to comfort humble believers and apply them to encourage proud ones. The careless, the stubborn, whose hearts neither bleed nor bend, have no business with the balm prepared for the *bruised reed!* But to the *bruised* reed the *box of ointment* shall not be sealed up, though impiety should venture to steal out of it when it is opened. Therefore,

I. In this life there is a connection established between bodily senses and passions on the one hand, and thoughts and affections on the other. Souls and bodies sympathize—they have a thousand reciprocal influences. We know not how. We only know they do. An agitated mind often shakes down the frail tabernacle it inhabits. A disordered body often produces a bewildered mind and a melancholy heart. One can not study intensely and study for ever, because the mysterious and material organs of the brain will give way, and the expected majesty of mind may be only the awful majesty of maniac thought.

To this connection sin has some special relations. The Fall brought its influences not on man's mind alone—it caused "the corruption of his whole nature." Bodily passions are different from what they would have been if man had never sinned. In the cultivation of holiness in this life the believer experiences many a sad trial, because his depravity makes his blood circulate differently; affects his muscles and bones; and if he suffers sinful affections to affect his mind at all, they soon produce an influence upon bodily sensations, which turns back upon the mind itself to hurry it on into deeper sin. The heat of anger which fires the blood, the restlessness of impatience which thrills the nerves, are bodily affections which, when once excited, tend to drive on the soul to more glaring guilt. Through this connection betwixt body and soul many sins assail us, and many a believer has need of the solemn purpose of Paul, *I keep under my body and bring it into subjection.*

Now, dying is going to dissolve this connection. The animal functions shall cease. The cessation of them *is* death. The blood stops. The limbs stiffen. The tongue lies still. What was activity, and bloom, and beauty, and gracefulness, a little while ago, becomes a cold and ghastly corse; *the dust returns to the earth as it was, and the spirit returns to God that gave it.* It may be, indeed,

> "Not there to dwell,
> But hear its doom and sink to hell"

But it is easy to understand that this separation of the soul of a believer from his mortal body, must have a most powerful influence upon his holiness. His body was a medium through which sin assailed him. Its *passions warred against the soul.* He has now left it behind him. It belongs to the worms, not to him. All those sins and all those defects in holiness which he experienced by reason of the flesh, he will experience no more. His weak nerves will no more hurry him into fretfulness and impatience. No more will his hasty blood prompt his spirit to unholy anger. And ah! no more will bloom of beauty and gracefulness of carriage be a temptation to vanity and a worldly forgetfulness of God. That beauty lies down where the worm has his banquet! In all respects, as far as sin has advantage over a believer, by reason of this union which death is going to dissolve, that death will help him to holiness.

But here we wish you to give one idea a fixed lodgment in your mind. It is this: that this effect of dying will be a very different thing with those who die in unbelief. Mark it well: believers sin, through their soul's connection with the body, on a very different principle from that on which unbelievers do. Believers sin in the body by infirmity, by surprise, by sudden temptation—we had almost said by accident. They never do it on principle, by design, by contrivance and permission; and invariably they mourn over it: *Oh, wretched man that I am, who shall deliver me from the body of this death?* Not so with unbelievers; sin is their choice. It is more: they delight in it. They have no fixed and solemn purpose like believers, to *keep under the body and bring it into subjection—to crucify the flesh with its affections and lusts—to mortify the deeds of the body that they may live* for ever. Dying, therefore, will have a very different effect upon these two classes of men. It will deliver a believer from one of the clogs and hindrances of his holiness. The moment his spirit is released from its prison of clay, it will be free to pursue unimpeded its own gracious and holy preferences. Once the flesh hindered it. It shall hinder it no more. But now—its prison bars broken—and seeing up to the city of God, it will be free to take its flight upward to the arms of that Saviour it has loved so well. God it had chosen *before* death, and *to* God death lets it go. Heaven it had longed for, and now it shall " walk the golden streets." But the effect of dying with an unbeliever is not to release him, but to rob him! *He* lived for the flesh, not for the spirit—for the world, not for heaven. While the believer in this world had the supremacy of his desires after spiritual good, and shed many a bitter tear because the flesh hindered him, the unbeliever had the supremacy of his affections on things of the flesh, and made the body the medium and instrument of his chosen delights. Consequently, death robs him. The body gone, all is gone. He loved it, lived for it: the grave has got it—and as the disembodied spirit surveys the wide circle of eternity, there is nothing there it wants! It never chose heaven and lived for it; it never loved God and served him; and now, when it has *returned to God who gave it*, under the curse, it hastens from an injured God to hide itself, if it may, in shame and everlasting despair!

There is no ground for the most remote idea that even to believers there is any thing necessarily sanctifying in death itself. Its pains do not purify, or its fears, its faintness, or its agitations. No, not at all. God, indeed, will hear prayer then—will verify the promises; and every one of us may have hopeful reasons, as we approach that hour, for seeking more grace, or even when it has come, for at least putting up the prayer of the penitent thief upon the cross. But we insist upon it, no believer even, much less an unbeliever, has the least foundation for thinking that the mere circumstance of dying will, in itself, have any tendency to make him holy. We insist upon it that the reigning love of Christ and of holiness in a believer's heart *before* death, is the only just ground for his hoping that at the hour of death he shall be "made perfect in holiness." But just so far as the flesh is a clog to the spirit and checks the influences of its supreme and spiritual aims, just so far the believer who *groans, being burdened*, can understand how dying shall tend to send him away with additional preparation to join the company of the *spirits of just men made perfect*. Bodily pains shall no more put him out of patience; bodily appetites shall no more hinder the appetites of his regenerated spirit; bodily health shall never again plunge him into those animal delights it qualified him to enjoy, whose remembrance often *bites like a serpent and stings like an adder;* and bodily weakness, making the mind dim and heart sad and languid, shall no more clip the wings of the spirit aiming to soar to God.

II. We may partially have anticipated it, but it is worthy of separate notice that believers are, in this world, less holy than they would be if worldly temptations were not so powerful and frequent. One of the cautions they need to exercise constantly is, to beware of the world; and they are wise when they enter into the spirit of the song:

> "Is this dark world a friend to grace,
> To help me on to God?"

When they die, they leave the world behind. While they are here, although they have yielded it up as a portion most certainly if they are Christians, and have prized another world and the favor of God in it far more, still they are liable to the world's solicitations, for they are men—they are living men, and have worldly interests and worldly business which they may not despise or neglect. To hold an even balance amid worldly interests and duties—to prize the world gratefully and not love it too much—to do its duties faithfully and not suffer them to infringe upon duties more especially relating to eternity, are things of importance, but they are things which few believers are so happy as uniformly to accomplish. In the ranks of ambition many a believer sins, and the high places of an earthly distinction are memorial spots of the weaknesses of our brethren. Amid the scramble after riches many a professor of religion so far forgets himself as to adopt and think he may adopt modes and principles of business which have been formed to his hand, and received all their nature and fashion from men who had no fear of God. Among those who spend many industrious hours over their books, you may find many a believer whose very industry is sin, as it proceeds from no better principle than a desire to be amused with some silly story, and qualified to talk about it in some silly circle, or from a desire to outstrip in fame some poor fool who never studied a day for the world to come. In some form or another the world tempts, distracts thought, dissipates purposes of holiness, and flings many an obstacle to holiness in the believer's path toward heaven.

Now, it is easy to understand, therefore, how his dying may promote his holiness most wonderfully, because it takes him away from a world that has troubled him, and that he long has been trying to put under his feet. As the soul leaves this tabernacle it leaves this world. Never again will it be compelled to enter into worldly cares and employ, and be compelled to seek those things in the sufficiency of which it had not virtue enough to stop, but was miserably tempted on beyond necessity, beyond competence, and fell into the shameful sins of pride, of avarice, of haughtiness, of indulgence. Never again will the soul on the other side of death, as many a one has on this side, while cold in rags and perishing with hunger, find itself sinning by envying and hating the rich, and by distrusting the goodness of God. If you consider, for only a moment, what a heavy hinderance the world is to grace, and how many of the sins of believers come from its temptations, and how many of them are hindered from humility, and from prayer, and from aiming after *durable riches*, because they have so much of the world and so much worldliness of spirit; you will see at once that dying shall give them a high advantage. It will lift the world's weight off from their heaven-bound spirits! It will unloose the trammeled soul! It will cut the strings and let it soar to God. On the other side of death believers will not be tempted with the world. They will not be lifted up because they have got it—or covetous and avaricious after it—or discontented and peevish and envious because they can not get it. They will be free to soar away to the God and heaven they have chosen,

"Nor cast one longing, lingering look behind."

Hence dying must and will aid a believer's spirit, and plume its wing for the flight.

Must we ask you again to bear it in mind, that it is not merely dying which gives believers any additional holiness, and that dying will have a very different effect upon two different classes of men? It will deliver a Christian from a snare; but it will rob an unbeliever of his all! It shall put Lazarus away from the difficulties of his hunger and his sores; but it shall put Dives beyond all the *good things* of his *life-time*, where no *drop of water* shall *cool his tongue!* Forget not, ye worldly, if ye do not love something better than the world before death, ye will have nothing better after it! Dying is one thing and regeneration is quite another. But ye who find the world plaguing you, may be comforted. It shall not plague you long. If you love heaven more, dying will soon let you go beyond this hinderance that troubles you now, to enter in among the *spirits of just men made perfect.*

(Bear with me, my brethren. I will curtail these articles as much as I can. I will only mention the ideas, and leave your meditation to discover their force.)

III. Dying will be an event to make believers more holy, because it will put them beyond the influences of *evil example*. A Christian is nothing but a man, and in this life frail in virtue and always peccable. He is liable to sympathize with those around him; and through the power of his sympathies he is liable to the contagion of sin. As other men feel he is exposed to feel. As other men act he is exposed to act. The fashions of the world do often check and stunt the growth of a believer's grace. More than Solomon and more than Samson, have fallen into sin by reason of connection with the Egyptian and the Philistine. More than one Hezekiah has, like the worldly, made vain show of his treasures and forgotten they were God's. Christians are exposed to copy the example of the worldly, especially when taste and poetry and outward decencies are hung around the deformities of sin and hide them from view.

Now dying, will remove all this hinderance to holiness. At the hour of death, the believing and the unbelieving do part to meet no more. Death's icy hand shall quench for ever in the believer all power to sympathize with the wicked and become assimilated to them in sin. On the other side of death, the example of the ungodly will have no more attractions. Its hideous deformities will be seen by every eye; and the believer will no longer be obliged, in order to be holy, to stem the strong currents of an ungodly world. Separate from sinners—superior to all sympathy with them, and away from the danger of their example—the believer will be left free at death to soar away to the heaven he has chosen, while the wicked will take their awful way down to the hell they have never shunned!

IV. In every quality that constitutes an element of holiness, believers would become more eminent in this life if they had more faith. Lack of faith hinders them. Sometimes it makes them indolent, sometimes prayerless, sometimes distrustful of God and without due dependence of spirit to go through the wilderness after the *pillar of cloud* and *pillar of fire;* and often, oh! how often, does a weak faith reluctate and refuse before that direction of a strange agriculture: *Cast thy bread upon the waters,* and that promise: *He that soweth to the Spirit shall of the Spirit reap life everlasting.* Some of you know very well that if you had more faith you would be more holy: you would pray more; you would labor more; you would love more.

Now the believer's dying is not going to strengthen his faith, but is going to render it unnecessary for him. If he could exercise it after death, it would indeed be powerful enough; but he will have no need of it. Then he will *see* all things. Now he *sees only in part; but when that which is perfect is come, then that which is in part shall be done away. Now he sees as through a glass darkly; but then face to face.* He shall see God; and that *love that never faileth* shall draw him upward to

"The bosom of his Father and his God."

In the open visions of eternity, as he steps out at the other end of the dark valley of death, there will be none of those defects of realization caused by weak faith here, and which so often left him to the influences of sin. Oh, no! then God will be a reality! Christ, with the nail-prints in his hands and the spear-gash in his side, will be a reality; enough for every slow-hearted Thomas! Heaven, hell will be a reality! All about God, and all about himself and about Christ that his Bible ever asked him to believe, he can not ever doubt any more.

Dying, therefore, must do much for a believer's perfection in holiness, as it will fling around his spirit the influences of a realized and amazing eternity!

But if one dies in his unregenerated condition, those realizations, instead of being the fullness of all he has hoped, will be the fullness of more than all he has feared. He will *see* God, but he does not love him! He will see Christ, but he is none of his! He will see heaven, but he has laid up no treasures there! He can have no part with the *spirits of just men made perfect!*

V. Some of you, I know, will believe it, when I say that in this life believers fail in holiness when they fail to secure the presence of God. *Walking with God* is no fiction or figure; it is a fact. Our Enochs and Elijahs and Pauls have proved it. Souls prosper by the presence of God. They can not prosper without it. But often here backslidings provoke him to depart! His Spirit is taken away, *grieved* from the soul. Then soon the Christian moans: *Oh that I knew where I might find him, I would come even to his seat!* He *will* know very well as soon as he is dead. Dying is the end of his distance, the last act of his disciplining God; and it will tend to a wonderful increase of holiness, because it will bring the believer's soul out into the loved light of God's countenance for ever. Oh that we were *all* believers—all loved the presence of God! If we do *not* love it, dying will never make us love it! We shall say: *Mountains fall upon us; rocks, hills, hide us from the face of Him that sitteth upon the throne, for the great day of his wrath has come!*

VI. The dying of believers will be an event tending powerfully to their perfection, because, in that event, they pass for ever beyond the temptations of the Devil. Even in the hour of death that malignant spirit may assail them! But his *time is short.* A few more breaths and the redeemed soul shall be safe from his deceptions and his *fiery darts* for ever. Satan may prowl around a death-bed, but he can not follow the soul beyond it. Leaving the body, it bids an everlasting farewell to Satan, and all his deep and dreadful malignity. But again I am obliged to say to you that dying brings this benefit to believers only. It hastens the wicked to that *everlasting fire prepared for the devil and his angels.*

In my opinion, this discourse would not do justice to the mercy of God, if it did not mention, finally, that,

VII. In the hour of dying, the God of infinite mercy does make, ordinarily, special communications of grace to his beloved and redeemed ones—such communications as rapidly enhance the holiness of the soul. Many of the phenomena of dying make me think so. Many blessed texts make me think so. *Precious in the sight of the Lord is the death of his saints* (Psalm cxvi. 15). *Blessed are the dead which die in the Lord* (Revelation, xiv. 13). *Oh death, I will be thy plagues* (Hosea, xiii. 14). Moreover, it comports with the whole economy of Divine mercy to suppose that in the believer's last hour, when the ascended Saviour verifies the promise, *I will come again and receive you to myself*—and when quivering lips pray him, *Come, Lord Jesus, come quickly*—I say, it is *like* the mercy of God to do, then, a more than ordinary work of grace, as he finishes the soul's redemption, and dismisses it to depart to the *spirits of just men made perfect.* Then, in the trials of dying—the world receding—heaven opening—the body cooling—and God, the Christian's own God, standing in faithfulness by his dying child; surely the departing spirit may expect such transformations as it never had before. Then, as death is finishing up his work rapidly, the Holy Spirit is finishing up his! And now the *body is death because of sin, but the spirit is life because of righteousness.* Clothed in Christ's righteousness and perfect in its own, it shall leave the trials of dying to enjoy the triumphs of heaven for ever! Blessed spirit! it has done with sinning and done with dying! Happy in God, and like him, it rests in its sinless and eternal heaven! Blessed spirit! we may well envy thee!

These considerations are enough to remove the difficulty we mentioned about believers at their death being made perfect in holiness. They ought to be enough to remove the despondency of many a sad-hearted believer here, whose remaining sin makes him write bitter things against himself, as if it were impossible he should ever reach the heaven he longs for. But certainly every one of these considerations warns you not to defer to the hour of death that *holiness without which no man shall see the Lord.* Death regenerates nobody. That is God's work. I beseech you, ask now of him, who is willing to give the *Holy Spirit to them that ask him,* if you ever expect to be found among *the spirits of just men made perfect.*

The Chief of Sinners.

This is a faithful saying and worthy of all acceptation, that Christ Jesus came into the world to save sinners, of whom I am chief.—1 TIMOTHY, i. 15.

IT was a characteristic of the religion of Paul, that it was eminently personal and practical. It was never speculative *first*. He did not commence at that end of the matter. It was not his way to take the attitude of a mere observer, and looking out on an economy or system, aim to understand all its principles and notice all its workings, as a curious spectator. He began at the other end of the business. He had *first* in mind, and he *kept* it first in mind, what religion was after, what it had to do, what end it proposed to secure, and especially for himself. With this full in his view, as the prompter and guide in all his deep thoughts, he enters into the subject; and while he is the most logical and purely argumentative of all the Divine writers, and goes further, and dives deeper, and soars higher in all matters of great thought, he does all this, not as a philosopher, not as a mere student, but as a sinner, himself a sinner, seeking to know how to be saved.

This was the characteristic of his religious mind. You may detect it in all his writings. The seventh chapter of the Epistle to the Romans is a remarkable example. Aiming to make the law of God understood in its nature and obligations, he gets on but a little way in his explanation and argument, before he brings *himself* in. His language imperceptibly slides into the experimental, and the experimental of his own heart. The abstraction of the first verse (*the law hath dominion over a man*), becomes the personal in the seventh (*I had not known sin but by the law*), and when he had got his mind into this personal direction, he could not leave the track—he holds on in it to the end of his argument: *I was alive without the law once; but when the commandment came, sin revived and I died. The commandment which was ordained unto life, I found to be unto death. The law is spiritual, but I am carnal, sold under sin. In me, that is, in my flesh dwelleth no good thing. To will is present with me; but how to perform that which is good I find not.* And so he goes on till he comes to the sweeping conclusion of the whole matter: *O wretched man that I am, who shall deliver me from the body of this death?* And this conclusion just turns his soul from the propriety of law to the preciousness of Christ. *I thank God through Jesus Christ our Lord.* Experimental at every step! Not an explanation, argument, or even a single idea of mere speculation! In the very depths of his ocean of thought, he not only keeps in mind *himself*, a sinner to be saved, but his ideas of himself constitute the starting-point and the stopping-place of every great argument, and throw over the whole an aspect of practical solemnity and earnestness, which demonstrates that his speculations were not for his curiosity's sake, but his soul's sake.

It were to be wished that Paul had more imitators. Where a mind approaches the field of doctrine merely to see what is in it—merely to look over the fence and examine it, or climb some eminence and look down upon it—inevitably the contents will be misunderstood. To every carnal and curious eye there will be such a fog and dense mist hanging over it, that if a dim outline *is* seen and seen correctly, the boldness of the outline will *not* be seen, while all the filling up, the substance and soul of the matter, will not be discerned at all. Divine truth is to be justly learned only through the heart. Man that would be saved must learn it, not as a mere student—not as a mere observer—but as one who is accountable to God, and *intends* to prepare to meet the day of the final reckoning. You who come here should come with prayer.

The last clause of the text before us (the matter to which we propose in this sermon principally to attend) shows us that Paul felt himself to be the chief of sinners. *Christ came into the world*, says he, *to save sinners;* and then the religious habit of his mind, his mode of religious thinking, comes out—*of whom I am chief.* Just as in the argument of the whole chapter (if you will examine it) he keeps the personally experimental in the fore-ground of thought, and makes the doctrinal only auxiliary to its purposes; so here, in one of its special ideas, he does the same thing. As an Apostle and as a Christian he knew well the Gospel system, and exulted in it: *The grace of our Lord*, says he, *was exceeding abundant with faith and love which is in Christ Jesus.*

He knew well the reach of that love and grace—and they sufficient for all sinners that wanted them—that the proclamation of God's mercy to sinners through the atonement and mediation of Jesus Christ was a proclamation which all men ought to heed: *This is a faithful saying, and worthy of all acceptation*, says he, *that Christ Jesus came into the world to save sinners;* and then, just at the moment when his believing soul exults in the fullness of redemption for sinners, he can not avoid flinging in the idea—*of whom I am chief.*

There can be no reasonable doubt that the mind of Paul was here in the full exercise of a true and happy faith. There can be no reasonable doubt that at the period when he wrote this he was much advanced and confirmed in the light and strength of grace—a more wise and more holy man than *when he first believed*. But still he regarded himself as peculiarly a sinner. To him it appeared he was *the least of all saints*, the greatest sinner among them. His faith, his hope, his joy in God, and the matured growth of his holiness, did not make him forget this. He remembered what he had been and what a miracle of grace had saved him. He attributed his salvation to no meritoriousness of his own. He gives an opposite account of it: *For this cause I obtained mercy that in me* FIRST (*as the chief of sinners*, in whose pardon grace would peculiarly shine), *Jesus Christ might show forth all long-suffering for a* PATTERN (an encouraging example) *to them which should hereafter believe on him to life everlasting.*

The idea, therefore, to which we direct your attention is this: That true religion, and great experience in it, cause the believer to regard himself peculiarly a sinner. More and more, he sees and feels that he *is* a sinner; and though his *reason* may not convince him that he has sinned really beyond all others, yet his *heart* will feel, amid his experiences of grace, that few, if any other hearts, have ever been as bad as his own. *Sinners* are *saved of whom I am chief*, will often be the expression of his exulting yet humbled soul.

We have several considerations to prove this:

I. The view which a believer has of his *own heart* is more minute, and more extensive also, than any view he can take of another's. He can not draw upon another's memory as he can upon his own. His quickened recollections furnish him with many a dark chapter, as his mind roves back upon forgotten years; and there is a vividness and freshness in the recollection of what a sinner he has been, which throws over his own experience an aspect of peculiarity. He can number his own sins as he can not another's. He can recollect the smallness of temptation, and the tender, and touching, and terrible motives which would have restrained him from his sins if he would only have felt them. Parental instructions and parental anxieties, which were around him when he was a child, will float over his mind, mingled with the recollection of parental prayer at the family altar—all which did not avail to win him off from the way of obstinacy in evil. The early, cogent, and yet tender strivings of the Holy Spirit with his youthful conscience will come up as memory recalls the past—all which did not win him to God. Conscience, with an eye of fire, will look into his soul, and the aggravations of sin, which arose from a thousand circumstances of *his* condition and *God's* forbearance toward him, will seem to invest his sinfulness with a criminality and an abomination beyond any thing that he will dare to attribute to other people. If others may have gone further in the overt act, it will seem to him that he should have out-stripped them all, if a power not his own had not held him back. Oh! how many times his heart sinned when his hands were pure! How many times he stood on the very verge of ruin—a thousand wonders that he had not sunk beyond recovery!

Thus the minuteness of the knowledge, and the extent

of the knowledge which a careful believer has of his own heart, tend to make him feel that he is the *chief of sinners.*

II. Very much in proportion to the extent of a believer's gracious attainments is pure *conscience* brought into exercise. We mean by this pure conscience an exercise of that faculty *as* such, in its own nature and *for* its own ends, not mingled with other affections. In a careless state of mind, and even in a convicted state of mind, the operations of conscience are very much mixed up with such emotions as remorse and fear. These often take the lead, if they are not all. And they are so much occupied with considerations of personal interest, that the mind of the sinner is really kept back from just conceptions of right and wrong, just apprehensions of his own character. Fear may tremble in every joint, and remorse may strike with more than the fangs of the serpent, while at the same time there is but a very limited conception of right and wrong, and a still more limited conception of the high place which belongs to pure rectitude of soul. And one great difference betwixt the convictions of a believer and the convictions of an unbeliever consists simply in this: the different impressions they have of the *mere wrong* of sin. A believer sees that wrong as an unbeliever does not. In sin itself he sees an evil which an unbeliever does not. Aside from remorse, without fear, looking simply at righteousness and unrighteousness, and affected about them on account of what they are in themselves, the believer has such conceptions of sin as an unbeliever never reaches. Would to God that we could make our unconverted hearers perceive that we desire their conversion for some other reason than their escaping the just anger of the Almighty! Would that they could be induced sometimes to forget hell, and be led to perceive that in mere unholiness there is an infinite evil, and in mere holiness an infinite good! Right and wrong come up before a sanctified conscience. An unsanctified one is jostled out of its place. Grace reinstates it; and the more grace carries on its operations in the soul the more purely does conscience look at rectitude and proprieties, let benefits be as they may.

And now, when a believer has been a considerable period under the tuition of this pure conscience—a conscience put right, exercised, and enlightened; and when *right and wrong* stand out before the contemplating and convicted soul in letters of fire; and when not only fear of punishment but the love of pure holiness has led him into the inner chambers of his own soul to detect its sin, then it is natural—it is unavoidable that he should be astonished and amazed at himself, and ready to conclude there never was a heart so bad as his own. He appears to himself the *chief of sinners*. He has new ideas of the high station of rectitude—the high moment of being right. To be *just*, to be what he ought to be, (benefit or no benefit connected with it,) appears to him to be a thing infinitely obligatory and eternally desirable. And as more and more he detects selfishness, and worldliness, and pride, and vanity, and impatience, and obstinacy, and covetousness, and envy within him, it is no wonder that his conscientious impressions make him appear the worst sinner that grace ever saved.

III. The *rule* of conscience is not a thing well understood by an unconverted sinner in his ordinary frame of mind. The deceptions of sin have been flung over it.

This was the experience of St. Paul: *I was alive without the law once; but when the commandment came, sin revived and I died.* He did not understand God's spiritual law in his careless state. He did not feel himself to be literally under condemnation, dead in law.

But when the Holy Spirit justly convicted him, he saw sin in himself that he never saw before, and hope died within him. He discovered what God's law meant and where it applied. He saw its extent, strictness, propriety and beauty. He saw that the *law was holy, and the commandment holy, just and good.* And this was what troubled him. He saw that the law was in the creature's favor, a good law; and that it turned against him and gathered up its terrors only because he was a sinner. The ordinary conviction of sinners includes the same thing. They understand then God's law better, its excellence, its rectitude, and eternal obligations upon the conscience. And for this reason they wonder at themselves. They are amazed at what they have been doing all their lives. Not a week since one said to me, "I wonder how I *could* have lived so."

Now, when grace makes progress in a believer's soul, this understanding of law is carried on. At every stage of advancement the believer understands it better, if not in its essence, at least in its applications. He has tried to obey it, and at last he is forced to exclaim, *I have seen an end of all perfection, but thy commandment is exceeding broad.* Not the act only but the passion—not the passion only but the emotion—not the emotion only but the very thought of evil, a thought checked in an instant and hated as soon as known, is seen to be sin. Law reigns; and now, better and better understood, *sharper than any two-edged sword, a discerner of the thoughts and intents of the heart;* it is no wonder that every just conception of God's law should tend to make the grace-enlightened believer conceive of himself as the *chief of sinners.* He sees that that code of spiritual purity has strange applications to his erring soul. His very spirit can not hide from it for a single moment. It pursues the soul every where. It drags every thought out of its hiding place and holds it up before the light and blaze of eternal law. And it is no wonder that a believer, as he goes on in the increasing knowledge of law, detecting one sin after another, one evil no sooner mastered than another comes to sight, detected every where, hunted into his very soul—it is no wonder that his conception of himself takes the turn of the text: *Chief of sinners! Chief of sinners!*

IV. The religious attempts of a believer constitute another consideration. They have been many, and he is fully conscious that they have sometimes been sincere and earnest; but oh! how often have they been baffled! What vain purposes! How little his strength! How many sinful desires! What vain thoughts! What pride! What obstinacy and worldliness! What vanity! What folly! How many purposes to study God's word more, and prize and frequent the place of prayer more, have been utterly and shamefully defeated! And if any attempt has been successful, and a victory over any sin has been gained, how often does the error and the meanness of a spiritual pride spring up, when humility of heart and gratitude for the grace that gained the victory ought to have been the exclusive affections. A believer aiming after fidelity in duty and conformity to the mind and spirit of Christ, finds a weakness in himself, a changefulness and besettings of sin which he little expected beforehand :

> "His soul with many a tempest tossed,
> Its comfort gone, its wishes crossed,
> Sees every where new straits attend,
> And wonders where the strife will end."

These baffled attempts and bitter experiences, these falls, these defeated purposes, and this ever-recurring struggle of corruption within him against all the aims of conscience and reason, urge him to the conclusion that no sinner was ever plagued with so bad a heart as his own. He utters the deep-toned cry, *Chief of sinners! Chief of sinners!*

V. Throughout all the successful attainments of grace, a believer is invariably becoming *better acquainted with God*. The knowledge he has of the Divine character constitutes one of the most efficacious aids and impressive influences. The better he knows God the better he knows himself; and while his knowledge of God increases both his reverence and his attachment, his knowledge of himself fills him with humiliation and shame. Sin appears worse and worse to him as he knows God better. He sees more and more of it as his soul comes out into the light of God's holy perfections. He perceives the malignity of its evil to be incapable of description, as it is against the greatest and best Being in the universe. He exclaims, *I thought on God and was troubled. I have heard of thee by the hearing of the ear, but now mine eye seeth thee, wherefore I abhor myself and repent in dust and ashes.*

As the believer's increasing acquaintance with God

goes on, and God's adorable majesty, his holy justice, his awful omniscience, and his tender love and matchless goodness, make deeper and deeper impression upon the heart. As the contemplative soul aims to measure the distance between God and itself, and as the light of the Divine perfections comes over the sin-stained spirit, surely it can not *but* be that sin shall put on a new aspect of deformity and odiousness in a believer's sight; and it can not *but* be that by the blaze of God's character he should discover more imperfections in his own. His impressions will be both natural and deep that he is the *chief of sinners*. He will be far from a readiness to attribute to others such an amount of vileness and impropriety as he is compelled to mourn over in himself. Let him reason as he will, let him have what views he may of the common origin, common nature and course of men, still the impressions he has about sin will be deepest and strongest when he turns to that lesson of fire which his knowledge of God's character has enabled him to read within his own sinning spirit. And he will gather up the whole matter about himself into the humiliating conclusion, *Chief of sinners! Chief of sinners!*

VI. A Christian, especially amid his attainments in grace, is a creature of no little reflection. His knowledge increases, especially his knowledge of himself; and amid his reflections and increasing knowledge in Divine things, again and again he is surprised and disappointed in a most painful and humiliating manner. Sometimes he is astounded, and disheartened, and driven to prayer by a wave of despondency that rolls over his soul. His reflection discovers sin as he did not expect, discovers it wherein he had little suspicion of its existence. He finds the imperfection of his repentance, that his very *repentance* (according to the graphic description of the Apostle) *needs to be repented of.* He finds his faith little, his love languid, his worldliness coming back upon him, and amid these tearful and struggling experiences, he would be unwilling to think of any other sinner in the world as he thinks of himself. He does not. He can not. He has had no other believer's heart to read and to be troubled with. *The plague of his own heart* has been his most distressful lesson. And as he finds more evil within himself than he expected, and less gain than he expected, his service of God more imperfect, and his gracious affections more frequently interrupted than he expected, it seems to him that he is indeed the very weakest Christian living. It seems to him that other sinners have not sinned as he has, and other believers have repented better.

VII. That process of sanctification carried on in a believer's heart by the omnipotent power of the Holy Spirit is very much carried on through the influence of two spiritual operations; *first*, the discovery of sin, and *second*, faith in the Redeemer of sinners to procure pardon and justification unto life eternal. There is the combined influence of compulsion and attraction; of violence and persuasion. The believer is driven off from himself at the same moment he is drawn toward God. The fullness of Divine mercy is set over against the sinner's guilt, and by both guilt in himself and mercy in God he feels urged on to aim after attainment in all the powers of a Divine life. His conceptions of sin are not more bitter than his sense of Christ's goodness is sweet; his wants are not more appalling than the fullness of Divine bounty is free. Humiliation and thankfulness blend together their influences upon his soul, and he knows not which is best for him, to be sweetly humble or sweetly grateful. He would be both. He would lie low before God and be grateful for the hand that lifts him up; or, as he treads pensively along the valley of humiliation, he would cheer his humbled spirit with his grateful and happy songs. He would *walk with God*, and wonders and adores that God will let him do so. By this united influence of humiliation and self-emptiness on the one hand, and of gratitude and love on the other, the process of sanctification is promoted within him as he *dies unto sin*, and loves to die unto it, and *lives unto righteousness*, and loves this *life from the dead*.

But this process and these affections are sometimes interrupted. His soul wanders from God. And that it *should ever* wander seems to him one of the strangest anomalies in the universe! How he *could* unite the two evils of forsaking the *fountain of living waters* and of attempting to *hew out for himself cisterns*, he can not conceive! And his wonder at himself deepens, that when he has found them *broken cisterns that can hold no water*, he should still stand by the empty fragments and expect any good! The world put in God's place has not answered his purpose, and nobody knows this so well and so bitterly as himself. And that he should forsake and forget God's love, God's wonderful love—what an evil and ungrateful thing! That he should exchange the calms of humility for the tumults of a wicked and worldly pride—that he should ever exchange the love of God for the love of the world—that he should not only forsake but at once offend and dishonor the best Friend, and most prized Friend he has in the universe, is something he can not account for and can not understand. To his sin against law he has added sin against LOVE; and if he trembles *most* when the thunder-peal breaks on Mount Sinai, he is *most ashamed* when the death-groan of redeeming love dies away on the hill of the crucifixion! Surely no heart, no heart in vile ingratitude can have surpassed his own! No friend ever asked so little as Christ, and no friend ever loved so much! He knows it and feels it all, yet he has backslidden from him! After God has reached so far and done so much—after he had redeemed him and sent the Holy Spirit to pluck him out of the whirl of the world—after he had comforted into peace his distressed and tempest-tossed soul, and dried up his tears and taken him as an adopted child to his heart—that after all this he should half forget his adoption, and only half love and half serve the Saviour that bought him, seems to him to be an extent and strangeness of evil that renders him indeed the *chief of sinners*. Few so guilty, few so guilty as he! And he would utterly despair, and never think of returning to God, nor think he might, if he did not know *that this is a faithful saying and worthy of all acceptation, that Christ Jesus came into the world to save sinners, of whom he is chief.*

The conclusions from this subject are worthy of remembrance.

1. Never despair. There is mercy for the chief of sinners. Your just convictions may trouble you, but they need not extinguish hope. Turn your face toward Christ, and flee to him in faith as a penitent sinner, but never despair. Let the depth of your convictions unite its urgency with the invitations of God's love: *Ho, every one that thirsteth, come ye to the waters!*

2. Never seek hope, consolation, or any comfort or encouragement to your soul by diminished ideas of sin. All such consolation is false, and will be found empty at last. Let Christ stand over against unworthiness and sin; and take all your comforts of hope and all your encouragements of soul from the infinitudes of his boundless grace and love for sinners.

3. Never judge of your Christian condition by the smallness of your humiliating conviction. Rather judge of it by the magnitude of them. Just as surely as grace prospers within you, more and more will you be sensible of your weakness and imperfections, and *that* experience will help to attach you to Christ, your sufficiency and strength.

4. Never allow pride to have any place in your religion. Self-complacency all rests on ignorance and deception. Spiritual pride is all founded on a lie. Humility is founded on truth; and the truth it rests upon will just as surely be discovered and kept in mind, and will just as surely lead to prayer and the hanging of the soul helpless (but hoping) upon God, as grace prospers within you.

5. Never imagine that a deep sense of sin and all the humiliating ideas that grow out of it, are things of unhappiness and gloom. Quite the contrary. They are matters of peace and joy to a believer. They lead to the full fountains of God—to *Christ Jesus, who came into the world to save sinners, even the chief.* Resting by faith on him, you may be happy now and blessed for ever God grant you may. Amen.

Delay of Conversion.

[ARGUED FROM THE NATURE OF MAN.]

To-day, if ye will hear his voice, harden not your heart.—PSALM xcv. 7, 8.

IT will not be disputed that the religion of the Bible requires man to turn from the course he is prone to pursue. In order to be saved he must become acquainted with truths to which, by nature, he has little inclination; he must be subject to rules of a heavenly bearing; and his affections, taken off from their scenes of earthly rioting, purified and elevated, must find joy in God. From that course of prodigal profligacy where he wanders in willing forgetfulness of all but the present, where the little play-things of earth occupy him, while the great interests of a measureless eternity are never suffered to enforce their legitimate claims; he must be called back to the sobrieties of truth, the laws of righteousness and the love of God.

About the proper requisites for salvation there is not, indeed, any material dispute among most of those favored with evangelical instruction. All acknowledge that God must be loved, sin hated, and holiness sought. All agree that religion is a reasonable duty, and that its benefits are not to be expected without some definite attention and some personal interest in its requirements and its provisions. And among all the inattentive in that busy throng of rushing worldliness who crowd the marts of commerce, throng the scenes of amusement, press eagerly on in the chase of honor, or, in the industry of their habits, strive by patient labor to attain a competence or rise to affluence, while all the demands of religion are little heeded and all the interests of eternity are disregarded—among all these, the devotees of wealth, of honor and of pleasure, there are very few who do not intend at some time to become men of religion and the friends of God. Some entirely neglect for the present, and some give partial attention; but all design at some other time to become men of piety and secure an interest in the kingdom of God.

This is the common state of mind among the irreligious. They defer. They do not so much reject religion as delay it; they reject it *by* delaying.

To this state of mind our text addresses itself: *To-day, if ye will hear his voice, harden not your hearts.* God speaks to us. His *voice* comes from the united testimonies of Creation, Providence, and the more special revelations of his Word. He fills heaven and earth with arguments for religion. Every where he shows that he is a *great God and a great King. In his hand are the deep places of the earth. The strength of the hills is his also. The sea is his and he made it; and his hands formed the dry land.* Thus Creation calls to us: *O come and let us worship and bow down, let us kneel before the Lord our Maker. For he is our God, and we are the people of his pasture and the sheep of his hand.* Our provision and preservation are arguments for piety: *To-day, if ye will hear his voice, harden not your hearts.*

But men delay. Their attention to religion, so far as

it is to be any reforming, controlling matter, they defer to another period.

On this delay we are going to make some reflections, and in the present discourse will strive to show the impropriety and folly of it by considerations taken from *the Nature of man.* That Nature cries out to you, *To-day, if ye will hear his voice.* We divide our discourse into two parts:

I. The uncertainty of future opportunity for conversion.

II. The increased difficulty and improbability of conversion, if death should not cut us off from an opportunity. These both have respect to the Nature of man.

I. Let us attend to the first. The uncertainty of the future is an argument for immediate conversion.

There are few things in which men more sadly deceive themselves than in their reckoning upon the continuance of life. They *know* that death is abroad in the world. They have seen its victims cut down around them ever since they were capable of any observation. They have seen the strength of the vigorous, the health of the healthful, the most salubrious climates, the most assiduous care, and the best medical skill, all baffled and rendered vain before that Death who claims the indisputable right to select his victims from any spot contaminated by sin. They have seen the diminutive length of the little hillock that rises so frequent in the grave-yard, beneath whose sod sleeps the little child, that lived only to bless its mother with its smile, and then died upon her bosom! The entire uncertainty of human life is a thing well known by every human mind. But still, when we come to look for the proper results of this conviction, how sadly are we disappointed! That work which must be done while life lasts, if it is done at all—that work which must be done while life lasts, or it had *been better* for us that we had *never been born*—that work is as wantonly neglected as if this perfect uncertainty were not hanging over all the future.

> "To-morrow?
> Where is to-morrow? in another world!
> For numbers this is certain, the reverse
> Is sure to none."

Yet on this *perhaps*, this mere *peradventure* that we shall live, we hazard all the interests of future existence! The soul, its eternity, its heaven, its hell, are hung up upon the brittle thread of human life, quivering to break! Let the sick man delay his remedies; let the poisoned suffer the venom to circulate in his veins, and carry death along with it in every pulse that beats; let the man whose dwelling is wrapt in flames suffer the fires to draw around him the circle of a dreadful death; we will call them wise compared with that delay which jeopards ALL ETERNITY on the uncertainties of human life!

"But there is a probability that we shall live." Yes, and there is a probability that you will die. I am aware that no demonstrations of reason, no proofs from facts, can fasten the reality upon the human feelings. I am aware that loved impression and cherished desire will triumph over every tale of truth, and after the mind is conquered by light, the heart will still hug its deceptions: I am aware that it is extremely difficult for us, even when we most earnestly desire it, to bring home to our bosoms a realization of our uncertainty, or of the improbabilities of human life. But we will draw one picture, and hope you will see in it an enforcement of the text. That picture is this assembly. I suppose myself to behold here a congregation of two thousand souls :

    In the course of one year,   66 of them will die.
    In ten years, ...   588 will have died.
    In twenty years, . . .   1,078 will be gone.
    In thirty years, . . .   1,477 will be no more.
    In forty years, ...   1,744 will be in eternity.
    In fifty years, ...   1,922 will be dead men.

Only seventy-eight left in the land of the living! What a picture of the probabilities of life! How rapidly we are rushing into eternity! At the beginning we behold two thousand; but how rapidly that number is diminished down! Seventy-eight only left in fifty years! One half century, according to the common chances of life, will not leave eighty in the land of the living!

Would that this picture were as effectual as it is appalling! Would that the hearts of the two thousand in a promiscuous assembly were so affected with the idea that sixty-six of them will die in a single year, that sixty-six of them in a single year would hear the voice of the Son of God and live! My hearers, your days are fast numbering up! the sands in your glass of life are rapidly falling! for you the shroud is weaving! for you the bed of death is spread! Your seat here will soon be vacant, and the ear that now listens to me will be sealed up, till the trump of the archangel shall awake the dead! Death is certain. Life is uncertain. *To-day, if ye will hear his voice, harden not your hearts.* To-morrow may be too late to hear.

II. But if you *should* live—if, amid all the dangers and uncertainties of our present state, you should continue on in life as you are, till you have reached the utmost limit fixed to human existence, the *effect* which continuing in irreligion will inevitably produce, according to the very constitution of human nature, should enforce the text, and forbid the delay of your conversion. This is our second topic.

What we mean is this: That we are ourselves such creatures, and true conversion to God is such a thing, that our conversion to God becomes more and more difficult by delay—more and more improbable. Let us enter upon the topic.

As forming the foundation of our argument, let us carefully premise four things, which all confess to be true, and which are plain to every body.

The first is, that although conversion is a work of Divine grace, yet it is an act of man, in such a sense at least that it requires the exercise of his own powers and faculties. Nobody disputes that.

The second is, that in true religion there are things to be known: the mind itself is to be *enlightened, renewed in knowledge;* the truths by which men are sanctified are to be understood. Not that religion is such a hard science as to defy the efforts of a very ordinary understanding, nor that mere speculative knowledge is to be our chief aim, but that religion has reason in it—that it requires for its exercise an intelligent mind, an understanding capable of apprehending truth. Nobody disputes that.

The third is, that in true religion there is voluntary obedience to God; that the converted man willingly renounces the ways of sin, and though his efforts are marked with imperfection, yet he possesses a fixed principle of obedience. Nobody disputes that.

The fourth is, that in true religion the sensibilities of the heart are affected. This needs no proof. All confess that if we do not love God we are not the children of God. Speculative knowledge alone can never save. With the *heart* man believeth unto righteousness. Nobody disputes that.

Fix these four ideas in your mind, and carry them along with you. On these premises (which none will dispute) we may be able to see that an increased difficulty and improbability of conversion must arise from delay. Because,

1. Such delay will tend to *unfit the mind for Divine knowledge.* We do not pretend to decide what, or how much a man must *know* in order to conversion; but the nature of religion, the course of Divine instruction, the whole procedure of God in saving men, (so far as *we* can understand it,) and all the vital exercises of religion itself—its hopes, its fears, its high and heavenly bearings as it reaches forth to pluck the fruits of eternal life—these, all these contain demonstration enough that man need not expect to become a true Christian without some enlightening in his mind. Besides this, it is worthy the consideration of those who live under the means of grace, and who are not influenced on common matters by superficial views, whether *their* mind will ever be influenced to faith, except by such maturity or extent of light as in other affairs it is wont to follow. It is easy to see how a man who, in the common affairs of life, is accustomed to act on very limited knowledge, may follow the same rule in religion—his mind being satisfied with the same extent of knowledge therein to which it has been accustomed in other matters—in mechanism, or agriculture, or trade, in history, or science, or the arts. But it is not easy to conceive how a mind, accustomed to mature instruction, to thorough intelligence, to an extensive

understanding of the subjects of thought, will ever be influenced in religion in a manner contradictory to all its fixed habits; will ever *believe*, ever yield, ever act on such little and limited knowledge as it has been accustomed to refuse. If, therefore, the Divine bounty is not something more than *grace for grace*—if God does not proportion his influences of sanctification not to the diligence but to the *negligence* of his creature, we can scarcely expect that one living under all the means of religion, and accustomed in common matters to thorough light, should fail of receiving a strong warning against delay. There is a balance in the human mind. There is habitude in intellect. Thought cleaves to analogy. And we are not to expect that on the subjects of knowledge in religion the mind will, by manner of its procedure, contradict all the principles of its ordinary action. To delay, therefore, may squander so much of life, forego so many opportunities for instruction, and crowd the whole business of religion into such a narrow space of time, that there will be little probability of attaining saving knowledge of the only *true God and Jesus Christ whom he has sent.*

This idea is susceptible of striking illustration if we had time to pursue it. But we must pass to others.

Our point is, that delaying religion may so unfit the mind for religious knowledge as to forbid our acquiring light enough to be saved. On this point let us name a few items of illustration.

(1) The man who delays his religion will not have his mind utterly unemployed. His thought and study will be mainly devoted to worldly and sensible objects. In these the intellect will find its range, the heart its interest, habits will become fixed. Go into your circles of trade,

and solicit those men whose minds have been employed for years in the calculations of commerce, to investigate some philosophical theory, to solve some abstract proposition, to exchange the subjects of sense for the abstractions of speculation, and though you should be able to array all the motives of interest in favor of your proposal, and wake the most eager wish for compliance, compliance is impossible. The mind has not been used to such investigations, and when such subjects come before it, they are a wilderness—they are all confusion and darkness, and the mind turns from them with a kind of instinctive horror. So in religion. Let the world educate us, let it form our mind, mark out its range, and hold us year after year under the sway of its influence, and we shall find it extremely difficult to dismiss *things seen and temporal;* religion will seem all dark to us, and, not accustomed to its study, we shall have small prospect of getting into the clear blaze of its light. *To-day, if ye will hear his voice.*

(2) With the man who defers religion, time does not defer the silent changes which it works upon his powers. True, the mind never dies; time never blots out one of its faculties. They are the birth of immortality, and eternity is their life-time. But *here* the mind is in close connection and sympathy with a material body. In youth the blood is warm. It circulates freely along its channels. The bones are full of marrow. The sinews are elastic. The step is light and motion easy and delightful. Their perception is quick, memory tenacious, recollection easy, and all the powers of the mind in seeming sympathy with the body, present their freshness and facility for action. Time passes on. Age has come. The chilled blood moves with retarded pace. The

elastic step has given place to the heavy tread, and the change which has passed upon the outward man finds its mournful parallel within. Now perception is slow, memory fails, recollection is difficult, and the whole faculties of the mind seem enveloped in darkness or trammeled with the weight of years. That mind is slow to receive any unwonted impressions—to take any new direction. Its circle of ideas seems fixed, and it is all but impossible to learn any thing new. *To-day, if ye will hear.* Time will soon hurry you on to that spot, where you will find it extremely difficult to learn enough about religion, to have its light lead you securely to the Son of God.

(3) Again: Delaying the study of religion renders saving knowledge more difficult of attainment, because the ordinary subjects of thought will be perpetually diverting the mind. Man is not the creature of demonstration alone. Proof can not wear out the impression of years. Already many of you have reached that unhappy point in your irreligion where you find it extremely difficult to avoid in your religious study the undesired intrusion of worldly things. Not that the subject seems dark to you only, (that was our first item,) but that other things have made such impressions on you, have so worn themselves into your minds, that you can not dismiss them when you desire. The man who has long chased the world will find the world chasing him. It will go after him into his closet, it will follow him into the sanctuary, it will damp and dissipate the spirit of devotion in those solemn moments when he would send up his most earnest prayer. After continued study of other things to the neglect of religion, you will find it more and more difficult to throw off the diverting influ-

ences of the world long enough to attain knowledge in religion, sufficient to satisfy the mind and hold it in firm faith on Jesus Christ.

(4) Delay, finally, (for we must end these items, and I am sorry to be obliged to end them with an idea like this; but my knowledge of the state of mind in which some of my hearers now are compels me to it;) I say, delaying religion will unfit the mind for attaining its light because of the prejudice which delay engenders. Let us explain the idea. You know very well that the Bible speaks to your reason. Its demands all court examination. What it asks is enforced by the monitions of conscience, and in the first part of life, when the mind learns easily, when the affections are generous, when the man is not guarded by some rampart flung around him; it is not easy to hear the subject of religion pressed upon us and remain unmoved. In these seats there has been more than one indication that the calls of the Gospel are enforced by the uneasy feelings of irreligious minds. But repentance is delayed. You retire and pacify your excited sensibilities as well as you can, by alleging the difficulties in your way, by gathering up excuses for your delaying, by endeavoring so to present the subject of religion to your own thoughts, its hard truths, its difficult doctrines, its deep mysteries, that your consciences shall be more at peace with your impenitence. Instead of walking in the light so far as you do see, you neglect all that is plain, and weave your apologies from the intricacies of things that are dark. This process is constantly going on. And this is the process by which men are led to *believe a lie.* Soon that lie occupies the mind. It wards off the truth. It comes up like a magic shield, to turn aside every arrow of truth,

and ward off every blow of the *two-edged sword*. When you are troubled you flee to your refuge and hide yourselves in its darknesses. You are forced to do this in order to delay in peace. And doing this you are fastening a falsehood upon your mind which will render it extremely difficult for you at any future period, to attain sufficient light in the truth to lead you to an established, consoling and saving faith.

We conclude, therefore, that delay does exceedingly diminish the probabilities of conversion to God, because it unfits the mind for receiving Divine illumination.

II. But we have a second source of argument. We find it in the influence of delay upon the principle of voluntary obedience.

We have nothing to do at this moment with any theories on the freedom of the human will. We take the plain sense of Scripture, *My people shall be willing in the day of my power*, and we maintain that there is no true conversion which does not include a voluntary submission to the Divine will. Not that Christian obedience is perfect, nor that we are to be saved by the law, but that true piety is willing to serve God, and that those who are justified through grace are desirous to be holy. We speak on these principles.

Now, our delaying religion renders our salvation difficult and more improbable because it increases the difficulty of willing obedience. It is true there are no chains woven round the will. Man is as free in sin as he is in holiness. He chooses in view of the motives before him; but still there is a sense in which a man may become a slave in sin. By delaying religion a man is not merely at a stand. He is perpetually exercising his volitions.

And, unhappily for him, he is exercising them in sin. By exercise they become strong. Every new act of disobedience to God gives them an additional power of disobeying. In a little time, the obstinacy of the will is unmoved by all those considerations which once made its choice slow and trembling. You see an exemplification of this in the disobedient child. A sense of duty, filial veneration, and it may be filial love, at first made disobeying a very difficult thing. After a little it is easy. You see an exemplification in the man of intemperance. At first there was not willingness to proceed to those lengths in sin to which in the later stages he moves on with unhesitating obstinacy. No man can continue in any sin without losing more and more of the powers of self-control. It requires some denying of self to follow Jesus Christ. The *thoughts* must be *brought into* captivity. The cross must be taken up.

"Deny thyself and take thy cross,
Is the Redeemer's great command;
Nature must count her gold but dross
If she would gain that heavenly land."

And if the duty demands an arduous struggle now, delay will make that duty more difficult still. If you are not equal to the self-control of Christianity now, you never will be equal to it. Every day's impenitence will only add to the obstinacy of an unyielding will, diminish your powers of self-control, and make you more and more the slave. The difficulties and improbabilities of conversion are increasing at every step. The delaying sinner is not only guilty of neglecting the most favorable period for his conversion, but he is perpetrating the madness of rendering himself incapable of it hereafter. Like a man in a gulf, who, instead of availing himself of the aids afforded for his deliverance, madly plunges further down the chasm that stretches its unfathomable depths beneath. To-DAY, *if ye* WILL, ye may hear. But delay will make you more and more the slave, and diminish with inconceivable rapidity the probabilities of your saving submission to the will of God.

But we must dismiss the rest of our materials on this point.

3. Delay will do much to destroy the sensibilities of the heart.

On this point we might proceed in the same method of illustration as when we showed how delaying tends to unfit the mind for attaining light enough to be saved. The sensibilities of the heart surely will feel the palsy of time quite as extensively as the faculties of the understanding. Quite as rapidly will worldly attachments weave themselves round our affections, and worldly endearments restrain us from the love of Christ. Man is so constituted that after proceeding far in life he is not apt to change the objects of his affections.

But above all, sin possesses a most deadening influence upon the religious sensibilities. Not to say any thing about age, to pass over all the influences of years of worldly attachments, to make no mention of the filling of the heart with things that shut out the love of God, it is enough for us to notice how the mere continuance in irreligion possesses a palsying influence over our sensibilities to religious things. If the shock of the fall left any thing unimpaired in human nature, it seems to have been the sensibilities of the heart. Its love, its tenderness, its hopes, its fears are neither dull nor weak. To the feelings of gratitude and love, the God of heaven seems to have made his most frequent appeal, as he would win us to himself. He calls us his children. He proposes to be our Father. He speaks kindly to us in our sins; and when we might justly expect the voice of his indignation, he only expostulates: *Come now, and let us reason together; though your sins be as scarlet, they shall be as white as snow; though they be red like crimson, they shall be as wool.* *As I live, saith the Lord, I have no pleasure in the death of the wicked.* He gives his Son to die for us, and promises with him also freely to *give us all things.* It is plain that God would win us to his bosom and have his *goodness lead us to repentance.* His eye is on the returning prodigal *when he is a great way off,* and he silences the agony of confession: *Bring forth the best robe and put it on him; this, my son, was dead and is alive again, was lost and is found.* Such mercy, such condescension, is designed to attract our hearts. And if we do not *love him who first loved us,* if we do not find our sensibilities softened and sanctified, our affections attracted to Christ and the love of Christ, we can not be the children of God. But what a wonderful influence continuance in sin is having over us! It hardens the heart. Who can not remember the time when he thought of the goodness of his heavenly Father—how he loved his sinful child, spared him, fed him, healed him when he was sick, and offered to forgive him and take him to heaven when he died—and as he thought of these, felt his bosom heave at the tenderness that solicited him? Who can not remember the time when he heard the tale of the crucifixion, and was almost ready to die for the Saviour who died to ransom him? But delay in sin hardens the heart! Where now are your generous sensibilities at the compassion of God? where the tears which you were ready to pour at the feet of Jesus? Oh! if sin darkens the mind, it does still more to harden the heart. Deferring religion will give bad passions power, mortgage the affections to earth, steel the sensibilities, and if you can not be affected, and melted, and won over to religion now, it will become more difficult, and your conversion will become less probable by delay! *To-day, if ye will hear his voice, harden not your heart.* If your sensibilities are unmoved *now* by all the touching tenderness of the love of God, what shall move them hereafter when your heart has become as *hard as the nether mill-stone? If such things are done in the green tree, what shall be done in the dry?* The uncertainty of any future opportunity for conversion, and the increased difficulty and improbability of conversion at any future time, if death should *not* cut us off from the opportunity, give an alarming emphasis to the cry, TO-DAY, TO-DAY, TO-DAY!

My aged fellow mortal, yet delaying your conversion to Christ, your race is partly run! Sin has long been passing its blighting influence upon you! Every moment's delay is making your salvation more difficult, and furnishing new reason to fear that you will never enter heaven! God forbid that I should treat your gray hairs with irreverence; but God forbid that I should see you, unwarned, tread on your dismal pathway to the tomb! Already your course has done much to impair those faculties whose action is necessary in securing your salvation! Let your gray hairs preach to you! Take warning from the dimmed vision of your eye! Be admonished by the influence of old age upon your mind! But I forget. There is a better voice than these. *If ye will hear* HIS *voice.* It is *God* that speaks to you. It is God, and therefore you need not despair. There is encouragement for you after all. You need not perish. True, you have much to do, and your *time is short.* But *to-day.* Oh wonderful, wonderful mercy! when only a day remains, there is some room for hope. *Turn your feet,* then, *to God's testimonies. Strive to enter in at the strait gate.* Pray for Divine aid. Even yet your hard heart may melt, and your old bosom thrill with generous tenderness, as you embrace Jesus Christ: *Lord, now lettest thou thy servant depart in peace, for mine eyes have seen thy salvation.*

You who are young in years are now in the most promising period for salvation. The world has not yet so far occupied and so sadly corrupted you. Your mind, your heart, your power of self-control, are now in a better state for obtaining salvation than they ever will be hereafter. Seize this happy moment. *Remember now your Creator in the days of your youth.* Even now it will be no easy thing to break loose from the attractions of sin. But delay will change its cords of silk into bands of iron. Yours is now the season when prayer may be breathed with most hope: *They that seek me early shall find me.* Lose not this auspicious moment. The hour is on the wing. Now, when the dew of your youth is upon you, you may more easily attain salvation than in any future period.

Why should any of us delay? Middle life, youth, old age, are tending to the tomb. Mercy solicits every class. *It is Christ that died, yea, rather, that is risen again.* We know God is gracious. We know conversion is needful. And we intend to secure *that better part which shall not be taken away.* Then *why* delay? Oh why? Alas! the mournful cause is too plain! Sin has already darkened your mind, diminished your self-control, hardened your heart, till you find it no easy thing to reform, and you defer the unpleasant task to a more *convenient season. But if such things are done in the green tree, what shall be done in the dry ?* Delay will multiply your difficulties. But you have *no hope* in exertion. Well, delay will not furnish any. And remember—*no man ought to have any hope in himself.* But there is a God in heaven. There is a Holy Spirit. There is a Throne of Grace. God never *said to the seed of Jacob, seek ye my face in vain.* What will you do ? Oh God, soften these hearts by thy Spirit. Draw them by the cords of thy love. Dispose us all to-day to hear thy voice, and we will praise the Father, Son and Holy Ghost. Amen.

Delay of Conversion.

[ARGUED FROM THE ECONOMY OF THE HOLY SPIRIT.]

To-day, if ye will hear his voice, harden not your hearts.—PSALM xcv. 7, 8.

THESE words may properly be considered as a solemn caution against a very common error, and a very disastrous result growing out of it. That error is delaying our conversion to God; that dreadful result is that we shall *not enter into his rest.* These words of caution (or, if you please, of command) stand connected with the mention of mercies here used as an attractive argument to draw the heart to God. *He is our God and we are the people of his pasture, and the sheep of his hand. To-day, if ye will hear his voice, harden not your hearts.* Like a good shepherd he would lead us *beside the still waters and in green pastures.* His *voice* is heard. His benefits are given. We have *means* enough to lead us to make God *our* God, and learn to rejoice in the *Rock of our salvation.*

While surrounded with these means, this goodness, these arguments for piety, we hear the emphatic caution against delay: *To-day, if ye will hear his voice, harden not your hearts, as in the provocation and as in the day of temptation in the wilderness, when your fathers tempted me, and proved me, and saw my work. Forty years was I grieved with this generation, and said, It is a people that do err in their heart, and they have not known my ways, unto whom I sware in my wrath that they should not enter into my rest.*

It appears to me, therefore, that our delaying religion is a practice here censured by considerations drawn from especially three sources:

First: From the effect of delay upon our own nature: it *hardens the heart*, and thus renders our salvation more improbable according to *the nature of man.* This was the topic of the first sermon.

Second: From the connection of our delay with the means and the spirit of holiness. Our delay grieves the Spirit of God, and thus renders our salvation more improbable according to the principles which regulate the actings of the Holy Ghost. This is the topic of this morning.

Third: From the history of grace. That history shows us that procrastination is the path of a dreadful hazard; and therefore our own observation ought to preach to us: *To-day, if ye will hear his voice, harden not your hearts, as in the provocation in the wilderness.* *History* enforces the caution. This shall be the topic of a future sermon, if God pleases to spare us to preach it.

For the present, we attend to the Economy of the Holy Spirit.

We do injustice, my brethren, both to the intelligence and the conscience of unconverted men, when we suppose them contented and happy in their irreligion—thinking themselves fit to die and meet God in the judgment. They are *not* contented. They are *not* happy. They do not live on in their impiety because they have any assured hope that they have now any interest in the mercies of the Son of God. They are at peace on quite another principle. They are flattering themselves that they shall *hereafter* become true converts to Jesus Christ, and before the messenger shall arrive to call them off from the fields of their earthly service to the reckoning of their Lord, they hope to be prepared to hear that plaudit, *Well done, good and faithful servant, enter thou into the joy of thy Lord.* On this hope, this flimsy hope, on this half-formed purpose of future piety, on this deceitful resolve hereafter to *seek the Lord*, the immense throng of unconverted men live on in sin. They *intend* to repent. They *mean* to be Christians. And though they are somewhat sensible of the hardening influence of sin—though they find themselves more and more inclined to forget God—though temptations multiply as they tread further and further along the *broad road that leadeth to destruction*—though they are warned by the uncertainties of life, the abuse of mercies, the worth of the soul—still they delay! It is *delay*—just delay. It is not the rejection of religion once and for ever with a determination never to attend to it. *Delay* keeps the irreligious away from Christ. And all that can be said about sudden and unexpected death—about the habits and hardening influence of sin—about the growing dispositions of worldliness—about weakened and darkened mind—perceptions dimmed by age—the sensibilities of the heart blunted or steeled or worn away—the obstinacy of will confirmed by years of disobedience—all this is not sufficient to wake immediate effort to gain eternal life; because it is all warded off by the idea of the power of the Holy Ghost, or the power of human purposes. The delaying sinner believes himself quite adequate to carrying out his good purposes, and hopes to find hereafter in the aids of the Holy Spirit enough to compensate for all his deficiencies. When he shall have lived on to that *uncertain* period (for he never fixes it—which of all the impenitent here has determined how long before he will seek God?)—when he has lived on to that uncertain period at which he shall set out to become a Christian, he hopes the omnipotence of the Holy Spirit will compensate for the hardening of years. He hopes the Holy Spirit will then subdue his hardness, irradiate his beclouded mind, eradicate his long-cherished propensities, and lead him in the way of faith. He hopes the aids of the Holy Spirit will be as easily procured then as now; and since that Spirit is omnipotent, he hopes his power will suffice for all the weakness and the hardness of heart which may need his agency. He does not tremble much at growing hardened, because God can soften the hardest heart. Thus he turns a doctrine of grace into an encouragement for delay.

For this reason we devote this sermon to the principles which regulate the converting influences of the Holy Spirit. These principles furnish no ground for this presuming procrastination.

It is true God can convert whom he will. There is no blindness, no hardness, no obstinacy beyond the power of the Holy Ghost. We limit not the Holy One of Israel. It is true also that his converting agencies are entirely sovereign. He works according to his own will, and in an infinitely wise and independent manner. It is also true that the principles of his economy may not all be revealed to us. Why *one is taken and another left*, we can give no other account than, *even so, Father, for so it seemed good in thy sight.*

Still we know something of the general principles on which the Holy One chooses to act in leading men to repentance. These principles (and here we form the division of this sermon)—these principles must be consistent with—

   I. His displeasure against sin.
   II. His appointment of grace.
   III. His requirements of justice.
   IV. His promises of kindness.
   V. His threatenings of indignation.

I. The converting operations of the Holy Spirit must be consistent with his displeasure at sin.

Sin and all continuance in sin are infinitely displeasing to God. *He is of purer eyes than to behold evil, and can not look upon iniquity.* There is nothing against which the whole mind of the Deity is so turned. Sin is his abhorrence. It dishonors him. It defeats the benefits of his love. Its continuance renders vain the treasures of his grace, and tramples on the blood of his Son. It belongs to the perfections of the Divine character to manifest every where a holy hatred of sin. It is manifested in the witherings of that curse which fell on the garden planted by his hand. It is manifested in the thunders of Sinai—in the terrific denunciations of that law which fell from the lips of Deity amid thunder and fire and smoke! It is manifested in those affectionate plaints which the God of love utters over perverse sinners, who will not turn to him and be forgiven: *Oh, Ephraim, what shall I do unto thee? Oh, Judah, what shall I do unto thee? Oh, Jerusalem! Jerusalem! how often would I have gathered thy children together!* It is manifested above all in the agonies of the eternal Son when his soul was made an offering for sin, and the earth drank the blood that gushed from his opened veins!

Now the principle of the sanctifying operations of the Holy Ghost must be entirely consistent with this. The Holy Ghost does not convert sinners on any system which will not manifest his displeasure at sin. When the irreligious man delays his religion, expecting that he shall hereafter find relief in the powers of the Holy Ghost for all the difficulties which continued impenitence has produced—expecting those powers to be granted just as readily after years of continued impiety, as in the beginning of life; he is expecting the operations of the Holy Ghost on a system which will manifest no displeasure at his delay and his continued sin. He will be disappointed! The Divine Spirit does not renew the hearts of men on such a system. Sovereign and dark to us as are his principles of operation, they are not principles which encourage delay. In the system of his converting agency he will manifest his disapprobation of protracted impenitence. Whatever may be his power to diminish the dispositions of worldliness—to dispel the darkness of the carnal mind—to break the iron chains of sinful habit—to soften down the adamant of a heart hardened by years of impiety; let us be assured he is not going to exert that power on principles to encourage sin, and therefore not on principles to encourage procrastination. No, no! The Holy Spirit is not acting on such a system. For his converting work he is *not* given as readily to *the sinner of a hundred years*, as to those that *seek him early!* To furnish you the aids of his grace, he will not be as ready at any future time you may appoint for your repentance, as while you are listening now to his call: *To-day, if ye will hear his voice!* He is *not* as ready to renew the heart of the profligate whose *steps take hold on hell*, as the heart of the child in the Sabbath-school whose lessons are conned with prayer.

It is true, that many an aged and long-procrastinating sinner has been converted. But it is also true, that *more* have *died accurst!* The subjects of grace among those long delaying conversion have been few enough to show that the genius of converting economy frowns on delay and manifests the Divine displeasure against sin.

You who delay, expecting hereafter to attain Divine aid just as easily, thinking that God will be just as near to *you*, and just as ready to subdue you to himself, and willing to compensate by his power for your hardness and habits and blindness, have greatly mistaken the system on which the Holy Ghost operates. His system agrees with his holiness. It frowns on your delay. You are the subjects of a miserable delusion! Think of this, ye that delay, and, delaying, prevent the economy of grace. *To-day, if ye will hear his voice, harden not your hearts.*

II. The gracious appointments of the Holy Ghost—the principles which control his converting agency, must be such as to do no dishonor to his appointments. For the purpose of leading sinners to heaven, God has made appointments in his Church, has given the ministry of reconciliation, instituted ordinances, hallowed one day in seven, and furnished all things necessary for holiness. He loves his appointments. He values them—honors them. He will in no wise cast any dishonor upon them. The economy of gracious operations by the Holy Spirit will be such as to conspire with that Spirit's own appointments, and do honor to them. God in action will not be inconsistent with God in appointment. The Holy Ghost in conversion will not act on such principles as to show that the appointments he has made are of no utility and no promise. Consequently, if we would procure the assistance of the Holy Spirit most securely, we must attend to the appointments of the Holy Spirit most assiduously.

If it had been the system of the Holy Spirit to enlighten without attention and study—to sanctify without our aims and efforts—to correct without our caution, and console without our coming to the fountains whence issue the streams of consolation; he never would have made such appointments. But he has made them. He tells us, *faith cometh by hearing, and hearing by the Word of God.* He sends his ministers to give *line upon line and precept upon precept;* to preach *Jesus Christ and him crucified.* *Strong meat* is to be prepared for those of mature age, and *milk for babes* in Christ. Every thing is arranged on the principle of a practical system. Apostles must teach —prophets foretell. *Some evangelists, some pastors and teachers* are given *for the work of the ministry—for the edifying of the body of Christ.* All this is practical. It all demands the attention and application of every sinner that would be saved.

Now when a man delays his religion, with the hope that hereafter he may be just as secure of attaining the aids of the Holy Ghost, he is expecting the Holy Ghost to cast contempt on his own appointments; he is expecting the Divine Spirit to sanctify him aside from his obedient and reverential use of the means which God has appointed for his salvation; he is expecting that Spirit to act on principles for his conversion utterly at war with the practical system of means, and motives, and instructions to which God calls him to attend. He neglects, delays now, hoping for as ready aid from the Divine Spirit hereafter. He will be woefully disappointed! God is not going to bestow his Spirit of conversion as freely, and readily, and constrainingly on those who delay and neglect and will not aim to improve the appointments of God, as on those who aim to *seek first the kingdom of God*—to *seek him early;* who, when God says, *Seek ye my face,* reply to him, *Thy face, Lord, will we seek.* And the delaying man who expects him to do so, is entertaining a delusive expectation directly at war with the system of the Spirit's operations.

Be assured you will not have the freeness of grace corresponding to your freeness in sin. It will correspond with your duty, but not with your delay. The system of heavenly influences is favorable to your industry, but not to your neglect. God helps those who aim to help themselves. Under the appointments of God you ought now to be *working out your salvation with fear and trembling.* Why this Bible? why this ministry we exercise? why these seats you fill? why these temples of worship—these Sabbaths for instruction—if you may as well expect to be converted after you have abused them all, as after you have improved them all? Delaying man! You are presuming on grace! You are running a dreadful hazard! You have mistaken the system of God's converting mercy! That system cries out to you: *Today, if ye will hear his voice, harden not your heart.*

III. The requirements of the Holy Spirit. His converting operations must be consistent with his requirements. Grace must *have* requirements. It would be licentiousness without them. Sinners must be reformed. *Without holiness no man shall see the Lord.*

In the *words which the Holy Ghost teacheth,* we find he makes requirements of those who would be saved. His requirements relate to many subjects. They are intended to secure the active exertions of men. Free as grace is—full and flowing as are the channels in which it is offered—sovereign as is the agency which renews men after the image of God, it is still true that efforts are demanded of those who would be saved. Take three items on this:

1. Notice the requirements relative to continued indulgence in sin. *Put away the evil of your doings; cease to do evil; learn to do well. Make you a new heart and a new spirit, for why will ye die? Let the wicked forsake his way and the unrighteous man his thoughts.* The requirements of God demanding our abandonment of thoughtlessness, and vanity, and sin, are made with just as much earnestness as if no grace were provided to aid our endeavors. And does this cast no light on the principles which regulate the agency of the Holy Spirit? Are we to believe after all this that the economy of renewing grace is of such a nature that we are as likely to be benefited by it in our negligence, as by our attention and vigorous exertions? May we indulge the hope that after we have continued our neglect of these requirements as long as our brief existence here will allow—after we have rushed madly on in sin—after we have run in the way of evil with willing feet, and cherished the dispositions of sinfulness in our hardening hearts; the power of the Holy Ghost will correspond to our disobedience and its results? May we hope that we shall as easily attain his aids, when hereafter we design to turn from worldliness and fit for heaven? Delaying sinners think so and thus encourage their delay. But they are encouraged by a falsehood. The Holy Spirit will do honor to his commands. By his converting agency he will pour no contempt upon his holy prohibitions. He

will not operate on the hearts of sinners on any system that will show his prohibitions of sin, his cautions and his calls were needless and groundless. He will not as readily meet the delaying sinner after he has gone on to all the *superfluity of naughtiness*, and then thinks to be converted. No, no. He will honor the obedience that honors him. He will verify the promise, *hear and your soul shall live*, in more senses than one.

2. Notice the requirements relative to the attentive study of religion. How emphatic are the commands: *Search the Scriptures; get wisdom, get instruction, incline your ear and come unto me; to-day, if ye will hear his voice; with all thy gettings get understanding; wisdom is better than rubies.* Will the economy of conversion pass unheeded all the disobedience of these commands of which the delay of conversion is guilty? Has the delaying man any right to suppose that the Holy Ghost will be as ready and sure to enlighten him in saving knowledge of our Lord and Saviour Jesus Christ, after his continued neglect of instruction, as before it? May he hope that his ignorance will be harmless, and that the darkness of his delaying mind will be as readily dispelled by the Holy Ghost when hereafter he chooses to seek God, as if he had not *despised instruction* and hated reproof? No! The Holy Spirit adopts no such system of conversion. The economy of his agency will be consistent with his commands; and the delaying man who hopes hereafter to find the Holy Spirit compensating for his present inattention will be sadly disappointed. The man delays, expecting special grace to enlighten him at once—to relieve him from the labor of learning, and make him wise unto salvation, as much as if he had vigilantly framed his heart to the Divine instructions. But he is perverting

the economy of the Spirit's operations! He is fast flinging himself beyond the sphere of the Spirit's agency! Be assured, the system of conversion will never demonstrate the uselessness of Divine instruction. The omnipotence of the Holy Ghost in enlightening will never justify the impiety of that *delaying* of religion which renders more deep the darkness of the carnal understanding! If you would attain the assistance of the Holy Spirit, *To-day, harden not your heart.*

3. Notice the requirements relating to prayer. *Seek ye the Lord while he may be found, call ye upon him while he is near; ask and it shall be given unto you; seek and ye shall find; knock and it shall be opened unto you. If any man lack wisdom let him ask of God.* The Holy Spirit is given in answer to prayer. A throne of grace is set up in heaven. A God of grace has made it his residence. Invitations are sent out to even ungodly sinners to approach it, that they may obtain mercy and find grace to help in time of need. But the lips of the delaying man are sealed up. No *effectual, fervent prayer* is sent up for even that gift, without which his soul must die! The last offer of God is unheeded! The last gift of Heaven— the Spirit to seal redemption and make the blessings of the *everlasting covenant* over to the sinner on the veracity of God, is trifled with! And is it so, that in some future day of intended penitence the delaying man will find it just as easy to obtain that Spirit as if he were not now resisting him? May the requirement of prayer be disregarded till the soul is just departing into eternity, and prayer then be offered with the same hope of converting answers by the Holy Spirit? Oh, no. The dying find it different from this! They want more time to pray! If they could recall the months of their negligence, how earnestly

would they devote them to *cry day and night unto God!* Their dreadful experience teaches us a useful lesson. The system of the Holy Ghost in fitting souls for heaven is not such as to sanction delaying.

In one word, the requirements of God meet us every where. The system of salvation no more passes over our efforts than God's operations. Have we any right, then, to presume on the agency of the Eternal Spirit to do for us, without our efforts, all that he demands our efforts in accomplishing? And when we have spent our best years, and squandered our most precious powers in delaying our conversion, are we to expect the Holy Spirit will do every thing for us in a little remnant of our life which needed the exertions of our squandered years? As we are the more disobedient will he be the more ready and powerful at last? No, no! It is all different from this. The principles of converting economy are perverted by us if we expect such aids of the Divine Spirit. Those principles will honor our text: *To-day, if ye will hear his voice, harden not your hearts.*

IV. The principles on which the Deity chooses to give the Spirit to lead men to Christ will be consistent with his promises.

It is worthy of the most serious remark that no promise in the whole Bible, about the gift of the Holy Spirit, is made for any future period to any individual. God promises aid for the present but not for the future. *To-day, if ye will hear. Behold now is the accepted time, now is the day of salvation.* It should be remarked, also, that while many precious promises are made to the young there are none made to irreligious old age.

Now, what are we to understand by this? Have we

any right to believe there is no certainty in these promises—no meaning in them? May we, in the very face of them, maintain that God is just as likely to give converting grace to one who continues to delay all efforts for salvation till the palsy of years and gray hairs preach to him, as he is to bestow such grace upon those who *seek him early?* If so, what means the promise, *They that seek me* EARLY *shall find me?* If there is no difference after all, if *early* and late are equally promising periods, then there is no *meaning* in the limitation, and it ought not to have been uttered, for it is calculated to mislead! May we maintain in the face of these promises that we may delay our conversion year after year, and at last, whenever we choose to begin the working out of our salvation, find it no more difficult and unlikely to succeed on account of our delay? To maintain this is to pervert the Scriptures. We may rest assured that the principles which regulate the acts of the Holy Spirit will not *make the promise of God of none effect.* God's system of conversion (all sovereign and mysterious as it is) will do honor to his promises. And though some with gray hairs may be converted, though some of presuming procrastination may not die as they have lived, their number will be small enough to contain a dreadful enforcement of the text: *To-day, if ye will hear his voice, harden not your hearts.*

V. The threatenings of the Holy Spirit will be our last article.

Some of you, my dear hearers, (and it pains me to be compelled to say it,) some of you are flattering yourselves that your delay is not much endangering your souls. You have the unhappy impression that though you are not now seeking God, yet you are in no special danger of forfeiting the offer of the Holy Spirit. You hope grace will meet you and fit you for eternity, though you are at present deferring to another time your known duty. Though you lend little or no personal effort to be saved, though your heart has little anxiety, yet you hope the system of gracious Divine operation will take you within its compass, the power of the Holy Ghost will compensate for lack of exertion, and save you (in a manner) in spite of yourselves. Sad error! Fearful error! You are passing beyond the compass of that system! Yours is that course of action which takes you away from the bright and blessed region of the promises! It is fast hurrying you into that dark spot where nothing but threatenings are heard! Listen. You can hear them already. *Because I have called and ye have refused, I have stretched out my hand and no man regarded it, therefore will I laugh at your calamity, I will mock when your fear cometh.* Such threatenings are frequent. I need not pain myself to rehearse them now. You have often heard them. You know them well. And yours is the unhappy course which makes them your own. You who are still putting all efforts to seek God, hearing his voice but not obeying, *knowing your Master's will* but not attempting to do it, are preparing to be *beaten with many stripes!* You have delusive hope! You think of the omnipotence of the Holy Ghost to save you in spite of yourselves! I assure you, you are indulging a dreadful delusion! The economy of the Holy Spirit will be found consistent with his threatenings. The Spirit *will not always strive.* In a little while the *one talent* will be taken away from the negligent servant! *the harvest* will be *past! the summer* will *be ended!* Delay, more than any thing else, brings you under the terrific threatenings of an angry God! Delay, more than any other one thing, peoples hell with its victims!

Now if you will combine the force of these articles, you will find in the economy of the Holy Spirit little encouragement for those who procrastinate. In the exercise of his saving agency, the Holy Spirit will act in such a manner as to manifest his disapprobation of continued impiety, and to be consistent with his appointments, his requirements, his promises, and his threatenings. On this general principle he will act. What sovereign instances of grace there may be beyond this, we know not. There will be some, for God delights in mercy. But they are rare. They resemble the few clusters on the outer branches when the vintage is over. But when we delay, we presume. We have little reason for continuing in impiety, because the power of the Holy Ghost can subdue any heart. Remember it, that power will not be exercised on principles to encourage delay. God, in converting sinners, will select his converts in such a manner as to enforce the text: *To-day, if ye will hear his voice, harden not your hearts.*

What a dark prospect lies before a procrastinating sinner! Without God he must perish! and the very time that God has appointed to aid him, *he* devotes to other purposes and other hopes! He expects grace hereafter, but he expects it unwisely, while he supposes himself as likely to attain it. He is *not* as likely. *Behold, now is the accepted time.* Now mercy reigns, long-suffering waits, the promises are uttered. But delay is fast hurrying the unhappy mortal onward beyond the light of the promises to that dark spot which lies beyond the scene of the usual victories of grace! it is putting beyond the boundary on this side of which the Holy Ghost works his wonders of mercy! Delay is blind to the economy of grace! It sins against the system of the Holy Ghost! It expects Heaven to be inconsistent with itself, and mercy to surpass the economy that mercy has established! The Holy Spirit is not going to act as delaying sinners expect. They will *not* so readily procure his aid after long rejecting his invitations and his influence. In their times of trouble, in their days of despair, perhaps on their bed of death, they will first learn the dreadful evil of the course they are so madly pursuing! *Ye shall call, and I will not answer; ye shall seek me early, but ye shall not find me.*

My dear friends, may God grant that these words do not embitter the agonies of your dying hour! They need not. *To-day, if ye will hear.* Now the Holy Spirit waits for you. Now he invites, he entreats, he encourages. Now is the day of salvation. What will you do? Are you going to shut your ears to the accents that are poured from heaven? Are you going to retire from these seats this afternoon prayerless, and unresolved, and *grieving the Holy Spirit* of God? Oh, do not this wickedness! Set your whole heart to seek God. Already you have lingered till I am afraid there is anger kindling against you; till I am afraid you feel less strong and less frequent the strivings of the Holy Ghost to lead you to seek Christ! Is it not so? Quick, then! be quick! Lift up your heart in the most earnest prayer:

> "Stay, thou insulted Spirit, stay,
> Though I have done thee such despite;
> Cast not the lingerer quite away,
> Nor take thine everlasting flight."

Hear thou, most merciful God, the prayer, and pity and save the souls that make it. Amen and amen.

Delay of Conversion.

[ARGUED FROM FACTS.]

To-day, if ye will hear his voice, harden not your hearts.—PSALM xcv. 7, 8.

WHEN we first read these words in your hearing we proposed to enforce the counsel they contain by considerations taken from the *nature of man*. The counsel is that of immediate conversion to God. We attempted to enforce it (so far as the nature of man is concerned), by showing what conversion is, what it requires, how it affects the mind, the heart, the habits, the wills of men, and from the examination of human nature, by demonstrating the increased and ever-increasing improbability of conversion, as year passes after year over the heads of the delaying. This was our first sermon.

We attempted afterward to enforce this counsel by examining (as far as we were able) the principles on which God *bestows the converting influences of the Holy Spirit*, and remarking how these principles, as far as we are able to understand a subject so darkly revealed, contain a still stronger urgency for immediate conversion; how the improbability of conversion is increased and still increasing as year passes after year over the head of the delaying sinner. This was our second sermon.

Would that another were not necessary! Greatly

would we rejoice to find any further urgency needless. Gladly would we abandon the text, if the irreligious, abandoning their dangerous procrastination, would cry out as they have urgent need to do: *Men and brethren, what shall we do to be saved?* But we know what has been in the minds of those who are delaying; we know the arguments prompted by *the deceivableness of unrighteousness*. We must, therefore, enforce the urgency of the text by arguments taken from another source. History must teach us. From what has been we must learn to think rightly about what will be. Correcting the mistakes into which delaying sinners are always liable to run on account of some instances of tardy conversion, we must bring the teaching of *fact* to aid the enforcement of the text: *To-day, if ye will hear.*

We enter upon the subject. And

I. We notice the history of conversions coming under our own observation and capable of being examined. Look around you on the Church. Select from it (if you are not able to believe *all* its members true Christians), select from it those whom you acknowledge to be on the way to heaven. Then look at them. When did they become Christians? You say, some of them long delayed their religion as you are doing, and yet they have become the subjects of grace. You say truly. But do you not make more of this fact than you ought? Do you not take more encouragement from it than you have any right, and thus find in it, as you think, a sanction for your delay, which you could not find in it if you would examine wisely? Allow me to name two things which you have probably entirely overlooked or partially considered.

First, your ignorance of their temper of mind *before* their conversion. You say that many who have become subjects of grace neglected for a long time the offers of Jesus Christ, and yet have been brought to a saving knowledge of Him. From this fact you conclude there is good reason to believe it will be the same with yourselves. That is your argument. But are you *like* them? Are you certain that you are now as attentive to the study of religion, to its duties, as cautious against sin, as prayerful, as these persons were when, like you, they were still unconverted? Was their case parallel to your own? Do you know that while they once delayed as you are now doing, they delayed in the same course of prayerlessness and pride and inattention? No. You have no such knowledge. You can not have. Though their conversion may have taken place after the hazard of a criminal procrastination, perhaps during all that procrastination they never spent a week as you are spending years! For aught you know there is already a rankness in your offences that theirs never reached! Your course of impenitence may have already done more to harden the heart, more to darken the understanding, more to displease God, than ever theirs did. There is far more force in this remark than the careless are apt to imagine. Let me tell you a secret: in conversation with those who have become religious late in life, I have often been astonished to find for what a long time they had given much anxious attention to religion. It was not with them as you are apt to think. They were not indifferent when you thought them indifferent—not prayerless when you thought them prayerless—when I thought them prayerless. The encouragement you take from their late conversion may not be at all countenanced by their example. Before you find any sanction for your delay in these late conversions, you ought to be certain that these people were no more religiously inclined than yourselves, no more obedient and prayerful during the time of unbelief. Of this you can not be certain.

Delaying persons deceive themselves. They can not cite a single instance of conversion in the case of any person which they know to be parallel with their own. The fact which they mention is no just foundation for the conclusion which they draw from it. We could produce many proofs to show that theirs resembles the conduct of a man, who, because some had been *saved by violence, pulled out of the fire*, should rush still further into the flames, hoping the same salvation would meet him.

The *second* idea probably overlooked in respect to them who delayed and afterward became subjects of grace, is the *comparative smallness of their number*. It is true you may look around on the circles of the pious and find some who did, for a long time, live *without God and without hope;* here a Mary washing with her tears the feet of her Saviour, and *wiping them with the hairs of her head;* there a *maniac sitting at the feet of Jesus clothed and in his right mind;* here a Matthew called from his business in money; there a Paul arrested in his career of persecution; here a thief on the cross regenerated while dying; there a Simeon thanking God that his purblind eyes had seen salvation before his sight was extinguished for ever; but how many *more* Marys, how many more maniacs, how many more Matthews and Pauls, and dying thieves and aged Simeons, have been *lost* by delay! These few—these exceedingly few tardy converts—are only a diminutive little fraction of that number who delayed at the same time. *Where are the nine?* Where the rest of that mighty throng who rejected the Saviour? Alas, most of them rejected him to the end! And those who still live, how few of them have ceased their negligence and heard the voice of the Son of God!

The delaying do not think when they mention the fact of the late conversion of some sinners how many *more* delaying sinners were never converted! How exceedingly small is the proportion of the saved among those who put off repentance from youth to middle life. The facts do not sustain their conclusion. Some among them it is true are converted; but what multitudes of them die in their sins! To delay on such grounds is trifling with history—it is trifling with facts open to every body's eyes—it resembles the folly of that man who willingly rushes into the worst of dangers, because the history of the whole world furnishes him with some few instances of those who have escaped unharmed! We do not forget how the *long-suffering of God waits*. We remember the laborers employed at the eleventh hour. We are not narrowing down the economy of grace or limiting the Holy One of Israel. But while we see some called at the eleventh hour, we behold more at that hour still refusing to hear the voice that calls! While we bear in mind the long-suffering of God we remember it has its limitations. While we rejoice to acknowledge that grace sometimes selects its gray-haired subjects, and while some old Simeons with quivering lips tell of salvation, we do not forget that overwhelming caution to be gathered from the blood of the slain!

Let those who linger learn to be wise. Let them arrange two classes of persons. In one class let them put all those who became Christians at a late period of life. In the other class let them put all others who delayed like them. (Some of them, many of them indeed, are dead, and have left no evidence behind them that they rest from their labors with the just; others are still living in sin.) Let these two classes be counted over. What a vast disproportion! Have you any idea of what it is? Have you formed the most remote conception of the magnitude of one of these classes as compared with the other? And yet, on this ignorance—on this threatening ignorance, you delayers build your hopes! On this dismal and deceitful argument you countenance your delay. Standing on a spot marked with only here and there a monument of grace—on a spot reddened with the blood and whitened over with the bones of the lost—you are promising yourselves security—a happy end hereafter! Was ever argument like this? Was hope ever fostered on such principles? Was ever the voice of history perverted so cruelly? Where can you find any parallel to this *deceivableness of unrighteousness in them that perish?*

Let me aid your contemplations. An accurate examination into the periods of life in which those whose lives of godliness give evidence of true religion first began to be followers of Christ, furnishes an amazing demonstration of the folly and danger of delay! The probability of conversion diminishes rapidly as years roll on. Make up a congregation of a thousand Christians. Divide them into five classes according to the ages at which they became Christians. Place in the

    1st class all those converted under 20 years of age;
    2d class all those converted between 20 and 30;
    3d class all those converted between 30 and 40;
    4th class all those converted between 40 and 50;
    5th class all those converted between 50 and 60;

Then count each of the five classes separately. Of your thousand Christians, there were hopefully converted,

    under 20 years of age, ... 548;
    between 20 and 30 years of age, . . . 337;
    between 30 and 40 years of age, . . . 86;
    between 40 and 50 years of age, . . . 15;
    between 50 and 60 years of age, . . . 3.

Here are your five classes! But you complain of me: you ask, "Why stop at sixty years old?" Ah well, then! if you will have a sixth class, and can call it a class—converted,

    between 60 and 70 years of age, . . . 1.

Just ONE out of a thousand Christians converted over sixty years old!!! What a lesson on delay! What an awful lesson!!

I once made an examination of this sort in respect to two hundred and fifty-three hopeful converts to Christ who came under my own observation at a particular period. Of this two hundred and fifty-three, there were converted,

    under 20 years of age, ... 138;
    between 20 and 30 years of age, . . . 85;
    between 30 and 40 years of age, . . . 22;
    between 40 and 50 years of age, . . . 4;
    between 50 and 60 years of age, . . . 3;
    between 60 and 70 years of age, . . . 1.

Beyond seventy, not one! What a lesson on the delay of conversion! what an awful lesson! How rapidly it cuts off the hopes of the delaying, as they continue on in life, making darker and darker the prospect as they are nearing the tomb! How rapidly the prospect of conversion diminishes! far *more* rapidly than the prospect of life! Let the sinner delay till he is twenty years old

—he has lost more than half the probability of salvation he had at twelve! Let him delay till he is thirty years old, and he has lost three fourths of the probability of salvation which he had at twenty. Let him delay till he has reached forty years, and only twenty-nine probabilities out of a thousand remain to him. Let him delay till he has reached fifty years, and beyond fifty there remains to him only fourteen out of a thousand! What a lesson upon delay! what an emphatic lesson! As an unconverted man treads on into the vale of years, scarcely a single ray of hope remains to him! His prospect of conversion diminishes a great deal faster than his prospect of life! The night-fall has come—its shades thicken fast—truth trembles for him when his feet shall stumble on the dark mountains of death! But what an encouragement to the young is the striking arithmetic of this table! More than *half* of the whole number of Christians become such before they are twenty years old; far more than three fourths before they are thirty. Come, ye youth! come. This is your day of promise! Yours is now the season of hope. Come, set your hearts on heaven. You will not now seek God in vain. The history of grace encourages you. And God, our blessed Lord and Redeemer, full of tender compassion, will love you as his own dear children; he will wipe away your tears; he will take care of you in your troubles; you shall live in hope and die in hope, if you will come now to Jesus Christ! To your first relentings God will say: *Is Ephraim my dear son? is he a pleasant child? For since I spake against him, I do earnestly remember him still . . . I will have mercy upon him, saith the Lord.* Come then; *To-day, if ye will hear his voice, harden not your hearts.*

Adhering to our historical idea, let us look at the same matter in another point of view.

II. As the second general matter of our sermon, let us notice the instances of *sudden conversion mentioned in the sacred Scriptures.* On these instances the procrastinating are accustomed to found some hope. Let us see with how much wisdom.

We have some cases on sacred record, instances of men who never gave much definite attention (it would seem) to religion, till finally, after much delay, they were suddenly brought to embrace it. The delaying form some kind of indefinite hope it will yet be so with them. They can indeed name, if they would, the instances of such an occurrence. There are such instances. They might name the disciples of Christ—Peter and Andrew and James the fishermen, leaving instantly their nets at the call of the Master—Zaccheus—the three thousand converted on the day of Pentecost—and the dying thief who embraced the Saviour at the last hour of his life. Because there are some such instances, you flatter yourselves in your delay that you may become such; though disobedient now to the heavenly voice, you indulge the idea that you may hereafter be suddenly called. I beg you to listen, then, to *five* remarks in reference to these Scripture cases.

1. First remark. These instances *were exceptions*—signal exceptions to the general history of conversions: for his own wise purposes, it pleased God to convert these men in an extraordinary manner. Such instances do not often occur in the history of religion. These instances are uncommon actings of God. They resemble the miracles—and it will add enforcement to the idea we are

DELAY OF CONVERSION. 395

presenting, if you will please to remember, they occurred in the *age* of miracles. They resemble those extraordinary operations of God, by which he was pleased to suspend the common laws of nature. He sometimes did suspend them. It was the common rule or law of nature, that the paralytic should not recover in an instant—that the dead should remain cold and lifeless in their tomb. But Jesus Christ said to the sick of the palsy, *Take up thy bed*, and instantly the muscles performed their office, vigor and sensibility were perfect. Jesus Christ said, *Lazarus come forth*, and instantly the grave opened—the dead lived—Lazarus came forth *bound hand and foot with grave-clothes, and his face bound with a napkin*. And what would you say of that man among you who would not much dread the palsy—who would have no fear of death and the grave on account of these miracles? Would you not say that his perverse heart abused facts instead of improving them? Of very much such abuse, of such perversion is he guilty, who on account of some sudden conversions mentioned in the Scriptures is careless about his own. They were extraordinary conversions; they were a sort of miracles in grace; they were exceptions to the general laws of religion, much the same as Lazarus was an exception to the general laws of life and death. This is the first remark. I know not what the delaying will say to it, so I add,

2. A *second* remark. Connected with these recorded cases of sudden conversion, there were extraordinary circumstances which no procrastinating sinner can now expect. Around Paul on his way to Damascus shone a light above the brightness of the midday sun. Jesus Christ spake to him: he was blind: his sight was restored to him. On the day of Pentecost, *there was a sound from*

heaven, as of a rushing mighty wind—there were *cloven tongues like as of fire—Parthians and Medes, Elamites, and the dwellers in Mesopotamia, and in Judea and Cappadocia, in Pontus and Asia, Phrygia and Pamphylia, in Egypt and in the parts of Lybia about Cyrena, and strangers of Rome, Jews and Proselytes, Cretes and Arabians, all heard them speak in their own tongues the wonderful works of God.* That illiterate fishermen should speak fifteen languages was no small wonder. Zaccheus found a cluster of men gathered around the Saviour, so that he could not even see him. He heard their shoutings: he *climbed the tree to see Jesus:* Jesus called him by name: went to his house. Under such circumstances it was that he was converted: he exclaimed: *One half of my goods I give to feed the poor, and if I have wronged any man, I restore him fourfold.* The thief on the cross witnessed the agonies and dying patience of the Son of God. He saw that godlike submission, those unequaled sufferings: he heard that strangest of all prayers: *Father, forgive them*—and he was converted (if his was a case of sudden conversion) amid the darkness of the crucifixion, when dead men out of their graves were walking the streets of Jerusalem. Peter, Andrew, and James, from their fisherman occupation, and Levi from the receipt of custom, were called by Jesus Christ himself. These were no ordinary circumstances. All these sudden conversions took place under circumstances the most peculiar. How much the circumstances aided to give preparation of mind we know not. But this we know, there were such peculiarities attending these conversions as forbid their being made an argument for your delaying your own. You are not going to see the Saviour in the flesh, and hear his lips calling you. You are not going to see the tongues of fire. You are not going to behold the heavens darkened, and rocks rent at the crucifixion, and find yourself urged to religion by such demonstrations as accompanied the sudden conversions from which you take courage to delay your own. This is the second remark.

3. The third is, that these sudden conversions—these conversions without much previous thought and feeling and seeking God (if they were such), were not instances of men who possessed the previous *knowledge* which the negligent possess here. They had not *your* previous knowledge. Paul probably was the best instructed among them. But while he persecuted the Church, he tells us he did it in his ignorance, and (as if to guard his example from perversion) he says, that *for this cause he obtained mercy.* The converted thief probably never heard the name of Jesus till he met him in blood on the hill of the crucifixion. Much the same with the rest. They were ignorant, all ignorant of a thousand religious truths well known to those here brought up under the Gospel light. How far, then, how very far are these instances from furnishing any ground of hope for the delaying! Our delay here is not in the darkness. It is in light. We do not resemble these instances of remarkable grace. We bear strange resemblance to those servants who *knew their master's will but did it not*—a dreadful resemblance to Tyre and Sidon, to Chorazin and Bethsaida!

4. The fourth remark. In the case of every one of these sudden conversions, the individual appears to have *obeyed the* FIRST *call.* There seems not to have been a moment's delay. As soon as salvation was intelligibly offered, it appears to have been instantly accepted. The disciples, the dying thief, Zaccheus, had not been pressed Sabbath after Sabbath with such texts as ours, and such

urgency as you are familiar with. They made no delay. The disciples abandoned their nets, their ship, their father; Matthew left his money; Zaccheus *made haste and came down;* the Pentecost three thousand took their stand for Christ as soon as the Pentecost sermon was ended; and the thief on the cross had no time to squander when his life's blood was streaming from his opened veins! What, then, if they were suddenly converted? what if they were *saved* without much of that study, and attention, and care, and prayer which we enjoin so assiduously upon you? You can build no hopes on their example. You have delayed too long already. Already have your ears heard and your hearts refused more than ever did any one of these sudden subjects of grace. This cuts you off from your refuge. These are no examples for *you.* Among all those you can mention who appear to have devoted themselves but little to religion, or none at all, who were suddenly met and arrested and converted to God, there is not one, no, not *one,* in the condition of delayers here! They had never delayed (at least not under the Gospel call, the heaven-offered *life and immortality brought to light*). Not one of them, no, not one had contracted that habit of sin, that hardness, that strange habitude of refusing mercy which characterizes and which ought to alarm the negligent in this assembly.

5. The final remark is the *exceeding fewness of the number* of these sudden conversions from which delay strengthens its encouragement. How many instances can you find? A Paul, a Simon, a Zaccheus, an Andrew, a dying thief—we could name the whole of them in a single breath! And while we acknowledge all these, and have no disposition to diminish your catalogue, where is Sodom? where is Gomorrah? where is Tyre

and Sidon? where is Chorazin? Bethsaida? Yea, where is Jerusalem herself? What multitudes, what vast multitudes of the delaying were *lost!* were lost! What a vast throng rose before the mind of Isaiah as he cried: *Howl, oh ye gate! cry, oh city! thou, whole Palestina, art dissolved!* What multitudes rose before the saddened mind of Jesus Christ as he pronounced the funeral dirge of the delaying: *Oh Jerusalem, Jerusalem! how often would I have gathered thy children . . . . but ye would not! Oh! that thou hadst known the things that belong to thy peace, but now they are hidden from thine eyes!* How little, how very little is the sanction for delay from all the instances of rescue that we can name! These instances are but a drop to the ocean—one Lot from a burning Sodom—one Noah floating over the sepulcher of a lost world!

III. But you will say (and here I come to my third general argument)—you will say, there is the bed of death. When that is spread for us and we are placed upon it, we intend to seek God. Then, you say, the world will not captivate and hinder us any longer. It can do us no more good. It will have no more power over our hearts. Then we shall not be ashamed of applying to Jesus Christ; there is a propriety in dying piously. It is a pity you do not think there is a propriety in living piously. Last week, a sick young man of my acquaintance in this city, alluding to the acceptance of mercy in the last hour, said he thought it was *mean* to look to God for favor then, at the last moment, when one could do nothing to serve him, and after having disobeyed him through the whole of health and life. So it *is* mean. But sin is mean every where. Yet, you say, when we come to the last hour, the circumstances of the case will compel our reluctant hearts. Death coming, the grave opening, the world receding out of our sight, shrouds, coffins, eternity—a few more breaths and a few tender farewells—and then the judgment, the presence of the great white throne, the face of Him upon it—these ideas, you say, will constrain you to become Christians. I know you hope so. I know all these delusions, and therefore designed the history of the dying as the final argument of this sermon. But we have not time to consider it. We can only glance at it. Besides, we have an inconceivable reluctance to approach a subject wherein every demonstration is so painful to us. To us, to ministers of the Gospel, the idea that there is still some little ground of hope for the salvation of the dying is an idea most exceedingly dear. We cling to it; we can not give it up; we dislike to diminish it; indeed we are half unwilling to *examine* it, because it is this little hope, this very little hope which alone enables us to preach to the dying who has delayed his religion till that hour. Take this little hope away, and our lips would be sealed up by that bed of death! We should be obliged to stand there and witness the waning of life, the blood cooling, the body stiffening, the immortal spirit passing into eternity, and not utter one word, one single word of hope on the ear of the dying impenitent! But, thank God, praised be his mercy to you, we are not now preaching to you in such a state. The blessed One grant we may never be called on to do it. *Before* such a time for you has come, you may be the dear children of God. Therefore we cry: *To-day, if ye will hear his voice, harden not your hearts.*

I am not going, as I said, to enter into this subject;

but I must confess to you that I can think of no words, form no figure, to express the diminutiveness of that hope with which we preach the Gospel to the graceless on their bed of death! What becomes of those who *die*, we know not; thank God, we know not. They are in his hands. There we must leave them. But among all the instances of supposed conversion on a sick bed which I have known (and I have known many in a ministry of twenty-five years), only *four* of those who *recovered* gave in after life any evidence of the religion which they thought they had gained when they were sick! Only *four! Where were the nine?* yea, the more than ninety and nine? *Only four!* What a lesson on the delay of conversion! what an appalling lesson! The mists of delusion seem to be thickening around the bed of the graceless. He neglected religion, delayed it all his life, and now in his dying moments he seems to be most peculiarly exposed to the dreadful, damning hope of the hypocrite! The hour of dying! oh, what an hour for conversion! Distracted thoughts, disordered mind, increasing danger, strange alternations of hope and fear, contradictory symptoms, physicians and medicines to occupy attention! a pained body! weeping friends to minister their last offices of kindness before we leave them! parents, wives, children to be left in this cold, wicked world! the grave! eternity and all that is in it! these are some of the things which press upon the hour of death! My friends, my dear friends, leave not your conversion to that hour. *To-day, if ye will hear his voice, harden not your hearts.* May God save you from lingering. Ye are mortal! remember, ye are mortal!

Here we close our arguments. The nature of man, the

economy of the Holy Spirit, and the whole history of human conversions have been employed in these sermons to enforce the urgency of the text. If you have attended to these considerations, and if you ever mean to be a Christian, you can not fail to perceive that you have no time to spare—no, not a moment, every one of you who are *yet in your sins*. There is not the remotest probability that you will ever be converted to God while you linger in your delaying indifference. The probability that you will ever arouse yourselves from that indifference and seek God is diminishing every day. I have less hope for you than I had last Sabbath. If we live, I shall have less for you next Sabbath than I have now. It is nothing less than madness for you to defer. Look at it. As you put off your conversion to a future period human nature is against you, the Divine Spirit is against you, the history of all the conversions the world ever saw in the path of common life, or on the bed of death, is against you. Take then your stand, unconverted man, at once—*to-day* begin to seek God—*to-day, to-day.*

Old man, your gray hairs have not yet *gone down with sorrow* into the grave! Seize the little remnant of your time! Peradventure you may be hid in the day of the Lord's anger. Young man, gray hairs may never be yours. If they should be, you may find yourself as stupid and steeled in sin as the old man now before you, who still defers his salvation and lives only to fill up the measure of his iniquities! Never a sinner *gained* any thing by delay. Thousands have lost heaven by it! Will you lose it too? Will you go out from these courts still undetermined, undecided, and by that indecision braving the command of God and treading over hell? If your final salvation is any thing dear to you, if you think your soul worth saving, if you ever mean to look forward into another world with the least comfort of hope, stop now —stop short—take not another step till you have fully and finally resolved, by God's help, to be a Christian indeed! *To-day—to-day.*

If such is *not* your purpose, you will take a course not to be thought of without horror! You will forget these truths we have been uttering—you will form some covering of lies to ward them off from your heart, as if, for example, you could do nothing—you could not even ask God to forgive you—to save you. You will go on in sin, doing a work far more melancholy than if you were manufacturing your own coffin or digging your own grave! You will be working out your way into hell! You did some of that work last week; you will do more of it this week if you delay! Horrible work! The wages of it is death eternal!

My dear hearer, the ideas you may form, the excuses you may weave, will not alter these truths of God. You may forget them—deny them—laugh at them; but you can not change them. After all you can do their force and solemnity will be undiminished! You may shut your eyes against an opened heaven, but still it will be true that that heaven was offered to you and you refused it! You may shut your eyes against the hell which is under your feet, but you can not annihilate it—yea, yea, you can not avoid sinking toward it, unless *to-day ye will hear his voice,* and *harden not your hearts.* May God have mercy upon your soul!

The Rich and Poor meet Together.

The rich and poor meet together; the Lord is the maker of them all.—
PROVERBS, xxii. 2.

THE text before us has reference to the different conditions of men. Some are rich and some are poor. This is a distinction which has always existed in the world and always will. It is one of the most important distinctions in human society. Certainly it is one of the most influential. The influence of it is felt, and very much felt, from the very commencement of our observations and reflections upon things around us, and does not cease to be felt down to the solemn period when the mortal makes his will, and prepares to enter into that world where this distinction must cease. The young, especially of the male sex, have but commenced to think of the world and of their interest and business in it, before the different states of the rich and the poor come before the mind with a very powerful influence upon it; and throughout the course of study, in the choice of a business or profession, in the common associations of life—indeed in almost all the reflections, desires and habits which help in the formation of character, the ideas taken from riches and poverty have a very powerful sway. If any one (of the male sex especially) will but take a serious hour and spend it in carefully recollecting and examining the processes of his own mind—

what his thoughts have been busy about, what his desires have been upon, what his contrivances and industry have sought, what feelings of hope, or fear, of pride or envy, have affected him—I am persuaded that he will be astonished to find to what an amazing extent he has been occupied with the distinction between the poor and the rich, and how much his character and life have been influenced by it.

Whatever we may think of the good or evil of this distinction, it *exists*, it *has* ever existed, it *will* exist; and it affects us to a very important extent. Its influences are deeply felt in the very formation of our character; then in directing our pursuits in life; and then in the adoption of not a few of our most important principles— principles social, moral, political, and perhaps sometimes religious. "Perhaps?" No *perhaps* about it! At the present moment the very system of Christianity is encountering a very vigorous assailment from this quarter, and not a few are prepared to raze its very foundations, if they can, unless they can bend its principles into an agreement with those ideas they themselves entertain about the distribution of wealth.

The importance of this matter, therefore, on many points, not only justifies, but calls for a very calm and serious consideration of it. And this must be our own justification, if we shall find it necessary to consume more of your time on this subject than at first thought you would think you could well afford. You may remember, if you please, that we are speaking of a matter whose influence in the very formation of human character surpasses that of any other mere earthly thing.

In the distinction between the rich and the poor there is something not altogether pleasant to the human mind.

We are apt to recoil from it. Without much thought, by the mere spontaneous promptings of our feelings, we are apt to have some dissatisfaction as we behold the advantages of riches so unequally distributed among men. And frequently the dissatisfaction increases as we can discover no just *rule* of this distribution; and as we behold more and more of the contrasted advantages and disadvantages of this distinction between the rich and the poor.

Something like this was, in my opinion, the feeling of the writer of this text. He saw the distinction between rich and poor; he felt amazed; he had a disliking for it which set his mind at work. He thought the matter all over patiently and religiously. And when he had done, he gathers up the whole substance into a single aphorism of wisdom and writes it down: *The rich and the poor meet together; the Lord is the maker of them all.* That was his satisfaction; there he left the matter. In this manner (in my opinion) he coined the proverb. His mind had been over the whole field. He had studied it as he studied botany: *From the cedar-tree that is in Lebanon to the hyssop that springeth out of the wall.* He had contemplated the loftiness of the rich and the lowliness of the poor; wherein they differed and wherein they agreed, and especially who made them to differ. And then he makes a proverbial condensation of all that he knew—such a condensation as soothes down into quietude the dissatisfaction he felt at first: *The rich and the poor meet together; the Lord is the maker of them all.*

I do not suppose that his mind employed these two ideas of the text separately. He probably blended them somewhat together. If he was a pious man he would naturally do so. His faith in God and constant recognition of Him would lead him to take along with him, in all his contemplations, the idea of the One Great Maker of all; and then when he found things strange, dark or revolting to him, growing out of the distinctions between *the rich and the poor*, he leaves all that with God. But *before* he comes to this, and while he is engaged amid things which he *can* understand, he finds another side of the question than that which at first disquieted him. He was disquieted—just as you or I are apt to be—with the *distinction* between *the rich and the poor ;* the advantages of the one class and the disadvantages of the other. But, coming to examine the matter, he finds that distinction is not the real affair after all; that there are more *agreements* than *distinctions*—more resemblances than differences—*the rich and the poor meet together :* the Maker of all has made them more alike than unlike.

This we suppose to be the general sense of the text. We suppose that the author's mind, led by the Holy Spirit, was corrected of its error—was turned over to the other side of the question—was led away from the distinctions between these two classes, to notice agreements between these classes. And he finds that, after all, their agreements or resemblances are so many and so important that they may well make us satisfied with the existing distinction.

Now we propose to follow as well as we can the course of the author's mind on this subject, and pick up along the track the materials out of which he coined this proverb.

The rich and the poor meet together (there is a substantial agreement between them) in their *origin and their situation* as they enter the world. They are equally dependent, equally helpless, equally miserable. The affluence of parentage can not prevent the cry of distress; and if it can do something which poverty can not do to minister comfort and to gain relief from science and skill, that something is very little for the alleviation of infantile distresses. Parental affection and fondness among the rich will find as many distresses to weep over, and will as often find the weeping vain, as among the poor. It may happen and sometimes does, that one may be born with a feeble and unpromising constitution of body, and be obliged in all future life to carry the evil along with him—an evil owing to the luxury and consequent effeminacy of his parentage. It may further happen and sometimes does, that fashion and the cares of other things, a heart absorbed amid show and indulgence, will go far to diminish parental affections and solicitudes, and leave the dependent child to guardianship and kindness different from a parent's. If on either of these points there is any difference, the difference would seem to be in favor of being born in poverty. Ordinarily there is more health and strength there; and ordinarily the parents, having little else to prize and love, center their hearts and cares where nature dictates. As we enter the world there is a substantial agreement among all: there is the same feebleness, the same dependence, the same helplessness and want; and the same kind of instinctive affection to care for us. Affluence can give us nothing better. Nor does the Maker of all, in the body or mind he gives to us, leave any imprint upon us whereby the most sagacious can discover whether in after life we shall make our way into the ranks of the poor or the rich.

Take another step. *The rich and the poor meet together* on the point of their training and preparation for after life. Education is ordered by circumstances and prospects. Parents aim with equal solicitude to fit their children for what they suppose is before them—for what they must do—for the station they are to hold. And the one class positively does succeed about as well as the other. There are all varieties on this point; but if there is any advantage it would seem to be on the side of the poor. In proportion to the number of the two classes, there are more of the children of the poor who work themselves out into the ranks of the affluent than of the children of the rich who continue to stay there. It is quite as common (in proportion to the number) to behold one educated in wealth sinking afterward to poverty, as it is to behold one educated in poverty and unfit to take care of himself. The training which childhood and youth receives does not necessarily keep one in poverty if he is trained there, nor keep him in affluence if he was trained there. The unwise indulgences extended to the children of the affluent, and the pride, thoughtlessness, and idleness so apt to characterize these children, go very far indeed to balance all the *dis*advantages of being educated among the poor. The poor young man learns to feel that he has himself to take care of, and this feeling (as it throws him upon his own resources) develops his powers, brings out his mind, leads him to take care of his character, his time, his opportunities, and this does as much for him, or *may* do as much, as any wealthy inheritance. Parental anxiety and affection can not do every thing. Men are born with corrupt natures. And there are very few, if any, of our early sins and errors which are so unfortunate for us and lead to so much misery in future life, as the foolish unwillingness of children and youth to demean themselves as parental anxiety would have them. In both poverty and affluence, this folly, and not want of affection or want of means in the parents to educate them rightly, leads to future unhappiness. There is a substantial agreement between *the rich and the poor*, in their opportunity to rear their offspring for felicity, honor and usefulness in life. They *meet together ; the Lord is the maker of them all.* He has made them so, and rules the world so as substantially to equalize their condition.

Take another step. With the exception of (I hope) some few instances wherein riches are valued merely for their own sake, and the soul is utterly debased by such a passion—a value is set upon them as *a means of enjoyment or usefulness.* And if we look upon the successful and unsuccessful aspirants after them, we shall not find all the felicity of the world with the rich nor all its miseries with the poor. The two classes are very much alike in their amount of happiness. Each has its troubles and each its joys. There will be always something coming up at every step to diminish the extent of those advantages which were expected from affluence, and to make the evils of poverty less than fear pictured them. The rich man is not necessarily happy, nor the poor man necessarily unhappy. Riches do not give wisdom, nor poverty ignorance. Virtue and vice are not dependent upon circumstances. Neither the rich nor the poor can monopolize all the friendship of the world, or the privilege of exercising those affections of kindness and good-will on which so much of the felicity of life depends. The passions which make men miserable can be exercised, and are exercised by both classes, with no visible difference in their effects. They may be different in their *nature ;* in the one class you may find pride, in the other envy—in the one ambition, in the other discontent—in one vanity, in the other fear; but when you come to weigh their results, you will find the pride, ambition, and vanity, have done about as much as the envy, discontent, and fear, to undermine the felicities of life. It is as easy a thing for a poor man to be contented as a rich one. It may be, for aught we know, more common. It is as easy for him to be kind, to be gentle, to be forbearing, or charitable. And if you will take notice of those in what you call the humbler walks of life, you will see there are as many happy faces, and healthy bodies, and laughing eyes, as much buoyancy of spirits, as much sprightly and joyful activity, as you can find any where. Between the rich and the poor, advantages and disadvantages for an earthly felicity are not indeed equally distributed; but yet, men so *use* them as very *nearly* to equalize them, if not entirely.

On the point of *usefulness* it may be more difficult to form a correct judgment. Riches are *valued* on this account, and sought on this account, to some little extent at least. The idea about the utility of them hangs around one's own self and family perhaps more exclusively than we should all be willing to admit. And this limitation of the idea has sometimes been unwisely blamed by the moralist and in the pulpit. To aim after wealth with no *other* idea indeed than that of being useful to one's own family, does not seem to be in accordance with the expansive benevolence of the Gospel: hope and aim of usefulness ought to reach further. But to censure the aim of being useful to one's own family by the acquisition of worldly things, is to act on a very dim and shortsighted wisdom. To maintain the dreamy principle that men should act *first* for the good of society in general, is nothing less than to put a crazy dream into the place of God's word, of nature, and of sound sense. *He that pro-*

vided not for his own hath denied the faith and is worse than an infidel. Nature has implanted in the parental heart a set of affections which lead to an anxiety and carefulness for one's own children, and these affections are not the results of the fall: to be *without natural affection* is to be in one of the last and lowest stages of sin. To have no more care for one's own children, and to aim no more to benefit them than we care for or aim to benefit the children of society in general, or of a community, is just setting up a silly speculation to combat God and nature. And the attempt will be vain. Good sense is against it. The family constitution as God ordained it, and the parental affections and kindness and care which grow out of them, are the great safe-guards of common virtue. Cut man off from these and he will soon fall low in the scale of being. Break him loose from family and family affections, and put him to work only to make gain and do good for society in general, and you have broken the strongest bond which holds him to industry, frugality and forethought. You have made his labor a drudgery instead of a pleasure, and he will soon quit it. You have perpetrated a fraud upon his heart, you have robbed it; you have stolen at once its stimulus and its solace. You have perpetrated an equal fraud upon his mind; you have ordered it to think and plan for a vision instead of a reality—for a cold world instead of a warm family—for a world-wide wilderness of interests which it can not even understand, instead of those plain and visible family interests which it can study every hour of the day. It will not do to make joint-stock of every thing. To societyize every thing is just to ruin every thing. For leading men to a proper course of life, for securing their industry, prudence, and carefulness and frugality and forecast, you need the aids and influences of a heart that is baptized with the spirit of home. That man, in all ordinary cases, is the most useful to society, who is the most useful to his family. God deliver us from those patriots and those philanthropists and statesmen who have got above the idea of being useful to their own family. There is indeed a just limit to this idea. We owe something to society, but not every thing. The extremes are to be avoided.

Now, with the *rich and the poor* there is a desire for wealth which arises from the hope of making it useful to one's own. The rich and the poor are more *alike* in this matter of usefulness than a casual observer might imagine. There is a great agreement between them. Many, very many of the affluent are far from being very useful to their own children. They can give them wealth, but they can not give them sense or virtue. They can not *prevent* those false ideas and those wrong feelings which will arise from the corruption of nature, and which are awakened into exercise by the expectations of an affluent inheritance. They can not, therefore, prevent the evils and unhappiness which must grow out of these. In the end, much of the advantage they have turns out to be a *disadvantage*. Many of the poor are just as useful to their own families as they. They make them really as comfortable. They educate them as fitly. They set before them as good an example. They do as much to train them to virtue, usefulness, felicity and honor. Look at the facts all around you. What a vast proportion of your most useful men were born and reared in poverty! Your first merchants and mechanics and teachers and professional men have, very many of them, struggled with the difficulties of early embarrassments, and worked themselves out into a condition of usefulness and competence. They are the children of the poor. The children of the rich, side by side with whom they commenced the journey of life, have certainly not done as well in general. Some have, and some have failed. But surely the whole advantage is not on the side of the rich. And since the poor do positively become about as *useful* to their own families and make them as happy, as honorable, as good, as beneficial to society; the advantages of wealth on this point are small; the two classes are very much alike— *the rich and the poor meet together.*

On the matter of a social or public utility the same thing may be said. The usefulness of the one class is of one kind, and of the other class of another kind. But both may be useful in nearly the same degree. The laborer who tills the soil, the mechanic who drives his tools, the poor man any where, who wields the implements of his industry with contentment and good-will, is a beneficial member of society. While he is doing himself good, he is doing good to the public. He is doing it in the best way. He is furnishing what the public need, without noise or ostentation. He is giving his talents and strength to minister steadily to the wants and comforts of his fellow-creatures. The man of wealth who employs him is doing the same thing. He is spending his wealth where it is needed. He is devising new enterprises, and searching out new fields of industry, and founding schools of education, and devising new means of social improvement. And between these two classes of men who shall strike the balance? who shall tell which is the most useful and does the most for the comfort, honor and virtue of society? No man can tell! Both classes are much alike. *The rich and the poor meet together.* You may find idlers and vicious among the poor, and you may find misers and vicious among the rich; and that avarice which just hoards money in the love of it, will go far by its social inutility to form an offset against that idleness and lack of thrift which sometimes make poverty a state of uselessness. A rich man may deny to society the benefits of his wealth, and the poor man may deny to it the benefits of his muscles and his mind. They *meet together*. Neither has a necessary disadvantage about doing good.

In regard to those public matters of social good in which the rich and the poor act together and seem to have an equal interest, there are erroneous notions in both classes, and perhaps we may despair of ever correcting them. They are rooted too deeply in the depths of a common depravity. In such public matters as our schools and colleges and churches and charitable societies of every name, the rich and the poor seem to have an equal interest, and they act together. The contributions of the poor man can not equal those of his wealthy neighbor, and both of them know this very well. And out of this there spring erroneous notions, against which it were perhaps vain to contend. Probably you could not find a poor man who thinks, with entire justice, of his duty and interest on the matter of his donations, interest and action for such matters. There are others so much abler than himself, the amount he can bestow is so small, and other ideas of this sort come to his mind, so that he is tempted to draw back entirely, or to give very little, or to regard all such matters as the duties and interests of the wealthier class far more than his own. No errors could be greater. They are *his* duties, and especially *his* interests, just as much as if he were in affluence. Churches, schools, benevolent societies, improvements are his, just as much as if he were rich. He has a soul, has children, has a heart which ought to be a heart of benevolence. If his benefaction must be small, let him, on that very account, be the *more careful* to give that: its diminutiveness does not annihilate the duty; and the virtue of his heart, if he would keep it alive and be like Christ, can not afford to dispense with his *doing* the duty; and his feelings of manliness, and feelings of a deep and common interest in this our social life, call on him to do his little (if little it must be) with unfailing punctuality and right good-will. Oh, if Divine Providence has made him poor, let him not make himself degraded, and stand back and shrink away as if he were not a man, and had no interest in the common welfare of society! If he does shrink back, he diminishes his manliness, his virtue, his honor, his independence; he takes a false position, and makes both his neighbors and himself think less of him than they ought to have occasion to do. But he says, he can do so little. Stop, stop! the poor can do much. They are the major part of every community. There is not the least occasion for their thinking that they must be in entire dependence upon the rich for building churches and seminaries and hospitals and orphan asylums, and giving the Bible to the world. Let them put aside their errors—errors which favor penuriousness, and not manliness or virtue—and the poor will find that they can *do more* in all these things than the rich can do alone. Their thousand streams united will swell beyond the measure of the few benefactions from the other class.

On the other hand the affluent have their errors. Almost invariably they judge unjustly. Scarcely a man of them knows his due proportion for matters of social utility. The man of wealth would be amazed at you, as a maniac or a fool, if you should tell him that his benefactions ought to take so much of his income that he shall add to his capital at the end of the year no more than the poor man by the side of him adds to his. Well, we will not tell him so; though if either of them shall be called on to give for social good all that he could add to his capital, it would seem that the poor man can least afford it.

If it were not for these erroneous notions, the rich and the poor would act together with more efficiency and more good-will. Public good would be more promoted. Both classes would be more useful, and both more happy—linked together by common action, common feeling, and common interests. Their errors may make them different from one another; but God has made them very much alike. *They meet together.* Alike and equally, or nearly so, they may do good. The poor can give as much as the rich the world over; not just here, perhaps, but in general. The rich can not do without the poor, and the poor can not do without the rich, in matters pertaining to public and social usefulness. There is no occasion for the poor to feel that they can do nothing, and have nothing to do. There is no occasion for the rich to feel that nothing can be done without them. The poor, if they will, can benefit society as much as the rich can. They can do much. . God has not cut them off from usefulness. Let them not cut themselves off. And let not the rich disregard the presence, feelings and action of the poor in matters of common interest and public good. They meet together. God has made them more alike than they are prone to think: their resemblances are more than their distinctions. There is little ground for pride on the one hand and envy on the other—for arrogance on the one hand and servility and feeling and meanness on the other. *The Lord is the maker of them all.* They may equally serve him, equally enjoy and love him, and in the great day may equally hear the welcome, *Well done, good and faithful servant.*

The Rich and Poor meet Together.

The rich and poor meet together; The Lord is the maker of them all.—
PROVERBS, xxii. 2.

IN a former sermon on this text, we proposed to follow, as well as we could, the course of the writer's mind, and pick up along his track the materials out of which he coined this proverb.

In aiming to do so, we found (as we thought) resemblances rather than differences between the affluent and the indigent.

1. In their origin and condition as they enter the world.

2. In their training and preparation for after-life, in their duties and stations.

3. In their means for enjoyment in the world.

4. In their power of usefulness in society.

And here we mentioned their utility to their own families—their utility to the public—and their utility in sustaining those public and costly institutions so necessary to the common good. On all these points we found between them more of similarity than of difference.

We now continue the same subject:

5. Between the rich and the poor there is a substantial agreement in all the organs of perception and enjoyment. Much of our felicity here, and not a little of our

improvement and usefulness, depend upon the organic constitution which makes us men. And herein we are all alike to a very remarkable degree. One class as well as another has all the limbs and bones and muscles and senses of humanity. The Maker of all has put no difference between them. The glory of the sunrise is as visible to the poor man as to the rich, and the penciled wild flower blushes just as sweetly upon his eye. The breeze fans his bosom as blandly, and music falls on his ear as sweetly, and he can lay hold on the furniture of the world by an organization for perception and enjoyment as vivid and as far-reaching as his wealthiest neighbor. The rich can not monopolize the fragrance of the morning—the sound of the thunder—or the tints of the rainbow. The poor man's organization throughout is as perfect as his own. His hands are as many, and his feet are as swift. With as keen perception, and as keen enjoyment too, he can lay hold upon the offerings of the world. If his Maker had given him an inferior organization, duller senses, or half-formed nerves; had denied him strong bones, or quick blood, or two eyes; he might have had some just ground for his discontent. But since he stands a man in organism, and equal to any other man in all the machinery for his purposes; and since the field of the world is open before him, and no monopoly can take it away from him; he has no ground for discontent. *The rich and the poor meet together.* Their equality in physical organization is of far more moment than all the adventitious circumstances which attend upon wealth.

6. In the intellectual faculties there is the same strong resemblance. The perception, the memory, the imagination, the reason which God has given to men, he has

been pleased to give with an impartial hand. Such faculties may be more cultivated indeed, and made instrumental to more usefulness and enjoyment among the rich, on account of their leisure and the means of culture which wealth can command. But even here, the advantages of riches often turn out to be practically disadvantages; and while many of the opulent fail of much intellectual excellence, many of the poor make attainments in knowledge which princes might envy. There is nothing in povery which necessarily forbids the attainment of as sound discretion, as good judgment, as well regulated mind, as graces any other condition of life. In the high gifts *of mind*, God bestows with an impartial hand. *The rich and the poor meet together.* There is not an item of distinction but such as arises from the circumstances and sins of life. The reflection of the poet over the graveyard of the poor is just:

> " Perhaps in this neglected spot is laid
> Some heart once pregnant with celestial fire;
> Hands that the rod of empire might have swayed,
> Or waked to ecstasy the living lyre."

7. In the original passions of men there is the same exact resemblance. The primary elements and implantation are equal. If there is "no royal road to learning," neither is there any royal road to virtue. The same care, the same caution and self-control and self-denial which are requisite in a poor man, for the formation of a character of excellence, are just as needful among the affluent. Self-indulgence will be as fatal to the rich as to the poor, both in respect to virtue and to an earthly felicity. And when we consider in how many things the natural passions of the poor are crossed and restrained

by their condition, and how often the rich are accustomed to an indulgence invited by their means of gratification, it would seem that for the mortification of evil passions, for the formation of a character of excellence, for any real virtue, the poor are the more favorably situated. They are more restrained by circumstances beyond their control. They are less tempted perhaps. They are more accustomed to crosses and to a voluntary carefulness. So that the elements of disorder and vice to be found in the evil passions, checked in the bud, or accustomed to restraint, may, perhaps, be radically subdued with more ease. But if there is a disposition to evil, it will find opportunity to operate in both classes. If there is a disposition to good, neither class lack field nor materials. That spirit of domination which makes a rich man a tyrant, makes a poor man a tyrant also; if the latter can not be a tyrant in society, he will be a tyrant at home. That spirit of ambition which makes a rich man proud, arrogant and forward in the face of a whole community, makes the poor man equally forward, arrogant and proud in his narrower sphere. That spirit of avarice which makes the rich man eager for gain and unjust in making it, will make the poor man envious and equally unjust in his sphere. The same justice, gentleness and good-will which make a man of affluence a public benefactor, to spread good around him by both example and activity, will make a poor man a benefactor also, whose *example* may do more, perhaps, if his *activity* does less, for the general welfare of society; his means furnish him less to give, but his example is right in the midst of the multitude where its influence will tell. In all these passions, elementary of character and promotive of activity for good or evil, the rich and the poor are alike. Their *Maker* has put no difference between them. Nor is there any difference in their opportunities for felicity or unhappiness by their just or unjust control of them. *The rich and the poor meet together; the Lord is the maker of them all.*

8. The rich and the poor are alike in their natural and equal dependence upon one another. Neither class can dispense with the other and stand independent and alone. Each is necessary in its place, like different members of the human body. The foot can not say to the head: *I have no need of thee;* nor the head reply: *I have no need of thee.* The poor have need of the rich to take off from their hands the produce of their toil and reward their labors; and the rich have need of the poor to furnish them the necessaries and elegances of life. The Divine penman was right when he said: *The king himself is served by the field.* By means of the mutual and equal dependence of these two classes upon one another, it has pleased God to give order and steadiness to human society, such as no philosophy could contrive or imitate. He puts men in such a mutually dependent condition, that while each aims at the furtherance of his own good, he really is promoting the general welfare; that while even the selfish feelings of humanity are at work, and are the promoters of activity, they are made to operate with an order and general utility not their own, and which yet they can not dispense with. As the poor gain their living by their daily toil, they are at once rendering themselves the more happy, and society the more happy also. As the rich reward that toil, living generously or even elegantly in the enjoyment of what they purchase from the hands of labor, they are thus encouraging industry, meeting the wants of others, and doing

more for the general good than if they scattered abroad their money without any equivalent for it in return. If the rich were to live parsimoniously, they would be less useful—less useful to themselves and to the world. If the poor were to live without labor and by the mere munificence of the affluent, *they* would be less useful to themselves and to the world. Wealth would be worth nothing if it could procure nothing; and labor, just as far as it can procure, is equally valuable with riches. The rich and the poor, the high and the low, are equally dependent upon one another. The rich could not stand alone. The poor could not stand alone. *They meet together*. They are mutually and equally dependent upon one another. The toil of the poor man furnishes the elegances which the rich man enjoys; and the wealth of the rich man, who buys at the hands of labor, is the reward which makes that labor contented and profitable. If wealth could not purchase any thing, it would be useless—only a burden or a gilded bauble to its possessor. If the laborious classes could not dispose of the avails of their labor, industry would be discouraged and society would languish. As it is, each class leans upon the other, and each contributes to the other's felicity. That equalization of wealth and earthly possessions, which some superficial and wicked reformers aim after, could do nothing for the good of the whole. It would discourage industry and all improvements to a vast extent. It would undermine parental affection and all filial requitals. The child would feel under no more obligations to his parents because they had done much for him than if they had done nothing. They could *not* do much. He would just come on the equal footing, of course. And *because* they could not, their industry, carefulness, frugality, their talents and virtues would not be peculiarly stimulated and secured by the strength and tenderness of parental solicitudes. And hence the family constitution, that highest earthly safeguard for felicity and virtue, would be almost entirely destroyed. The reciprocal and equal dependence of the rich and the poor is the very thing which gives to human society, under God, its security and its felicity and virtue. "Socialism" is as silly as it is heartless.

9. Betwixt these two classes of men there is a very nearly equal distribution of the disappointments, vexations and distresses of life. Human happiness is nowhere perfect and uninterrupted. Some trials fall to the lot of every mortal. Care goes every where. So does apprehension. So do pains and sickness. The storms of life beat upon every head, and there is no earthly shelter. Some of them may beat the more heavily upon the one class, and some upon the other. There are many of the most disastrous evils from which the poor are comparatively secure. The shock falls only upon those in high places:

> "The bolts that spare the mountain's side,
> His cloud-capt eminence divide,
> And spread the ruin round."

Revolutions, great commercial reverses, and things of the like nature, spend their worst violence upon the high and affluent, and pass over the rest with comparative harmlessness. Eagerness, ambition, and high hopes have been aroused by their situation, in the breasts of the rich, and have thus prepared them to suffer *more* by coming disappointments, than is suffered among those of less lofty aims and more contented disposition. The passions and hopes in general which distinguish the affluent are more in danger of being interfered with and dashed in the course of life than the hopes and passions of humble life. It is the oak of the hills which must struggle with the career of the tempest, and sometimes break because it can not bend. It is the humble reed at its foot which bends uninjured, and when the tempest has swept by stands erect and verdant as before. The cares and distresses of life, vexations, annoyances, pains of body, griefs of heart, are very equally distributed among men. The Lord, the Maker of all, has so ordered.

10. There is a perfect equality among men in their capabilities for religion. Here the affluent have not an item of advantage. Those poor in earthly things, can with equal ease become *rich in faith and heirs of the kingdom which God has promised to them that love him*. There is the same faculty of conscience, the same power of love to God, the same amount of ability to serve God, and the same opportunity for the full enjoyments of faith furnished to all men. The devotion of the lowly may be as pure and as felicitous as that of the lofty. Their love may burn as blandly and as constantly. Their faith may be as firm. Their hope may reach as far. Their communion with God may be as intimate and as tender. The temptations of affluence seem to constitute as serious a hinderance to all the duties and advances of the Divine life *practically*, as the destitution of poverty. If the affluent through the advantages of means and leisure, can become the more extensively intelligent in religion, the indigent have some advantages to equal this; for they are less tempted to a self-reliance, and are led by their condition to know and feel better what it means when they pray: *Give us, day by day, our daily bread.*

Those who have little of this world to rely upon, are more likely to realize their dependence and to recognize the constant care of a Divine Providence. They have not their mind called off from God by so many of the *cares of this world, and by the deceitfulness of riches.* No man can furnish an item of proof that there is any practical inequality among men for all the advantages of religion. All *meet together.*

11. The spiritual condition and necessities of human souls are all precisely the same by nature. One man has the same repentance to exercise as another—the same faith—the same self-denial. One man can do without regeneration no better than another. The path which leads to Christ is the same for every human being. Earthly distinctions vanish entirely the very moment our attention is turned upon the nature and wants of the soul and upon our preparation to meet God. A rich man's heart is as depraved as a poor man's. It is as obstinate, as perverse, and as unbelieving. He needs pardon just as much—needs Christ just as much—the Holy Spirit as much. He must take as lowly a place before God as the veriest beggar that lives. The poor man's prayer is no more necessary for him than the rich man's for him; and it may take as direct a pathway up to the throne of equal and eternal mercy; and it may bring back from thence as sure and as sweet an answer. The same promises of God are written for all men alike. Light, aid, comfort—all there is in religion here, and all that it provides for us hereafter, are things equally within the reach of all. The prince upon his throne and arrayed in his splendor, can no more walk with God and in no more intimacy and tenderness of communion, than his humblest subject. The poorest child of poverty and tears

can lift his eye to as lofty a seat in heaven as the most affluent. *There is one Lord, one faith, one baptism.* There is one heaven for all, one Christ, and one way of entrance for all. All will not reach it indeed, but it will not be the necessary hinderance of any earthly distinctions which shall prevent. There may be some temptations of riches indeed more dangerous to souls than the most pinching poverty, and Jesus Christ seems to have referred to them in this sense when he said: *How hardly shall they that have riches enter into the kingdom of heaven!* And James seems to have reiterated the same idea, when he says: *Let the brother of low degree rejoice in that he is exalted, but the rich in that he is made low, because as the flower of the grass he shall pass away.* But neither riches nor poverty constitutes any necessary hinderance to eternal life, or any necessary advantage for attaining it. Their distinctions vanish before God. On the foundation of the promises, and in the name of a common Saviour, they may look forward toward that eternal world of light and glory where earthly distinctions shall be no more.

12. There is one common end to all our common humanity. The rich and the poor, liable alike to the same disorders and decay of vital functions, are approaching alike that solemn hour which shall level all earthly distinctions. In the grasp of death they are equally helpless, equally distressful, and, when the blood stops, equally cold in death. The vast resources of the most opulent can not bring to expiring nature a single item of advantages. His pain will be as keen, and his condition as helpless, and the path before him as dark, and his spirit immortal as needy of spiritual support and consolations. At the hour of death all earthly distinctions sink together into nothing: one man is just as poor as another. All the

appendages of wealth and grandeur are laid aside, and all the marks of poverty which distinguish one man from another, disappear at that solemn hour when the mortal passes the narrow gate of death into the invisible and eternal world.

13. *The rich and poor meet together* in the same moldering of the tomb. There is no difference between them down in that spot where the grave-worm has his banquet! Among the darkness, dust and putrefaction—among *dead men's bones*, you can find nothing to minister to human vanity. The loftiest and the lowliest rest side by side, and mingle their dust together in the bosom of their common mother, earth. Affluence seeks, indeed, an external distinction in the burial spot; but it can not even seek for any other, and all it can do is only to rear some more imposing sepulcher, or more proudly-sculptured marble, which may arrest, for a little while, the passing stranger. It is *only* for a little while. As time sweeps on his course, the chiseled marble gives way; the letters are worn off; the proud name is gone; the splendid tomb is crumbled down; the plow-share passes over the moldering heart, or the spade of the grave-digger flings up the dust and bones of the mighty as unceremoniously as those of the mean. In a few centuries after they have left the earth, the high and the mighty of Babylon, Tyre and Egypt—of Nineveh, Rome and Etruria, have not even a man left upon the earth; and if their sepulchers are known at all, they are only known as matters of curiosity to the antiquary, or to be rifled of their bones by the rude hands of some heartless barbarian! The decree has gone forth over all the walks of humanity alike, and will be every where executed just alike—*dust thou art, and unto dust shalt thou return.*

14. The rich and poor meet together on the common platform of another world. The time is coming when sepulchers shall be emptied of their tenants. The earth and the sea shall give up their dead. The rich and the poor will come back from their equal place of corruption and worms and oblivion, to appear on a new scene, wherein there will be only one single point of interest or distinction. They will stand together at the *judgment-seat of Christ*, and be judged together out of the same book of God. They shall alike give account of themselves in respect to the *deeds done in the body*. The rich shall tell how he used his riches, and the poor how he used his poverty. Their daily life shall come up in that solemn review. There will be no exception, no disguise, no concealments, and no partiality. The same Maker of all will be the final judge of all. The mighty Redeemer on the throne, once a poor man—a *man of sorrows and acquainted with grief*, who had not *where to lay his head*, will equally arraign the rich and poor before him—the possessor of ten talents and of one. Not the possession, but the *use* of them will then be the question. The poorest man that ever lived will then be on a perfect equality with the richest, and may receive just as magnificent and glorious a reward. According as he served God and loved him here, and following Christ in faith aimed to glorify God and do good on earth, he shall then receive at the hands of the final Judge. If it shall appear that his poverty only increased his discontent, his envy toward his fellow-man and his murmuring against God, he will fall under the curse of a just indignation. If, on the contrary, it shall appear that his poverty was borne with patience and faith, and made him *rich toward God*, he will have no occasion to mourn that his life was

not spent in opulence, but he will bless and praise the God who made him poor, and made his poverty an aid to his salvation. If, then, the rich man shall be found to have loved and served God, avoiding the temptations to pride, indulgence and worldliness, he will meet the approval of his Judge. If, on the contrary, it shall be found that his wealth made him forget God and neglect Christ; if then he should be compelled to look back to the days of his flesh, and recollect talents perverted, means of good misapplied, his Saviour and his heaven forgotten; instead of being led by the *goodness of God to repentance,* and employing his means and his mind and his time and his world for his Lord and Master, he will have deep occasion to curse the wealth he coveted and misapplied, and sinking lower in perdition, will become an example of what Christ warned him about: *In hell the rich man lifted up his eyes, his soul being in torments!*

At that final bar the *rich and poor shall meet together.* The character of every man shall be weighed by the unerring and omniscient God, and the destiny of every one shall be fixed for ever. From among both rich and poor some will fall under the final displeasure of God, and *go away into everlasting punishment.* Before some of both rich and poor the gates of heaven shall open, and they shall *enter in through the gates into the city.* They *shall walk with Christ in white.* They shall bathe their immortal spirits in that sea of glory; and as the ages of eternity sweep by, their ceaseless anthem of grace shall come up before the throne of God and of the Lamb. *The rich and poor meet together; the Lord is the maker of them all.*

There is no necessity for any other particulars in this

sermon. Those we have mentioned are enough to make it manifest that the resemblances between the rich and poor are far more, and far more remarkable, than the distinctions between them. We suppose that it was the notice which his mind took of these resemblances that led the author of this text to utter the proverb before us. He had wondered at earthly distinctions. He had felt a dissatisfaction about them. He studied the matter more deeply, and more religiously; and after his mind had gone over the whole field, he just embodies the whole matter in a proverb, *the rich and poor meet together*—they are very much alike often—the *Maker of them all* has acted wisely and beneficently.

The subject before us ought to receive from this audience a practical application.

The poor ought to employ it for their personal direction. It ought to be enough to hush to rest every emotion of envy toward those in more affluent circumstances, and every emotion of discontent with their worldly lot. They have no occasion to repine. Riches do not confer happiness necessarily—nor render one better or more useful. If you are poor in this world's goods you may be *rich in faith and heirs of the kingdom*. Your riches, if you are Christians, are not *put into a bag with holes*, nor treasured where *moth and rust* can reach them. Your recompense is above. You may rise above all the sorrows and ills of an earthly poverty, by the enjoyment of God and contemplations of the glory to be revealed. In faith, in hope, in holiness, in prayer, in communion with God, in living in the world rightly, and dying out of it happily, you have all the advantages that you ever could have, if the wealth of the world were yours. Jesus

Christ was a poor man, and his life of humiliation has thrown a bright beam of comfort and promise on the path of the poor.

Those who are rich ought to recollect their resemblances to the poor. They have no very signal and essential advantages over them. They have nothing which ought to fill them with pride or with feelings of haughtiness and security. They must give an account for the manner in which they employ their possessions. If they live only for the world and for themselves, the day of their reckoning will be a dreadful day. They will have a heavy account to render in—an account which shall reach back upon all their possessions and all their earthly transactions. Unless they are Christians and live to the glory of Christ, in the love and service of God with all their heart and all their riches; it were a thousand-fold better for them that they had walked in the poor man's path and gone down to the poor man's grave. God has given them an important stewardship, and he will not forget it. If they will, their stewardship may be profitable to them. But it can not be so if they forget God and his dominion. Their riches are sacred trusts put into their hands. Human dependence, the dictates of an enlightened conscience, the precepts of God, the blood of atonement, and the opening gates of another world, all conspire to demonstrate to us that we are not our own, and all call on us to use our possessions according to the will of him who gives them. If we do so we shall serve him in a more glorious field hereafter. The affluent should remember his equality with the most lowly. He needs pardon as much—Christ as much—prayer as much. All earthly distinctions will soon cease. At the threshold of eternity they must be laid down together. There will be one eternity and one judge for all.

This subject, too, ought to make a deep impression upon the *young*. Young men are prone to look upon the distinctions and supposed advantages of wealth with a mistaken eye. They devote to its acquisition hopes and fears and calculations and genius and talents and precious days, of which all the wealth of the world is not worthy. Their eye is dazzled with a deceitful splendor. Their young mind is entranced with a delusive dream. Riches will not necessarily render them more happy or more useful—better in life or more fit to leave it. First of all they ought to seek to be *rich toward God*—to be renewed by the Holy Ghost, washed in atoning blood, and fitted for eternal life. What will it avail to you, young men, that you should attain what you must so soon lose? What will riches alone confer upon you that will do you any good? The distinctions of wealth all vanish and sink down together into nothing at the door of the sepulcher; and you will be swallowed up in the ocean of a vast eternity. Garner your wealth there. Do that *first*. The only distinction which shall survive the day when your bodies are deposited in the grave, must be found in that holiness which saves, or that sin which ruins for ever. Whatever be your lot here, life and bliss eternal you may have; for *the rich and poor meet together; the Lord is the maker of them all.*

Lessons from Ecclesiastes.

Therefore I hated life; because the work that is wrought under the sun is grievous unto me; for all is vanity and vexation of spirit.—ECCLESIASTES, ii. 17.

THERE are few parts of the sacred Scriptures more difficult of interpretation than the one which contains this text. The style of the book is peculiar; and the rapid transition of thought from one subject to another, and from one state of mind to another—a transition often made without any express mention of it—throws an air of obscurity and, indeed, sometimes an appearance of contradiction over the sentiments uttered.

Hence the most extravagant ideas have sometimes been deduced from it—the most mischievous, the most absurd. Some expressions in it have been employed in a manner which might well rejoice libertines; and the licentious themselves have sometimes seized upon ideas contained in it to justify all the extravagances of an unbridled licentiousness. They have very eloquently repeated that passage in the seventh verse of the ninth chapter: *Go thy way, eat thy bread with joy, and drink thy wine with a merry heart*, as if it were a fit motto for a man of pleasure. With equal animation and eloquence, they have recited that passage in the twenty-fourth verse of the second chapter: *There is nothing better for a man than that he should eat and drink, and that he should make his soul enjoy good in his labor,* as if it was designed to give loose reins to indulgence.

And infidelity, as well as libertinism, has made itself merry over the supports supposed to be found in some of these chapters. It has called ideas found here contradictory—the whole book a jumble of inconsistencies. Bringing together the second verse of the second chapter—*I said of laughter it is mad, and of mirth what doeth it;* and the fifteenth verse of the eighth chapter; *Then I commended mirth, because a man hath no better thing under the sun than to eat and drink and to be merry,*—Infidelity has put on a malignant smile, as if she had found at once a refutation of the Bible in its inconsistency and liberty for the indulgence of chosen *amusements* and sensuality.

Libertines and infidels are not always worth noticing. Most of their pretences are a compound of folly and falsehood, both silly and dishonest. And when men have descended so low as *that*, they are ordinarily best treated when left to become wise and right or not, just as they shall choose. Many a foolish man has become confirmed in error when his error has been dignified by noticing it. But some of these ideas are worthy of notice, especially as the notice of them may lead us to a just understanding of the writer of this book; and as some serious minds also have been embarrassed by expressions contained in it.

The text before us has not escaped misconception: *I hated life; because the work that is wrought under the sun is grievous unto me.* This has been said to justify an entire disgust with life. It has also been adduced as a proof that a man of religious sentiments must be so far led off from the ordinary feelings of humanity as to *hate life* and the world, and must therefore be unfit for society in respect to enjoying it, or aiming to promote its good. And it may be that a true believer sometimes, in dejection and trouble, may seek to justify the gloom of his sentiments and his dark dislike of a wearisome life by supposing himself to resemble the author of the text—*I hated life.*

Before, therefore, we enter upon the special consideration of the text itself, we propose to furnish an explanation of the peculiarities of this book—a matter which seems necessary, not only for a just explanation of the text itself, but for *justifying* the explanation, and for guarding the book in general from misconstruction.

On this point we have several ideas to present. We want your entire attention. We are going to teach you a matter for you to remember whenever you read this book of Solomon. To this object we devote this sermon. We will attend to the particular idea of the text hereafter.

Let us enter upon the subject. Let us learn how to interpret the book before us—a book containing some expressions which sound strange to many ears.

We make one remark, as a clew to the meaning of the author, as a key to unlock the mysteries hidden here, as a wand to sweep away the fogs and clouds which infidelity, worldliness and libertinism (always superficial) have hung round the expressions of this author. The remark is this: That almost the entire sum of this book is composed in the style of *experience* and *observation*. In some passages the writer speaks from experience. In others he speaks from observation. In others still he mingles both these together, grounding his ideas on both what he had *seen* and what he had himself *felt*.

I. He speaks as a man of *experience*. Examine the sixteenth and seventeenth verses of the first chapter: *I communed with mine own heart, saying, Lo, I am come to great estate, and have gotten more wisdom than all they that have been before me in Jerusalem; yea, my heart had great experience of wisdom and knowledge. And I gave my heart to know wisdom, and to know madness and folly.* So in the second chapter, to the end of the tenth verse, he speaks of his own experience: *I said in mine heart, Go to now, I will prove thee with mirth, therefore enjoy pleasure . . . I sought in mine heart to give myself unto wine . . . I made me great works; I builded me houses; I planted me vineyards; I made me gardens and orchards.* And he goes on to tell of his *servants* and *cattle* and *singers* and *silver* and *gold* and *delights,* not *withholding his heart from any joy.* In the same style of experience he utters the fifteenth verse of the eighth chapter (already cited): *Then I commended mirth, because a man hath no better thing under the sun than to eat and to drink and to be merry.* The same style of experience, of history, of autobiography, runs through the book.

If ever there was a man qualified by the experience of it to tell what pleasure is worth, that man was Solomon, the author of the book before us. He was *king over Israel in Jerusalem,* in the days of its highest splendor. His proud city glittered with gold. It abounded in luxury—in every refinement. To its glory all the civilized world had contributed. Egypt had sent thither in profuse abundance the finest of her wheat. The East had sent the choicest of her delicacies—the aroma of her plants to breathe their perfumes on the air of Palestine, and the glitter of her gems to flash in the sun-light abroad, or adorn the persons that moved amid the splendor of her proud palaces at home. The South and the West had contributed all the adornments of architecture. Science and art contributed to the enjoyments of taste. Arabia had sent in her mathematics. Tyre and Sidon their purple and fine linen. Poesy sang. Music found a home there. And amid all these resources and all this splendor, Solomon gave loose reins to his desires to enjoy them all, better situated than ever man was before or since, to prove by his own experiences what the pleasures of the world are worth. And in this book he has given us an account of the whole matter. He has summed it up in five words—VANITY AND VEXATION OF SPIRIT. He summed it up (just as you would have done if you had his wisdom and trial) on the ground of his own experience. He had tried it all and knew what was its value; and as he recapitulates to us in this book his experiences, he tells us how he turned from one pleasure to another, and one earthly promise to another, with the sickening feeling, *this also is vanity.* It is on this principle that he makes this remarkable introduction—an introduction which has no parallel or resemblance in any other writing that we have ever seen: *Vanity of vanities, saith the preacher, vanity of vanities, all is vanity.* He spake from the heart: he was a man of experience. He had tried *amusements.*

Now let me ask you to notice, in his own phraseology, how this remark about his style is applicable. Commence with the text itself: *I hated life, because the work that is wrought under the sun is grievous unto me.* When did he hate it? How are we to understand him? Is he telling us what he thinks *now?* or what he thought while his reason was entranced and he was pursuing the vanities of the world? If you were to write your own biography, how would you write it? Suppose you had been eagerly pursuing some object for a time, and afterward had altered your sentiments in distaste and disappointment, and still afterward had set your heart upon something very different, and suppose you were going to employ your own experience as an argument to persuade other people to take a wiser way than you had taken at first, how would you be apt to express yourself? You would have three different points to hold up. At one time you would mention the sentiments you entertained at *the period* when you were eagerly pursuing your favorite object. At another time you would mention the sentiments you entertained at *the period* when you had concluded to abandon it. At another time you would mention the sentiments you entertain *now*, when, having set your heart upon another object, you are aiming, by the force of your own experience, to induce your friend to shun the error and copy the wisdom of your example. And if you were much gifted in the art of persuasion, your ideas would move backward and forward from one of these periods to another, in order to bring into frequent contrast the benefits of one course and the evil of its opposite. Well; Solomon has done precisely this in the book before us. He has done just as you would have done. He states his sentiments *after* his recovery from error, and while he is under the direction of Divine wisdom. He states his sentiments in the outset. And he states his sentiments in the intermediate time—in the day of his disappointment, when he had got no further than to hear and feel the *rebuke* of truth, but had not yet taken its positive direction. And he passes from one of these to another, under no rule but that of the heart's logic, more intent on persuasion than on the name of scholarship. And when he says, *I hated life, because the work that is wrought under the sun is grievous unto me,* there is no difficulty in perceiving to *what period* of his heart's history he alludes. Manifestly he does not express his *present* sentiments. He speaks of the past; he employs what the grammarians call the "past tense," *I hated life:* he does not say he hates it now. Just as manifestly he does not express the sentiments he entertained when he was pursuing, with all the zest of his heart, the vanities of the world. The expression refers to the other period—to the time of his disappointment, disgust and dissatisfaction—to the moment when he awoke from his dream, and found it *was* a dream: *I hated life.* Nothing is more natural. He had been living for mere pleasure. It did not satisfy him. It could not. He knew of nothing better to live for. His pleasures palled upon his senses—his heart was sick—he was disgusted with life itself: *I hated life.*

It may be that some of you can sympathize with him, far enough at least to understand him. Tax your recollection. Has there been no moment when you were disgusted with life itself? Have you not felt so? When your plans have been dashed, or your pride mortified, or your hearts have sickened amid your worldly vanities, or your health has failed and your spirits sunk and all the world seemed to you a bubble, a dream; have you not wondered what you lived for; and, amid this empty and sickening scene, been disgusted with life itself? Very well; Solomon would have you feel so. He would convince you that sooner or later you *must.* He would employ this feeling as an argument, *first* to turn off the heart from the world's deceitful promises, and *second,* to turn it to something better—to that love and service of

God, wherein life shall be as valuable as, spent upon the world, it ought to be disgusting. Do not stop with your disgust. Follow Solomon further. Heart-sick of the world, do not ask merely, in distaste and despondency, What do I live for? or, in disgust and despair, do not wish you had never lived at all. Turn to the great and valuable ends of your existence, which Solomon has summed up in the closing sentence of this book, and calls the *conclusion of the whole matter: Fear God and keep his commandments, for this is the whole duty of man; for God shall bring every work into judgment with every secret thing, whether it be good or whether it be evil.*

On the same principle we interpret the verses immediately after the text: *Yea I had hated all my labor which I had taken under the sun, because I should leave it unto the man that shall be after me. And who knoweth whether he shall be a wise man or a fool?* So he felt when he had become disgusted with his dissipation, and *before* he had turned him to labor for another life and another world. How natural his expression! It is an artist-sketch of the heart of a selfish man! *I hated labor, because I should leave it unto the man that shall be after me,* wise or fool. He must leave it, be it crown, or gold, or splendor. He must leave it, and perhaps the son that inherits it shall be a *fool!* He must leave it; and this was the lament of his selfishness, at the time of his disgust with life. If he had now been a man of benevolence, it might have given him some satisfaction, that what he should leave behind him might contribute something to the good of his successor. But he was not yet a man of religious benevolence. He was a man of selfishness, and of selfish disgust and dissatisfaction, mourning that he must leave his gold to his heir, and exchange his royal purple for the shroud of the tomb.

In the expression: *Who knoweth whether he shall be a wise man or a fool, yet shall he have rule over all my labor*, possibly Solomon utters his present sentiments, and not the sentiments of his period of disgust. We told you that the sentiments of these two periods were sometimes mingled together in his argument. Take your choice betwixt the two. Neither is very unnatural. A wise man, a pious man, may very well feel that his living for another world has an enforcement from the fact that his heirs may be fools, and the inheritance he leaves them may do them no good; this reflection may very well come in to check his remaining worldliness of spirit, or to induce him to do good with his possessions *before* he is dead and others shall employ them to do hurt. A man disgusted with life and the world may very well find his sentiments of disgust strengthened by the idea, that all his labors and possessions may be as vain for his children as they have been for himself. *Fools* may be his heirs! *fools* may take the avails of his labor! and as he thinks of it, his increased disgust may exclaim: *This also is vanity*.

On the same principle we interpret the fifteenth verse of the eighth chapter. It is a piece of autobiography. The author is telling, not what is his opinion *now*, but what his opinion was once; not what it was in his period of disgust with life, but what it was before that, in the period of his dissipation. *I commended mirth*—(he does not commend it *now*)—*I commended mirth, because a man hath no better thing under the sun than to eat and to drink and to be merry*. So he thought in his season of pleasure and dissipation. He thought there was *nothing better*.

He thought just as the silly sons of pleasure think now. He confesses it to them. He tells them that he has been over their ground, he has tried the whole matter, he was once foolish enough to feel as they feel: *That there is nothing better under the sun than to eat and to drink and to be merry.* And now, as a man of experience, as an old hand in the business, who has been through the whole, and knows all about it, he claims to be heard, when he tells them; *This also is vanity; it shall not be well with the wicked, neither shall he prolong his days which are as a shadow; because he feareth not before God* (viii. 13). Young men would do well to hear him. He ought to be heard. Beside his inspiration, he was now an old man. He was an experienced man. He had run the whole round of pleasure. He had justified it. He had said as they say, that *there is nothing better than to eat and to drink and to be merry.* Now he knows better. He knows those of such merriment and dissipation do not *fear God;* it can not be *well with them;* and when he says that *the wicked shall not prolong his days which are as a shadow,* young men should remember that he who lives *to eat and to drink and to be merry* will not live long; and, however screened and hidden may be this drinking and merriment now, it will not be hidden long: *God shall bring every work into judgment with every secret thing.* He does not plead for *amusements.*

On the same principle we interpret a multitude of other expressions found in this book. *I sought in mine heart to give myself unto wine. . . . I made me great works; I builded me houses and planted me vineyards; I made me gardens and orchards; . . . I gathered me silver and gold; I got me men-singers and women-singers; . . . I commended mirth; . . . I said, Drink thy wine with a merry heart;*

. . . *live joyfully ; let thy garments be always white, and thy head lack no ointment;*—these, all these, are expressions of the sentiments which Solomon entertained in the days of his pleasure.

You can not err in fixing upon the passages which express his sentiments *after* the days of his pleasure were ended. The book is full of them. After pleasure palled upon his senses, and his heart sickened with disgust of life, he chose something more wise than either—he turned to religion. His sentiments *now* are uttered in such passages as these : *Remember now thy Creator in the days of thy youth, while the evil days come not, nor the years draw nigh when thou shalt say, I have no pleasure in them. Fear God and keep his commandments ; this is the whole of man*—his duty, felicity, and interest. *Though a sinner do evil an hundred times, and his days be prolonged* (as sometimes they may be), *yet surely I know that it shall be well with them that fear God . . . but it shall not be well with the wicked.* (Ch. xii. 1, 13 ; viii. 12, 13.) Looking on the world, all its pleasure, pomp and promise, he turns from one thing to another—*this, this also is vanity.* Looking at the trials and fears that cluster around the pathway of life, he says, *He that feareth God shall come forth of them all* (vii. 18). Looking forth into another world, he sees that the retributions of *that* shall clear up the confusion of this: *For God shall bring every work into judgment with every secret thing, whether it be good or whether it be evil* (xii. 14).

Let this suffice on the head of *experience.* It is plain that Solomon in this book gives much of his own heart's history as an argument for religion ; and he makes three points prominent : *first,* his sentiments in the period of his indulgence ; *second,* his sentiments in the period of his digust with life; and *third*, his sentiments in the afterperiod—the period of his piety.

II. A second characteristic of the style of this book is a little variation from this: much of it is in the style of *observation*. The author not only states what his heart had felt, but what his eyes had seen. He does this for the same purpose, namely, to persuade men, especially young men, to religion. He draws an argument for it from things that met his eyes. And while he is pursuing the argument, he sometimes unites with the account of what he had noticed the sentiments he entertained at the different periods we have mentioned. This, also, is perfectly natural. You would have done the same thing. If you had wished to persuade any person, you would both have mentioned the facts, (what your eyes had seen,) and your own feelings in view of them—your feelings at different times.

You can not but be convinced that Solomon argues as an observer, when you notice the abundance of passages like the following: *I have* SEEN *all the works that are done under the sun, and behold all is vanity* (i. 14). *I* SAW *under the sun the place of judgment, that wickedness was there, and the place of righteousness, that iniquity was there* (iii. 16). *There is a sore evil which I have* SEEN *under the sun, namely, riches kept for the owners thereof to their hurt* (v. 13). (If he had lived till this time he might have seen the same thing.) *There is an evil which I have* SEEN *under the sun, and it is common among men: a man to whom God hath given riches, wealth, and honor, so that he wanteth nothing for his soul of all that he desireth, yet God giveth him not power to eat thereof, but a stranger eateth it* (vi. 1, 2.) *All this have I* SEEN, *and applied my heart unto every work that* is done under the sun: there is a time wherein one man ruleth over another to his own hurt (viii. 9). When I applied my heart to know wisdom, and to SEE the business that is done upon the earth, . . . then I beheld all the work of God, that a man can not find out the work that is done under the sun, because though a man labor to seek it out, yet he shall not find it (viii. 16, 17). I have SEEN servants upon horses, and princes walking as servants upon the earth (x. 7). (He would see it now if he were alive.) I returned and SAW under the sun, that the race is not to the swift, nor the battle to the strong, neither yet bread to the wise, nor yet riches to men of understanding, nor yet favor to men of skill, but time and chance happeneth to them all (ix. 11). He knew no better. He thought so then. He could see no further. He was a fool. He thought it was mere *time and chance* at that period, the period of distaste which preceded his pious recognition of God.

All these passages, and an abundance of others, prove to us that Solomon composed this book as a man of observation: that he makes use of the things which his own eyes had SEEN *under the sun*, to point the maxims and give strength to the arguments he utters.

We said it would be perfectly natural that, while aiming to persuade young men to religion, he should tell them not only the facts which fell under his observation, but also his feelings in view of them at the time. He has done this—just as you would have done. Notice his account of some facts in the first verse of the fourth chapter, and his feelings in view of them in the second and third verses: *So I returned and considered all the oppressions that are done under the sun, and behold, the tears of such as were oppressed, and they had no comforter, and on the side of the oppressors there was power: but* THEY *had no comforter.* You may judge of the keenness of his observation by this last clause. Then follows an account of the feelings he had in view of all this, when he noticed it at first: *Wherefore I praised the dead which are already dead more than the living which are yet alive. Yea, better is he than both they which hath not yet been, who hath not seen the evil work that is done under the sun.* So he thought *then.* He thought *the dead* were more to be envied than *the living.* He thought it would have been better still never to have been born. Who would *not* think so, if he had only eyes to see earthly things; and had no faith, the substance of things hoped for, the evidence of things not seen?

A similar account of his feelings at that time is recorded in the second verse of the ninth chapter, when he felt more like a Deist than a believer: *All things come alike to all; there is one event to the righteous and the wicked: to the good, and to the clean and to the unclean; to him that sacrificeth and to him that sacrificeth not; as is the good so is the sinner; and he that sweareth as he that feareth an oath.* So he thought *then.* He knew no better *then.* Mere observers are apt to think so. He thought differently afterward; he extended his contemplation beyond visible things—things *under the sun*, as he calls them so often and so significantly. Though it may be true, as far as eyes can see, *that there is one event to all*, yet he did not therefore adopt that pernicious maxim, *Let us eat and drink, for to-morrow we shall die.* He came very near doing so; he wishes young men to know it. But he avoided that rock on which so many made shipwreck of their faith and their philosophy at the same time. He said, *I know it shall be well with them that fear God; it shall not be well with the wicked* (viii. 12, 13).

III. There is a third characteristic of the style of this book, not necessary to mention indeed for the interpretation of this text, as the others were, but, considering the nature of this sermon, and to complete the ground-work for the interpretation of the whole book, we mention it here—it is Solomon's *keen irony*. He was aiming to persuade men, especially young men, to religion. No easy task! Their blood warm—their hopes ardent—death to them apparently far off, and the world dressed in such tempting smiles and splendor before their eyes, they will naturally cling to its gayety and merriment. They will say they were made for it, and *it* was made for them; they do not see any harm in it, and they *do* see there is *one event to them all, to the righteous and the wicked;* they are about alike in misery here, and they die alike. Solomon responds to such sentiments in his keenest irony. He affects to agree with them. He takes up these sentiments and just preaches them back into the bosoms they came from—preaches just as these merry young men want him to preach. *Go thy way; eat thy bread with joy, and drink thy wine with a merry heart, for now God accepteth thy works* (ix. 7). That is the way they want him to preach; and in irony, in cutting sarcasm, he does it. He yields to them, and tells them that their wine and merriment are acceptable to God on their own principles. Then he goes on with the sermon for which they have furnished the text: Carry out thy principles, then: *Let thy garments be always white, and let thy head lack no ointment. Live joyfully with the wife whom thou lovest all the days of the life of thy* VANITY, *which he hath given thee under the sun. All the days of thy* VANITY (he can not help repeating it), *for that is thy portion in this life,* (all you are good for,) *and in thy labor which thou takest under the sun* (all you can get on your own principles). *Whatsoever thy hand findeth to do* (music, merriment, mirth, wine, no matter what foolery), *do it with thy might* (now or never), *for there is no work, nor device, nor knowledge, nor wisdom in the grave whither thou goest.* What cutting irony! Their own principles, carried out, just about make beasts of them! (iii. 18). They must labor here for nothing but vanity, and die but to rot. Go on, then, if that is all you were made for—eat and drink, for to-morrow you shall die (Isa. xxii. 13).

The same species of irony may be found in the ninth verse of the eleventh chapter. The author is preaching back his own sentiments into the bosom of a young man, *expecting to live many years and rejoice in them*, and therefore indisposed to religion. With severe sarcasm, he reminds him that youth vanishes, as the young man wishes to live in pleasure, and neglect God. Go on, then! carry out your principles! *Rejoice, O young man, in thy youth, and let thy heart cheer thee in the days of thy youth,* (they will soon be gone—haste in mirth or you can not have it,) *and walk in the ways of thine heart* (if you will), *and in the sight of thine eyes* (live as you list); and then the preacher adds a solemn idea of his own, for this merry youth to carry along with him in his pleasure : *But know thou that for all these things God will bring thee into judgment. Therefore, remove sorrow from thy heart, and put away evil from thy flesh ;* fear nothing, care for nothing but pleasure, if you will, in this "childhood and youth," which are vanity: and *because* youth is soon gone, and death soon comes, and the judgment after it, be a fool and be merry ; you say there is nothing better! If Solomon was deep in experience and extensive in observation, he was also as remarkably keen in his irony.

The discussion of the text itself will come hereafter. These remarks on the style of this book lead me to utter some counsels.

1. Beware how you interpret its expressions. For example, when you read in the second chapter: *To every thing there is a season, and a time to every purpose under heaven; a time to be born and a time to die: a time to kill and a time to heal; a time to mourn and a time to dance; a time to hate; a time of war;* do not be so superficial as to suppose that Solomon is enjoining or justifying war, and hatred, and dancing, and killing. Put the whole chapter under its proper head. It belongs to the chapter of *observation*. He is only stating facts as they were—things he saw—and not telling how they should be. Apply this advice to his expressions of experience and of irony also. Hence,

2. See what is the great drift and purpose of this book; namely, to persuade young men, especially, to fear God, keep his commandments, and fit for the day of judgment. This is its sole aim. In accordance with this, all its particular expressions are to be interpreted. If you interpret them wisely now, *in the days of your youth*, they will give you an eye fixed on the judgment-seat of Christ.

3. Aim to copy Solomon's mode of reasoning—spread out his argumentation as wide as you will. *Be* observers. Look at the world—its life, death, gold, honor, merriment, wine, wisdom, labor, laughter, tears—all that is in it, all that is visible of the works of *God under the sun;* and then ask yourselves solemnly if all this does not amount to an overwhelming argument that there is something better for you *beyond the sun*, which you ought first and forthwith to seek after. Add your own expe-

rience to Solomon's. He found the world vanity. What have you found it? He sometimes even hated life. So will you, if you do not employ it for the life to come. Have you not found it *vexation of spirit* already? Deeper vexations are in store for you if you will not live unto God. Do you need any deeper ones? Have you not enough already to convince you that your heart runs wrong when it runs upon the world; and that your affections and purposes ought not any longer to lie supremely upon a world which can only furnish you, as an unbeliever, two things—vanity and a grave?

Lessons from Ecclesiastes.

[CONTINUED.]

Therefore I hated life, because the work that is wrought under the sun is grievous unto me: for all is vanity and vexation of spirit.—Ecclesiastes, ii. 17.

WE directed your attention to this passage on a former occasion. At that time we desired to lay the foundation of a just interpretation of it. We could not *then* do more in the space of time your indulgence allowed to us. We propose now a more close attention to the text itself. But it will be necessary to advert to the principle we then laid down—a principle needful to be kept steadily in mind by any and every man who would have a right understanding of the book of Ecclesiastes.

The principle was this: that Solomon wrote this book to persuade men, especially young men, to religion by an argument drawn from his own life. On the ground of that love, he holds up the world before the eye of a young man, simply to have him look at it as it is, in all its forms and promise, and then make up his mind whether it is worth the consideration he gives to it, while for its sake he continues in his irreligion, and does not *seek first* the favor of God. To show the world in its just light, Solomon speaks as an old practitioner and an old observer—a man of feelings and of eyes. And while he adverts so constantly throughout the book to his own experience and observation, as a man who had tried riches and pomp and pleasure, and who had lived long enough to see all that the widespread shiftings and fluctuations of this world can heave up; he distinguishes three points of his own heart's history.

First, Sometimes he tells what he felt and thought at the period when he was going on in the full tide of worldly enjoyment and hope.

Second, Sometimes he expresses the sentiments he entertained at the period when he had found that the world could not answer his purpose, and found himself heart-sick and disgusted with it all; and *before* he had turned to God, placing his affections and directing his aims upon something better than earth.

Third, Sometimes he expresses the sentiments he entertained *now; the fear of God* and *the keeping of his commandments;* and when, as an old hand in the matter, he could tell irreligious young people what the world's offers were good for, and what was the only thing that was worth living for.

The text before us expresses the sentiments he entertained in the second of these periods, which we have denominated the period of disgust. You perceive he speaks of the past—he speaks of himself—he speaks as a man of experience and observation: *I hated life, because the work that is wrought under the sun is grievous unto me; for all is vanity and vexation of spirit.* You perceive, he saw the world in its true light, so far as it is considered by itself, and *not* considered in its relation to another. He was heart-sick of it all; he even *hated life; i. e.,* he was disgusted with it—he saw it useless, and found it distasteful. Things met his eyes which threw a cast of vanity over all human existence; and feelings came up in his heart which made even life itself in such a world as this a sickening portion, a burden, an empty and distressful dream. So he felt without religion. So he found life. So he would have all the irreligious feel. So he would assure them that they shall find life, sooner or later, just as surely as they live in this world without God. Sooner or later (much as they live in this world, and eagerly as they pursue it), they shall half wish, or quite wish, they had never lived at all.

Let us enter into this subject. Let us spread out this lesson. Let us cast our eyes over the whole scene of an irreligious life, and see if any where we can discern any thing which ought not to make an irreligious man sympathize with Solomon in his period of disgust: *I hated life.*

Not to exhaust this subject, but to give some hints of its extent, we name to you six ideas:

1. The confusion and darkness which cover life.
2. The results of a worldly experience.
3. Knowledge of men.
4. Excessive fondness for the world.
5. Failure in worldly endeavors.
6. Failure of even that intellectual excellence which rises above "amusements" and sensuality.

I. It needs no argument to prove that the dispensations of God are often shrouded in impenetrable darkness. But the *depth* of that midnight hovers over the head of an irreligious man. God's promises cast light where nothing else can; and one of the present and often realized advantages of religion is to be found in the fact, that the Divine dispensations are all of them confirmatory of the Divine promises, and all illustrative of their significance. There is not a thing so strange, a distress so deep, a night so dark, but the very unacceptableness of the matter brings along with it to the Christian some lesson of profit, as it bears on an immortality to come, or some balm of comfort, as God stands by his people in the furnace of trial. With the wicked, with the worldly, it is not so. They read time by the light of time's own torch, flickering and fitful. They read the world aside from the light cast back upon it from the anticipated fires of its coming conflagration. Hence they can not read rightly. Time, the world, life, are all misunderstood; and *so* misunderstood by an irreligious man that he is compelled to be disgusted with life, or else act very much on the proposal of licentiousness: *Let us eat and drink, for to-morrow we shall die.*

How can a man be satisfied here, or be any thing better than sickened with life, when at every glance over society his eyes meet with instances of virtue depressed and vice prosperous? Where is the equity in this? On what principle is it that the man who has done most good to society is often least rewarded and least esteemed by society; and the man who has done most evil to his generation shall be the very man upon whom earth confers most of her advantages and men of the world lavish most of their smiles? The wicked often prosper. The righteous often suffer. Confusion seems to reign over life. As a man looks upon it, his eyes behold strange things; and as he thinks in the days of his youth of entering upon that capricious scene wherein awards are distributed not according to merit, to industry, to worth, how can he avoid being disheartened and disgusted with a life which proposes to him he knows not what? He has no religion. He can not think or feel on religious principles. He sees only uncertainty and confusion. On the one hand he beholds men whom he is compelled to despise seated in high places of honor and trust; and on the other hand he beholds men whose transactions are detestable gifted with every desired prosperity. He says to himself: *The race is not to the swift, nor the battle to the strong; neither yet bread to the wise, nor yet riches to the men of understanding, nor yet favor to men of skill, but time and chance happeneth to them all* (ix. 11). So he thinks. He knows no better. He sees no further. And can you wonder that he should be thoroughly heartsick of a life which he must go and spend amid such a scene of turmoil, confusion, and uncertainty? Is it any wonder, if, disgusted with all that life and the world can offer, he should just let *time and chance* dispose of them as they will? Or if he looks forward to the end, all the end that his now worldly soul cares any thing about, how can he avoid dissatisfaction, the most perfect disgust with life, while he says: As man *came forth of his mother's womb, naked shall he return to God as he came, and shall take nothing of his labor which he may carry away in his hand. And this is a sore evil, that in all points as he came so he shall go; and what profit hath he that hath labored for the wind? All his days also he eateth in darkness, and he hath much sorrow and wrath with his sickness* (v. 15–17). How can he avoid disgust with life while his lips, untaught in the language of Israel, are saying:. *All things come alike to all: there is one event to the righteous and to the wicked; to the good, and to the clean and to the unclean; to him that sacrificeth, and to him that sacrificeth not; as is the good, so is the sinner; and he that sweareth, as he that feareth an oath. This is an evil among all things that are done under the sun, that there is one event unto all. yea, also the heart of the sons of men is full of evil, and madness is in their heart while they live, and after that they go to the dead. For to him that is joined to all the living there is hope: for a living dog is better than a dead lion: for the living know they shall die; but the dead know not any thing, neither have they any more a reward, for the memory of them is forgotten* (ix. 2-5). As the mind of this irreligious man sweeps over all human life, from the time of man's birth in nakedness down to the period when time has worn the letters from his tomb-stone, and the *memory of all is alike forgotten*, is it any wonder if such a life disgusts him? if, sick at heart, he turns away from its darkness, distresses, and perishing memory? Life, the world, time, were never designed to be read in their own light simply. They were designed to be read in the full blaze of eternity. A wise man can not be any thing else than dissatisfied with life while all his ideas linger on things this side the tomb. He may prosper here—he may not. And whether he does or not, he deems a matter of *chance*—and since all die alike and alike are forgotten, a matter of indifference. He is dissatisfied with the world; he is dissatisfied with God when he thinks of him; and dissatisfied with himself, whether he considers his experience or contemplates his prospects. *I hated life, because the work that is wrought under the sun is grievous unto me.* He should look *beyond* the sun; beyond the world; beyond time. His disgust with life can not be easily cured in any other method. Eternity alone can explain the darkness and disorders of time.

II. After all the earthly bounties of God, and all the provisions he has made to meet the wants, capacities and tastes of our common humanity; there never yet has been a man who arrived at any thing like a full satisfaction. This was one of Solomon's stings of experience. He tried hard to attain contentment. He ran the full round of pleasure. He tried wealth. He tried honor. He tried pomp and splendor. He tried science. He tried wine. He was resolved to be happy: *Whatever mine eyes desired I kept not from them: I withheld not my heart from any joy, for my heart rejoiced in all my labor, and this was my portion of all my labor* (ii. 10). But it all would not do. He tried in vain. His hopes were blasted, and his heart saddened and sickened by the very profusion in which he sought satisfaction. And then he sums up the matter in a method most instructive to a votary of the world: *I looked on all the works that my hands had wrought, and on all the labor that I had labored to do, and behold all was vanity and vexation of spirit, and there was no profit under the sun* (ii. 11). *I hated life.* The difference between Solomon and our worldlings is this: *He* succeeded; most of our worldlings fail! He was disgusted by success; most of our worldling are disgusted by failure! His disgust with life bore off his mind toward the *life that is to come;* THEIR disgust, confined to experienced things, and not calling their thoughts to things hoped for, only fastens their mind more fixedly on the *life that now is.* But it will all be in vain. They can not compel the world to satisfy them. They will be as much disgusted when the next year is closing upon them as they are now when the last sands of this are falling, and when their hearts are so far from satisfaction. No matter what a worldly man attains, it does not answer his purpose. It disappoints him. It cheats him just as much in successes as in failures, *neither is his eye satis-*

fied with riches (iv. 8). And it is a thousand wonders that he does not become more disgusted with life than he is, and sooner disgusted. It is a thousand wonders that he does not *perceive* that his dissatisfaction springs, not from the limitation of his successes, but from the very nature of the objects he pursues. Such objects never can satisfy him. Give him any thing, and he will crave more. And if he would only stop now and take one sober thought about the ashes, the phantom, the dream he is pursuing, he could not avoid being disgusted with a life distressfully expended on such vanities. Every unbeliever in the world would be disgusted with life if he would only notice the emptiness of that for which he is spending it. He is doomed—*no*, he dooms *himself*, to walk in a valley of trouble. Its end is as dark as its portion is troublesome; and it is no wonder that as long as he is an irreligious man his most sober and deep thought compels him to wish, or half wish, that he had never lived at all! There is but one rock of repose for an immortal soul, and *that rock is Christ*.

III. The same, or a worse species of dissatisfaction with life may very well result from what is often experienced amid once valued and sought intimacies and attachments. Let us do the melancholy justice. Let us not attribute all their downcast feelings to a dark and gloomy disposition, nor to the east wind that has shattered their nerves. Where is the man whose heart has not saddened at the recollection of professions once made to him? Who is there that has not found occasion to exclaim, What a world! what friendships! what friends! How soon their affections cool! How readily they fly from me in trouble! They could love me in prosperity, but they forsake me in adversity! Perfidious wretches! They could bask in the sunshine of my favor, when my favor was good for any thing for them; they could desert me in trouble unshamed at their perfidy and their mean selfishness! *Two are better than one, for if they fall one will lift up his fellow; but woe to him that is alone when he falleth, for he hath not another to help him up* (iv. 10). Such laments do not all come from a disordered fancy, from unstrung nerves, or from a melancholy disposition. They come sometimes from the realities of distressful experience; and that distress strikes so deep and so disgustfully upon the heart (not now to say so common) that there is little ground to wonder if life itself, to be spent among such sunshine friends, becomes a matter of disgust: *I hated life.* If you can realize it, I can only say, the realization is yet in store for you. You have but one way of avoiding it. You must have a *friend that sticketh closer than a brother*, to whom you may flee in every time of trouble, and with whose spirit you must be so deeply imbued that instead of hating the treacherous that pierce you, you shall pity them and pray, *Father forgive them, for they know not what they do.* It is very common that an unbeliever's own companions make him hate life itself.

IV. There are instances in which this detestation of life results in its strongest measure from an excessive valuation of what one proposes to gain from the world while life lasts. As ministers of the Gospel, we have something to do sometimes with this strange aspect of human nature. Let us tell you a secret: the most extravagant *fondness* for the world which we are ever called to notice and compelled to deplore, is indicated to us in the language of laments and dissatisfaction. Our acquaintance is unbosoming himself to us. He tells how he feels. He says, I detest the world; I despise it; I could wish to be dissolved from it; it has done me injustice; life in such a world is little more than a burden! How is this? Does this complainer realize the world's emptiness? Has he risen superior to its charms? No such thing. Its charms are as dear to him as ever. He is heart-sick, but does not half know what makes him so. Its charms have escaped him, and his contempt of the world just springs from that fact. He had an excessive love for it, and his lamentations *now* are just in proportion to his fondness once—aye, his fondness still. He is not sorry for sin; he is only sorry his sin can not find the means of indulgence. He is not about to repent; he is only taking revenge upon a world that has cheated him, by calling it hard names, and pouring contempt upon it. Take a little leaf of his heart's biography. I write it in this way: He commenced life in raptures with the world: his heart bounded to its embraces: he did not imagine that friends would be treacherous, fortune capricious, hopes vanishing, riches have wings, and the blood of youth and health soon circulate pain through his bones instead of pleasure. But his dream of fancy was soon broken. Its gilded spell gave place to a hated reality. And now he is disgusted with life in such a world as this, just in the very proportion as he loved, and loves still, the things beyond his reach; he hates life just as much as he loves the world; and he rails at the world simply because it eludes him. This is a leaf of his heart. He does not own it; he does not believe it, simply because he does not know himself, because his *heart is deceitful above all things and desperately wicked.* His disgust with life is just the result of an excessive worldliness. It does not result from the serious reflections which an immortal soul ought to have—reflections controlled by the contrast between *the life that now is and that which is to come.*

V. A disrelish for life often springs from the cutting contemplation of the end of all man's endeavors (ii. 11). One does not like to labor in vain. It is disheartening to expend much toil for little good; and it becomes the more so when the good falls nowhere, either to the man himself or to those who come after him. If there could be any fixed certainty that beneficial results shall come *somewhere*, and that though the laborer does not reach them himself, yet his labor shall bless his successors, the recollection of this might bring some solace to weary mind and weary muscles; pride, if not benevolence, might then extend its regards onward beyond life, and as far as the results of present exertion shall reach—and the man might value life on much the same principle as some men put value on the tomb-stone that shall tell where they lie—it gives their earthly existence a kind of extension.

But behold the reality. Even worldly men are often compelled to see it. There *is no* certainty; none that is solacing. Toil and labor must be expended very much in vain. At least the wicked think so whenever they really think at all. Solomon thought so. Hear him. He asks (ii. 23): *For what hath man of all his labor and of the vexation of his heart wherein he hath labored under the sun? For all his days are sorrows, and his travail grief, yea, his heart taketh not rest in the night. This is also vanity.* (ii. 11): *Then I looked on all the works that my hands had wrought, and on the labor that I had labored to do; and behold all was vanity and vexation of spirit, and there was no profit under the sun.* So much for the present. And what in the future? The future is no better. *There is no remembrance of the wise man more than of the fool for ever, seeing that which now is, in the days to come shall all be forgotten. And how dieth the wise man? as the fool. Therefore I hated life.* And the future is no better when contemplated in respect to those who shall take the fruits of our labor. *Yea, I hated all my labor which I had taken under the sun; because I should leave it unto the man that shall be after me; and who knoweth whether he shall be a wise man or a fool! Yet shall he have rule over all my labor wherein I have labored and wheren I have showed myself wise under the sun. This also is vanity* (ii. 18, 19). Fools may take our possessions. Fools may be our heirs. All our labor, instead of profiting them, may only be a curse to them. Rehoboams may inherit the crowns of our Solomons! and personal dissipation, and divided and ruined kingdoms, may be the fruits of all our earthly successes! Who, then, can blame a disgust with life? If this is all, who ought *not* to be disgusted? Oh, that men would see it! Certainly we do not live here for life's sake! most certainly, the world's history, almost every heart's history, is made by God himself, as bold a lesson to turn man's eyes toward the life to come as could be written by the sunbeams on the ashes of a burnt world! There is only one thing which never cheats endeavor, and never cheats hearts.

VI. But Solomon tried other resources. He was a man of science. Seldom if ever hath he been equaled. The wisdom embodied in his book of Proverbs is unparalleled. Not to speak now of its religion, it is unequaled in its wisdom in reference to the common principles and economy of life. You have been taught how he coined these proverbs. To make a single one of them demanded great labor—extensive and acute observation. His mind examined and weighed every thing connected with the subject; and having attained its knowledge and formed its judgments and made its discriminations, it condensed the whole matter in one short proverb, the embodied wisdom of a world of thought. There never was such a man. He studied every thing. He says, *I turned myself to behold wisdom* (ii. 12). *I gave my heart to seek and search out by wisdom concerning all things, that are done under heaven* (i. 13). He applied himself to the sciences, and he expresses the superiority of his opportunities and means, by the question (ii. 12): *What can the man do that cometh after the king?* i. e., who can have such advantages for science as royalty furnished him? And he improved them. In the first book of the Kings, fourth chapter and thirtieth verse, it is said: *Solomon's wisdom excelled the wisdom of all the children of the east country, and all the wisdom of Egypt, for he was wiser than all men.* The twelfth verse of the third chapter of that book tells us what God himself said to him: *Lo, I have given thee a wise and an understanding heart, so that there was none like thee before thee, neither after thee shall any arise like unto thee.* The thirty-second and thirty-third verses of the fourth chapter furnish us a catalogue of some of the subjects on which he composed treatises, part of which are lost to the world: *He spoke three thousand proverbs, and his songs were one thousand and five. He spake of trees, from the cedar-tree that is in Lebanon even unto the hyssop that springeth out of the wall; he spake also of beasts and of fowl and of creeping things and of fishes.* A moralist, a poet, a philosopher, a historian, a botanist, a master in the natural history of beasts and birds and fishes and creeping things; there is no danger of extravagance in affirming that his extent of science has seldom or never been equaled. He *gave his heart* to it, as he says, and he signally succeeded.

If, therefore, there was ever a man, or ever will be one, qualified by the knowledge and experience of the matter to estimate literature and science justly, that man was Solomon. And what does he say? Does he deem all this worth living for? Does it give him a relish for life any more than his pleasure—*I said of laughter it is mad, and of mirth what doeth it?*—or any more than his labors and his possessions, which might fall into the hands of *a fool?* Not at all. Take his own testimony. He does, indeed, in one sentence, express a preference for knowledge. He says: *A wise man's eyes are in his head,* i. e., a man of knowledge is not blind, while a fool *walketh in darkness.* But after all, the whole array of his literature and science could not hinder his disgust of life, or make him feel it was worth living for. Read the eighth verse of the first chapter: *All things are full of labor; man can not utter it; the eye is not satisfied with seeing, nor the ear filled with hearing;* science cost him more labor than it furnished him satisfaction: it could not fill an immortal soul. Read the eighteenth verse: *But in much wisdom is much grief; and he that increaseth in knowledge increaseth in sorrow.* How is *this?* How *is* it? Why, it comes in a hundred ways; one is, that the point of satisfaction is never reached, not only, but is pushed further off, and appears more inaccessible as knowledge increases—*that which is far off and exceeding deep, who can find it out?* (vii. 24). This is an affliction. Another is, that as knowledge increases you will see more and more to deplore in the world, and more and more to detest in its inhabitants. As your skill unmasks selfishness and sees through the disguises of insincerity, and as you find the very man who has a smile for your presence will have a sneer for you in your absence, you will have less bliss than when you had more ignorance; you will be disgusted with men, and blush to think that you belong to the race. Another way is, that your increasing knowledge will have little justice done to it. You have laboriously fitted yourself for a station that the world will not give you. A dolt, a simpleton, a profound blockhead, whose stupidity is his only qualification, will be ushered before you into the station, place or business for which you have laboriously qualified yourself in vain. Another way is, that knowledge will bear hard upon an irreligious pride. Fools may be vain. Vanity is a vice of the superficial. But men of extensive knowledge can not have the stupid bliss of a high self-esteem. To say all in one word, when you have explored the hights and depths of all earthly science, and gratified your zeal for knowledge in all that is knowable among men, you will be compelled to an *increase of sorrow*, because all this comes no nearer to satisfy your immortal soul than did the ignorance in which you began. You will say, like Solomon, *As it happeneth to the fool so it happeneth even to me; and why was I then more wise? Then I said in my heart that this also is vanity* (ii. 15). Considered in view of eternity, the longest periods of time are no more than the shortest; and, measured by the wants of an immortal soul, the most extensive science hath no more sufficiency than ignorance and stupidity. And if you could try it all, and on the ground of your experience should desire to leave your advice as a legacy to your son, you would just copy the twelfth verse of the twelfth chapter of this book: *By these, my son, be admonished: of making many books there is no end; and much study is a weariness of the flesh. Therefore I hated life, because the work that is wrought under the sun is grievous unto me; for all is vanity and vexation of spirit.* Disgust with life, when life is spent for any mere earthly purposes, will be an inevitable result of all sober thinking. Men can not avoid it but by avoiding thought, by shutting their eyes, by drowning their senses in the intoxication of thoughtless merriment, or gilded and baseless hopes.

It were easy to add to these items. Let these suffice.

But we can not close without some other ideas—some lessons by way of inference.

1. Man was made for religion. He must have been. If not, he was made by an enemy, made for *vanity and vexation of spirit*. His life, and all he gains as he spends it, will sooner or later become matter of disgust, contempt and sickening: just as surely as he lives and must die, if he does *not* live for immortality and die to inherit it. If an immortal life is not within his reach, his life is itself a dark riddle, his world a riddle, his heart and conscience and hopes are only curses to him, all cheats; and it matters scarcely a song, whether he dies this year or the next, or lives a century! If he will not live for immortality, he will soon hate life, and soon wish he had never lived at all! He was made to *fear God and keep his commandments, for this is the whole of man.*

2. The felicities of the irreligious in this life, all depend upon lack of thought, and the power of deception. They cheat themselves; the world cheats them; their hopes, their aims, all cheat them! They are not what

they think, and the world is not what they think it. Life, spent as they are spending it, will do them no good. How mournful to see young people, (while life is on the wing, and its years one after another are rushing by), spending their hours, their hopes, their energies, in a way not only to do them no good, but in a way which, if not speedily abandoned, will force them to curse the day in which *they were born!* Let me tell you, my young hearers, your life was not given for this world's purposes; and if you spend it for them, you will spend it very much in vain. Your souls—your immortal souls, can not be satisfied as you hope. You need what the world can not give. The sooner you are convinced of it the better. You need the favor of God. You need the blood of atonement, and the sustaining grace of the Holy Spirit. As you pass on in life, your hopes will be often disappointed, your world will become a blank to you, and your life a burden! What gives you most happiness will soon give you most pain; what now multiplies your joys will soon multiply and embitter your sorrows; for death will cut down your friends around you! It will make the world a solitude, and life itself a distress. As you part with them, as you bear away their bones to the land of silence, your hearts will sink within you: and how will you bear the superadded distress of the thought that your impiety embittered the dying hours of the friend, the father, the mother you will see no more? Oh, if you but had then that sweet hope that you should see them in heaven, how it would blunt the sting that enters into your soul! how it would make you realize that life is something more than a sickening scene, and death something else than an eternal separation. Therefore,

3. How greatly desirable is early piety. This was one

of the conclusions which Solomon drew from his varied experience and extensive observation. He had tried the world. He well knew its worth. He had tried religion too; and having felt how strong an enforcement for religion could be gathered from all that the world contains, in this book his mind takes a truly philosophical sweep over the whole range of an earthly existence, and then comes to the conclusions which such a view could not avoid. Early piety is one of these conclusions—*Remember now thy Creator in the days of thy youth.* Notice how he arrives at this conclusion. Both observation and experience help him to it. *Vanity of vanities, all is vanity,* is an expression containing the condensation of all that he felt and knew about the world. *I hated life,* is a description of one of his bitter experiences after he had tried to force the world to make him happy. He wished to save young people from the toilsome and tearful career that he had himself run, while seeking his happiness in luxury and splendor, and "amusements," in songs and science, and *whatsoever his heart desired under the sun.* He holds up before them the whole world as it is, when taken as a portion; *vanity, vanity, vanity,* written in letters of fire all over its splendor and pomp and merriment, and even science. He opens to them his heart, his own heart, torn with *vexation,* and sick of life even, while its fondness hung round things *under the sun.* They may glance at the picture and then at the heart; and having done so, may take their choice, whether they will spend their earliest and best days for such *vanity,* only to give such *vexation.* But if they will hear him, an old practitioner, an old observer, he tells them, in the twelfth chapter, the sentiments which he now entertains, burnt into his heart by the bitterness of an experience from which he would dissuade *them. Remember* NOW *thy Creator in the days of thy youth, while the evil days come not, nor the years draw nigh when thou shalt say, I have no pleasure in them; while the sun, or the light, or the moon, or the stars, be not darkened, nor the clouds return after the rain. In the day when the keepers of the house shall tremble, and the strong men shall bow themselves, and the grinders shall cease because they are few, and those that look out of the windows shall be darkened. And the doors shall be shut in the streets, when the sound of the grinding is low; and he shall rise up at the voice of the bird; and all the daughters of music shall be brought low; also when they shall be afraid of that which is high, and fears shall be in the way, and the almond-tree shall flourish, and the grasshopper shall be a burden, and desire shall fail; because man goeth to his long home; and the mourners go about the streets; or ever the silver cord be loosed, or the golden bowl be broken, or the pitcher be broken at the fountain, or the wheel be broken at the cistern. Then shall the dust return to the earth as it was, and the spirit shall return unto God who gave it.*

What is it all? all the world? all life? *Vanity of vanities, saith the Preacher, all is vanity. I hated life.* And shall the young run the same round? Shall they lend their minds to the same dream, and their hearts to the same sickening? Shall their best energies be expended in vain? Will they not *believe*, without the bitterness of a trial, that the world can not answer their purpose? Will they not believe philosophy, gathering up all the worth of the world, and labeling it all *vanity?* Will they disbelieve history, biography, experience, the grave and God—all which urge them to the *conclusion of the whole matter*, that to *fear God and keep his commandments is the whole of man?* (xii. 13.) But by-and-by (if they should live), their best days spent, old, worn out, and good for nothing, their bones shaken at the grave's mouth, will they then first begin to think that *God shall bring every work into judgment, with every secret thing, whether it be good, or whether it be evil?* (xii. 14). Early piety would save them from a world of vexation. Nothing *but* early piety can save many of them from hell. Few of them will live to be old.

My young friends: living in such a world, and hasting to such a tribunal, does thoughtlessness or merriment become you? Must you live to be "amused," and then die to be lost? Remember, you must have a meeting with God! Hide you can not! Shrink you can not! You must stand *there* where the throne blazes and endless ruin or eternal bliss begins! Despair, perdition, are unnecessary. God *waits to be gracious*. He calls you to Christ. He offers you heaven. You may be saved if you will. But let me tell you he will soon take back his offers of fatherly and gracious kindness and love. That *throne of grace* on which he sits shall soon be taken down, and he will rear on the spot his throne of judgment! *Every man's work shall be made manifest; for the day shall declare it, because it shall be revealed by fire; and the fire shall try every man's work, of what sort it is* (1 Cor. iii. 13). *For behold the day cometh that shall burn as an oven; and all the proud, yea, and all that do wickedly, shall be stubble; and the day that cometh shall burn them up, that it shall leave neither root nor branch* (Mal. iv. 1). *If the righteous scarcely be saved, where shall the ungodly and the sinner appear?* (1 Peter iv. 18). In view of that dreadful day and all its results—*now* in your youth—*now* before you hate life—make your choice betwixt vanity and heaven—truth and falsehood—sin and holiness—the eternal friendship and eternal enmity of God! But, oh! choose wisely and live for ever.

If you will not choose so, reflect,

4. How strong is the power of sin over the human heart! Men will spend their lives in the very way to make life itself a distress. They will live for the world in a way to poison life's good and force from their own lips the bitter confession: *I hate life, because the work that is wrought under the sun is grievous unto me; all is vanity and vexation of spirit.* It need not be. This life, as an introduction into heaven, may be joy in God, and the triumph of hope over gloom, dissatisfaction, and anguish.

5. Finally, this discussion ought to be a lesson to us on the matter of a worldly prosperity. One of the most amiable sins (if I may speak so), certainly one of the most excusable (if again I may speak so), is the anxiety of parents for the prosperity of their children. But amid that desired prosperity, their very children may *yet hate life*. Let us not expend our affections unwisely. Let us be more anxious that our children shall be disgusted with a life spent for the world than that they shall be satisfied with it. Let us be more desirous that they shall be happy in heaven than prosperous on earth. Let us consult for them, not merely as formed for this world, but as accountable, immortal beings, formed for eternity. If we live to the next Lord's day, let us come to the Lord's table with prayer for them, that our life and our death may not be embittered with the thought of their impiety. If the God of mercy will hear our prayers and bring them yet to that table with us, we will no longer say: *I hate life;* we will exclaim: Lord, *now lettest thou thy servants depart in peace, for our eyes have seen thy salvation.* God grant it. Amen.

A Pastor's Sketches 1 & 2
by Dr. Ichabod Spencer

"*A Pastor's Sketches* is a sobering and challenging reminder that the Holy Spirit is the true agent of conversion. This book is urgently needed today when so much of our evangelism is patterned after current marketing methods. It has deeply convicted me to always seek to be in tune with the Holy Spirit as I minister to others." **Jerry Bridges**

"Dr. Spencer's *Sketches*, reprinted after a lapse of many years, are a veritable treasury of pastoral wisdom. They will amply repay careful reading by pastors and serious Christians in our day." **Maurice Roberts**

"The Spencer extracts are superb and will be of great benefit when printed. This is very sobering but enlightening material. It is quite contrary to much of today's practice and all pastors need to read it." **Peter Jeffery**

"Spencer is a master at flushing sinners out of hiding and directing them to Jesus Christ for salvation through Spirit-worked, simple faith. The responses he makes to inquirers is, in the main, biblical, doctrinal, practical, and experiential. His perceptive counsel certainly has produced much fruit. *A Pastor's Sketches* is a compelling read for pastors and Christian workers; its pages contain the nuts and bolts of biblical evangelism." **Joel R. Beeke**

"The republication of Spencer's sketches gives a rare opportunity for contemporary pastors, who have few if any models of pastors who understand the 'work of evangelism.' These sketches show a doctrinal depth and an experiential savvy perfectly meshed in one who had the cure of souls as his passion." **Tom Nettles**

"Ichabod Spencer was gifted by God with a passion for the pastoral care of souls. Any pastor desiring to shepherd the sheep, or to see God's elect drawn to Christ, will find page after page of wise and sage counsel in this work. It is practical, pious, personal, and precious." **James White**

List Price for each volume **$12.95**
Purchase both from SGCB for **$22.00**

Solid Ground Christian Books
Call us toll free at **1-877-666-9469**
E-mail us at **sgcb@charter.net**
Visit us on the web at **solid-ground-books.com**

Other SGCB Classic Reprints

In addition to *The Bunyan of Brooklyn* which you now hold in your hands, Solid Ground Christian Books is honored to present the following titles, many for the first time in more than a century:

THEOLOGY ON FIRE: *Sermons from the Heart of J.A. Alexander*
A SHEPHERD'S HEART: *Sermons from the Ministry of J.W. Alexander*
A GENTLEMAN & A SCHOLAR: *Memoir of James P. Boyce* by *John Albert Broadus*
OPENING SCRIPTURE: *A Hermeneutical Manual* by *Patrick Fairbairn*
THE ASSURANCE OF FAITH by *Louis Berkhof*
THE PASTOR IN THE SICK ROOM by *John D. Wells*
THE NATIONAL PREACHER: *Sermons from the 2nd Great Awakening*
THE POOR MAN'S OT COMMENTARY by *Robert Hawker* (6 vols)
THE POOR MAN'S NT COMMENTARY by *Robert Hawker* (3 vols)
FIRST THINGS: *The First Lessons God Taught Mankind* by *Gardiner Spring*
BIBLICAL & THEOLOGICAL STUDIES by *the 1912 Faculty of Princeton*
EVANGELICAL TRUTH by *Archibald Alexander*
THE LORD OF GLORY by *B.B. Warfield*
CHRIST ON THE CROSS & THE LORD OUR SHEPHERD by *John Stevenson*
SERMONS TO THE NATURAL MAN by *W.G.T. Shedd*
SERMONS TO THE SPIRITUAL MAN by *W.G.T. Shedd*
HOMILETICS AND PASTORAL THEOLOGY by *W.G.T. Shedd*
A PASTOR'S SKETCHES 1 & 2 by *Ichabod S. Spencer*
THE PREACHER AND HIS MODELS by *James Stalker*
IMAGO CHRISTI by *James Stalker*
A HISTORY OF PREACHING by *Edwin C. Dargan*
LECTURES ON THE HISTORY OF PREACHING by *John A. Broadus*
THE SCOTTISH PULPIT by *William Taylor*
THE SHORTER CATECHISM ILLUSTRATED by *John Whitecross*
THE CHURCH MEMBER'S GUIDE by *John Angell James*
THE SUNDAY SCHOOL TEACHER'S GUIDE by *John Angell James*
CHRIST IN SONG: *Hymns of Immanuel from All Ages* by *Philip Schaff*
COME YE APART: *Daily Words from the Four Gospels* by *J.R. Miller*
DEVOTIONAL LIFE OF THE SUNDAY SCHOOL TEACHER by *J.R. Miller*

Call us Toll Free at 1-877-666-9469
Send us an e-mail at sgcb@charter.net
Visit us on line at solid-ground-books.com

"Uncovering Buried Treasure to the Glory of God"

www.ingramcontent.com/pod-product-compliance
Lightning Source LLC
Chambersburg PA
CBHW021757220426
43662CB00006B/91